MW00326023

Olivia Manning

A Woman at War

DEIRDRE DAVID

OXFORD
UNIVERSITY PRESS

OXFORD
UNIVERSITY PRESS

Great Clarendon Street, Oxford, OX2 6DP,
United Kingdom

Oxford University Press is a department of the University of Oxford.
It furthers the University's objective of excellence in research, scholarship,
and education by publishing worldwide. Oxford is a registered trade mark of
Oxford University Press in the UK and in certain other countries

© Deirdre David 2012

The moral rights of the author have been asserted

First Edition published in 2012

Impression: 2

All rights reserved. No part of this publication may be reproduced, stored in
a retrieval system, or transmitted, in any form or by any means, without the
prior permission in writing of Oxford University Press, or as expressly permitted
by law, by licence or under terms agreed with the appropriate reprographics
rights organization. Enquiries concerning reproduction outside the scope of the
above should be sent to the Rights Department, Oxford University Press, at the
address above

You must not circulate this work in any other form
and you must impose this same condition on any acquirer

British Library Cataloguing in Publication Data
Data available

Library of Congress Cataloging in Publication Data
Data available

ISBN 978–0–19–960918–5

Printed in Great Britain by
MPG Books Group, Bodmin and King's Lynn

For John Richetti

Preface

In 1969, a journalist from the *Guardian*, preparing to interview Olivia Manning, did some asking around among friends and colleagues. Most knew Manning was a writer, but few could come up with titles of her novels. Wasn't she rather 'difficult', someone ventured; others recalled she'd had a rough time during the war; and almost everyone seemed to know she was married to the BBC producer, Reggie Smith.[1] Beginning this book, close to forty years after the *Guardian* interview, I also quizzed friends and colleagues: had they heard of Olivia Manning? Read any of her novels? Discovered anything about her life? Almost everyone knew the name, some had read the Balkan and Levant trilogies (transparently autobiographical novels about Olivia's wartime adventures), and no one had heard of Reggie Smith. All remembered *Fortunes of War*, the 1987 BBC adaptation of the wartime books and recalled that Emma Thompson was terrific as Harriet Pringle, Olivia's barely disguised fictional surrogate.

The biographical challenge became clear: while remaining attentive to the wartime experience, I needed to show that Olivia Manning had been a woman at war on a number of fronts. From the time of growing up in Portsmouth, a seaside city she forever despised, to living in London in the 1930s as a young woman with little money but plenty of wit and sexy good looks, through her traverse one step ahead of the Germans across the Balkans and the Middle East, to her immediate post-war years back in Britain where she confronted an indifferent literary culture, she had battled her way through adversity.

At one time or another, all biographers are queried about their subject, asked to explain why they are traveling to libraries, tracking down documents, reading primary texts, manuscripts, letters, diaries, medical reports, and wills, and, whenever possible, interviewing

---

[1] Ruth Inglis, 'Who is Olivia Manning?,' *Observer Colour Supplement*, 6 April 1969.

people who knew the person they are writing about. In the case of
Olivia Manning, my answer has been simple. Knowing the trilogies
were heavily autobiographical, I became curious about the rich and
risky life of the writer, and also to wonder what else she had written in
addition to these six novels. But as I began my education in her life,
I realized I was being drawn to writing her biography because of
certain similarities between that life and my own, improbable as this
may seem.

Like Olivia, I left school at sixteen and went to work, reluctantly, as
a typist. Like Olivia, I survived World War II, far less dramatically, to
be sure, since rather than being a woman in her early thirties dodging
the Germans in the Balkans and the Middle East, I was a child dodging
V1 and V2 rockets sent over London at the close of the war. And like
Olivia, I had lived in post-war Austerity Britain, less troubled than she
by poor food, bombed-out streets, and washed-out faces, since I was
used to ration books and doing without. And when I read Olivia's
descriptions of the stress of wartime conditions in Bucharest bringing
about dirty fingernails, sour breath, nicotine-stained fingers, I recalled
my own memories of sleeping in the Clapham South tube station: it
reeked of too-long brewed tea, soured milk, sweaty bodies wrapped in
multiple jumpers to stave off the icy drafts that came hurtling through
the tunnels. Even though I was disinclined to make a fictional appearance in the biographical narrative (could I have become Olivia's
wartime friend?) or to weave my own memories with her autobiographical recollections, I readily recognized much of her experience
and I shared her ambition to move to a world elsewhere (in her case
away from the provincial swamp of Portsmouth and in mine far from
the dismal seediness of South London). I'd like to think that this sort of
empathetic affiliation makes for good biography.

At a cultural moment of nostalgic reconstruction of World War II,
with the Imperial War Museum offering the Blitz Experience, Jamie
Oliver urging Britain to adopt a healthy wartime diet featuring many
root vegetables and not much meat, and a global recession turning
people's thoughts to allotments and make-do-and-mend, a reconsider-
ation of Olivia Manning's wartime fiction would seem to be in order.
But she did not just write about World War II. She published
novels about the struggle for survival by young women in 1950s
still-diminished London, about desecration of the environment
through uncontrolled commercial development, and about the painful

adjustment to post-war English life for young men (her work is especially notable for its subtle portrayal of male, sometimes homosexual, characters). And in her short stories, relying upon memories of her Portsmouth childhood, she writes brilliantly about unhappy children trapped in an adult world of quarrels about money and disappointed expectations.

For thirty-five years after the end of World War II, she was a visible, hard-working presence in the British literary marketplace: as the author of thirteen published novels, two volumes of short stories, and four works of non-fiction, and as a regular writer on contemporary fiction for *The Spectator*, *The Observer*, and the *Sunday Times*. Over her long career, she reviewed some four hundred novels and many collections of short stories. But despite becoming a polished woman of letters with a wide circle of intelligent friends culled from Reggie Smith's world of BBC colleagues and actor pals, and from her own group of fellow-writers such as Francis King, Margaret Drabble, and Beryl Bainbridge, she felt herself exiled as much from the London literary establishment as she had from the provincial world of Portsmouth. Claire Tomalin remembers her in the 1970s as 'slim and chic, hair well done, lively face, the very embodiment of a successful and worldly literary woman,'[2] yet despite her smart appearance and confident manner, Manning bitterly resented many of her female contemporaries—figures such as Iris Murdoch, Muriel Spark, and Edna O'Brien—who, she believed, received an unwarranted amount of critical attention and were paid more money than she ever commanded for her novels and reviewing. But even though she never made the short list for the Booker prize and never got that solo *Sunday Times* review for which she lobbied vigorously, she remained a dedicated, ambitious writer until the end of her life. As a young woman, writing sustained her as she witnessed the dispiriting battles between her adored father and her nagging mother; it kept her going throughout dislocation from Romania to Greece and from Greece to the Middle East; and from 1945 until her death in 1980, writing was her daily work, despite periods of dark depression and ill health that were a legacy of the war.

---

[2] Correspondence between the author and Claire Tomalin, 26 November 2011.

With a recurrent emphasis on the autobiographical nature of Olivia Manning's writing, authorized by her admission that she wrote best about things she had experienced 'at first hand,' I've discussed all her fictional and non-fictional work. But I have also regarded that writing as much more than provision of factual evidence for the actual life. To be sure, she wrote versions of herself, her husband, and many of her friends into her fiction, but the unsentimental dry prose, the brilliance in creating a visual scene, the deft construction of narrative—all this would be lost in a sole focus on fiction as autobiography. Olivia Manning was a woman at war who came through, victorious by virtue of her dedication to the work of writing, whether conducted in the Portsmouth public library, a London bed-sitting room, a Bucharest flat, an Athens villa, the Jerusalem YMCA, or a St John's Wood house. My hope is that this study of her embattled and plucky life, and all the writing she produced in addition to the trilogies, will prompt a reassessment of the work of one of the most under-valued and under-read British women novelists of the twentieth century.

Acknowledgments

In the early stages of interviewing people who had known Olivia Manning, I was very fortunate to meet the novelist Francis King, who died in July 2011. His generosity in talking about his friendship with Olivia and in steering me to others he thought might be helpful was invaluable. I remain deeply indebted to him for his kindness, his hospitality, and his willingness to share memories of many other twentieth-century British writers. Through Francis King, I met Victoria Orr-Ewing, the daughter of Olivia's close friend, the novelist Isobel English (June Braybrooke). It is no exaggeration to say that it would have been impossible to write this book without her help. She allowed me free access to all the papers that Olivia had left in care of June and Neville Braybrooke, and we spent many hours at Grove House on the Isle of Wight going through letters, manuscripts, typescripts, and many odd scraps of paper and envelopes on which Olivia had jotted notes to herself. I am deeply grateful for her help and also for the friendship we formed while sorting through dusty documents and enjoying a glass or two of wine. All these papers are now safely housed at the Harry Ransom Center. I am also indebted to the historian Roy Foster, who was kind enough to share his keen interest in Olivia Manning's life and work, to point me in the right research directions, and to help in arranging interviews with many people who knew Olivia and her husband Reggie Smith.

I am grateful to Margaret Drabble and Elizabeth Jane Howard for taking time from their writing lives to share their memories of Olivia Manning and their opinions of her work. Julian Mitchell was extraordinarily generous not only in talking at length about Olivia, but also in giving me access to their correspondence and in reading to me from his private diaries for the years when he knew her. Backstage at the National Theatre, between matinee and evening performances of Alan Bennett's *The Habit of Art*, Richard Griffiths chatted wittily and at length about Reggie Smith's kindness to him when he first arrived in London as a young actor; as he put it, he was a penniless bloke with few friends and Reggie took him immediately under his BBC wing. I am grateful also to Andrew Biswell, Director of the International Anthony Burgess Foundation, for sharing with me important correspondence between Burgess and Manning, and to Claire Tomalin, who was kind enough to recall her memories of Olivia Manning in the 1970s as a hard-working literary figure.

A number of Olivia Manning's close friends provided valuable insights into her life and work. In particular, I was fortunate in interviewing Johnny Slattery, who reminisced about her long friendship with Olivia and Reggie; many thanks must also go to Parvin and Michael Laurence, who generously shared memories of happy times in St John's Wood and on the Isle of Wight. Anna Davin recalled the close ties between her father, Dan Davin, and Reggie Smith; Joanna Hines spoke to me about her mother Nancy's marriage to Lawrence Durrell, whom Olivia and Reggie knew when they were in Cairo; and John Tydeman and Helen Miller-Smith had many jolly stories to relate about Reggie's career at the BBC and Olivia's forceful personality.

All biographers know that without helpful librarians they would be lost. Those at the Harry Ransom Center, the University of Texas at Austin, the McFarlin Library at the University of Tulsa, the BBC Written Archives at Caversham, and the Sound Archives at the British Library, offered invaluable assistance. Mareike Doleschal, Collections Librarian at the Shakespeare Centre Library and Archive, Stratford-upon-Avon, answered my queries about various Royal Shakespeare Company productions. Christian Panaite did some invaluable translating from the Romanian. Equally important to the biographer is assistance in tracking down illustrations and obtaining permissions: Mark Paul at Getty Images, Mark Vivian at the Mary Evans Picture Library, and Bernard Horrocks at the National Portrait Gallery were most helpful in this regard. In addition, Diana Hogarth gave permission for the reproduction of many significant photographs in her possession; I am grateful to her and to Simon Robson for their cooperation and assistance. Finally, Penny Hoare at Chatto and Windus was kind enough to forward images that had been reproduced in *Olivia Manning: A Life* by Neville and June Braybrooke.

I owe a debt of gratitude to a group of dear friends, women in my New York reading group, MFIV. Some six years ago, having discussed Tony Judt's *Postwar*, we decided to read some World War II fiction:

the subsequent lively discussion of *The Balkan Trilogy* led me to begin work on Olivia Manning. Two old friends, Barry Qualls and Lily Hoffman, read some of the early chapters and their insightful comments helped me see what needed bringing out and what needed elimination. Their careful readings pointed the way forward, as did those of two anonymous readers for Oxford University Press. I feel very fortunate in having worked with Jacqueline Baker at the Press: with great professional skill, she helped steer this biography from its beginnings to its publication. Heartfelt thanks, also, to Jane Olin-Ammentorp for her superb work as production editor, and to Dorothy McCarthy and Veronica Ions for astute copy-editing and vigilant proofreading. Whatever errors might have crept in remain my sole responsibility. Lastly, over various convivial lunches, Eileen Gillooly, Pamela McCorduck, Charlotte Sheedy, and Louise Yelin encouraged me to talk about Olivia Manning and her work, and to test out various approaches. I am indebted to them for their insights, for their patience, and for their friendship. John Richetti read an almost final version of the manuscript and his sharp yet tactful editing helped tremendously in bringing the book to its close. My gratitude for that is immeasurable, as it is for much else in our life together.

Santa Fe, New Mexico
Summer 2012

Contents

List of Illustrations

Plates

1. Olivia Morrow Manning, with baby Olivia, aged three months. With permission of Victoria Orr-Ewing.
2. Lieutenant-Commander Oliver Manning. With permission of Victoria Orr-Ewing.
3. Olivia Manning, with doll, aged five years. With permission of Diana Hogarth.
4. Olivia Manning (seated) at Portsmouth Municipal School of Art, c.1934. With permission of Diana Hogarth.
5. Olivia Manning, studio portrait, just before leaving Portsmouth for London in 1936. With permission of Victoria Orr-Ewing.
6. Hamish Miles, editor at Jonathan Cape, and Olivia's lover until his death in December 1937. With permission of Victoria Orr-Ewing.
7. Stevie Smith, c.1950. Mary Evans Picture Library/Robin Adler.
8. Reggie Smith, in Bucharest, 1939, shortly after his marriage to Olivia Manning. With permission of Diana Hogarth.
9. Louis MacNeice, 1946, Reggie Smith's mentor at the University of Birmingham in the mid-1930s. Getty Images.
10. Athénée Palace Hotel, Bucharest, February 1940. Getty Images/Margaret Bourke-White.
11. Calea Victoriei, Bucharest, February 1940. Getty Images/Margaret Bourke-White.
12. Romanian Iron Guard, December 1940. Getty Images/Hulton Archive.
13. Olivia Manning's brother, Oliver, 1941, who died in an airplane accident in the same year. With permission of Victoria Orr-Ewing.
14. Reggie Smith, broadcasting from Jerusalem, 1942. With permission of Victoria Orr-Ewing.
15. Olivia Manning, studio portrait, Cairo, c.1942. With permission of Diana Hogarth.
16. Olivia Manning, studio portrait, on her return to England in 1946. With permission of Victoria Orr-Ewing.

Figures

List of Abbreviations

OMC, HRC	Olivia Manning Collection, Harry Ransom Center, The University of Texas, Austin
OMC/C, HRC	Olivia Manning Collection/Correspondence, Harry Ransom Center, The University of Texas, Austin
FKC/OM, HRC	Francis King Correspondence, Harry Ransom Center, The University of Texas, Austin
OMP, UT	Olivia Manning Papers, McFarlin Library, The University of Tulsa
SSP, UT	Stevie Smith Papers, McFarlin Library, The University of Tulsa
V.O-E	Victoria Orr-Ewing

Introduction

Never a Day Without a Line

'All official biographies are stodge. They are too close to the subject
to be anything else. The perceptive books come much later.'

Olivia Manning to Francis King, 30 December 1969.[1]

On a hot and humid day in Bucharest in early September 1940, not
long after leaders of the paramilitary movement known popularly as
the Iron Guard had forced King Carol II to abdicate in favor of his son
Prince Michael, a German Trade Delegation drove into the city.
Romanian citizens had been well prepared for the arrival of their
German visitors by a speech to the nation delivered on 9 August
1940 by their Prime Minister, Ion Gigurtu. He declared that although
Romania had sensibly followed a pro-Allied policy for almost twenty
years after World War I, since 1935 the adoption of a pro-Axis position
had proved more to its advantage: such an alliance had supported
the workers and peasants, shielded the country from harmful price
fluctuations, and protected Romanian cultural and economic life
against Jewish influences. Now it was time for all Romanians to
embrace their German allies—well, not quite all, for on the same
day the government published a statute governing the future status
of the Jews: henceforward, they were barred from the professions and
from government service.[2]

---

[1] FKC/OM, HRC. [2] *The Times*, 10 August 1940.

The Trade Delegation made straight for the luxurious Athénée Palace hotel, situated diagonally across from the Royal Palace on Bucharest's main square, and the broad driveway in front of the hotel portico quickly became filled with German cars and military lorries, each bearing a prominent swastika on a red pennant. The lorries were packed with military equipment and the Delegation was accompanied by a phalanx of SS men in black uniforms. As the young officers entered the hotel a gigantic Nazi flag of scarlet, white, and black unfurled above them. Long a favored meeting place for the English colony in Bucharest, which usually clustered in the bar, and also for sundry down-on-their-luck Romanian princes who monopolized the plush sofas in the lobby, the hotel customarily flew a small Union Jack or a Romanian flag. Now a new gilded flagpole had been fixed on the roof and the enormous swastika that hung from it fell four floors to touch the main portico.

The Germans were delighted by the reassuring sight of the swastika, a symbol of the military might that had, within the space of a year, vanquished Czechoslovakia, Poland, Belgium, the Netherlands, Norway, and France. Romania's turn for occupation was imminent and a few weeks after the arrival of a Military Delegation on 8 October 1940, some five hundred thousand troops crossed the northern borders while German bombers flew in formation over Bucharest and German officers requisitioned an entire floor of the Athénée Palace to accommodate two divisional generals, three major generals, and eleven colonels. On 23 November 1940 Romania joined the Axis Powers. Soon thereafter, the industrial and agricultural riches of the country (primarily oil and cereals) were requisitioned to become an important source of fuel and food for the Nazi armies and Bucharest became less enthusiastic about its glamorous visitors. But on that warm September day when the Trade Delegation and the SS officers arrived, the Athénée put on a welcoming show. Inside the hotel, clusters of attractive, well-dressed Romanian women sipped coffee, the light veils that shaded their dark eyes barely hiding a feverish desire to attract the handsome officers. Their sensuality heightened by the proximity of these conquerors of Europe, they gazed spellbound at the young men, their eyes agleam, their ample curves displayed to seductive advantage by Parisian silk frocks.

Throughout the year preceding the riveting entry of German officials and SS men into the crowded lobby of the Athénée (from

September 1939 to September 1940), a slim thirty-two-year-old English woman with creamy olive skin, sharp dark eyes, and very pretty legs had been a regular presence in the bar of the hotel. She was a member of the English colony, composed principally of British embassy staff, businessmen, and journalists, that had huddled daily to glean news of the domino collapse of Europe and to wonder when and how it was going to get out of Romania. The young woman was Olivia Manning, a wry and witty observer of the political and social scene in Bucharest, and the author of several short stories and one well-received novel, *The Wind Changes*, published in 1937, whose setting is the Irish 'Troubles' and whose theme is the eventual futility of political protest. Her novel had impressed critics with its seamless integration of historical actuality into fictional narrative. Recently married to a teacher of English literature working for the British Council, she had left London in late August 1939 and arrived in Bucharest on the fateful day of 3 September to find herself an official enemy of those elegant officers now sauntering into the hotel.

Some twenty years after this dramatic moment in Bucharest, Olivia Manning, back in London and now well established as a talented writer, published *The Spoilt City*, the second of three novels about World War II in Romania and Greece, known familiarly as *The Balkan Trilogy* (1960–5), and I have quite deliberately begun this book about her life and work with a virtual paraphrase of a passage from this novel: her description of the theatrical arrival of the German Trade Delegation at the Athénée. Naturally, she embellished for dramatic effect—perhaps the flag was not quite so enormous, the day so stifling, the women so eager—but *The Balkan Trilogy* is transparently autobiographical in its evocation of Bucharest in September 1940 and in its staging of the displacement from Romania to Greece of the principal characters Harriet and Guy Pringle. They are barely disguised representations of Olivia and her husband Reggie Smith: Harriet a witty young woman who worked in a London art gallery before her marriage and Guy a lecturer in English literature for the British Council. Reggie readily admitted a strong resemblance between Olivia and Harriet, but he always insisted that his wife was never as 'sour and nagging' as her fictional counterpart.[3] Olivia, however, identified so

---

[3] 'Never a day without a line,' BBC Radio 3, 21 November 1981.

closely with Harriet Pringle that when she learned, just before her death in July 1980, that Emma Thompson was a possible candidate to play Harriet in the BBC adaptation of the trilogies (eventually aired in 1987 as *Fortunes of War*) she announced that Thompson was absolutely wrong for the part: quite simply, her feet were too big. 'Look at my dainty feet!' she exclaimed, 'Hers are enormous!'[4] Actually, it was Kenneth Branagh who was wrong for the part of Reggie Smith: Branagh is short and slight where Reggie was tall and bear-like, and he was dreamy and brooding where Reggie was ebullient and almost manically expansive. Despite her large feet, Emma Thompson did play Harriet Pringle and she tried not to base her performance on what she had learned of Olivia's life, although she suspected, finally, that a great deal of that life came through 'of its own accord.'[5] Twelve years after the publication of the third novel in her Balkan trilogy, *Friends and Heroes* (1965), Olivia returned to Guy and Harriet Pringle, and the three novels about their perilous adventures in Egypt and Palestine that constitute *The Levant Trilogy* (1977–80) are similarly faithful to the recorded facts of her wartime experiences.

Never uneasy about discussing the thickly textured weaving of historical event, personal memory, and imaginative fiction that characterizes her writing, Olivia Manning regularly declared that she intended the trilogies to work both as history and as autobiography. After completing the first draft of *The Spoilt City*, she wrote to a friend that it was 'almost an historical novel as it is about our year in Roumania.'[6] And when asked in 1964 by a skeptical interviewer for *The Times* where she had managed to ferret out so much extraordinary material, she replied crisply that she had experienced it 'mostly at first hand . . . In effect the characters in the books are real . . . all the background comes from my own or my husband's knowledge and experience.'[7] Throughout Olivia's writing life, Reggie Smith was a veritable archive of information about their shared adventures, a reliable source for confirmation of what she recalled and for additional detail that might have escaped her capacious storehouse of memories of their life together. In the way that Robert Graves and Vera Brittain had written

---

[4] Author's conversation with Roy and Aisling Foster, 27 November 2008.
[5] Emma Thompson to Neville Braybrooke, 5 August 1987, OMC/C, HRC.
[6] To Rupert Croft-Cooke, 4 December 1957, OMC/C, HRC.
[7] 'Speaking of writing,' *The Times*, 30 January 1964.

histories of World War I through autobiography, in *Good-Bye to All That* (1929) and *Testament of Youth* (1933), Olivia mined the rich material of her wartime experience and her years in Portsmouth from early childhood to the age of twenty-six, and fashioned it all into compelling narratives.

During her writing life, which began with adventure serials published in the *Portsmouth Evening News* in the late 1920s and ended with her last novel, *The Sum of Things* (the third volume of *The Levant Trilogy*) that appeared a few months after her death in July 1980, she published thirteen novels (counting the trilogies), four works of non-fiction, some fourteen short stories, and innumerable reviews of contemporary novels. As she openly confided to friends and fellow-writers, she felt happiest and most confident when writing of things she had known first-hand. Ruefully declaring that she possessed neither a capacious imagination nor a feel for fantasy, she insisted she wrote completely 'out of experience,' something fully understood by many of her readers, one of whom wrote to say "I felt instinctively that much of your material must be autobiographical."[8] That Olivia wrote most powerfully out of her own experience is undeniable, but the self-deprecating denial of a feel for fantasy is contradicted by her earliest publications—the thrilling adventure serials that appeared in her local newspaper when she was in her early twenties. From that time until just before she died, writing was everything to her: without it, she wrote to her close friend June Braybrooke (the novelist who published under the name Isobel English), life was 'a nightmare.' When she wasn't writing, everything seemed 'difficult, a source of fear and anxiety.' At such times (and there weren't many since she wrote almost every day), she would be overwhelmed by a terrible sense of her own 'inadequacy.'[9]

After the Nazis settled into Bucharest in 1940, first forming alliances with the green-shirted Iron Guard and then crushing it in late 1941 when the disruptive street violence with which it had sporadically terrorized the city no longer served the German cause, as a British citizen Olivia began to fear Romanian retribution. She was exiled from England in an alien city described by one of her most memorably

---

[8] Letter from Ann Griswold (3 Ickburgh Road, London E5) to Olivia Manning, 1 March 1974, OMC/C, HRC.

[9] To June Braybrooke, 12 July 1969, OMC/C, HRC.

comic and selfish characters, the scrounging Prince Yakimov in *The Balkan Trilogy*, as being 'on the edge of Europe,' a place where one can almost smell the Orient. In fact, from the unforgettable date of her arrival in Bucharest, Olivia Manning had been, quite literally, a woman at war. But feeling embattled was hardly new to her, albeit in a less frightening way. Back in England, first in Portsmouth and then in London, where she had lived for five years before her marriage in August 1939, she had been at war on different, domestic fronts. Her father's meager income from a naval pension had precipitated social embarrassment and feelings of class inferiority that never entirely evaporated—as she put it, 'we were very, very poor, in the way that only a naval officer's family can be. There was never a farthing to spare';[10] she had been driven to sullen distraction by her mother's grumbling about the family's finances and the fecklessness and infidelity of her husband; and as a young and ambitious writer she had both solicited and resented the influence of indifferent publishers to whom she sent her short stories. And she had spiritedly confronted 'the petty social tyrants of provincial life' (for Olivia, nowhere was more provincial than Portsmouth) who failed to understand and appreciate her artistic ambitions. In 1940, however, the sight of wealthy Jewish families being taken from their sumptuous Calea Victoriei apartments and the rapid deterioration of glamorous Bucharest as it came under fascist rule placed her pre-war battles in a sobering perspective. As she and Reggie witnessed the acquiescence of fascist Romania to German rule in the autumn of 1940, her familial and professional struggles faded in the sobering context of European war.

Not all of Olivia Manning's fiction is openly autobiographical, of course, yet in almost all the novels we encounter characters, landscapes, and exotic streets that return us to the verifiable details of her actual life. The British Council types lounging around the Athénée English bar in *The Spoilt City* are modeled on her husband's colleagues; the beautiful Aran Islands captured in her first novel *The Wind Changes* were visited in 1936 by Olivia and her lover at the time, an editor at Jonathan Cape; she climbed the rock faces at Petra and walked many times on the Jaffa Road in Jerusalem, the sites of crucial scenes in *Artist Among the Missing* (1949), a novel that depicts the psychological

---

[10] Olivia Manning in conversation with Kay Dick. Kay Dick, *Friends and Friendship: Conversations and Reflections*, 27.

disintegration of a character who survives the desert war in North Africa. What, though, makes Olivia's reliance upon her real-life experiences different from any other novelist's? Doesn't Dickens return again and again (for some, a little too often) to his miserable childhood; doesn't the magisterial mapping of early nineteenth-century provincial England to be found in *Middlemarch* (1871–2) derive its power from George Eliot's rural girlhood as the daughter of an estate bailiff; and isn't the high hilarity of Kingsley Amis's *Lucky Jim* made that much funnier by his tortured time as an assistant lecturer in English at the University College of Swansea? Consider, too, the detailed description of London's Fitzrovia neighborhood in Ian McEwan's *Saturday* (2005) that gains authenticity by virtue of the fact that he lives right there, knows intimately all the intricacies of one-way streets that set the plot in violent motion. It hardly needs saying that all novelists derive inspiration and verisimilitude from memory, experience, and observation.

Yet with Olivia Manning two things make this grounding of fiction in actuality particularly engaging and also highlight her attraction for the literary biographer. First, even though we can say that Dickens, Eliot, Amis, and McEwan, each in their different way, experienced tumultuous times of political and social upheaval—for Dickens and Eliot, the growth of an exhilarating and terrifying metropolis and an incremental shift in political and cultural power from the upper to the middle classes, for McEwan, a post-11 September climate of fear and suspicion—Olivia Manning lived through particularly disruptive times, above and beyond the way that any English person born in 1908 (as she was) may be said to have survived two world wars, the crippling depressions of the late 1920s and 1930s, and the dispiriting social climate of post-World War II Britain. Buffeted actor and cool commentator on the stage of European history in the latter half of the twentieth century, she was an eyewitness to the way ordinary individuals are caught up in the sweep of cataclysmic events, an attestant, as the historian Roy Foster put it in 1981 on the BBC Radio program about her life and work, to the way people behave under pressure.[11] Fusing private and public histories, however, she did not insert her biographical presence into the fiction merely to

---

[11] 'Never a day without a line.'

describe herself: as Rachel Cusk observes, that presence existed in order 'to witness.'[12] A spectator to history graced with incisive vision and recording what she saw in her spare, dry prose, Olivia Manning watched Romanian gypsies quiver with terror as the Iron Guard smashed the windows of the British Information Office in Bucharest; she was one of the lucky few who made it out of Greece just ahead of the Nazi takeover in 1941 (after having barely escaped Romania); she sailed from Piraeus to Cairo on a leaky overloaded ship and lived on an orange a day; and as she lay in a Jerusalem hospital in the late summer of 1944, on cots stretched out below her window she saw the mangled bodies of British soldiers convalescing from injuries sustained in the desert war. Olivia Manning's wartime story is dramatic, harrowing, rich in graphic incident, and it is also a writer's story framed by pre-war artistic ambition to escape the stifling provincialism of her childhood and post-war determination to gain recognition by the English literary establishment.

Second, what makes her story unusually appealing for the literary biographer is the frank and lucid transformation of actual experience into fiction, regardless of whether the characters are real and the events fictitious or the characters fictitious and the events real (she said both of these things about her work). What drew me first to Manning was the story of a highly intelligent woman's tumultuous life that could be discovered in and behind the writing, and as I read and re-read I began to see her as a seriously under-appreciated mid-twentieth-century English novelist.[13] Like many readers, I was enthralled by the way one almost hears the thunder of German bombers swooping down on Piraeus harbor and feels the Cairo night-air that envelops British

---

[12] Rachel Cusk, Introduction, *The Fortunes of War: The Balkan Trilogy*, p. viii.

[13] She also remains one of the most under-read of first-rate British writers, despite the fact that the *New York Review of Books* published in 2009 an edition of *School for Love* (with an introduction by the American novelist Jane Smiley) and in 2010 *The Fortunes of War: The Balkan Trilogy* (with an introduction by Rachel Cusk), although it was heartening recently to see *The Fortunes of War* ranked as number four by the historian Anthony Beevor in his list of the 'Five Best' works of WW2 Fiction (*Wall Street Journal*, 21 November 2009). Philip Hensher's observation that Manning seems to fall 'into the category of novelists whose name is somehow familiar but whose novels are not familiar at all,' contradicts, perhaps, a general transatlantic familiarity with the Balkan and Levant trilogies. Certainly, Manning is not as well known as some of her female contemporaries, figures such as Iris Murdoch, Margaret Drabble, or Muriel Spark. I aim to remedy this neglect and also to correct Hensher's dismissal of Manning as possessing only occasional 'flashes of interest as a novelist' (*The Times*, 30 October 2004).

officers sipping Stella beer on the lawns of the Anglo-Egyptian Union. I became increasingly curious about the experience that had created this visceral immediacy. Inevitably, I wondered how Olivia Manning became a writer. From where did she derive the skill to reconstruct after many years the experience of being an on-the-spot witness to momentous historical events? Essentially self-educated through disciplined reading in the treasured volumes of Dickens, Thackeray, and Rider Haggard she found on her father's bookshelves and then through immersing herself in Virginia Woolf and D. H. Lawrence in the Portsmouth Public Library, as a young girl she learned to write through reading, and in almost all ways her life is in her writing. And yet, of course, her work is not just unmediated transcription of experience into fiction. Where does autobiography end and fiction begin? Always to take the writing as solely autobiographical would be to diminish Olivia's literary imagination and to fail to appreciate the prose in which one 'never hears the creak nor feels the labour of invention.'[14] But by the same token, to ignore the resemblance between a tracing of the life and a reading of her work would be to evade exploration of the enticing interstices between what actually happened and how what actually happened gets shaped into compelling stories. This biography tackles such an exploration and investigates the ways in which a lifelong devotion to reading and writing shaped the lucid prose, the supple narrative line, and the vivid creation of character and landscape through visual description.

Biographical exploration sometimes gets complicated, but always in fascinating ways, by Olivia's tendency to relate her life in literary, often highly dramatized terms: in interviews with friends and journalists, she often figured herself as a literary character who might have stepped out of an Olivia Manning novel. Fashioning fictions more exotic than the tedious contingencies that she felt had shaped her early life, she created a self freed from the unexciting stuff that Virginia Woolf noted can be omitted when writing a realistic novel: 'The fascination of novel writing lies in its freedom; the dull parts can be skipped, and excitements intensified.'[15] Olivia was also given to a good deal of

---

[14] Olivia used this phrase to criticize a collection of short stories by G. F. Green: *The Spectator*, 23 April 1948.

[15] Virginia Woolf, 'Sterne,' *The Essays of Virginia Woolf*, I: 281 (this essay appeared originally in the *TLS* on 12 August 1909).

self-fabulation, about her family, her lovers, and her perceived profes-sional injuries. In fact, researching and writing her life has, at certain moments, seemed to me like writing a novel, or perhaps, more accurately, it has seemed as if I were tracing a life that already possessed literary shape by virtue of familiar literary tropes. The yearning of the provincial individual for the city, the voyages to exotic locales packed with thrill and risk, the struggle to forge professional identity, the imperishable imprint of familial conflict upon the psyche: are these not virtual commonplaces of the novel form?

Taking the novelistic 'material' that she experienced 'mostly at first hand' (as she put it), Olivia Manning forged for herself a working writer's life in which she scrupulously followed some advice she had received before the war from the prolific English novelist Marie Belloc Lowndes (sister of the writer Hilaire Belloc): 'Never a Day Without a Line.' Generally, Olivia wrote for between three and five hours every afternoon, and she allowed nothing to interfere with her regime. At one point, she confided to her close friend and fellow-writer Francis King that a psychiatrist had told her he found her novel *Artist Among the Missing* (1949) 'the best and most exact account of a neurosis which he had read. It is just a matter, of course, of putting down one's wretched symptoms, but I have wondered since if such a thing is justified. It must be so horrid to read. I rather hoped to cure myself, but failed to do so.'[16] She knew, of course, that she did much more than put down her 'wretched symptoms.' Troubled by memories of a peevish mother and a henpecked father, often hobbled by grudges against a literary marketplace that seemed to favor every British woman novelist but herself, and shunted about the Balkans and the Middle East by the forces of war, she did very much more than put it all down. She took it all, laced it into her writing, and created herself as a highly professional and hard-working figure in post-war literary London.

When Olivia returned finally to England in 1946, she found a post-war nation exhausted by battle, preoccupied with the coming of the Welfare State, and already being wrung to the bone by an Age of Austerity. It felt to her as if she were still a woman at war. It's very likely she read Cyril Connolly's introductory comments to the first

---

[16] I November 1957, FKC/OM, HRC.

post-war numbers of *Horizon*, and her melancholic tendencies certainly would have inclined her to share his pessimism. Connolly elegized a lost England in this way: 'The great marquee of European civilization, in whose yellow light we all grew up, and read or wrote or loved or travelled, has fallen down . . . the roses are withered on their stands . . . the grass is dead.'[17] Before the war, Olivia had not exactly moved in the world of garden fêtes that Connolly takes as his emblem of pre-war serenity, but she nevertheless abhorred the grind of post-war British life. For her, it was a bit too much like the misery of pre-war Portsmouth where she had witnessed daily quarrels about money and seen the effects of a grim economic climate caused by post-World War I recession and the Great Depression of the early 1930s. Hampered by having to leave school at sixteen to work in a solicitor's office and harboring the sense of class inferiority attendant upon such necessity, her prospects for social escape from the grimmer side of Portsmouth life had been pretty dim. That she made it to London, survived many days on not much more than beans on toast, and managed not only to write but also to get her work published, speaks to the dogged resilience and unquenchable ambition that sustained her through World War II and beyond.

After the war, Olivia also led a vibrantly public life, in contrast, say, to that of Elizabeth Bowen, a contemporary whom Manning called one of the 'genteel Georgians' and whose writing she dismissed as tediously pretentious: 'I cannot stand E.B.'s attempts at Style . . . what a tiresome writer she is. The attitudes and grotesqueries of style, all to say nothing much. It is like someone eating bread and milk with their legs crossed over their heads.'[18] By contrast with this peculiar image, Olivia Manning's style is elegantly plain—much like someone eating bread and milk with their feet sensibly planted on the floor. Olivia was candid in discussing the real-life sources of her fiction, whereas Elizabeth Bowen wrote to Francis King that she just wanted people to read her books and leave her life out of it: any connection between her stories and her experiences she would find 'damagingly public to explore.'[19] Olivia relished a risky public life—giving BBC talks, getting herself reviewed as often as she could, and throwing lively parties

---

[17] Sissons and French, *The Age of Austerity*, 216.
[18] 12 July 1970, OMC/C, HRC.
[19] n.d., FKC, Box 1, folder 1, HRC.

in her St John's Wood flat where gin and water, cheap wine, and cold cuts from the local delicatessen constituted the drink and food (she loved literary parties when she could entertain friends such as Beryl Bainbridge and J. G. Farrell but she hated the preparation). Kay Dick, the editor, translator, and writer with whom Olivia had a long and turbulent friendship, noted in her diary after one of these gatherings, 'Olivia's parties are the end. Nine drunks, all Irish, praising Edna O'Brien. Wine filthy. Where does Reggie find it? Notice he drank whisky. Olivia looked dead tired. No wonder—so was I.'[20] Francis King recalls that the lettuce would be gritty, the tomatoes hacked into chunks, and that the charming sitting-room decorated with rugs from Damascus and antiques from the King's Road would be packed with a hard-drinking crowd composed of Olivia's literary friends and Reggie's actor and politician pals.[21]

But however popular her parties, however well-received she was as a novelist, and however much in demand she was as an astute reviewer, Olivia always felt like the wallflower at literary gatherings—the one who never received a solo review in the *Sunday Times*, the one who never made the short list for the Booker prize. Never entirely surmounting nagging insecurities about her work and her background, she often appeared grudging and bitter to her contemporaries. For example, the historical novelist Peter Vansittart recalls, 'Olivia I admired, without very much liking. She seemed permanently discontented, aggrieved by what she considered critical neglect, and undue attentions awarded lesser writers.'[22] Yet the coexistence of her psychological fragility with the strength that drove her to write, to escape her provincial origins, and to translate her World War II experiences into compelling fiction, is, I think, the principal key to understanding Olivia Manning's life: tough and fragile at the same time, fighting her way to literary success and also retreating into sour complaint, delighting in many of her male and female friends and also

---

[20] *Friends and Friendship: Conversations and Reflections*, 172.

[21] Francis King, *Yesterday Came Suddenly*, 238.

[22] Unpublished letter from Peter Vansittart to Gerry Harrison, October 2006. I am grateful to Gerry Harrison for allowing me to quote from this letter. In this connection, it's possible, though, that Vansittart had been made none too happy by a review of one of his novels (*Sources of Unrest*) that appeared in *The Spectator* in 1962: Olivia declared that he was 'clearly struggling to impart something profoundly felt, but what it is I am not sure that I know.' 'Historical-fantastical-comical,' *The Spectator*, 2 February 1962.

denigrating other women writers whose experiences she failed to acknowledge had been similar to her own, she was a woman very much at war with herself.

Her female contemporaries in the 1960s—the more intellectual Iris Murdoch, of whom Ivy Compton-Burnett said had she trained as a nurse rather than as a philosopher she would have written less tedious books, or Muriel Spark, whose money-making abilities Olivia much envied, together with her diamonds, and whose Edinburgh girlhood had hardly been more privileged than Olivia's Portsmouth experience, or Pamela Hansford Johnson, one of the 'Snows' she hoped would soon melt away (Hansford Johnson was married to C. P. Snow)—seemed to get all the attention from literary editors and to make all the money. Much of Olivia's spiteful griping was voiced at lunches at Ivy Compton-Burnett's flat in Braemar Mansions off the Cromwell Road, where Compton-Burnett lived for many years with her companion, the furniture historian Margaret Jourdain. As Nicola Beauman notes in her biography of the novelist Elizabeth Taylor, in Braemar Mansions the 'conversation consisted almost entirely of fairly malicious gossip and complaints about the difficulties of post-war Kensington life: the male guests were mostly homosexual, the women almost all success-ful writers such as Kay Dick, Kathleen Farrell, Olivia Manning.'[23] Elizabeth Taylor was decidedly not one of this crowd. Her novels of middle-class domesticity in places like High Wycombe (where she lived for a number of years), together with what seemed to be a tedious existence married to a businessman, identified her as dull and 'feminine,' especially for someone with a racy wit and cosmo-politan sensibility like Olivia Manning. But despite feeling superior to novelists such as Elizabeth Taylor, Olivia still moaned about slaving away (Francis King's nickname for her was 'Olivia Moaning') and she noisily complained to her publishers and to the newspapers for which she produced reams of reviews that she was overworked, underpaid, and insufficiently appreciated.

At the historical moment in 1940 when the German Military Delegation made its swaggering entry into the Athénée Hotel, Olivia was known mainly to her husband's friends and the English colony as Mrs Reginald Smith and hardly at all as the novelist Olivia Manning.

[23] Nicola Beauman, *The Other Elizabeth Taylor*, 247.

When she married Reginald Donald Smith at the Marylebone Register Office on 18 August 1939 she had known him for only three
weeks. Always affectionately hailed as 'Reggie' by everyone from
high-level officials at the BBC where he worked as a Features and
Drama editor for many years after the war to waiters in Cairo cafés and
pub-owners in Hampstead, he was a large teddy-bear of a man six years
younger than his wife: carefree, ebullient, and promiscuously affectionate. He embraced life in a manner very different from her droll and
caustic approach to the world. After a boozy wedding party in the bar
of the Ritz Hotel attended by Reggie's best man and former tutor at
Birmingham University, the poet Louis MacNeice, and by Olivia's
bridesmaid, the poet and novelist Stevie Smith, less than a week later
Olivia found herself on a train to Bucharest where Reggie was to
resume his duties after a hectic English holiday.

At the Marylebone Register Office she had sliced three years off her
age, an instance of her characteristic fondness for self-invention.[24]
Despite the persistent reliance upon fact for fiction, Olivia was also a
great spinner of seductive stories about herself that served to romanti-
cize her background: her mother's Belfast Protestant family history as
the daughter of a publican sometimes got elevated into a romantic
narrative to do with Anglo-Irish country houses, and she confided to
friends details of affairs with the writers William Gerhardie, Henry
Green, and Anthony Burgess. It's possible she slept with all three
(although there is no persuasive evidence to support the truth of her
confidences), and possibly she had affairs with other, less well-known
men, given her sexual attractiveness and the relaxed nature of her
marriage to Reggie, but much more to the point (at least for this
biographer) is her need to tantalize and hold an audience with stories of
Anglo-Irish heritage and sexual conquest. The paradoxical confluence
in Olivia's life of appropriation of fact for fiction and invention of
fiction to glamorize prosaic facts, together with periods of hobbling
depression and professional self-doubt, tend to prohibit a tidy biographical narrative. Her life as a woman at war is scrambled and

---

[24] Sustaining this fiction to the end of her life, she told an academic interviewer in
January 1980 that she was born in 1911 (she was actually born in 1908). Professor Helen
L. Jones, interview with Olivia Manning, 21 January 1980: I am grateful to Professor
Gordon Jones for allowing me to refer to his late wife's meeting with Olivia Manning.

disjunctive, punctuated by the violence of public history and of private trauma.

When the Orient Express train nosed its slow way into Romania in late August 1939, Olivia Manning was on her way to war and to becoming an observer of a violent period in mid-twentieth-century European history. As the broadcaster and writer Joan Bakewell recently declared when nominating Olivia as a 'Woman of Achievement' who deserves to have her face on a British stamp, her resolute commitment to her work should be 'brought out of the shadows.'[25] With a controlling emphasis, then, on Olivia's enduring commitment to her writing, this story of a life that became the stuff of so much fiction begins in a semi-detached house at 134 Laburnum Grove, Portsmouth. For Olivia it was 'the longest, dreariest avenue in England.'[26] It was here that she was born on 2 March 1908, her birthplace registered as the North End and Buckland sub-district of the city. At the time of her birth her father, Oliver Manning, was forty-nine and her mother, Olivia Mary Manning, thirty-five. When Olivia's brother arrived five years later they christened him Oliver, having decided to name their children after themselves.

[25] *The Times*, 16 October 2008.
[26] Francis King, quoted in *The News*, Portsmouth, 26 June 2008.

I

Laburnum Grove

'My journey out of literary darkness reads like one of those
post-Wellsian novels much written in the 30s: lower middle-
class hero, unlettered but aspirant, comes upon a copy of *John
O'London's Weekly* and never looks back.'

Oliver Manning, 'Books I have read.'[1]

The avid uncertainty of the poor

At the beginning of the twentieth century, Portsmouth had long been
a significant major dockyard and base for the Royal Navy and so many
officers lived in Laburnum Grove (in the North End neighborhood of
Portsmouth) that it was nicknamed 'Brass Button Alley.' It was also
called Lavatory Lane because the white tiles on the outside of the
terraced houses looked like those on the walls inside public lavatories.
The son of a naval officer who lived right around the corner from
Laburnum Grove when Olivia was growing up remembers vividly that
the neighborhood had some 'local importance in a city not distinguished for its social cachet' by virtue of its throngs of navy personnel
in their smart uniforms who lived with their families in the white
glazed brick houses.[2] The Manning family occupied the last but one in
a terrace of twelve built in the late nineteenth century.

---

[1] *Bookmarks*, ed. Frederic Raphael, 116.
[2] Letter from Kenneth Holmes to Neville Braybrooke dated 30 December 1987,
written in response to an appeal for information that appeared in the *Portsmouth Evening
News* on 26 October 1987. OMC, HRC.

Laburnum Grove is also situated just over a mile from 393 Old Commercial Road, where Charles Dickens was born in 1812, the son of a clerk in the navy pay office, and as a child Olivia Manning often gazed at the large gold letters blazoned across number 393 that announced his birthplace. What's more, as an avid reader of almost everything on her father's bookshelves, she was well acquainted with most of Dickens's early novels, although a full appreciation of his genius came only after she married and Reggie urged her to read *Our Mutual Friend*. Going through a period of 'great anxiety' and unable to sleep, she found the first pages 'unpleasantly melodramatic . . . then, suddenly, the magic took hold of me and I became a Dickens addict . . . entranced, knowing myself fortunate that I had found him in time of need.'[3] Before becoming a true Dickens 'addict', however, Olivia had recognized his preoccupation with childhood unhappiness, wayward fathers, and punitive mothers, and early in her writing career had drawn upon his fiction for her own work. Although never as furious as Mrs Jo in *Great Expectations* nor as cunning as Mrs Skewton in *Dombey and Son*, the mothers in Olivia's short stories behave in similarly nasty ways to the dreadful parents who torment Dickens's unhappy children.

The boyhood of Olivia's father Oliver Manning was undeniably Dickensian, marked as it was by the obstacles, fortitude, and eventual success that we associate with boys such as Oliver Twist and David Copperfield. Born in the working-class district of Clerkenwell in London on 21 April 1859, he was the son of a house painter who when sober was a decent enough fellow but when drunk would grow obstreperous, thump the table (and occasionally his children), and announce he was the illegitimate son of the Earl of Warwick. Olivia would often announce ironically that she must have inherited her inventive gifts from her paternal grandfather. Oliver Manning was the last of eleven boys and, the family having run out of ordinary names, his father and brothers opted for something grander: Oliver, after the Great Protector. When he was four his mother died of consumption, and by the end of the century all his brothers had been carried off by the same disease, which left him much like Pip at the beginning of *Great Expectations*, a guilty survivor contemplating the gravestones of his dead parents and brothers. Barely literate but innately clever, he taught himself to read by

---

[3] 'Books I have read,' 124.

studying music hall posters, and since he had a good voice and did a plausible comic turn, his brothers thought he might be good material for the music-hall stage. Petrified with stage fright, however, he failed the one audition they could arrange for him and so, at the age of twelve, he was packed off to a naval training ship on the Thames.

Happy to be warm and reasonably well fed, Oliver bore up well under the harsh discipline and was eventually promoted to the rank of First Class Boy. Having survived the early morning winter rituals of being beaten up the rigging with a frayed rope end, his bare feet sticking to the frosted rungs, he was given an initial assignment on HMS *Impregnable*, which sailed to the West Indies in the early 1870s. Oliver Manning did not return to England until 1878 and by then he was a seasoned member of the military and naval forces that maintained governance in the far-flung outposts of empire. To the end of his life, he remained a loyal defender of British imperial power and a supporter of the Tory Party. Schooled in the Victorian ethos of self-help and spurred by memories of a rough and tumble Clerkenwell boyhood, whenever he could snatch a moment as a trainee, he studied navigation and mathematics while his companions rousted around below decks, and later, whilst on watch, he learned by heart complete scenes of Shakespeare and passages from Tennyson and Longfellow. To his daughter, he was a model of the unlettered aspiring 'hero' she evoked when recalling her 'journey out of literary darkness.'

In 1892, Oliver Manning was promoted to Gunner, and in 1911 at the age of fifty-five to Chief Gunner; when he retired in early 1914 he had reached the rank of lieutenant. On the outbreak of World War I in August 1914, he volunteered eagerly to serve once more and commanded patrol boats working the inland waters along the south coast, and when he retired for the second time in 1924 he had become a lieutenant-commander. But much as he relished his well-deserved promotion he loathed being ashore and hoped that the General Strike of 1926 would mean a return to active service. Ready to sign up, he hurried down to Portsmouth Town Hall, and when asked if he could take a boat across the harbor, proudly replied, 'Yes, or around the world, if you like.'[4] His was a story of some forty years of hard work under stark conditions, strict adherence to orders, and progress

---

[4] Typescript notes for 'Voyages around my father,' OMC, HRC.

through the ranks. Despite her awareness of the heavy price exacted by the navy for her father's elevation, his daughter cherished forever a fond preference for the navy over the other armed forces: 'The Navy is not like the army; it cleans up after itself, it leaves things shipshape. It is always a professional service while the army is always amateur, always dirty, wasteful indifferent, leaving its grimy touch on things like a sluttish house-wife.'[5]

Writing about her father after he was long dead, Olivia remembered he used to have a collection of pewter pots, one of which had been given to him on his twenty-first birthday: it was inscribed 'Oliver Manning, 21st. April 1880.' As she mulled over the fact that her father had been born in the year Charles Darwin published *On the Origin of Species* and that he had been forty-nine years old when she was born, she remembered how old he had appeared to her when she was a child: with his white hair, gray beard, and naval bearing, it seemed 'He did not belong merely to another generation, he belonged to history'—as indeed he did, to late Victorian history.[6] Around the time he received the pewter mug in 1880, he married a young woman named Phoebe, about whom little can be discovered except that she died in childbirth, together with her infant. For the next twenty-five years Oliver Manning enjoyed himself as an attractive widower: he was an entertaining storyteller, a splendid lead in all the Gilbert and Sullivan ships' productions, and a tremendous flirt when ashore. But the climb from lower to upper decks was painfully slow and bitterly demanding: to reach a commissioned rank, Oliver Manning needed to give twenty years of service. By December 1904 he was a lieutenant, and when he remarried in that year he chose the dark-haired daughter of a Northern Irish publican, but having neither the money nor the class confidence to mingle at ease with those who had once been his commanders and were now his colleagues, his life with Olivia Mary Morrow soon settled into bickering about penny pinching and social slights.

A pained witness to her parents' quarrels, Olivia never overcame her feelings of deprivation and liminality. As a child, she felt shut out from a better world elsewhere by her social inferiority, her pitiful wardrobe, and her provincial manners, and even when she had achieved considerable professional success, spoke in a remarkably polished accent, and

[5] Olivia Manning, *The Dreaming Shore*, 12.
[6] 'Voyages around my father,' *The Times*, 24 May 1975.

was surrounded by a bevy of bright and accomplished friends, she sometimes appeared almost forlorn, according to Victoria Orr-Ewing, the daughter of Olivia's closest friend.[7] Even taking a rented cottage on the Isle of Wight was often unmanageable for the Manning family and summer holidays were spent at the Northern Ireland home of Olivia's maternal grandparents. Her eventual biographer, June Braybrooke, remembers that when Olivia was invited by Francis King to lunch with Antonia Fraser at a Chelsea restaurant in 1960 she said, before setting out, 'Pour me a stiff gin. I'm nervous. How proud my old father would be to know I was lunching with an earl's daughter.'[8] Perhaps as solace for the parsimonious childhood, when she began to make some money in the 1960s, a lot of it went into the acquisition of nice furniture and some good paintings, in particular a David Hockney that featured a rather well-endowed young man. Olivia told her friends Roy and Aisling Foster that Reggie hated it because the young man was, indeed, so well-equipped. She kept the Hockney in the kitchen.

Olivia's recollections of her mother and a preoccupation with the figure of a disappointed and rancorous woman in her short stories suggest much bickering and unhappiness at the white-tiled house in Laburnum Grove. Olivia Mary Morrow was the daughter of David Morrow, an Ulster Presbyterian and the proprietor of 'The Old House at Home' on Ballymagee Street in Bangor; throughout her married life she remained strongly opposed to alcoholic consumption at home and spitefully contemptuous of her husband's fellow naval pensioners. To her, they were a bunch of boozy layabouts far too fond of listening to her husband's colorful yarns of life at sea and adventures ashore, the latter mostly to do with women. Johnny Slattery, a close friend and neighbor of Olivia and Reggie from their days in St John's Wood in the 1970s, remembers visits to London from Olivia's mother; the unconcealed grim demeanor and spiteful resentment of her daughter's material and professional success (attributable in Johnny Slattery's charitable opinion to a hardscrabble upbringing in Northern Ireland) did not make for joyful occasions.[9] On the other hand, Reggie's mother when visiting London was all accommodating admiration of

[7] Interview with Victoria Orr-Ewing, 8 April 2009.
[8] *Olivia Manning: A Life*, 103.
[9] Author's conversation with Johnny Slattery, 4 April 2009.

her son's intellect and his wife's professional success: she insisted that Reggie not be asked to undertake any menial tasks like taking his own supper out of the oven when he arrived home two hours late. She would, as Olivia puts it, leap up and announce that she didn't want him to 'tire his brain, or his feet, or something.'[10]

In remembering her father, Olivia Manning says that even if his happy days did not end completely with remarriage to a woman so temperamentally different from himself, whatever joyful moments they had enjoyed were soon overshadowed by squabbles about money and other women. By the time of Olivia's birth, Oliver Manning had come to bear a strong resemblance to George V and when serving on the Royal Yacht had even been mistaken for him. With his upright bearing, gray beard, and handsome face, he was a striking figure on Brass Button Alley, charming old ladies out for their constitutional and hailing his fellow naval retirees. His daughter adored him—for his generosity, his gentleness, his love of language, and a simple decency that might be seen as bordering on sentimentality but that to her was precious: on Christmas Day he always wept during the King's speech (regardless of which king) and he remained a fierce conservative to the end of his life, his Tory politics handed on to his daughter, albeit in gentler form. He died at the age of ninety, never having truly recovered from the death of Olivia's brother, who was killed in the Fleet Air Arm in 1941; for many months, he refused to speak and could scarcely be persuaded to eat. When Olivia visited Laburnum Grove on her return to England at the end of World War II, she was horrified by her parents' desolation—'they were quite shut away from me in the tragedy that had fallen on them.'[11] Lieutenant-Commander Manning was also much diminished by fading eyesight and recurrent bronchial infections. Once a man of great physical vigor who for many years looked younger than his age, in his last years he seemed to his daughter 'an absolutely unbearable figure.' On his deathbed, he murmured to her, 'I never thought I would break up like this,' to which she responded that he could live another ten years: 'his face lit at the thought of ten more years in a world he had loved so much.'[12] Olivia's special name for her father was 'Dumps,'

---

[10] Olivia Manning to June Braybrooke, 24 March 1969, OMC/C, HRC.
[11] 27 April 1971, FKC/OM, HRC.
[12] Typescript notes for 'Voyages around my father,' OMC, HRC.

affectionately intended, to be sure, but undeniably suggestive of a tendency to be down-in-the-dumps when around his discontented wife.

The Portsmouth of Olivia's childhood memories is a place of seedy desolation: depressed by the sight of a polluted harbor and dull stony beaches littered with paper bags, banana-skins, and broken bottles left by day-trippers, she found her primary comfort in the Portsmouth public library with the air smelling of mackintoshes and 'the desolate glimmer of a wet, foggy evening touching ten thousand books, all stoutly bound against assault.'[13] A rare childhood treat would be tea at the George Hotel with their father, where Olivia and Oliver were always shown the rooms where Nelson and Emma Hamilton slept before he left in the chill, early morning for victory and death at Trafalgar. After tea and the ritualistic inspection of the bedroom, the children were usually taken for a look at the house where Dickens was born, where they would gaze admiringly at the large gold lettering across the front door. By far the happiest memory of Olivia's Portsmouth childhood features the return of her father from long commissions: not only did this bring some relief from the morose nagging of her mother, it also meant exotic presents such as Chinese silks, tins of quinces, and jars of ginger and kumquats. To his children, Oliver Manning was a magical figure, magnificent in his gold braid as he whisked them past the sentries onto Whale Island (a small island in Portsmouth harbor and the oldest shore training establishment within the Royal Navy), where he would show them the mysteries of the Gunnery School and the zoo to which returning sailors brought gifts of emus and kangaroos, and odd, long-legged tropical birds. After visits to Whale Island, he would take them to the Dockyard where they explored the great painted and gilded *Victory*, Nelson's ship that sailed to Trafalgar.[14]

As a child of three or four, Olivia Manning vowed to her parents that when she grew up she would become a painter. Her favorite book was Charles Kingsley's *The Water Babies*. She would pore over the Noel Paton illustrations of the boy-hero Tom's transformation from grimy chimney sweep to endearing sprite. At the time, her father was in charge of what was known as the Naval Stationery office and he

[13] Olivia Manning, 'Buried alive,' *The Times*, 6 November 1961.
[14] Olivia Manning, 'The Irish coast and Portsmouth,' *The Palestine Post*, 2 June 1944.

used to bring home for his daughter enormous books used for keeping accounts. She filled them with 'scribble, scribble, scribble, like Mr. Gibbon,' and when she tired of writing she got down to illustrations for her nonsense, filling the hefty books with her own fanciful drawings, eager to win her parents' admiration of her talent. As a teenager dreaming about her grown-up future and a world elsewhere, she oscillated between fantasies of becoming a famous writer housed in a Bloomsbury square or a moody painter holed up in a Paris garret; the question was settled eventually by her acceptance of the fact that painters need studios, paint, canvases, and so on—'I could afford pen and paper but not much else.'[15]

Until about the age of five, Olivia Manning was thought by her mother to be an appealing child with dainty features, very dark hair, and beautiful olive skin, all attributed by her Bangor relatives to direct descent from the Spaniards who had been shipwrecked off the west coast of Ireland with the Armada in 1588. Delighted by her prettiness and sprightly intelligence, her mother paraded her before the Laburnum Grove neighbors. But everything changed with the birth of Oliver Manning in 1913. Olivia recalls that she became so sulky and difficult that her mother announced chidingly, 'You're a terrible disappointment to me. When you were a small child, I used to think you were going to be something remarkable. Everyone said how unusually intelligent you were. You were delightful, you were charming, you amused everybody, and now look at you, wretched, sulky, shut in, disagreeable.'[16] Olivia began to see herself 'as somebody who nobody could possibly like.' And not only did she endure her mother's unkind commentary on her behavior, her brother began to make fun of her beak-like features—when she was in her mid-fifties she told Kay Dick, 'I have this sort of irregular profile which has been the agony of my life; my brother used to make fun of my nose—I never got over it.'[17] (See Figure 1.)

That her father was frequently caught in compromising situations with other women and that her mother made it painfully plain to her children she remained in the house with their erring parent for their sake only, further increased the sullen misery Olivia had begun to feel

[15] Olivia Manning, 'Books I have read,' 116–17.
[16] Kay Dick, *Friends and Friendship: Conversations and Reflections*, 33.
[17] *Friends and Friendship*, 28.

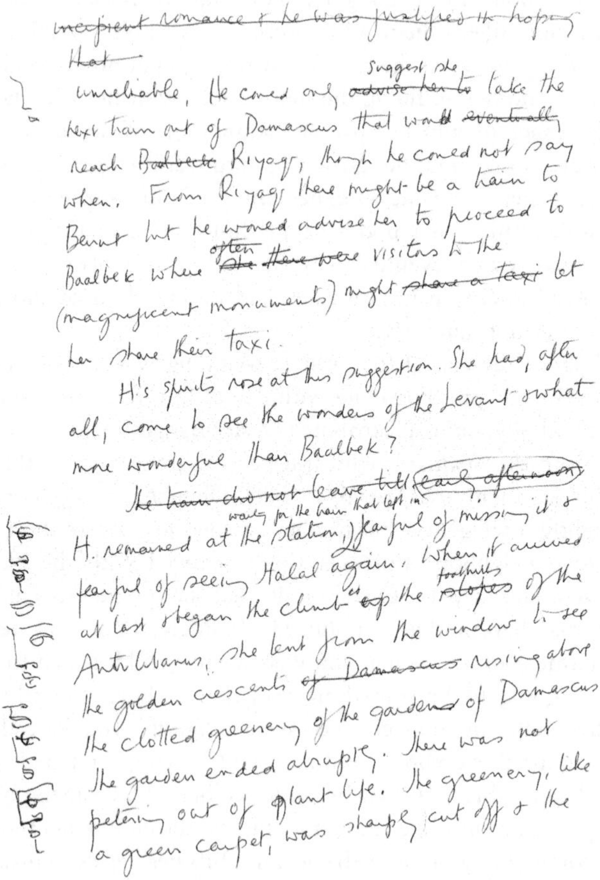
~~incipient romance & he was justified the hoping~~
~~that~~
unreliable. He could only ~~advise her to~~ suggest she take the
next train out of Damascus that would ~~eventually~~
reach ~~Baalbeck~~ Riyaq, though he could not say
when. From Riyaq there might be a train to
Beirut but he would advise her to proceed to
Baalbek where ~~there were~~ often visitors to the
(magnificent monuments) might ~~share a taxi~~ let
her share their taxi.
H's spirits rose at this suggestion. She had, after
all, come to see the wonders of the Levant & what
more wonderful than Baalbek?
~~The train did not leave till early afternoon~~
H. remained at the station, waiting for the train that left in fearful of missing it &
fearful of seeing Halal again. When it arrived
at last & began the climb up the ~~slopes~~ foothills of the
Anti Libanus, she leant from the window to see
the golden crescents ~~of Damascus~~ rising above
the clotted greenery of the gardens of Damascus
The garden ended abruptly. There was not
petering out of plant life. The greenery, like
a green carpet, was sharply cut off & the

Figure 1. Olivia Manning, manuscript pages from *School for Love.* The sketches of profiles with prominent noses appear frequently in the margins of Manning's manuscripts. Olivia was sensitive about the size and sharpness of her nose. With permission of Victoria Orr-Ewing.

with the birth of Oliver. Driven to vengeful fury by the Commander's philandering, one awful day his wife bundled the children on to the top of a tram-car to ride down Portsmouth High Street so they might see him arm in arm with his latest paramour: 'My brother and I felt guilty that because of us our parents lived in a state of alternating uproar and

sullen sulks.'[18] After her mother's death, Reggie, always sweetly benign
and the treasured son of an adoring mother, advised Olivia to forgive and
forget: her acid response was that Olivia Manning had been an outrageous, tactless woman with a mind as rigid as a cast-iron mangle, not
clinically deranged but definitely psychologically unbalanced.

Olivia's education began at a Dame's School a few doors down from
the house in Laburnum Grove. With the outbreak of World War I in
1914, she traveled to her mother's home town of Bangor and attended
a Presbyterian School in Main Street for several terms; on her return to
Portsmouth she was enrolled briefly at Lynton House School in King-
ston Crescent (how her parents could afford school fees remains mysterious) and at the age of fourteen, in 1922, entered Portsmouth Grammar
School with her brother Oliver. She left when she was sixteen. This was
the extent of her formal education, although as a child, like almost all
writers, she was an avid reader and her 'journey out of literary darkness'
began at precisely the moment she began to hang around the public
library, 'sensing that somewhere there, if one could find it, was the
answer to the mystifying boredom of existence.'[19] She discovered that
books were 'Important.' As a teenager, she was delighted by Shaw's
contempt for the English middle classes and until she died she treasured a
few first editions of his plays purchased with precious pocket money.
She was also devastated by D. H. Lawrence's portraits of tormented
family life, stunned by his searing depiction of fights between husbands
and wives that resembled battles she witnessed at Laburnum Grove.
After Shaw and Lawrence, she moved on to Wyndham Lewis, Aldous
Huxley, and Virginia Woolf.[20] In a notebook inscribed 'Olivia Mary
Manning, February 1929,' she jotted down her thoughts on what she
termed a 'decadent style,' something she struggled to define in relation
to the 'classic style' displayed, say, in *Hamlet*. In themselves not particularly revelatory, the value of these notes is their evidence of the serious-
ness with which Olivia undertook her reading. She may not have been
attending university, or even have gone to school beyond the age of
sixteen, but at the age of twenty-one she was creating her own world
through solitary reading and note taking, like her father before her
heroically determined to rise through the ranks.

[18] 'Books I have read,' 119.
[19] 'Books I have read,' 117.
[20] 'Books I have read,' 117.

Before arriving at the challenging complexity of Woolf's novels, however, at around the age of thirteen she had retreated from the gloom of Portsmouth into popular English schoolgirl fiction of the time—principally, thrilling books by Angela Brazil (1868–1947) with titles such as *The Jolliest Term on Record* (1915) and *A Patriotic Schoolgirl* (1918). Reading about middle-class schoolgirls running around playing lacrosse and vying with each other to become Head Girl led her to become inventive about her own background and she told her fellow-pupils at the rather posh Lynton House School that she had a nanny and that she would be going to boarding-school. Quickly, she earned a reputation for lying and showing-off and so she moved from Angela Brazil's athletic schoolgirls to Rider Haggard's muscular young men; after reading through all of the Haggards to be found on her father's bookshelves and in the public library, she declared herself to be an authority on Zulu history. Before taking up Rider Haggard she had wanted to read George Eliot and had started with *Adam Bede* (a suggestion from her father), but her mother had quickly interfered, banned the book from the house, and declared its depiction of seduction and illegitimacy unfit reading for an extravagantly imaginative girl of fifteen. She was equally disapproving of Rider Haggard (not good for girls) and of the *TLS*, which Olivia took to reading around the same time; worried that her daughter's bookishness and sharp intelligence would diminish her chances of marriage, she declared that young men were not attracted to young ladies who favored such reading material. 'A lot I cared,' Olivia thought to herself: 'I was going to a city where there were young men with more advanced ideas.'[21]

At the age of sixteen, rather than going to a boarding-school of the sort depicted in her once treasured Angela Brazil, Olivia Manning left Portsmouth Grammar School to become a typist. Her father having retired from the navy at the close of World War I on a pension that Olivia termed 'absolutely pitiable,' it was essential that she begin contributing to the family finances. In a rocky economic climate she was lucky to find employment. During the eleven years that elapsed between leaving school in 1924 and arriving in London in 1935 (the city where she hoped to meet young men with advanced ideas), Olivia worked in various solicitors' and architects' offices, usually earning

---

[21] 'Books I have read,' 121.

around fifteen shillings per week (now approximately £30 per week), and she gave ten shillings to her mother as a contribution to room and board. Never free of what she later called 'this awful thing' of money worries and the painful absence of any kind of higher education, she would chide more socially privileged friends such as Francis King for their failure to remember her absence of a 'classy sort of background,' announcing sarcastically that while they had lived on their investments and had been fed things with a silver spoon, she had lived on her wits and had fought for everything.

When Olivia started earning her living, she somehow managed to scrape together enough money to attend evening classes at the Portsmouth Municipal School of Art, still hoping to become a painter but having no idea how she might manage to support herself and find a place in the art world. What she did know with complete certainty was that she needed to leave Portsmouth: she vowed not to sink into the swamp of a seaside town she later described as situated on 'the outer rim of provincial ignorance,' and she longed to escape the pitiful sight of her henpecked father and the constant carping of her mother. The evening classes were a consolation and a spur to improving her life. To one of her fellow-students, she remained an 'enigma . . . a Modigliani type female' with her pale skin, sharp features, and almost black hair, an aloof young woman intellectually superior to everyone around her who never rushed across the Guildhall Square during a break in classes to buy succulent cream buns.[22] (See Figure 2.)

But even if she achieved a measure of recognition in April 1928 when one of her paintings ('A Study in Tempera') was chosen for an annual art exhibition on the South Parade Pier in Portsmouth, she knew that painting would not propel her departure for London. Even if she had been an exceptionally talented artist, which she suspected was not the case, she lacked the financial resources to keep going through hard times, something brought painfully home to her when she was invited to tea at an amiable fellow-student's country house. She had never been inside the gates of such a house, and the shrewd eye of her friend's mother took in her 'old, washed-out dress and skinny limbs,' seeing in her 'the avid uncertainty of the poor.'[23]

---

[22] Letter from Kenneth Holmes to Neville Braybrooke, 30 December 1987, OMC, HRC.

[23] 'Nothing but the best,' *The Spectator*, 14 May 1977.

Figure 2. Sketch of Olivia Manning at Portsmouth Municipal School of Art, 1928, by Kenneth Holmes. With permission of Victoria Orr-Ewing.

As a means of saving money to get to London, while at art school Olivia also took to writing popular serials and sending them to the *Portsmouth Evening News*. Hours spent in the public library devouring Rider Haggard's romances and Angela Brazil's plucky tales paid off, literally to the tune of £25: starting in October 1929 the newspaper began publication of the first of nineteen installments of 'The Rose of Rubies.' Advertised as 'A Sensational Story by a New Writer' named Jacob Morrow (Olivia took Jacob from Virginia Woolf's novel *Jacob's Room* and added her mother's maiden name) and liberally sprinkled with research into alchemy and gemology conducted at the public library, it traces the perilous adventures of an English governess in Paris caught up in searching for an exquisite brooch set in the shape of a rose and fashioned from rubies that is the centerpiece of a cult,

'The Religion of the Rose.' 'The Rose of Rubies' delivers on its promise of sensation as Helen Massey, the English governess, races around Paris in plucky pursuit of the villainous Madame Paul who has stolen the precious brooch from its rightful owner (Olivia must have spent many hours with a Paris street map since the plot involves much dodging in and out of obscure alleyways). 'The Rose of Rubies' was a hit with Portsmouth readers and Olivia quickly followed up with 'Here is Murder.' Delighted with the success of 'Jacob Morrow,' the *Evening News* hailed him as a 'brilliant young author' who shows 'a complete mastery of the technique of thrills, as well as a very keen insight into human psychology': Morrow's third serial, 'The Dark Scarab,' promised the *News*, will display 'his knowledge of Egypt and Egyptology,' another remarkable testament to the hours Olivia spent in the Portsmouth Public Library swotting up on all things Egyptian. Little did she know that some twelve years later she would actually be living in Egypt, soaking up the atmosphere first-hand as preparation for the fiction she published after the war.

In addition to working up the serials, Olivia was writing short stories, one of which, 'The Sunwaite Ghost,' appeared in the *Hampshire Telegraph and Post* on 29 December 1929: the winner of fourth prize in a short-story competition, it reveals Olivia's sharp memory for detail in its copious description of a country house at Christmastime. Modeling the house on that of her art school friend, she describes many grand rooms decorated with holly, ivy, and mistletoe and a snow-covered lawn similar to the one where her 'avid uncertainty' and lower-class origins had been detected by the sharp eye of her friend's mother. She also continued work on a novel begun when she was eighteen, 'very word and beauty conscious,' as she described it in 1958 when sending it to Neville Braybrooke as possible contribution to a collection of early writings by well-known authors. The typescript fragment that remains (thirteen pages), among other wordy and colorful moments, describes a young man standing on board a ship, staring down into the water 'where the sun, striking in wide emerald bars through oil-dark obscurity, glanced over a swiftly flickering flight of purple and amber fish.' More lush description follows; rock faces, for example, are overhung by 'escallop pink bushes and grey-green creeper.'[24]

---

[24] 'Christmas Eve,' OMC, HRC.

In February 1929, she began keeping the first of her literary note-books, those records of an ambitious self-education, in which she entered quotations from current reading (books by Havelock Ellis, Herbert Read, Robert Graves, George Moore, and Bertrand Russell) and also ideas for her stories. Aldous Huxley, Virginia Woolf, and Katherine Mansfield were an exhilarating inspiration, writers who kept her scribbling away in her small and drafty bedroom, and what had begun as a somewhat cavalier fling at writing serials for the Ports-mouth newspaper to supplement the wages from office typing began to supplant the earlier ambition to become a painter. Although two probably not very good novels written in the early 1930s were rejected by Jonathan Cape, she soldiered on, determined that writing would take her to London. Sad to say, no manuscripts exist for these two novels. After her mother's death in 1954 (she left her daughter a diamond ring, shares in the United Premier Oil Co., and interest on four houses in Bangor owned by the Morrow family), Olivia had a big bonfire in the garden into which she flung all her early writings, having decided they were 'too embarrassing to preserve.'[25] One of them was probably an astonishingly long opus that she titled 'The Hobbyhorse,' a tragic story of a misunderstood young painter starving to death in a Paris garret whose suffering conjures up the sad saga of a young writer struggling away in a Portsmouth terraced house on Lavatory Lane. Predicting at the mid-point in writing this tome that the total length would be three hundred thousand words, Olivia wrote naively to James Joyce's Paris publisher offering them a novel as long as *Ulysses*, to which they replied that length was not all that was required for publication. Jonathan Cape, however, did send her a reader's report on 'The Hobbyhorse'—'the first encouragement I had ever received.'[26] What is so remarkable about all this is the intellectual isolation of Olivia's life in the 1920s and early 1930s. No one advised her, few encouraged her, yet after typing all day in a solicitor's office, she managed to write an enormously long novel, made it her business to discover the name of Joyce's Paris publisher, and having no luck with that approach, valiantly sent the manuscript off to Jonathan Cape.

---

[25] Isobel English (June Braybrooke), Introduction, *The Wind Changes*, p. xi.

[26] See the brief summary of her writing life that she sent to William Gerhardie in 1953. Correspondence of William Gerhardie, Cambridge University Library, 4 September 1953. She never finished 'The Hobbyhorse.'

Learning to write

Signing herself as Olivia Mary Manning, on 22 June 1933 she wrote from Laburnum Grove to the literary agents Curtis Brown enclosing two short stories, 'A Scantling of Foxes' and 'A Change of Mood.' Her letter was addressed to Geoffrey West, one of the assistants, who was also a biographer and critic, and it reveals her touching ambition and insecurity: 'I am still learning to write. I live and work amongst people who have no interest in literature and who would only make fun of anything I write. I have, therefore, only my own untrained judgement on which to rely.'[27] As things turned out, West had recently joined the small group of proprietors of a new journal, *New Stories* (the others were H. E. Bates, Arthur Calder-Marshall, Hamish Miles, Edward O'Brien, and L. A. Pavey), and the autumn issue of 1934 carried Olivia Manning's first short story published somewhere other than in a local newspaper, 'A Scantling of Foxes.' It is an amazing tale of sadism, male obsession, and female suffering, its depiction of sexual pathology derived doubtless from Olivia's readings in Havelock Ellis. Father Sheehan—'ridden by sexual lust which, suppressed, inflicted, by way of revenge for its suppression, moods in which, half-demented, he felt more suffering and imprisoned beast than human creature'—serves as priest for a convent on the Irish coast. The sight of the nuns compels him in his imagination to strip them of their 'concealing robes' and to fantasize breaking with 'savage fury, beneath the strength of his own lean limbs, those women's bodies.'[28] A pregnant village girl taken into the convent becomes the abused scapegoat for his suppressed desires, and intuitively sensing his sexual torment, she registers that knowledge in a sideways glance; he, in return, determines to ruin her beauty with physical labor: 'He believed now he could destroy his lust only by destroying in her all her beauty, her youth, the contagion of her desire' (p. 344). After three years of unremitting work scrubbing the convent floors, she dies of consumption: on her deathbed, refused forgiveness by the priest, she murmurs 'Fool' as she expires. Since no foxes appear in the story, the title remains mysterious, but the sketch (a scantling) of

[27] OMC/C, HRC.
[28] *New Stories*, 1/5 (October–November 1934), 340–1.

male fear of female sexual contagion testifies to Olivia's extensive
reading and bold imagination.

After 'A Scantling of Foxes' was accepted by *New Stories*, Olivia
continued to labor over the fatally long 'The Hobbyhorse' but again
wrote dispiritingly to Geoffrey West on 12 July 1934 that she has
neither the heart nor the energy to do any more revisions: 'As I have
to keep myself I am working until quite late each evening and have
therefore very little time for writing. I am also very tired and prefer to
work up new ideas. To return to old work, lacking the impetus of the
sense of exploration and discovery that comes with new work requires
more energy than I seem to have.'[29] Dispirited, then, by her inability
to undertake sustained revision of her epic novel, she turned once
more to short stories. In a pattern that was to shape much of her later
fiction, the miserable saga of her family life gave them focus and
intensity, and in common with all autobiographical writing, the stories
are rooted in actual experience and molded by the imaginative power
of memory. Most were completed at various times before the war and
appeared in various journals when relative stability returned to publishing after 1945. Inspired by Joyce (for her, 'one of the greatest, if not
the great short story' writer in the English language), she set them all in
Ireland.

'The Children,' written in 1938, is related through the wounding
experiences of Vanessa and Joseph Clandavy, a sister and brother who
bear strong resemblance to Olivia and Oliver Manning. With a philandering father and a needy, resentful mother who asks, 'What life is
there here for me? What happiness? I have nothing now but you two
children,'[30] as often as they can, the children escape their decaying
Galway house to explore the beach and rock face. The familiar family
narrative of parental squabbling and damaged children that resonated
for Olivia through her reading of D. H. Lawrence, if no one else, is
enriched through her evocation of a child's joy in discovering the
natural world, and her talent as a painter vivifies her descriptions of
the landscape, the clouds, the storms, the sea, and the rock pools where
the children search for crabs: they look down into the pools, and 'see,
through the clear, smooth water, the film of fawn-coloured, speckled
sand at the bottom. All over the sides the delicate anemones were

---

[29] OMC/C, HRC.   [30] *A Romantic Hero, and Other Stories*, 14.

pearl-pink and flamingo pink. Beside them grew little blood-dark, unvarying jellies.'[31] The bulk of the story is taken up with a visit to the children of neighbors, Sir James O'Neil and his English wife: it is a visit tainted by the resentment and social inferiority felt by Vanessa and Joseph when in the company of the privileged O'Neil children who taunt them for their gauche manners and shabby clothes. In a traverse through Elizabeth Bowen's Anglo-Irish country, Manning brilliantly conveys the sad envy of the Clandavy children, while at the same time showing us the rugged beauty of the Irish coast as seen through their eyes. And this was a beauty remembered from childhood visits to her grandmother's house in Ireland where she and Oliver would play for hours on the beach and see no one except a man with his donkey gathering sea-wrack; believing that the heaped, slippery seaweed hid sea monsters, they would pick their way carefully over the jagged gray rocks that ran out into the frothing, dangerous sea.[32]

'Two Birthdays,' written in 1939 and first published in *Modern Reading* in 1947, follows the same family one year later when the father is dead, the house has been sold, and the mother remains the same resentful and despairing figure we see in 'The Children.' 'The Visit,' written in 1939 and first published in *Kenyon Review* in 1944, is narrated by an unnamed girl whose jealousy of her brother, admiration of her father, and dislike of her mother spring virtually unmediated from Olivia's own family life. The story begins with the brother's admission that his first memory is of being pushed downstairs by his sister; as an adult, Olivia ruefully confessed to Reggie that when Oliver Manning was still a baby she would place toys on the staircase in the hope that her mother would trip and drop him. The brother in 'The Visit' has very fair skin, large gray eyes, and soft blond hair, exactly like Oliver Manning. And like Lieutenant-Commander Manning, who was a talented drawer and encouraged his daughter's artistic ambitions when she was a little girl, the father in 'The Visit' is a draftsman, a man who 'drew beautifully in pencil or ink—animals, flowers, houses with gardens overhanging the sea.'[33] The mother in the story is jealous and mean-spirited (no surprise here), alienated from the artist crowd into

---

[31] *A Romantic Hero*, 4.

[32] For Olivia's memories of these visits to Ireland, see 'The Irish coast and Portsmouth,' *The Palestine Post*, 2 July 1944.

[33] *A Romantic Hero*, 75.

which her husband had taken her, a situation analogous to the social elevation from publican's daughter to naval officer's wife experienced by Olivia's mother. Rather than living in Portsmouth, this family lives in Belfast, but the city's bleak atmosphere summons up Olivia's dislike of Northern Ireland and her hatred of the grim seaside town where she grew up: 'We knew all about the world. It was outside our window: the black river crawling under the drizzle of rain; the wet cobbles; the dirty pavements; the stale fishy smell from the docks; the women with starved and bitter faces beneath their shawls; the irritating chilliness of summer and the knife-edged winter cold; and the harsh-voiced schoolchildren whom we, the aliens, were always fighting.'[34]

The centerpiece of 'The Visit' is an invitation to tea at the home of Lady Moxton, the wealthy widow of a linen manufacturer and a distant relative of the mother. She is an appalling figure, somewhat like Mrs Skewton in Dickens's *Dombey and Son* (1847), that caricature of a woman of seventy who dresses as if she were twenty-seven and whose maid when she prepares her for bed removes the wig, the eyebrows, and the rouge, leaving her an old, worn, yellow, nodding skeleton with red eyes. In Olivia's story, Lady Moxton receives her guests in her bedroom, propped up in bed and wearing heavy make-up. Failing to charm the old woman, the narrator endures the fury of her mother, who shrieks, 'with the spite she showed when disappointed,' that if her daughter were a girl who could make herself pleasant she might have received a present. When the narrator cries that she does not wish to be rich, the mother responds that if she does not wish to make money for her mother, then the brother will: 'She smiled at him: he smiled back, and their understanding of each other made me feel excluded and afraid.'[35] Essentially, the story is about deprivation and exclusion—the mother deprived of the comforts and privilege of the family she has left for an improvident marriage and the daughter excluded from maternal warmth and the affectionate bond between doting mother and compliant son. This is Olivia's childhood story as she wrote it into her fiction and into her adult self-dramatization as an unloved and unappreciated figure.

When 'The Hobbyhorse' was returned to her by Jonathan Cape in 1934, it was accompanied by an encouraging and thrilling letter from

[34] *A Romantic Hero*, 76.   [35] *A Romantic Hero*, 81.

the assistant to Edward Garnett at Jonathan Cape, Hamish Miles, a name she knew already from the masthead of *New Stories*. He wrote to say that although 'The Hobbyhorse' was far too long and derivative, he could discern real talent in its writer. From her devoted reading of the *TLS* and her familiarity with the life and work of Virginia Woolf, Olivia was up on all Bloomsbury doings, enthralled by a shimmering world so different from her own. She knew that Edward Garnett was a writer, critic, and well-known editor with impressive connections in the English literary establishment. She knew that his wife was Constance Garnett, the distinguished translator of Russian literature, and that their son David Garnett was a member of the Bloomsbury Group; in 1942 Garnett married the daughter of Vanessa Bell and Duncan Grant, his one-time lover. She longed for Bloomsbury and so identified with the Ugly Duckling of fairy tales that she believed she had only to reach Fitzroy Square for those beautiful swans Virginia Woolf and Vanessa Bell to come sailing to welcome her and caress her with their beaks.[36] All that remained was to escape the claustrophobic horror of Portsmouth, and when she had enough money saved for the bus fare and could take a day off from typing, she would lug her portfolio of paintings and drawings from Portsmouth to Victoria Station and spend a discouraging day trudging from art agency to art agency. But despite the frosty lack of interest in her work, she was intoxicated by London—the rush of air in the underground seeming to her 'the most wonderful smell in the world'[37]—and seeing that she would get nowhere as a commercial artist, she decided to answer every advertisement in the 'Situations Vacant' section of *The Times* that might land a typing job in London. Finally, she got a nibble and again took the early morning bus to Victoria, a journey of about two hours and a half, but when she got to the prospective employer's office in the financial district, she found a dispiriting number of applicants ahead of her.

Temporarily at a loss, she remembered that in his encouraging letter Hamish Miles had suggested she telephone him if she were to be in London. She did so, and when they met in his office in Tavistock Square he was reserved but complimentary about her writing, telling

---

[36] 'Books I have read,' 118.

[37] 'Let me tell you before I forget,' fragment of autobiography by Olivia Manning, OMC, HRC.

her that Edward Garnett believed she had great talent. With work, he said, she might even become as good as D. H. Lawrence. At the sight of him, nervously moving the pens and pencils on his desk, she thought to herself, 'Yes. He is exactly right.'[38] On the bus back to Portsmouth that evening, she was exhilarated, lingering thoughts of becoming a painter extinguished by their meeting, and she felt sure she could become a very good, if not a great writer. She also decided that if it were not for his sensual, hedonistic mouth Hamish Miles might appear 'over-sensitive' with his fine, light-colored hair and ivory-colored skin. But she liked the way he looked at her when he suggested they have dinner when she was next in London, and walking home to Laburnum Grove after she got off the bus, she felt Bloomsbury might be within her reach. As soon as she escaped the domestic war zone controlled by her mother, she would be ready to enter the battle for survival in the exciting world of London, to dine with Hamish Miles, and perhaps, even, transformed from ugly duckling into beautiful swan, to chat with Virginia Woolf and Vanessa Bell.

[38] 'Let me tell you before I forget,' OMC, HRC.

2

The Most Terrifying City
in the World

'When we were young, I think what made life easier to cope
with was the fact that it was a much greater challenge. You had
nothing given to you. You had to fight, and people did fight.
They stood up to life better.'
                    Olivia Manning in conversation with Kay Dick, 1972.

Hamish and Stevie

In late 1934, with an introduction from one of her father's naval friends
and despite a high level of unemployment in the capital, Olivia
Manning finally found a job that took her away from Portsmouth:
'The time was the out of work '30s when anyone who had a job could
count himself lucky.'[1] Much as she had hoped for something in
Bloomsbury, close to Jonathan Cape and Hamish Miles, perhaps in
one of the many publishers' offices scattered around Bedford and
Tavistock Squares, she found herself typing out lists and addresses for
the van drivers at the Peter Jones department store in Chelsea—'the
only job that no one else wanted.' Situated on the west side of Sloane
Square and founded as a small haberdashers in 1877, the store had
been glossily redesigned in 1934 and featured the first steel-and-glass,
curtain-wall façade in Britain. This modern sleekness mattered little to
Olivia, however, since she spent her day closeted in a stuffy back

---

[1] 'Let me tell you before I forget,' OMC, HRC.

office, her contact with customers restricted to answering testy questions about their late deliveries. Peter Jones in the 1930s was where the upper crust of Chelsea and Kensington came to buy dresses for baby, uniforms for the boys before they went off to boarding school, and wedding presents for friends and family: it was also the most desirable place to select furniture, china, and linens for the elegant Georgian mansions and red-brick Queen-Anne-style mansion blocks that housed the majority of the store's customers. John Betjeman reputedly said that when the end of the world came he wanted to be in the haberdashery department of Peter Jones 'because nothing unpleasant could ever happen there,' and, in the early twenty-first century, its fashionable reputation remains unchanged from the time that Olivia Manning turned up at 8:00 one morning in 1934 to begin her new job. At the age of twenty-six, she had devoted a fair chunk of her life to planning an escape from Portsmouth, her humorless and hard-lipped mother, and those 'petty tyrants' of provincial existence. Now, in London, the smell of the underground was exhilarating, the plant pots in Sloane Square a riot of autumnal colors, the city an unexplored paradise.

Before leaving Portsmouth, she had secured lodging at the Girls' Friendly Society hostel near Euston Station, but she soon discovered that this noisy, crowded, and down-market dormitory was decidedly not what she wanted. Since Euston Station was also a long way from Peter Jones she immediately began scouring the handwritten advertisements in tobacconists and newsagents around Sloane Square and within a week moved to a bed-sitting room on Margaretta Terrace, situated just off Oakley Street in Chelsea and roughly halfway between the King's Road and the Embankment. It was only a ten-minute or so walk along the King's Road to Peter Jones. The rent was twenty-five shillings a week, which did not leave much to live on after it was deducted from her weekly wage of thirty-five shillings. But she was deliriously happy despite the dilapidated condition of the house in Margaretta Terrace: it was 'at a point of near decay.' The stairs with their torn scraps of carpet were never cleaned and a nasty smell followed her up from the bathroom to the second floor where she had a large front room.[2] But even if she had to deal with a smelly house, grumpy van drivers, and irate customers, she took great satisfaction in having defied her mother's sour

---

[2] 'Let me tell you before I forget,' OMC, HRC.

prediction that she wouldn't last five minutes outside Portsmouth. Also Hamish Miles had responded enthusiastically when she telephoned to say she was now in London. He suggested dinner at *Au Jardin des Gourmets* on Greek Street in Soho, and although the prospect of eating French food worried her a little (Portsmouth meals had generally run to mince and sprouts), she knew he found her attractive and that she was ready to go to bed with him. Since their encounter in his office, she had dreamt of conquering Bloomsbury with her wit, intelligence, and promising literary talent. Hamish would be her introduction. As things turned out, he matched all her dreams and expectations when he became her lover, ferried her from one literary party to another, and arranged for publication of her first novel.

Hamish's influence upon Olivia was immediate, profound, and long lasting. At the start, it was very much a mentor–acolyte relationship: he 'fatherly, informative and kind,' congratulating her on her wit, original mind, and fresh outlook, and she enthralled as she acquiesced to his authority, her mother's taunts that she was 'impudent and too clever by half' obliterated by his praise. Actually, though, the age difference between them was not that great. When they became lovers, Hamish was forty and Olivia twenty-six, and it would seem that in her memoir of their affair she painted herself as rather more sexually and intellectually naïve than she was in actuality, a pattern consistent with a lifelong practice of slicing several years off her true age. Initially, they met once a week for romantic dinners in various Soho restaurants, and she adapted herself quickly to *escaloppe de veau* and a delicious roast chicken quite unlike the bird accompanied by bread sauce that was occasionally served for Sunday lunch at Laburnum Grove. At these dinners, she played the part of adoring student to his seasoned role as instructor in European literature. When she fervently confessed that she admired Dostoyevsky above all other writers, he suggested she read *Madame Bovary* (Hamish translated Andre Maurois's *Byron* in 1930 and his *Voltaire* in 1935), and when she spoke longingly of wanting to write like Virginia Woolf he prescribed immediate immersion in James Joyce. Following his advice, she plunged immediately into Joyce's short stories and set her first published novel, *The Wind Changes*, in Dublin and the Irish countryside rather than in the London of *Mrs Dalloway*. Hamish also took her to Paris, where she strolled happily through streets that had been mere names on a map when she wrote 'The Rose of Rubies' for the *Portsmouth Evening News*, and until someone in what she termed 'the hungry post-war years' stole it from her flat, her most treasured book was a copy of Joyce's *Ulysses* that Hamish had bought from Sylvia Beach's bookshop in Paris, Shakespeare and Company, and then presented to her after dinner in a nearby bistro on the rue Dupuytren. Hand-bound in white leather, he inscribed it 'From Ulysses, the Wanderer and the Deceiver,' an ironic and apt sentiment since he was a married Roman Catholic with two children and the affair with Olivia was not the first of his extramarital adventures: as she rather decorously put it in her description of the first time they went to bed together in the smelly house in Margaretta Terrace (changing Hamish's Scottish name to its English equivalent), 'I had been inexperienced while James had made several forays into love.' Already a practiced adulterer, he explained that his wife was frail and no longer able to tolerate sexual intercourse. When Olivia took him back to her Chelsea bed-sitting room, they became less the mentor and acolyte and more equal partners in gratifying their sexual desire, both of them believing that 'sex was the motivating charm of life.'[3]

Hamish Miles also possessed strong right-wing political sympathies, expressed, for example, in his judgment that despite the dreadful carnage of the Spanish war being spread daily across British newspapers, Franco and the Falangists were preserving everything valuable about Spanish culture and society. When he and Olivia got caught up in an anti-Franco demonstration at Hyde Park Corner in the summer of 1937, Hamish declared, 'Franco is the only possible solution to the Spanish situation.' Recalling that day in her memoir, Olivia says, 'If anyone could have told me that among the crowd in the road there was a young man whom I would marry before the next two years were out, I would have thought my prediction absurd.' That young man, of course, was Reggie Smith, already an enrolled member of the British Communist Party and a fervent supporter of the Spanish Republican cause. But, feeling it was only now she was beginning to live, before that having existed in 'a limbo of loneliness, longing for someone I never seemed to meet,'[4] Hamish's right-wing views mattered little to Olivia. Hamish read her work, removing every unnecessary adjective (a lesson Olivia says she never forgot), arranged for *The*

[3] Fragment of Olivia's memoir of her relationship with 'James Sinclair,' OMC, HRC.
[4] 'Let me tell you before I forget,' OMC, HRC.

Wind Changes to be published by Jonathan Cape in April 1937, introduced her to interesting people such as Malcolm Lowry and Stevie Smith, and was a gallant and passionate lover. For her, the affair obliterated almost all awareness of the momentous political events that were taking place in England and on the Continent. It barely registered that Edward VII had abdicated on 11 December 1936, that Germany had staged a spectacular Olympic Games in the summer of that same year, that Hitler had accelerated his aggressive maneuvers in central Europe, and that hundreds of idealistic young British men were departing daily to fight Franco in the Spanish Civil War. She did not, for instance, express any interest in the pamphlet published in 1937, 'Authors Take Sides on the Spanish War,' in which one hundred and twenty-seven English writers were asked by W. H. Auden and Stephen Spender to express their support for the Republican cause.

In the late autumn of 1937, Hamish Miles began to suffer from severe headaches and would become strangely distracted when attempting simple tasks such as reading the 'A to Z' map for directions to a cinema where he and Olivia were planning to see a Marx Brothers film, an incident that she incorporated into a short story published in 1958, 'The Guillemot.' In that story, on a wet autumn afternoon, a middle-aged man and his younger lover plan to see a film at a cinema in the Elephant and Castle: the man is unable to read the tube map and the woman says, 'Edward darling... your brain is going to sleep.' Within weeks, he is dead of an 'abscess' on the brain. In actuality, within weeks of being unable to read the London 'A to Z,' Hamish became evasive and distant when Olivia telephoned him almost daily at his office at the *TLS* (he moved from Jonathan Cape to become its editor in September 1937), fobbing her off with stories about his wife's increasing frailty and the need to spend more time with her in the country. As the weeks went by, Olivia tried desperately to see him but with no success, even going to the offices of Jonathan Cape in search of information: as she describes this sorry visit in her memoir of the affair, she was greeted with envious annoyance and the snide remark that Hamish's love interests were well known but no one had suspected she could be one of them. In late November Olivia learned from a mutual acquaintance that he had been diagnosed with a brain tumor and admitted to an Edinburgh hospital where his father was a surgeon.

Unable to visit him and lacking anyone in whom she could confide her grief and anxiety, she fainted from fatigue and lack of food outside

Charing Cross Hospital: she weighed only seven stone (98 lbs) and was advised to go home, have a good meal, and rest. For the previous few months, she had usually arrived back in Bloomsbury at about 7:00 (she had moved from Chelsea to 446 Russell Court in Woburn Place to be close to Hamish's office), snacked on tea and toast after having eaten one full meal during the day, and worked until bedtime polishing *The Wind Changes* and drafting short stories. Living on less than £2 a week, distraught and undernourished, she only learned of Hamish's death from the obituary in *The Times* that appeared a few days after he succumbed to the brain tumor: there, he was celebrated as a gifted editor, translator, and critic and as someone who had never failed to support writers whom he admired, 'some of whom he was the first to discover and promote.' From his days at Balliol to his few weeks at the *TLS*, the obituary continued, he had been esteemed by friends and colleagues for his generosity, judgment, and sensibility.[5]

As she read the obituary, Olivia began to weep: 'I wept at home and in the street and on the bus and in the underground. I wept while I was reading and while I was typing...I gave myself up to a grief that can be suffered completely only once in a lifetime.'[6] A month after his death, she penciled a note to herself: 'The sound of his voice is fading even now in my mind and each day the lines on his face require more effort to recall. Yet still, and I know it will be ever so, I would give all the fifty years before me to live again the last one of my knowing him.' A few months after this, Olivia traveled to Edinburgh to find his grave in 'the dismal, raw-looking, new Catholic cemetery', and when she recalled his green eyes, his wide soft mouth, and his pale face, the dismal chilly day suddenly seemed a little less bleak. As things turned out, Olivia had slightly less than those fifty years in front of her that she would have relinquished to relive her last year with Hamish Miles (forty-seven to be exact). During those years, she traveled far more than she had imagined possible when plotting her escape from Portsmouth, and she never entirely overcame the searing shock of Hamish's sudden illness and death.

In the months before Hamish became ill, Olivia's life had undergone a number of significant changes. First, she had managed to escape the typing job at Peter Jones and get herself promoted to its furniture

---

[5] *The Times*, 29 December 1937.
[6] Fragment of Olivia's memoir of her relationship with 'James Sinclair,' OMC, HRC.

studio, an enterprise that transformed ordinary pine reproductions of Regency furniture into delicately painted ladies' desks and dressing tables. Unfortunately, the employment didn't last long, probably because by now writing mattered much more to Olivia than painting bluebells on dainty desks, and she was preoccupied with *The Wind Changes* rather than excited by the decoration of bedroom furniture. Peter Jones shifted her back to answering the telephone and typing delivery lists, and when this became intolerable, she left for a job at the grand salary of £4 a week at the Medici Society in Islington, a genteel business that dealt in the sale of copies of religious prints and paintings. Rather than being kept constantly on the go as she had been at Peter Jones, whether typing delivery lists or painting furniture, here she was able to snatch time between dealing with the Medici customers to work on her writing. But even with the improved salary she still felt pinched and deprived. In the hope that Marie Belloc Lowndes, a friend of Hamish's, might be able to get her a better-paid typing job at her publishers, William Heinemann, she wrote a despairing letter in October 1937 describing her pokey bed-sitting room and evoking the difficulty of feeding herself properly on a pitiful salary (by this time, Hamish had become ill and Olivia's Soho dining had come to an end). Mrs Belloc Lowndes was sympathetic and willing to help, but Heinemann proved uncooperative (ironically, they became Olivia's principal publishers after the war).[7]

To make things worse, the manager of the Medici Society decided that writing novels on office time was not acceptable. When Olivia was called into his office and asked to swear on the Bible to abandon fiction writing during working hours (this was a religious firm, after all), she refused, and was fired. Soon, though, with the help of Edward O'Brien, an American she had met through Hamish and who had recommended publication of her short story 'A Change of Mood' in *Best English Stories of 1935*, she managed to secure freelance work reading novels and short stories for Metro Goldwyn Mayer (O'Brien ran the reading department). Recalling this work, Olivia termed it 'absolute slavery'; forced to read 'intensively to make a living,' she scarcely ever ate a meal without a book propped in front of her. But she was fond of O'Brien (a 'kindly man') and grateful when he gave

---

[7] 4 October 1937, OMC/C, HRC.

her the job of putting his books in order in his Hampstead flat.[8] It was only with the advance from Jonathan Cape on *The Wind Changes* that she was able to eat moderately well, cut back on the freelance work, and imagine that she might, one day, become a full-time, successful working writer.

She had been in London for two years, had worked as a typist, furniture-painter, and general office person, had moved from one cramped bed-sitting room to another, and had lived through a passionate and wrenching love affair. Contact with her parents had been kept to the minimum and visits to Portsmouth out of the question, mostly because of lack of money but also because the prospect of her mother's nagging was intolerable. In a poem titled 'London, December 1937' and written in that year, Olivia Manning evokes these years:

You are still in this city, your adolescent samarkand,
Here, savage, homeless and determined,
You arrived three years ago.
Comforts were meagre. Your fire devalued them. Even the rain pleased you.
It rains still.
The same opaque, wet air obscures these steeples.
This is the city to which you laboured,
Rapacious, innocent and passionate,
A visitation on a noted man who, self betrayed,
Mistook your affirmation for his own.[9]

Soon after she returned to England from the Middle East after the war, Olivia looked back on her life as the 'savage, homeless and determined' young woman of her poem, and wrote a column for *The Palestine Post* in which she described her feelings as she unpacked a case of dusty books from what she calls her 'bachelor days' of six years ago: those days when, in the feverish language of the poem, she was 'rapacious, innocent and passionate.' During the war, the books had been kept by her friend Stevie Smith at her house in Palmers Green and the sight of each of them triggered more painful memories than Olivia had bargained for, particularly of 'those who will not return': dead friends. First is the detective-story writer John Mair, who was killed during the war and with whom Olivia probably had an affair after Hamish's death. She eulogizes him as a young man of unusual

[8] Olivia Manning to 'Mr. Simmonds,' 8 January 1980, OMC/C, HRC.
[9] Typescript, OMC, HRC.

brilliance and promise. Next, as one would expect, is Hamish Miles, whose translations dating, she says, from 'my very earliest days in London' to his death in 1937, recall for her exciting years of newly discovered freedom 'in the greatest and if you had no money most terrifying city in the world.'[10] But as thrilling and as transformative as the affair with Hamish remains in her memory, she bitterly recalls that her marginal existence as a woman alone in London before the war was an all too familiar story: the struggle to hold down a job, maintain independence, and have a room of one's own 'devoured the youth and energy of thousands of young women.' Because there were 'too many of them,' they were 'ruthlessly exploited' and since there were always dozens waiting to snatch their jobs, they could be safely underpaid and overworked.

An ally in these years of being underpaid, overworked, and living on macaroni and cheese at Lyons Corner House was the poet and novelist Stevie Smith (1902–71), although Stevie was better off financially than Olivia since she had a secure job as private secretary to Sir Neville Pearson at Newnes Publishing Company. Jonathan Cape had published Stevie's first book, *Novel on Yellow Paper*, to great acclaim in 1936 and Stevie had inscribed Hamish Miles's own personal copy in the following way: 'Thank you. Dr. Hamish. | For being so *beamish*. | If it hadn't been for you, believe me, | My child would never have seen the light | of day. Stevie.' When Hamish's son (also named Hamish) was asked by one of Stevie's biographers about her relationship with Jonathan Cape, he responded by saying that 'Miss Smith was, as you know, diseased with diffidence. I believe my father did much to give her confidence.'[11] In love with Olivia, fond of Stevie, and strongly supportive of the work of both women, Hamish believed that they would have much in common—and he was correct. Both were daughters of naval officers, both were notably quick-witted, and both had serious literary ambitions. Neither had gone to university. They wandered London together—exploring Soho streets, visiting the Victoria and Albert Museum (it was free), and, when they could afford it, seeing the latest French film at the Curzon in Mayfair, which opened in 1934 and was the first British cinema to import and show

---

[10] 'Against the past,' *The Palestine Post*, 14 December 1945.
[11] Inscription on fly-leaf of *Novel on Yellow Paper*; letter from Hamish Miles to William McBrien, SSP, UT, Series 1, Box 6, Folder 2.

foreign language films. And on lonely weekends, when Hamish visited his wife and children in the country, Olivia would often stay with Stevie at the house in Palmers Green in north London where she lived with her Yorkshire aunt. For her, it was a welcome change from the isolation of a bed-sitting room in what was the most 'terrifying city in the world' if you had no money. Before she came to London, Olivia had wishfully imagined that she would meet other writers, but at first (pre-Hamish) she met hardly anyone: 'I did not know how to contact the people I wanted to meet. The established intellectuals of the time were far out of my reach and beyond their circle, people were still conventional and suspicious of solitary young women without background or money.'[12] Even after beginning the affair with Hamish and starting to meet 'established intellectuals,' Olivia was often lonely and Stevie's friendship did a great deal to assuage her social isolation.

The meeting with Stevie was, in Olivia's words, 'momentous,' and although she occasionally felt a trifle patronized (probably because she was still shaking off her Portsmouth accent and manners, whereas Stevie, the older by six years, had spent more time maneuvering herself around London), they saw a great deal of each other.[13] They were both notoriously fond of gossip and loved to broadcast rumors of intrigues and affairs about their friends and acquaintances, especially women. Francis King believes they were a 'tricky and malicious' duo, although he argues that Stevie's tongue was more insidious; certainly as spitefully inaccurate as Olivia, Stevie was 'far more skilful—so that, whereas people often dismissed Olivia's gossip, Stevie's tended to be accepted. Far more damaging, therefore.' King admits that Stevie had many devoted friends but perhaps out of loyalty to Olivia he has always insisted that at root Stevie was not a 'nice character.'[14] To Walter Allen, the novelist and critic who was Reggie Smith's fellow-student at Birmingham University and who later helped him get a job with the British Council, Stevie and Olivia presented a fearsome front. When he met them both in 1937, he was reading scripts for Metro Goldwyn Mayer along with Olivia, who, he says, 'had a wit that was devastating and was as formidable a young woman as any in London . . . You could count yourself a friend of Olivia Manning the moment you were

[12] Fragment of Olivia's memoir of her relationship with 'James Sinclair,' OMC, HRC.
[13] Frances Spalding, *Stevie Smith: A Critical Biography*, 106.
[14] Jack Barbera and William McBrien, *Stevie: A Biography of Stevie Smith*, 161.

introduced to Stevie Smith.'[15] They were a compellingly eccentric
couple: Olivia with her creamy olive complexion, dark hair, lithe
figure, and stylish clothes (when she could manage to scrounge them
from various street markets) and Stevie with her intensely dark eyes,
quizzical demeanor, and deceptively prim outfits (often 1920s-style
dresses made from furnishing fabrics): both of them full of life, vastly
entertaining, and wittily subversive. Olivia especially loved Stevie's
eyes, which she described as 'circles of pure, deep, chocolate brown.'[16]

The shared love of intrigue and fondness for a tactless witticism at
the expense of someone's feelings led to a temporary souring of their
friendship, at least according to Olivia. As she relates the story, desolate
after Hamish's death, she confided her grief-stricken hopelessness,
whereupon Stevie suddenly let it drop that it was common gossip
Hamish had regularly visited a certain woman's flat while conducting
his affair with Olivia. Although Stevie begged to be forgiven, Olivia
felt it was a telling instance of her capacity for 'calculated cruelty,' and
after relating the story in a letter to the novelist Kathleen Farrell six
years after Stevie's death in March 1971 (an indication of how long she
had nursed her memory of this episode), she added that Stevie 'had the
most venomous tongue of any person I have ever known.'[17] She also
included this instance of what she felt was Stevie's unfeeling behavior
in her unpublished autobiographical fragment, 'Let me tell you before
I forget.' But despite Olivia's mixed feelings about Stevie and the fact
that she seemed resistant to Reggie's exuberant charm, she always felt
grateful for her efforts during the war years to get her short stories
published and to keep her name alive in literary circles. Stevie, however, remained immune to Reggie's boyish attractions, a resistance
that prompted Olivia to write from the Middle East in the early 1940s
that he was working terribly hard, that he had 'developed tremendously' since she knew him, and that the responsibilities of his job were
'making him much maturer.' In the long run, the sometimes rocky
friendship was too important to both Olivia and Stevie for it to wither
away because of transient upsets or war-caused separation.

[15] Spalding, *Stevie Smith: A Critical Biography*, 107.
[16] Manuscript notes for an unpublished memoir of Stevie Smith, OMC, HRC. Olivia
began this memoir of their friendship in 1975 but misplaced the notes. I discovered them
in the papers in possession of Victoria Orr-Ewing, now at the Harry Ransom Center.
[17] Barbera and McBrien, *Stevie: A Biography of Stevie Smith*, 162. For some twenty
years, Kathleen Farrell was the companion of Kay Dick.

In August 1939, when Reggie Smith and Olivia Manning decided
to marry after knowing each other for only three weeks—they had
been introduced by Walter Allen after Reggie, on leave from Bucharest, had told him how much he admired Olivia's novel *The Wind
Changes*—the first person to whom Olivia turned was, of course,
Stevie, even though she worried that Stevie might resent her absorption into Reggie's circle of Birmingham University pals. In a long and
affectionate letter written to her in early August 1939, Olivia confessed
that she was seriously undecided about getting married. Louis Mac-
Neice, Reggie's former tutor in Classics at Birmingham, had asked
them to go and stay with him in Ireland but she felt she should remain
in London to maintain her contacts for reading film scripts: 'I need the
money badly . . . what should one choose experience or money? Louis
has also offered us his house on Primrose Hill [he lived at 16A Primrose
Hill Road] for a reception should we marry. Such inducements,
dearie, make the problem harder.'[18] Adding that she was 'practically
penniless,' perpetually tired, and sick of the damp hot weather, she
ended by saying she hoped they could have lunch very soon after
Stevie returned from her holiday in France: 'You are lucky to be with
the Pernod.' As things turned out, 'experience' won out over 'money'
in terms of arrival in Bucharest on the day of England's declaration of
war against Germany—although Olivia's life after arriving in London
had hardly been without incident: a tumultuous love affair, various
awful jobs, and publishing a well-received novel.

Without question, Olivia's insecurities about her writing sometimes
strained her affection for Stevie. Much as she often claimed to love her,
she also called her a 'sly puss,' proclaimed her 'arch-bitchiness' to their
friends, and was jealous of her success. That they both published novels
with Jonathan Cape and that Stevie's received more exciting critical
notice did not help: *Novel on Yellow Paper, or Work It Out for Yourself*
(1936) was greeted with a flurry of newspaper and magazine articles
speculating as to the identity of the brilliant and mysterious author who
had written what seemed to be an autobiographical novel narrated by
one Pompey Casmilus, a name that combines Pompey, the Roman
military leader, with Casmilus, another name for Mercury. The narrator declines traditional plot structure and roams at will through the

18 SSP, UT.

comic trials of working for a high-level publisher (a little bit of autobiography here), the nastiness of suburban manners, and the horrors of trashy fiction for married women, Roman Catholicism, and sex education. The novel is stunningly clever. Influenced by the willful randomness of Gertrude Stein and the narrative playfulness of Lawrence Sterne's *Tristram Shandy*, it is packed with literary allusions, digressions, and parodies of traditional forms. As the narrator says at the beginning, 'this book is the talking voice that runs on, and the thoughts come, the way I said, and the people come too, and come and go, to illustrate the thoughts, to point the moral, to adorn the tale.'[19] Termed a 'curious, amusing, provocative, and very serious piece of work' by the *TLS*, in almost every way it differs radically from anything written by Olivia.[20]

Where *Novel on Yellow Paper* playfully and irreverently dismantles a nineteenth-century literary inheritance, just as Sterne had poked fun at the fictions of verisimilitude underpinning the rise of the English novel in the eighteenth century, *The Wind Changes* immerses itself in the tradition of social and psychological realism that Stevie tossed out of the window. And somewhat ironically in light of Olivia's early reverence for the lyrical modernism of Virginia Woolf, her first novel tends to favor the intense realism of, say, Joseph Conrad far more than it does the poetic stream-of-consciousness of her literary idol. Right after the war, when she had a bit of money, she bought the complete works of Conrad (probably the Complete Collected Edition first published in 1946) and always professed her great admiration for his work. Believing that she had 'a more masculine than feminine mind as a writer,' she acknowledged to herself and in her work a fundamental difference in literary imagination between her own writing and that of her friend: if Stevie was irreverent, fantastic, perhaps even contemptuous of her reader, then she devoted herself to the heavy task of making the reader 'see' (as Conrad puts it in the Preface to *The Nigger of the 'Narcissus'*).[21] But Olivia never forgot that the pleasures of friendship with Stevie had sustained her during her early months in London, and although her literary talent did not run to the strange and wonderful qualities of

[19] *Novel on Yellow Paper*, 39.   [20] 12 September 1936.
[21] 'Speaking of writing,' *The Times*, 30 January 1964.

Stevie's verse, she felt herself in perfect accord with the sentiments of 'The Pleasures of Friendship,' published in 1942:

> The pleasures of friendship are exquisite,
> How pleasant to go to a friend on a visit!
> I go to my friend, we walk on the grass,
> And the hours and moments like minutes pass.

A really accomplished piece of work

Despite the fact that Olivia Manning seemed indifferent to contemporary political events when enraptured by Hamish Miles, she set the action of her first novel, completed after they traveled to Ireland together in the summer of 1936, in the tense period that preceded the Anglo-Irish Truce of 1921. *The Wind Changes* is framed by memories of the rebellion against English governance lasting from Easter Monday, 24 April, to 30 April 1916. Brutally suppressed after six days of furious fighting and the court-martial and execution of its leaders, the rebellion of 1916 drives the novel's plot of redemption and revenge. This interest in Irish political history signals a preference, right at the beginning of Olivia's career, for writing historical fiction, even if, as is the case with *The Wind Changes*, that history is set a mere sixteen years in the past. This first novel also anticipates many of the defining characteristics of Olivia's work: violent political action vivified by closely observed detail (the cold winds, for instance, that whistle through bullet holes on Dublin tram windows); war itself as both subject and canvas for development of individual characters; sensuous landscape descriptions painted with opulent color; and a central narrative presence (usually female) whose exclusion from the action (usually male) fosters a skeptical detachment. The *TLS* praised the novel's 'rich, disciplined detail, its delicate perception of fleeting moods,' and declared that it showed 'unusual promise.'[22] And looking back in 1964, Walter Allen, Olivia's fellow-toiler in the reading department of Metro Goldwyn Mayer, lauded *The Wind Changes* for its 'exceedingly pure and exact style.'[23] It was clear that Olivia had heeded Hamish's distaste for superfluous adjectives.

Set mostly in Dublin, the plot revolves around two men and one woman bound in an erotic trio whose characterization draws upon Olivia's literal and emotional journey from Portsmouth to London.

---

[22] *TLS*, 24 April 1937.   [23] *Tradition and Dream*, 281.

Arion, a married English Roman Catholic journalist with Republican sympathies that may or may not be authentic (various clues in the novel imply he might be a spy for the British), voices the pain and exhilaration of being a writer in terms that foreshadow much of Olivia's lifelong oscillation (familiar to most writers) between the sheer hell of sitting down to write and the weary relief that comes at the end of the writing day. In addition, the intensity of his sexual encounters with Elizabeth, the central female figure, suggests the urgency of Olivia's affair with Hamish: they meet as antagonists, 'thrown together, body to body, in a sensual transport that was like the lust of combat' (*The Wind Changes*, 70). The third member in this not quite consummated *ménage à trois* is Sean, a rebel who comes from a privileged Dublin family; he bears little resemblance to Olivia or anyone in her life, but his graphic wasting from consumption owes something to family stories told to her by her father (the survivor in a family in which ten brothers and a mother died of consumption). And in anticipation of the subtle, allusive representations of male homo-eroticism that we find in Olivia's later fiction, Sean's infatuation with Arion is recorded in letters that are like those of 'an unhappy lover' and that are read by Elizabeth with 'bewildered distaste' (p. 194). Elizabeth herself is caught in the web of desire and conspiracy woven by Arion and Sean (she sleeps with both of them) and eventually frees herself from dependence upon men for romantic excitement and social identity.

The action in *The Wind Changes* opens with Arion and Elizabeth driving from Dublin to the western islands to rescue Sean from pursuit by Black and Tan forces: all three are quickly enmeshed in a political plot led by the mythical revolutionary Riordan and designed to redeem the ignominious memories of the Easter Rising. When Sean and Arion first greet each other, Elizabeth is immediately excluded, an angry outsider caught 'in a frigid numbness of resentment' (p. 15). As the trio eats breakfast in a forlorn hotel, she stays silent and watches the men closely, a contempt born of exclusion increasing by the minute: Arion seems fatuous and preening, 'his large, silver-coloured eyes half covered by heavy lids and his full lips set smilingly,' Sean a 'mixture of egoist and fool' (p. 17). Feeding her feeling of exclusion, she sits in petulant silence and feigned submission as they drive back to Dublin, irritated by the smug expression on Sean's 'pale, crooked face' and delighted by the fact that Arion is developing a double chin. In Dublin, they go immediately to the house of Sean's father in Merrion Square

where she stands back in the shadows and watches the men in a circle
of lamplight: 'She knew they were deliberately excluding her from
their consciousness—Arion with malice, Sean with anger . . . She went
and sat in a chair by the fire-place and watched them, seeming
tranquilly oblivious of being excluded' (pp. 51–2). Despite the fact
Olivia often declared she found most 'women characters rather tiresome' (in all fiction, not just her own), Elizabeth's burning resentment
at being shut out from male discussion strikes the reader as anything
but tiresome: her sense of injury fleshes out her characterization and
also signals the unspoken indignation of the woman artist seeking
public recognition beyond the sphere of romantic conquest. In its
depiction of an affair between a seasoned male philanderer with a
sensuous mouth and an ambitious young woman eager for artistic
success, in its persuasive description of Irish resistance to English
rule, and in its richly lyrical descriptions of the Irish countryside, *The
Wind Changes* signals the inception of Olivia's fusion of autobiography,
historical actuality, and economical yet vivid prose.

In a scene that celebrates Joyce's 'sweet mother' of the Irish Sea
(by the time of completing *The Wind Changes* Olivia had followed
Hamish's directive to read *Ulysses*), injury and anger are washed away
as Elizabeth swims naked off the beach at Howth, a fishing port just
north of Dublin. In a form of rebirth into a self formed before the affair
with Arion, travel to Ireland, and fascination with Sean, she begins to
feel 'a depth of satisfaction in her own nakedness, and in the movement of her muscles and the soft lap of water along her body . . . She
felt a delight in the beauty of her own body, a contentment in it for its
own sake that set her apart from need of Arion or Sean or any other
man . . . Deliberately, she was setting out to try and cure herself of her
reliance on others for the will to live' (p. 172). The delight and
satisfaction in herself erases the jealousy she has felt earlier of Arion's
narcissistic commitment to Irish rebellion and his complacent acceptance of Sean's adoration: now she begins to love the Irish countryside
for itself, rather than for the nationalistic meaning with which it is
invested by their revolutionary politics. Olivia's description of the
extraordinarily beautiful Galway landscape, derived in part from her
time in Ireland with Hamish in the summer of 1936, reveals the
painter's sensual eye for color with which she brilliantly evokes,
much later in the Balkan and Levant trilogies, the mountains of
Transylvania, the rocky hillside above Athens, and the magnificent

coastline of Alexandria. As she heads for Dublin, Elizabeth looks back and sees that 'Under the great arc of lavender-coloured sky, gilded at the horizon and set with long, static, gilt-edged lavender clouds, the bog-land heather quivered like creeping purple flame. . . . Here and there the peats were piled like bricks of wedding cake. Some had been left there so long new grass was poking out from them in emerald pins' (p. 24). The visual montage of lavender, purple, and emerald green draws richly on Olivia's night-time training at Portsmouth's Municipal Art School.

At a certain point in the novel when she describes Arion's 'unendurable consciousness of his own solitude,' Olivia touches upon the doubt that almost always plagues the life of any writer, whether journalist, novelist, or critic. Both desiring and fearing the terrors felt by the solitary artist, Arion finds himself 'being carried away painfully by the maniac distress of the uncontrolled creative imagination' (p. 130). Often announcing to her friends that all writers 'suffer a great deal' (hardly an original observation), Olivia would also voice the familiar frustration of a thwarted desire to express the inexpressible, to say more than the words at hand will permit. All writers, she would insist, wrestle with isolation, loneliness, and depression. Yet she also felt strongly that she could hardly go on living if she had nothing to do, if she had no chapter with which to struggle when she got up in the morning. When she was finishing *The Wind Changes*, she wrote under the pressure of having had two novels rejected by Jonathan Cape, of laboring to survive from day to day, and of feeling the exhilaration and sorrow of the affair with Hamish Miles. She poured those years of emotional and professional anguish into her first novel: they are the narrative source of a young woman's journey from dependence to liberation and of an ambiguous characterization of an egotistical male writer—part Hamish, part Olivia.[24] In a *Sunday Times* advertisement for *The Wind Changes* that appeared in April 1937, Storm Jameson praised it as follows: 'A really accomplished piece of work. She can create living men and women and allow them to develop by the logic of their own natures, which is the gift of a real writer.' Reading that,

---

[24] Saddened, perhaps, by memories of the bittersweet years when she was writing *The Wind Changes*, in 1971 she asked that this novel not be included in a list of her publications: 'a very juvenile piece . . . I cannot think it would interest anyone,' she wrote to James Vinson. 15 March 1971, OMC/C, HRC.

Olivia felt that Hamish's encouraging prediction that with hard work she might become a very good writer was on its way to realization.

If Elizabeth is not quite as cynical as the woman in a Grafton Street tea-shop in *The Wind Changes* who natters on about her new false teeth (sounding like a fugitive from the pub scene in *The Waste Land*)— 'When you're my age you'll know that romance is nothing more than the bit of tissue paper the toffee's wrapped in' (p. 238)—then she metaphorically rejects the tissue paper in favor of the toffee. As Arion leaves to return to London and pick up with a former lover, he offers to bring her work to the attention of his publisher friends: in the realm of war between the sexes, a truce between them concludes their corrosive combat, just as, on the grander historical canvas of tragic conflict between English rule and Irish resistance, the truce of July 1920 temporarily concluded a bloody conflict that lasted another seventy-eight years, and still resonates with periodic outbreaks of violence in Northern Ireland. Although Olivia admitted ruefully to her friend the Anglo-Russian novelist William Gerhardie (1895–1977) that *The Wind Changes* initially sold only six copies since it appeared around the same time as 'a major royal event' (perhaps the coronation of George VI on 12 May 1937), her first novel deserves critical revisiting if only for its introduction of major motifs in her fiction: representation of actual historical events and observation of male camaraderie by a skeptical female outsider.

Some say Olivia had an affair with Gerhardie, although there is no evidence in their correspondence to prove it.[25] When he reviewed her recently published fourth novel in the *TLS* in September 1953 (*A Different Face*), he saluted her as 'a writer of genius' and spoke warmly of *The Wind Changes*.[26] Undoubtedly basing his judgment on intimate knowledge of Olivia's temperament and views (she visited him regularly at his flat behind Broadcasting House in Portland Place until the squalor began to test even her affectionate loyalty), Gerhardie was the first to identify an important aspect of *The Wind Changes*. Deploying a theatrical metaphor, he astutely praises it for 'the revelation of the tragedy of the woman writer, who knows reality to be in the stalls, seeking a relationship with first one, then another, and a third

---

[25] In *Yesterday Came Suddenly*, Francis King asserts that Olivia verified the truth of the affair, 'By her own admission to me.'

[26] *TLS*, 4 September 1953.

young man who, being patriotic conspirators, conceive themselves as actors on a world stage.' Technically, of course, Elizabeth is an aspiring illustrator rather than a writer, but Gerhardie perfectly intuits the novel's eventual subordination of male political action to the struggle of the woman artist for recognition. As the male characters posture upon the stage of Irish history, the actuality that metaphorically resides 'in the stalls' of daily life is expressed through Elizabeth's desire for emotional and professional independence.

Gerhardie's approval, here and elsewhere, always mattered a great deal to Olivia. In the 1960s, she wrote about reading all his novels in the Portsmouth Public Library and declared that his work perfectly embodies his stated prerequisites of the novelist's art: 'humour, tenderness, and pathos.' His books now pushed to the hidden-away dusty shelves in public libraries, she wonders how he has become lost to view. Anthony Powell, Evelyn Waugh, C. P. Snow, Kingsley Amis 'all acknowledge his influence...We all come out of him.'[27] The correspondence between them that dates from 1951 to 1973 and that is housed in the Cambridge University Library reveals Olivia's devoted efforts to get his work more fully appreciated and her worried insistence that he take better care of himself. Their letters reveal much about an affectionate bond between two working writers.

Tractors on the horizon

Gregarious, bear-like, a grammar-school boy from Birmingham, Reginald Donald Smith could not have been more different from Hamish Miles. He was born on 31 July 1914 to working-class parents in Aston; his father was a master toolmaker and his mother an occasional charwoman when times were rough, and they were often very rough indeed in the depressed economic climate of post-World War I Britain. Following the customary escape from class-bound limitations that had been adopted by hundreds of bright, provincial boys before him, he first attended King Edward VI Grammar School in Aston, along with his two brothers and the literary critic Walter Allen, where rugby, chess, and cricket became his lifetime passions and where he

---

[27] 'Buried alive,' *The Times*, 9 November 1961.

worked on losing his 'Brummy' accent by acting in school plays. He excelled in French, Modern Poetry, and the study of Marcel Proust. In 1923 he went off to Birmingham University, where he supported himself in a colorful variety of part-time jobs: sorting mail at the main post office at Christmas, touring the Midlands with a local acting company, doing the odd bit of clerking and journalism, and hamming it up as a radio actor on the regional BBC. His tutor in Classics was Louis MacNeice and through MacNeice he became friendly with Wystan Auden and Malcolm Lowry, bright boys, provincial lads, like himself. According to Walter Allen, when he first arrived in Birmingham straight from Oxford, MacNeice was an ineffective lecturer, and Reggie concurred in this judgment: MacNeice 'droned on' in the lecture hall, although he steered his students brilliantly in tutorials.[28]

MacNeice's education at Sherborne preparatory school, Marlborough College, and Merton College, Oxford, provided him with a more privileged background than most of the students at Birmingham in the early thirties, and in his long dramatic poem, *Autumn Journal 1939*, an elegy for the twenty-one years of peace Great Britain had experienced since the end of World War I, he recalls how he came to the 'hazy city' of Birmingham, 'To work in a building caked with grime | Teaching the classics to Midland students; | Virgil, Livy, the usual round, | Principal parts and lost digamma; | And to hear the prison-like lecture room resound | to Homer in a Dudley accent.'[29] Since Dudley is less than seventeen miles from Aston, it's very likely that Reggie's booming voice was one of those MacNeice heard declaiming Homer, his Brummy accent not yet fully erased. All his life, Reggie loved to recite poetry and he knew a great deal of English verse by heart: while at Birmingham in a student production, he was word perfect as Othello within three days. Forty years on, listening to him introduce a group of young poets in a 1970s BBC radio program, *Poetry Now*, and also read some of the poems, one hears a richly mature and mellifluous actor's voice. For MacNeice, Reggie Smith was the best of his Birmingham students, someone who quite remarkably 'had no complex about class, thought nothing was so funny as the Oxford and Cambridge poseurs' who played at being Marxists. Although he had become a dedicated and enthusiastic Marxist through the influence of the Classics scholar and philosopher George Thomson, who joined the Communist Party in 1936 (Reggie was a founding member of the Birmingham University Socialists Society), he was perfectly at home with all classes, says MacNeice, equally happy drinking half-pints with factory hands and talking literary criticism with his tutors. Responding happily to Reggie's 'great supply of animal spirits and natural taste for poetry,' they spent many 'wonderful pointless nights walking through back streets,' and dropping into Reggie's family house at two in the morning to find his father playing chess in the kitchen with his brother.[30]

When he graduated from Birmingham, Reggie began teaching in various rather grim private schools and also in elementary schools in the Black Country, that area in the West Midlands which gained its name in the mid-nineteenth century from the smoke from the many thousands of ironworking foundries and forges, plus the working of the shallow thirty-foot-thick coal seams. The Black Country also encompassed Aston and Dudley. But, as temperamentally optimistic and as politically committed as he was to the education of working-class children, Reggie soon found the work tedious, uninspiring, and a definite dampener on his natural good spirits. He began to look around for alternative employment, not an easy task in the mid-1930s when poverty, poor housing, and dreadful infant mortality were creating a volatile atmosphere of social unrest throughout England, especially in the North. In October 1936, for instance, one of the most celebrated of the hunger marches that took place during the Great Depression of the 1930s began in Jarrow, a small shipbuilding town close to Newcastle upon Tyne where close to 75 per cent of the workers were unemployed. Like the Chartist marches of the 1840s, the Jarrow march ended in London where a petition with 11,000 signatures was presented to Parliament. It was in this uneasy economic climate that Reggie became quite open about his Communist sympathies: in notes for an unwritten autobiography, he recalls that he probably presented the notorious spy and art historian Anthony Blunt 'with a conundrum... Was I rough trade or a spy prospect?'[31] Reggie's good looks and charismatic personality caught the attention of both sexes:

[30] *The Strings Are False*, 154; 164.
[31] I am grateful to Gerry Harrison for kindly sharing these notes with me.

not only did he have a number of attractive girlfriends at Birmingham (MacNeice wrote to his lover, the actress Mary Wimbush, that the student she saw as Othello was 'living in sin' with one of these girlfriends), he also seems to have been fancied by Auden and his friends: Reggie recalls that Auden introduced him one day by saying, 'He's not one of us, my dear, but we have hopes for him.'[32] Without question, the sixty-nine-year-old Reggie who appears in *As I Was Walking Down Bristol Street* (the 1983 documentary narrated by David Lodge about Birmingham writers in the 1930s) is a handsome fellow: with a full head of wavy silver hair, dressed smartly in a blue V-necked jumper, and speaking in such a polished accent that he sounds somewhat like the current Prince of Wales, he more than validates all that has been written about his appealing presence and personality.

Through his connections with the Birmingham group of writers, Reggie managed in late 1938 to secure an interview with the British Council and arrived in London to stay with the close friend who had been his fellow-student both at King Edward Grammar School and at Birmingham, Walter Allen: Allen had moved to London, the cosmopolitan goal for all writers in the 1930s, a few years earlier and had settled into a bed-sitting room in Bloomsbury where he worked on his fiction and scrounged around for freelance writing assignments. Allen was astonished to see Reggie arrive wearing a splendid suit and tie (both borrowed and the suit not quite correct since the flies were held together by a safety pin) and 'all six-feet two or three looking very impressive indeed.' Something, though, was lacking to complete an ensemble that would impress the director-general of the British Council, Lord Lloyd. Allen dashed round the corner to a dentist friend in the Gray's Inn Road and returned with a rolled umbrella and the sort of trilby hat worn by Anthony Eden, which proved a little small so Reggie decided to carry it. When he arrived in Hanover Square, he was asked, among other things, whether he considered his French good enough to allow him to take a duchess in to dinner. Reggie genially replied that it certainly was (which Allen very much doubted) and Lord Lloyd promptly offered him a teaching post at the newly created British Institute in Bucharest, whose formation had been substantially supported with funds from the British Council. With an

[32] *Letters of Louis MacNeice*, 10 November 1936 (28); *As I Was Walking Down Bristol Street*, 1983.

opening scheduled for 12 October 1938, Lord Lloyd was hiring three English male lecturers to work with eight locally engaged English teachers, and twenty-three hundred students were already enrolled to take classes in English and English literature during the forthcoming academic year. When Reggie was hired, Walter Allen realized that he needed to revise his opinion of someone he had regarded 'as in some sense a protégé': 'I was suddenly made to realize that it was true no longer, even if it had ever been. He was a man very much in his own right, who went his own way, didn't give a damn for anybody and was governed only by his principles and affections. He completely transcended his background.'[33] That background, Reggie always insisted, had been left behind primarily because he had been 'lucky,' unlike countless other working-class boys in the 1930s who must also have possessed lively minds and exuberant personalities, but somehow lacked what Reggie called 'luck.'[34]

If Walter Allen is correct about Reggie's personality, and there is no reason to think otherwise since almost everyone who knew Reggie speaks of his generosity, his lack of snobbishness, and his endearing self-confidence, then some remarkable differences from Olivia Manning become very obvious. Artemis Cooper describes Reggie's wartime colleagues in Cairo as saying that his 'boundless capacity for enjoying people's company was only matched by their desire to be near him . . . Money and comfort meant little, and what he had was easily shared or given away.'[35] To the historical novelist Peter Vansittart, Reggie always appeared 'courteous, outgoing. At parties large, benign, spectacled, he was a reassuring presence, gathering the young, particularly girls, around him like an avuncular bear . . . though with reserves of intelligence, influence, power.'[36] And when Reggie took Olivia to Birmingham to meet his parents in August 1939 and introduced her to his university friends, she appeared cold and standoffish: one of those friends recalled that 'nobody took to her very much as she seemed to look down on provincials from a great height.'[37] Finally, whereas Reggie didn't give a damn for anybody (in Walter Allen's

[33] *As I Walked Down New Grub Street*, 111.
[34] *As I Was Walking Down Bristol Street*.
[35] *Cairo in the War: 1939–1945*, 154.
[36] Unpublished letter from Peter Vansittart to Gerry Harrison, October 2006.
[37] Memoir of R. D. Smith, sent by L. W. Bailey to Neville Braybrooke, n.d. OMC, HRC.

words), Olivia was obsessed by what people thought of her; where he was governed only by his firmly held political beliefs and effusive affections, she was often controlled by strong feelings of injury and resentment that tended to temper the warmth she might have felt for others. And she certainly never transcended her social background, quite simply because she had not enjoyed the liberating experience of university life that had proved so important in Reggie's formation. Rather than having tutorials with Louis MacNeice and going to the pub with Wystan Auden, she had been typing away in various offices in Portsmouth. If Reggie was equally at home in a Birmingham bar and at the Garrick Club, she tended to harp on the deprivations of her childhood, worried even in her sixties about using the wrong fork at the Ivy when having lunch with Lady Antonia Fraser. Most importantly, Reggie grew up in an essentially happy working-class household with a strong and deeply loving mother (this is most likely what he termed 'luck'); Olivia suffered through years of argument between her parents and constant maternal nagging. This determinative divergence must explain, in part, a difference in personality that was immediately and often astonishingly apparent to everyone who met them: Reggie always the cheery optimist, Olivia very often the sardonic pessimist. What then attracted them to one another?

In July 1939, Reggie returned to England from Bucharest on what he knew would be a brief leave since war was imminent, and Louis MacNeice was delighted to have him back in London and to put him up in his Primrose Hill flat. On the sixteenth of that month, MacNeice wrote to Eleanor Clarke that Reggie had told him he could get £8 a week and all expenses in Bucharest, and that he might just go, given his need to up his income. The summer of 1939, was, in MacNeice's words, 'a steady delirium, the caterpillar wheels of enormous tractors rearing on every horizon. As individuals there was nothing we could do—just mark time or kill it.'[38] Reggie camped out on the sofa in the sitting-room, scattering his clothes everywhere, but despite the untidiness, his 'irrepressible cheerfulness' was just what MacNeice needed to cheer him up as he agonized over the looming prospect of European war, finished a book on Yeats (*The Poetry of W. B. Yeats*, published in 1941), and wondered if he should accompany Reggie back to

---

[38] *The Strings Are False*, 208.

Bucharest. Since Reggie had decided that he was going to write a graduate thesis on the poetry of D. H. Lawrence, each day they repaired together to the Reading Room of the British Museum, where a sort of club had been constituted by four friends: MacNeice, Reggie, Walter Allen, and Ernest Stahl, a lecturer in German at Oxford. How much actual work got done remains uncertain since, as MacNeice recalls, when 'any of us arrived in the reading room he would walk around under the fantastic dome to find someone else and they would go out and have a coffee or beer.'[39]

By this time, Olivia and Walter Allen were close friends. They had met while reading film scripts for Metro Goldwyn Mayer, they lived close to one another in Bloomsbury, and they often rendezvoused in the local pub 'to commiserate over common grievances,' which were mostly to do with the dreary, underpaid labor entailed in working for their American bosses. They were pals, and never lovers. On Walter's recommendation, Reggie had read *The Wind Changes*: he liked the feisty independence of the principal female character and he considered himself a feminist after a fair amount of sexual experience with women at Birmingham—as he observed wryly in his autobiographical notes, 'this was exceptional in one of my class, which is fiercely macho and sexist.' On an evening in late July, Olivia, and Reggie were introduced outside a bar in Southampton Row—a handsome, rumpled man of twenty-five, over six feet tall and with unruly wavy hair, and an alluring woman of thirty-one with a slim figure, beautiful skin, and dark, intelligent eyes. In almost every way, Reggie was utterly different from Hamish Miles, and Olivia's magnetic combination of exotic attractiveness and incisive wit made her quite unlike any woman he had met before, whether in Birmingham, London, or Bucharest. Perhaps most importantly, he deeply admired her writing and her mind, and, given his tremendous love of language and English literature, his enduring support throughout their forty-one years together testifies to imaginative and intellectual gifts that she herself always questioned. Everyone felt that there was a bad time coming, and, looking back on these years, Olivia declared that 'Life was not much fun for people who grew up between the wars, because we all knew what the First World War had been like, and really thought the

---

[39] *The Strings Are False*, 209.

Second would be worse.'[40] Given their strong sexual attraction to one another and the frantic urgency that prevailed in August 1939, it is not surprising that Reggie moved immediately into Olivia's bed-sitting room and that they were married at the Marylebone Register Office three weeks after their first meeting.

Walter Allen and Louis MacNeice offer slightly different accounts of the wedding, although they do agree about who was present: themselves, Ernest Stahl, and Stevie Smith (for Allen, as 'formidable' as Olivia). MacNeice remembers that they were all late for the scheduled appointment with the registrar, and needing to fill in time until she returned from lunch, the party repaired to the bar of the Ritz. 'None of us had been in the Ritz before and we felt like Tambourlaine— "Holla, ye pampered jades"'; but on the strength of many mint juleps, 'the harsh leaves of the mint brushing against our lips, the titillation of a male kiss, the eternal vegetable world,' they quickly felt better and more at home, and well fortified to face the disgruntled registrar.[41] After the early afternoon ceremony, the six of them set off for a late lunch at Chez Victor on Wardour Street in Soho: seated in an upper room, they were looked at askance by the waiters since it was well after two o'clock when they arrived and they created further disruption by singing throughout the meal. In *his* memoir, Walter Allen confesses he does not really remember the sojourn in the bar of the Ritz before going to the registrar's office (perhaps one too many mint juleps) but he does recall that the registrar, 'who was a lady, invited the best man to produce the ring. Reggie came in with: "Is the ring obligatory?" The registrar, taken aback, said: "Well, not obligatory precisely but certainly customary." "In that case," Reggie said, "we'll dispense with it."' Five days later, Reggie having received orders that he was to return immediately to Bucharest, the newly-weds were off on the Orient Express crossing Europe towards Romania. Walter Allen and Stevie Smith saw them off at Victoria Station.

That Reggie Smith is Olivia Manning's model for Guy Pringle in the trilogies is indisputable: the multiple similarities between them are conspicuous and Olivia, as we know, is on record as saying that the six novels follow closely her experiences with Reggie in Romania, Greece, and the Middle East. But when excavating the trilogies for

---

[40] Kay Dick, *Friends and Friendship*, 41.
[41] *The Strings Are False*, 116.

impressions of Reggie Smith, it's important to remember that the
portrait to be found there was assembled some years after the event,
although the excavation almost always pays off in terms of uncovering
correspondences between the living, breathing Reggie and his fictional counterpart. Without question, Olivia's fiction provides a generous opening into multiple aspects of her personality, her career, and
her marriage, but it is important to bear in mind the length of time
between composition of the trilogies and their publication: the first,
nearly twenty years after Olivia and Reggie arrived in Bucharest
in early September 1939 (*The Great Fortune*, January 1960) and the
following five over the next twenty years. There does exist, however,
another key to Olivia's fictional reconstruction of Reggie in Guy
Pringle: the unpublished typescript of a novel titled 'Guests at a
Marriage' that she composed in the winter of 1943–4 while in Palestine. At the top of each page she typed 'Olivia Manning c/o Controller
of British Broadcasting, Jerusalem.'[42] Closer in writing time than the
trilogies to Olivia's wedding in London in August 1939, the manuscript suggests possible reservations about Reggie's personality and
about her hasty marriage.

The novel begins with Alex and Stella Linden sitting in a café; they
have been married for five days and the strong sexual attraction
between them is immediately apparent as Stella pulls her fingertips
over 'the glowing, very smooth skin' of Alex's arm, laying 'brown on
the white table-cloth . . . They smiled at one another. They felt they
knew all there was to know about one another then, but they had not
realized their knowledge. They were still mysterious, and excited and
tranquillised by each other's mystery' (p. 1). This conjuring of sexual
desire between two recently married people reminds one of the
conspicuous lack of such description in the trilogies. Extravagantly
packed with precisely observed detail, they offer virtually no evidence
of a sexual relationship between Harriet and Guy Pringle, and, by
association, create some questions in the reader about the relationship
between Olivia and Reggie.[43] How to explain this lacuna in six novels
that are, after all, not only about World War II but also about a
marriage? First, one might think that Olivia Manning was squeamish

---

[42] The typescript runs to 166 pages. OMC, HRC.

[43] Alan Munton notes that 'Manning has less to say about desire in marriage than many
novelists of the nineteenth century.' *English Fiction of the Second World War*, 189.

when writing about sexuality, but this explanation loses credibility if we consider the violent coupling between Edwina Little, a secretary at the British Embassy in Cairo, and Peter Lisdoonvarna, an Irish army officer, that Harriet hears through the wall when she is living in that city, or the graphic description of a sex show witnessed by Simon Boulderstone in a Cairo brothel (both incidents from *The Battle Lost and Won*). It's also possible that when she started writing the trilogies Olivia was no longer sleeping with Reggie and that this influenced her invention of Guy Pringle; Francis King believes that when he met them in the mid-1950s, they were 'no longer sexual partners... in addition, he was an energetic philanderer.'[44] That they were no longer sexual partners may or may not be true, and it's possible that writing about a sexual spark between fictional characters could have proved painful for Olivia, if it were absent from her own marriage. But for whatever reason, she writes sex into 'Guests at a Marriage' and pretty much leaves it out of the trilogies when it comes to Harriet and Guy.

Soon though, however attracted Stella may be to Alex's smooth brown body, she becomes dissatisfied with the rest of him: 'For the first time Stella found herself thinking: "He talks too much," and realized how much of his force was dissipated in speech. His personality was like radium flinging itself off, dissipating itself in brilliance. It seemed to her an indiscriminate giving for the sake of friendship' (p. 22). In the first volume of *The Balkan Trilogy*, *The Great Fortune*, Olivia deploys identical imagery to describe Harriet Pringle's observation that even when Guy's listeners weary of his energetic rhetoric, he remains unworried: 'On the contrary he seemed like radium throwing off vitality to the outside world—not that he thought of it as the outside world' (p. 160). Nothing much happens in terms of action in 'Guests at a Marriage,' which makes it totally different from the vivid accounts of battle, political intrigues, perilous escapes, and bombing that pack the pages of the trilogies. The tension between Alex and Stella remains unresolved, although Stella does announce at the end that she is leaving: 'I want to live alone—I don't want to be worried by being near you. If I'm away from you I won't care. I'll be quite separate. I'll get a job and live an intelligent life again. You needn't worry about me—I want to do it. I realize it's a thing I've wanted for

---

[44] *Yesterday Came Suddenly*, 240.

ages' (p. 125). If we accept imaginative affiliations between Olivia and Stella and Reggie and Alex, it would seem that Olivia, writing roughly four years after her marriage, had some reservations about its future.

Yet Olivia, of course, stayed with Reggie and we can assume from Harriet's teasing reply to Guy's pleading question, posed at the close of the trilogies ('You'll never leave me again, will you?')—'Don't know. Can't promise... Probably not'—that their fictional counterparts do not separate. For Olivia Manning and Harriet Pringle, Reggie Smith and Guy Pringle, despite their failings, remain attractive, open-hearted, and generous men of infinite good nature. Reflecting on the disenchantment that comes with marriage, Harriet concludes that, having entered it 'unsuspecting,' to live with reasonable happiness, one must accept the 'unsuspected' difficulties. According to Francis King, Olivia complained constantly about Reggie; she would bemoan the fact that 'He was unreliable, unfaithful, unpunctual, slovenly, hopeless about money.'[45] Yet she stayed with him throughout a tumultuous forty-year period in twentieth-century English history, and also he with her, despite his fondness for other women, some of whom were eagerly awaiting his return to Bucharest. And why? Because he admired her work tremendously, told everyone always that she was a genius, and because she deeply respected his love of language and literature and relied upon him for that support and for his generous willingness to read everything she wrote, and to tell her without reservation what he thought of it. Perhaps they did stop sleeping together at some point, but eventually that hardly seems to matter if we understand that their marriage rested upon a strong sense of companionship, mutual respect, and a shared experience of surviving World War II in the Balkans and in the Middle East.

---

[45] *Yesterday Came Suddenly*, 239.

3

Bucharest

'Nobody who has not experienced it can know what a trial that "warmth and benevolence" is to live with.'

Olivia Manning to Francis King.[1]

What a novel!

In August 1939 the Orient Express train usually left Victoria Station at six o'clock in the evening and would arrive in Bucharest sixty hours later, which meant Olivia and Reggie slept for three nights on the train, the first in cramped upright seats and the next two in a cozy *wagon-lit*. Having lived together for three weeks in Olivia's tiny flat in Woburn Place before their departure, they were used to close quarters and were not sorry to leave 'trench-digging, tree-chopping, sandbag-filling London.'[2] But for Olivia it was a 'dreadful journey.' In a long letter written to Stevie Smith shortly after they arrived in Bucharest, she says they had hoped to spend nights in Paris, Milan, and Zagreb but did not dare to do so because of an imminent declaration of war between Britain and Germany. She had arrived looking and feeling 'a wreck.' As the train roared through France, Reggie had buried his head in one of the many books he had crammed into a rucksack (he was getting ready to teach Romantic poetry to the Romanian students) and Olivia had mostly stared out of the window;

---

[1] 14 April 1970, FKC/OM, HRC.
[2] Reggie Smith, Preface to Olivia Manning, *The Remarkable Expedition: The Story of Stanley's Rescue of Emin Pasha from Equatorial Africa*, p. xi.

'Italy and Switzerland looked really lovely but Jugo-Slavia [sic] through which we spent one whole day was just a flat plain on which nothing seemed to grow but maize.'[3] As she thought about her last sight of England, the cliffs of Dover, she felt no sentimental regrets about leaving, even though the journey was a trial and she had been forced to pack in a hurry, abandon her small flat, and leave behind all her books. Writing to Stevie on 8 September 1939, she says she would be 'more than grateful' if she could get the books out of the flat and into her house at Palmers Green, which Stevie did and for which Olivia remained very grateful.[4]

On the train, Olivia thought about how far she had come from Laburnum Grove, how much she was physically attracted to Reggie, and how thrilled she was at the prospect of a new life in Bucharest, even on the eve of World War II with MacNeice's metaphorical tractors on the horizon. Her previous journeys had been on the bus from Portsmouth to London, brief trips to Ireland and Paris with Hamish, and now she was racing across Europe on the glamorous Orient Express, chatting with Foreign Office wives returning to Baghdad by way of Istanbul, Colonial Service officials traveling to Trieste, where they would pick up a boat to travel east, and bank clerks returning to their posts in Belgrade, Bucharest, and Athens. When the train entered Italy the windows were blacked out in the evening, but during the day signs of the impending European conflict became more apparent and as the train steamed past Lake Maggiore the passengers could see increasing numbers of grayish-green uniforms, camouflaged buildings, and the infantry on maneuvers. Describing the journey to one of her wedding guests, Ernest Stahl, who was lecturing at Oxford, she says that when the train food became unappetizing, she and Reggie 'bought bits and pieces from peasants selling things and so the long day wore on like a Russian novel.'[5] As they continued through Venice, Trieste, and Belgrade, the rumblings of imminent war made the journey one of hesitations, sudden movements, and stops at miserable little villages when weary inspectors would climb on board to check their tickets and passports. But at the Romanian border various handsomely dressed officials boarded the train, she reported to Ernest Stahl. The Romanian women passengers greeted them with delight.

[3] SSP, UT.   [4] SSP, UT.
[5] 31 August 1939, OMC/C, HRC.

Olivia's memories of entering Romania frame the first chapter of *The Great Fortune* (the first volume in the Balkan trilogy) and she constructs a scene that suggests as much about her early misgivings in regard to her marriage as it does about the preparation for war to be seen from the train windows. Olivia's fictive surrogate, Harriet Pringle, watches as her husband chats animatedly with a cluster of 'stout, little Romanian women,' putting his arms out to them 'as though he would embrace them all' and looking slightly drunk and foolish as he does so.[6] Married for just a week (as Olivia had been when she boarded the Orient Express), Harriet wonders how well she knows Guy, if, in fact she really knows anything about him at all. When one of the enraptured women recognizes him as the professor who taught her son English, he answers in Romanian, flushing with pleasure at the admiration he receives for his fluency and pronunciation. Harriet, understanding not a word, smiles at the fun, pretends to be part of it, and retreats into the attitude of amused, skeptical observation that pretty much remains her demeanor throughout the entire trilogy. As a factual correlative to this fictional attitude, before entering Romania as a woman at war, Olivia's droll wit and ironic detachment defined her personality. Although they were qualities that often alienated people to whom she was introduced, that wit and that irony sustained her through the difficulties and dislocations of the years to come.

Given the close affinity between the experience of two couples (one fictional, one not), it is difficult not to read the first chapter of *The Great Fortune* as Olivia's recollection of her resigned acquiescence in Reggie's compulsive need for attention and her discomfort with his habit of scattering affection like confetti, despite her strong attraction to his physicality and his genuine warmth. That he was irresistibly lovable is indisputable; for the English composer Elisabeth Lutyens, who worked with him at the BBC after the war, he was as 'amiable as a Newfoundland puppy, with a generosity as big as his huge frame . . . he befriended the world, giving jobs, money and cheer to all and sundry, almost indiscriminately. The only difficulty was in getting his undivided attention for one split second, even when work demanded it.'[7] The trilogies do nothing to undermine Reggie's essential decency as expressed through the characterization of Guy Pringle, however

---

[6] *The Great Fortune*, 8.   [7] *A Goldfish Bowl*, 143.

difficult it was for Olivia to cope with such things as his chronic inability to be on time, his annoying compulsion to flirt with every woman to whom he was introduced, and his refusal to leave a party or a café when she was ready to go home. What *is* remarkable is that Olivia chose to begin her novel about World War II, written almost twenty years after the fact, with a revelation of Harriet's uneasiness about the marriage, and, by extension, an admission of the doubts about Reggie Smith that were also suggested in Olivia's unpublished manuscript 'Guests at a Marriage.'[8]

At the close of the first chapter of *The Great Fortune*, Harriet says to Guy, 'I love you,' something she had hitherto been reluctant to admit, and she feels this romantic moment should 'expand into rapture.' But Guy takes it lightly, murmurs 'I know,' and returns to reading Coleridge. She begins to realize that the cuddly warmth that had enfolded her before her marriage had, in fact, provided a false kind of security: for Guy, personal relationships are merely means to gain the attention he needs from the outside world and Harriet is but one of a squadron of adoring people on whom he is delighted to bestow reciprocal adoration. At the time of writing *The Great Fortune*, Olivia had published five novels, one collection of short stories, two works of non-fiction, and had been a regular reviewer of new fiction, particularly for *The Palestine Post*. A seasoned novelist when she began *The Balkan Trilogy*, she had perfected the art of appropriating autobiography for the larger canvas of a historical novel, and perhaps her greatest achievement, here and elsewhere, is her skillful integration of private unhappiness into a larger narrative of war and violence. We feel Harriet's dissatisfaction with no diminution of our understanding of the tumultuous historical period in which she lives: the private unhappiness does not trivialize the historical tragedy, nor make it mere backdrop for romantic disappointment, yet at the same time Olivia shows the deepening of personal unease in a time of war.

We know we are in the hands of a practiced novelist when we encounter (still in Chapter One) an arresting paragraph that describes the Romanian women dispersing, Guy returning to his books, and Harriet remaining at the window. For a few uncomfortable minutes, she has been an embarrassed witness to her husband's fatuity, but she

---

[8] Francis King claims that Olivia told him 'constantly' of her dissatisfaction with Reggie's unreliability, infidelity, and hopelessness about money and he believes that what aggrieved her most was the squandering of a love she felt should be focused solely on herself—instead it was 'diffused on everyone.' *Yesterday Came Suddenly*, 239.

now returns to her position as fascinated observer of the alien landscape: 'Harriet remained a while at the window, watching the mountains rise and grow, ebony against the dim and starless sky. A pine forest
came down to the edge of the track: the light from the carriages rippled
over the bordering trees. As she gazed out into the dark heart of the
forest, she began to see small moving lights. For an instant a grey dog-
shape skirted the rail, then returned to darkness. The lights, she
realized, were the eyes of beasts' (pp. 8–9). It's very likely that Olivia
saw wolves coming out of the forest to run alongside the train since
Romania was a country with vast stretches of mountain and forest
where bears, wild boar, lynx, and wolves roamed freely, but this
description does more than set down a memory. Olivia takes that
memory and shapes it into an imaginative foreshadowing of mysterious and forbidding darkness. The mountains pitch-black against the
sky, the light from the carriages rippling over the trees, the eyes of the
wolves that seem, at first, to be lights punctuating the darkness—all of
this looks back to Bram Stoker's *Dracula* and forward to the darkness of
war into which Guy and Harriet Pringle are being transported by the
Orient Express. Impenetrably dark and inhabited by 'beasts' both
animal and human, Romania impresses itself upon Harriet's imagination in a manner that transcends a mere autobiographical record of
Olivia Manning's arrival in a strange country. In its depiction of
marital unease and alien landscape, this first chapter prepares us for
the story of a difficult marriage and the narrative of survival in a Balkan
country riven by political conflict and ripe for fascist rule.

At the end of World War I, as a reward for entering the war on the
side of the victors, Romania had acquired the territories of Transylvania, Bessarabia, and Bukovina and set itself on the path of forging a
powerful national identity. For prosperous Romanians, the 1930s were
a golden age in which the country fostered capitalist development of its
considerable natural resources—primarily the oil and cereals that
proved so attractive to Germany at the end of the decade as it beefed
up its military forces. Somewhat paradoxically, however, as it scrambled to gain economic autonomy, Romania still turned to western
Europe for cultural inspiration, a trend that had developed during the
late nineteenth century and that grew even stronger as the country
aspired to be a progressive, modern state: during the inter-war years,
Romanian artists, writers, and architects became increasingly aware

that a national culture could not exist independently of world culture.[9] Large numbers of young Romanians went abroad to study in Paris, Berlin, Zurich, or Vienna and their contact with the European artistic avant-garde, particularly in Paris, influenced the shaping of a Modernist aesthetic that was most apparent in the capital.

In the 1930s, as Modernism became a defining feature of Bucharest's architectural landscape, the city became dotted with Art Deco and refashioned classical buildings, some of them incorporating regional vernacular elements and all disclosing a broad range of western European sources such as the Bauhaus and classical features of the Beaux-Arts movement. The primary focus was on the development of a domestic architectural style, and dazzling new villas and apartment buildings appeared on Bucharest's wide, tree-shaded boulevards: as Carmen Andras observes, Bucharest was not only a city of monuments and up-to-date buildings, it was also 'a city of smart shops, picturesque open-gardens, shady retreats, parks, stylish restaurants and coffee houses, cabarets, a city with an intense night life.'[10] When the poet, translator, and travel writer Derek Patmore visited Romania in the late 1930s, anxious to gain his first impressions of the city he leaned out of the train window and was amazed to see in the distance tall white buildings gleaming in the early morning sunshine: 'But I noticed no domes or minarets. Instead, it reminded me of many of the great cities I had seen in America.' Patmore also much admired the principal train station where Olivia and Reggie arrived on the fateful day of 3 September 1939: he describes it as 'a large, fine modern building, very up-to-date and elegant in style, as befits the main station for the capital of a rich, proud, new country.'[11]

On their arrival, Olivia and Reggie settled into a room at the Anglo-Rumanian Society on a side street just off the main square on the side opposite the Athénée Palace Hotel, and their first few weeks in an excitingly beautiful city were marred only by Reggie being rushed to hospital for an appendectomy, from which he quickly recovered. But Olivia wrote to Stevie Smith that she was wretchedly homesick for a

[9] See Luminita Machedon and Ernie Scoffham, *Romanian Modernism: The Architecture of Bucharest, 1920–1940*, 33.
[10] 'In-betweenness and intermediality in British images of inter-war Bucharest (1930–1939)', in *New Directions in Travel Writing and Travel Studies*, 230.
[11] *Invitation to Roumania*, 3.

few days without Reggie as her Bucharest *cicerone*; she begged for news
of London and their friends—'Stevie darling, do write soon and tell me
lots... You know how much I want to see you again.'[12] She did add,
however, that Bucharest was 'charming—an extremely modern Wes-
ternised civilization imposed on an ancient Eastern one. The streets are
wide and the houses white. The sun shines every day and is very hot.'
But if the Germans come here, she concludes, there are plans for
evacuation to Turkey and 'from there there is no knowing. What a
novel!' After his rapid recovery from the appendectomy, Reggie took
himself off every morning to the British Institute housed at the University, excited about being back in Bucharest and untroubled by the
fact that, having returned to Romania, he had exempted himself from
any pressing need to join up (Francis King notes that Reggie 'being
young, able-bodied, and not a pacifist', could very well have volunteered while back in London, but clearly he had chosen not to[13]). The
British Institute represented a big investment by the British Council:
started in 1937 with seven teachers and sixteen hundred students, by
the time Reggie returned in September 1939 its student population
had doubled, many of them young Jewish men seeking to learn or to
perfect their English as preparation for leaving the country.

    While Reggie was happily re-installing himself at the Institute,
Olivia would spend her mornings exploring the streets around the
square. Excited by Bucharest's strange and wonderful potpourri of East
and West, her strong visual sense attracted to scenes such as modern
taxis vying for precedence with ancient *droshkies* (horse-drawn carriages controlled by drivers dressed in green costumes with wide
leather belts), she would wander down side streets full of little shops
and then head for the Calea Victoriei, the great boulevard named in
honor of the 1878 Romanian victory over the Turks and the end of
four centuries of Ottoman rule. Jostled by crowds of expensively
dressed women with carefully coiffured hair and exquisite complex-
ions, she would find herself stumbling into the gutter, so crowded was
the Calea Victoriei, a street of charming single-story houses, modern

---

[12] 9 September 1939, from The Anglo-Rumanian Society, 3 Boteanu, Bucharest.
SSP, UT.
[13] King says that Reggie's choice to go back to Romania and not join the armed forces
was pointed out to him by someone who had actually returned from Romania and joined
Fighter Command. *Yesterday Came Suddenly*, 239.

apartment buildings, cafés, and Orthodox churches. Most famously, the boulevard offered a procession of fancy shops where wealthy Bucharest residents purchased English cashmere sweaters and visited their tailors. When Olivia arrived at the famous grocer Dragomir's she could barely get inside to inspect the luxurious delicacies on offer: expensive cuts of meat, every kind of game bird, caviar, French cheeses, lobsters and crayfish swimming in tanks, button mushrooms flown in from Paris, and costly English jams and marmalades. Similar to Fortnum and Mason in London, where she had occasionally treated herself, and sometimes Hamish, to the odd game pie or rich chocolate tart, Dragomir's catered to the epicurean bourgeoisie of Bucharest. Prince Yakimov, that superbly realized comic character from *The Balkan Trilogy*, can barely contain himself when he enters Dragomir's: homeless, penniless, and wearing a sable-lined coat that may or may not have been given to his father by the tsar, he regards Bucharest as the last decent outpost of European cooking. Gazing longingly at the luxurious profusion, he furtively pockets a chunk of Roquefort newly arrived from France.

Visiting Dragomir's affirmed Olivia's belief that the Bucharest bourgeoisie essentially spent the day eating, talking, and sleeping, an impression that she incorporated in an introduction to a collection of Romanian short stories published in 1971. She writes that the day began with coffee and rolls, followed by coffee and cakes at a local café; lunch was preceded by an aperitif and tiny hot pies filled with cheese and mushrooms; lunch was followed by a siesta, and then by the famous 'Five O'Clockul' at which one drank coffee and ate more cakes; finally, dinner, where one ate even more than one had eaten at lunch.[14] After sampling the post-breakfast coffee and cakes, Olivia would often join the promenade along the Calea Victoriei, astonished by the sumptuous displays of jewelry, silver fox furs, Italian leather handbags, and cashmere twin-sets that filled the shop windows. In the brief time before she and Reggie left Victoria on the boat-train to the Continent, Olivia had frantically read up on Romania but nothing had prepared her for the visible displays of wealth and sensual indulgence that she encountered on the Bucharest streets, or for the inescapable

---

[14] Typescript notes for Olivia's Introduction to *Romanian Short Stories*, OMC, HRC. The Oxford University Press volume is out of print, unobtainable at the British Library, and only available from booksellers at a very high price.

presence of maimed beggars who pressed upon her when she left her flat. In *The Balkan Trilogy*, she writes that Harriet Pringle has read travelers' accounts of the Romanians as 'a rollicking, open-hearted, happy, healthy peasantry' and is shocked by the sight of 'starved, frightened figures, scrawny with pellagra, wandering about in a search for work' (pp. 132–3).[15]

Even if the gracious boulevards, elegant clothes, and inviting restaurants failed fully to convince Olivia that for western Europeans and Romanians alike, Bucharest was the 'Paris of the East,' a ride with Reggie in a *trăsură* (a horse-drawn carriage) that took them to the end of the Chaussée, the wide, tree-lined boulevard that led out to the open country, provided a literal sign of that claim: the Chaussée ended at Bucharest's own Arc de Triomphe, a symbol of its aspiration to rival the cultural capital of western Europe. On the way back they were dropped off at Pavel's, a large open-air restaurant that specialized in rotisserie chickens and gypsy violin music, and where Reggie seemed right at home and she felt distinctly out of place. Dining out with Hamish in Soho and running around town with Stevie Smith had smoothed out most of the provincialism Olivia betrayed when she first arrived in London: attractive, witty, and with one published novel to her credit, she had moved with increasing confidence in the bright Bloomsbury crowd of publishers and authors to which Hamish had introduced her, despite her lingering embarrassment about a lower-middle-class Portsmouth upbringing. But here, in Bucharest, surrounded by Reggie's university-educated British Council friends and a bevy of attractive young women, some of whom appeared to be alarmingly familiar with her husband, and plunged into a café culture where he flourished but where she was hobbled by a lack of fluency in the language, she retreated into a protective reserve that many interpreted as either social insecurity or active dislike. Ivor Porter, for instance, recalls that even though he found Olivia 'a little too severe,' he would often sit with her in Bucharest cafés 'surrounded by Reggie's crowd of which I was one, but she never really joined in.' Looking

---

[15] In arguing that British 'balkanism' served to enforce 1950s and 1960s Cold War ideology, Andrew Hammond claims that it 'certainly dominated' *The Balkan Trilogy*: the Romanian capital emerges as one of the major protagonists, a diseased and 'disintegrating presence, whose wretched streets are rife with poverty, corruption and political violence.' ' "The Red threat": Cold War rhetoric and the British novel,' 44–5.

back, Porter realizes that she must have felt vulnerable and resentful when she perceived that Reggie, returned to Bucharest, was continuing 'to sleep around as if nothing had changed.' Sympathetic to Olivia's plight, Porter excuses the bitter wit and social standoffishness: 'Cut off from her own country with war approaching, without friends or even the language to help her, she watched her young marriage breaking up, seemed incapable or unwilling to do anything about it, and hated the place where it was happening.'[16] If Porter is correct, then it would seem Reggie's cavalier views on sexual fidelity very early on became an accepted pattern in Olivia's marriage. On the other hand, the 'young marriage' did not break up, a fact which tends to undermine the reliability of Porter's conclusions about Olivia's feelings.

To Reggie's boisterous and less sympathetic friends, Olivia appeared wan, bored, and unhappy, unable or unwilling to join the fast and frenzied banter with which they amused themselves. To Adam Watson, an official at the British Legation in Bucharest and a model for the character of Dobson in the trilogies (admired by Reggie as a 'great and fast-talking scholar'), initially she seemed sadly out of her social depth, a provincial girl intimidated by her surroundings. However, when she and Reggie began to share his flat in Bucharest after they moved out of the Anglo-Rumanian Society, Watson revised his opinion. Like Ivor Porter, he understood that what people read as ennui or lack of sophistication was as much a symptom of Olivia's fear that she had married unwisely as it was a sign of self-protection in an unfriendly atmosphere. This uncertainty about a choice of husband is expressed by Harriet Pringle when she thinks about *her* arrival in Bucharest: she had been 'nervous, suspicious and isolated among strangers,' woefully conscious of the fact that 'Unmarried, she had been a personality in her own right. Married, she herself coming in, if at all, somewhere in Guy's wake' (p. 301). It was certainly true that Olivia did to some extent flounder in Reggie's wake when they first arrived in Romania: the crucial difference, though, between the novelist and the fictional character is that the former was already a working writer whereas the latter, despite her pre-war employment in an art gallery, seems to have neither work nor social identity independent of Guy. If Olivia at times

---

[16] *Operation Autonomous: With SOE in Wartime Romania*, 22–4.

seemed distracted and eager to leave whatever café Reggie was determined to linger in, often it was because she was working on various
short stories and reading books from the British Council library for a
study of Henry Morton Stanley's rescue of Emin Pasha from Equatorial Africa. As Reggie noted in his preface to the book when it was
republished in 1985 (it first appeared in 1947), as a novelist Olivia was
'lying fallow' in Bucharest but felt she needed 'to be writing about
something.'[17]

As the months went by, Romania began to look less favorably
upon its old British ally, and it was no longer willing to regard Great
Britain 'as the one country left in a distracted Europe which can
maintain the balance of peace,' as Derek Patmore observed in 1939
when traveling through the Balkans.[18] And at the same moment that
Bucharest was forging itself as a Modernist city with international
aspirations and a vibrant café culture, Romanian politicians were
turning inward, encouraging the exclusion of Jews from membership
in professional organizations and ignoring the growing and dangerous
popularity of the Iron Guard.[19] As the intelligentsia flocked to the
famous Capsa brasserie on Calea Victoriei and prosperous families took
sled rides out to the end of the boulevards, fascist gangs inspired by the
memory of the martyred Iron Guard leader Corneliu Zelea Codreanu
(King Carol had him executed on the grounds of treason in November
1938) were terrorizing with immunity persons who struck them as
dangerous outsiders. Moreover, Romania's strategic position on the
direct routes from Central Europe to the Black Sea and the Near East,
and from European Russia down to the Balkans and the Mediterranean, made it particularly vulnerable to German aggression. On 1
February 1940, King Carol reassured his country and its allies that
Romania would resist outright German invasion, but his speech did
little to alleviate the fears of the British colony.

Already exiled to the garden of the Athénée by a phalanx of German
officials who had taken over the English bar, the British colony

---

[17] *The Remarkable Expedition: The Story of Stanley's Rescue of Emin Pasha from Equatorial Africa*, p. xi.

[18] *Invitation to Roumania*, 23.

[19] See Irinia Livezeanu, Review of *Romanian Modernism: The Architecture of Bucharest, 1920–1940* by Luminita Machedon, *Slavic Review*; and Carmen Popescu, review of *Romanian Modernism: The Architecture of Bucharest, 1920–1940* by Luminita Machedon, *The Journal of the Society of Architectural Historians*.

huddled together for news of the war and waited to see how the Legation was going to get them out of the country. Olivia had written despairingly to Stevie Smith on 11 October 1939 bemoaning the 'stupidity' of their generation and ruing the loss of her 'old life': when she left London it had 'ceased almost at once to be the London I knew and seems to have become a blacked-out wilderness... it is dreadful to feel that my old life is no longer there to be returned to.' She had been delighted to get letters from old friends such as Walter Allen and Ernest Stahl but alarmed to learn that 'Margaret G.' had 'got to know Everything. Neither R. nor I told her... I can tell you, Stevie, that I am not letting everyone know my secrets and I am quite serious when I say I do not want people to know.'[20] Nothing in Olivia's letters or in other archival material provides evidence of what 'Everything' might be: possibly an abortion, but that is pure speculation. Olivia ended this letter by saying that she thinks often of Stevie and misses her wit and smart intelligence: 'For us the English community consists of the lecturers, R. and three Oxford men... The other English are pukka sahibs in Oil who have sent their Women and Children Home for Safety—quite unknowable. Some of the Roumanians are worth knowing—highly cultured, but I long for the horrors of Bloomsbury.'

Political instability and violence increased in the months to come. The execution of Codreanu, the Iron Guard leader, was quickly repaid by the assassination in the city's Chicken Market of the Prime Minister Cālinescu, the aftermath of which is viewed with horror by Yakimov (in The Great Fortune) as he tries to find his way from the railway station to the British Legation. Understandably, most troubling to the British colony was the fact that English citizens were being kidnapped, bundled roughly into cars, and imprisoned by the authorities. On 3 October 1940, for example, a Mr Miller, who was a manager in the Astra-Romana Oil Company, was arrested while playing bridge in the company's club. Eyewitnesses related seeing him marched off across the fields to a waiting vehicle: the police, the military, and the Iron Guard all vehemently denied giving any orders for his arrest. On the

---

[20] SSP, UT. 'Margaret G.' in all likelihood was Margaret Gardiner (1904–2005), the daughter of a wealthy Egyptologist, Sir Alan Gardiner. She had an affair with Louis MacNeice in the late 1930s and later became a notable patron of the arts and founder of the ICA in London.

same day, three green-shirted members of the Iron Guard escorted a Mr Percy Clarke from the Athénée Palace Hotel; Clarke had been running a wire-rope business in Poiesti, the city thirty-five miles north of Bucharest that was the center of Romania's oil refining industry. Miller, Clarke, and three other British subjects arrested the week previously were all charged with sabotage of the oil fields, and when the British Minister, Sir Reginald Hoare, was permitted to visit the prisoners, the Minister of Justice conceded that they had been maltreated by their captors, but at the same time informed Sir Reginald he was no longer *persona grata* with the Romanian authorities. On 6 October, *The Times* announced that, according to 'trustworthy reports,' the British employees of oil companies who had been arrested were subjected to torture in order to induce them to reveal alleged plans for sabotage: 'Their hands were tied high up on a wall, while blow-lamps were applied to their feet by members of the Iron Guard.'[21] After vigorous protests from the British Legation, all the prisoners were released and returned to their homes, but placed under house arrest. On 8 October 1940 German troops entered Romania, occupied the oil fields, and announced that they took a very serious view of the sabotage plots recently engineered by British subjects. From the moment of her arrival in Bucharest, Olivia had known she was, literally, a woman at war but it was only after the arrest of Miller, Clark, and others that Reggie woke up from his woolly dream that a Russian invasion from the north would protect Romania from the Germans. Increasingly distraught, she pleaded with him to get them out, and soon.

From 3 September 1939 they, and the entire city, had lived with the possibility of German invasion. When Derek Patmore reached Bucharest in the autumn of 1939, he found the people generally 'calm and collected,' laying in stores of tinned foods and anxiously scouring placards to read the latest news (p. 145); also, by the summer of 1940, many people had found it sensible to speak German, if they could. Yet, in that hot summer, Bucharest restaurants still stayed open until dawn, orchestras and singers still played as long as there was someone to listen, and the city was still full of wine and flowers. It was also abundantly clear that Germany attached great importance to

[21] *The Times*, 4 October 1940; 5 October 1940; 7 October 1940.

propaganda as preparation for their arrival. The German Travel Agency in Bucharest employed some six hundred people who were engaged mainly in spreading rumors about the dastardly Allies rather than arranging boat trips down the Rhine for interested Romanians. Olivia would watch in horror as the map of Europe displayed in the window of the travel agency daily acquired more swastika stickers. The packed cafés proved fertile ground for sowing rumors about perfidious financial transactions in which English businessmen in league with greedy Jewish merchants were swindling honest Balkan traders. BBC news broadcasts to the Balkans were pre-empted by German sympathizers and then re-recorded with insertion of glowing praise of Romanian–German friendship. English-speaking newsreels were blocked and Bucharest was treated to terrifying footage of Germany's military might. Olivia's description of these newsreels in *The Great Fortune* discloses her skill in vivifying cataclysmic history with stunning visual images: the German 'destructive lust was like a glimpse of the dark ages. The fires of Rotterdam shot up livid against the midnight sky. They roared from the screen. The camera backed, barely evading a shower of masonry as tall facades, every window aflame, crashed towards the audience. Bricks showered through the air. Cathedral spires, towers that had withstood a dozen other wars, great buildings that had been a wonder for centuries, all toppled into dust' (p. 280). In Bucharest, strange young men began to appear in the streets: white-faced, very grim, they were Romanian Blackshirts who had been trained in Germany by the SS.

While Olivia watched newsreels and coped with the challenge of getting a decent meal on the table (by late summer 1940 diminished supplies of sugar, coffee, meat, and eggs from the market stalls pretty much demolished Bucharest's reputation as one of the great food capitals of Europe), Reggie continued to teach for the British Institute at the University, where, despite the almost daily attacks upon the British, students clamored to be taught Coleridge, Wordsworth, and Byron. Jewish students now felt more than ever that fluent English could prove an asset in emigrating from Romania to another European country. When not teaching, Reggie distracted himself by arranging amateur productions of Shakespeare and, aided by volunteers from the British colony (some of them the pukka oil sahibs) and before the situation became truly alarming, at the end of May 1940 he mounted a production of *Othello* at the National Theatre Studio as a benefit for

the Red Cross. Romanian newspaper reviews were highly complimentary: professors and clerks from the British Council were com-
mended for turning themselves into plausible actors and Reggie in
particular received praise for taking on 'the very difficult lead role' and
for having a head resembling the young Oscar Wilde. Adam Watson
played Cassio 'with all the moral force this role requires' and everyone
'reenacted the story with energetic youth, calm, and a truthfulness that
proved to be quite moving.'[22] Reggie, of course, had acted Othello
eight years earlier when at university and his robust physicality and
mellifluous delivery were as successful in Bucharest as they had been in
Birmingham. Olivia did the costumes and make-up and worried about
when and how they were going to get out of the country—and, more
to the point, where they might end up. Lacking Reggie's cheerful
ability to carry on in the face of impending disaster, she became
increasingly wan and distracted.

During July and August of 1940, the British journalists gathered in
the English Bar of the Athénée brought news of the bombing of
Portsmouth, a site of strategic importance to the Germans as the
home of the Royal Navy, and, of course, a place of great personal
significance for Olivia. Nearly a thousand civilians were killed during
the aerial bombardment, many of Portsmouth's great civic buildings
were destroyed, never to be rebuilt, and almost all the principal
shopping areas were obliterated. In the late summer of 1940, the
London Blitz began and lasted until May of the following year; the
city was bombed every day or night from 7 September to 2 November.
When it was all over, twenty thousand civilians were killed and one
and half million people were made homeless. The news that Laburnum Grove and her parents had survived the Portsmouth bombing
was a tremendous relief to Olivia, but listening to what was happening
in England compounded the anxiety about what was happening in
Bucharest, and what might happen to her if she and Reggie were not
evacuated before the Germans officially took over.

In June 1940, the Nazis occupied Paris, and Olivia, terrified,
watched a newsreel showing the victory parade for Adolf Hitler on

the Champs Élysées, and then another that showed refugees trudging along poplar-lined roads, planes swooping down in a splatter of bullets, and children's bodies spreadeagled by the roadside. Between 24 May and 4 June, the British had retreated from the Continent via Dunkirk and on 28 June Russian forces marched into the capitals of Romania's northern territories, Bessarabia and Bukovina. Within days the Romanian cabinet had acceded to demands that the spoils gained at the end of World War I be ceded to the Soviet government. Two months later, on 30 August, Romania gave in to pressure from Germany and Italy and handed over two-thirds of Transylvania to Hungary. By now, Romania was a dismembered and virtually occupied country. The Prime Minister, Ion Antonescu, appeared in public wearing the green uniform of the Iron Guard; peasants were transported to Germany to work in the munitions factories; Romania's perennial outsiders, the gypsies and the Jews, were terrorized into either leaving the country (difficult for penniless gypsies to manage and not all Romanian Jews could afford the bribes) or being forced to face certain internment. In the late autumn of 1940, Olivia Manning, an official enemy of the Axis Powers, looked back over the previous six years of her life: she had escaped Portsmouth for London, loved and lost Hamish Miles, published a novel about the Irish 'Troubles,' embarked upon a perilous adventure in her marriage to Reggie Smith, and she had absolutely no idea where she might next find herself.

In the historically specific first novel of the Balkan trilogy, *The Great Fortune*, one year before this terrible autumn, on a late October day in 1939, Harriet and Guy Pringle are invited to lunch at the sumptuous flat of a wealthy Jewish family, the Druckers. In this brilliant set piece, Olivia's weaving of historical drama, fictional narrative, and personal memory both animates the tragic destiny that was fast overtaking Romanian Jewry and renders yet one more chilling recognition on the part of Harriet Pringle that she has married a man who remains blind to historical inevitability. The chapter also registers Olivia's memory of her frustration in late 1940 with Reggie's sunny assumption that Romanian politics would settle down, that he would continue unmolested as a teacher for the British Council, and that he and Olivia would remain unharmed by the Iron Guard.

Lunch at the Druckers

After the Romanian acquisition in 1919 at the Paris Peace Conference
of Transylvania, Bessarabia, and Bukovina, the Jewish population
increased considerably, particularly in urban areas and most noticeably
in Bucharest, and concomitantly with official efforts in the inter-war
years to forge a strong national identity and a distinctive national
culture, a Balkan anti-Semitism that had long existed acquired a fresh
intensity. The Iron Guard under Codreanu's brutal leadership
emerged to challenge and persecute the Jewish presence on Romanian
soil. As a means of pressuring the government to revoke their national
identity, the Guard spread insidious rumors that Jews had been clan-
destinely entering Romania in vast numbers, taking precious jobs from
the peasantry, and forging documents to prove their citizenship.[23]
From the mid-1930s, Jews of all social classes and professions found
themselves under attack. On 16 May 1937, the Confederation of the
Associations of Professional Intellectuals voted to exclude all Jewish
members from its affiliated bodies, calling for the government to
withdraw their licenses and reassess their right to remain in Romania.
On 21 January 1938, under the benevolently despotic eye of King
Carol, his cabinet passed a law aimed at reviewing criteria for citizenship and requiring all Jews who had received citizenship in 1918–19 to
reapply for it. On 10 February 1938, a law was passed requiring all
physicians and pharmacists holding foreign diplomas to submit documents proving their right to continue in practice.[24] In 1940, the
cabinet adopted Romania's equivalent to the Nuremberg Laws,
forbidding Jewish–Christian marriage and defining Jewish identity
along racial criteria. And after the arrival of the Germans in October
1940, the Iron Guard began a massive anti-Semitic campaign, looting
and beating with immunity from prosecution. By the time Romania
officially joined the Axis powers, on 23 November 1940, atrocities
against Jews had become common. It is in a climate of mounting
oppression and violence that Harriet and Guy Pringle arrive for
lunch at the Druckers, on a day that Olivia places almost exactly one

---

[23] Joshua Starr, 'Jewish citizenship in Rumania (1878–1940),' 69.
[24] Starr, 'Jewish citizenship,' 73.

year prior to the German invasion: that is to say, they come to lunch in late October 1939 and the Germans invaded in late October 1940. It is a day on which Harriet is able, for the first time, to see the mountains north of the city, 'crevassed and veined with glaciers that looked like threads of cotton', and she struggles to remain reassured by Guy's certainty that neither Russians nor Germans could possibly invade because the high passes in the mountains silting up with snow would prove an insurmountable barrier (Guy eventually relinquishes this mistaken belief when invasion becomes a real possibility). The Drucker family occupies the entire top floor of a large block of mansion flats owned by the Drucker bank (Drucker's son Sasha is one of Guy's students). The lobby has an atmosphere of France and smells of Romania. At the sight of Emanuel Drucker and his three sisters, Guy gives a cry of pleasure and throws open his arms: 'A tremendous babble of greetings, questions, and laughter broke out while Guy, breathlessly trying to answer all that was asked of him, bent about him, kissing the women and girls . . . Harriet stood back, watching, as she had watched the similar excitement in the *wagon-lit*' (p. 99). Just as she had stood by, amused and troubled, when Guy relished the squealing admiration of the Romanian women on the Orient Express, so here she remains silent, watching, and feeling equally uncomfortable. Troubled observation, in fact, becomes the primary motif of this tightly constructed chapter, titled 'The Centre of Things.' Most remarkable about its presence in an overtly autobiographical work of fiction, however, is the lack of evidence that Olivia ever met a family on which she might have modeled the Druckers, although she did write a very powerful piece about a boatload of doomed Romanian Jews titled 'Struma: The Ship That Never Had a Chance' (this appeared in the *Observer Magazine* in March 1970 and I discuss it in Chapter 10). 'The Centre of Things' is pure fictional imagination, a splendid example of Olivia's ability to bring the reader directly into the moment and make us feel the violent press of history, and also to remind us, whether she intended it or not, that she did actually witness what happened to Romanian Jews.

Drucker, heavily built and elegant in English tweeds, leads the Pringles into an enormous drawing room, packed with mahogany furniture and 'hemmed in by walls of so dark a red they were almost black' (p. 100). Many portraits heavily framed in gold pack the walls and a very large Turkish carpet covers the floor. Drucker introduces his three sisters to Harriet, one of whom is reputed to have been a mistress of the King and all of whom inspect Harriet with critical eyes, disappointed that their beloved Guy should have married someone so thin, so pale, so lacking in vitality (many who knew Olivia Manning in Bucharest in 1940 were concerned about her frail appearance). Harriet knows that she is not what they expected, not what they felt she ought to be. In this flat and in this company, she feels she would be a stranger forever. They chatter in French and English and she becomes increasingly isolated in a 'tumult of vivacious enquiry,' whereas Guy, flushed and excited, seems as distanced from her as she is from the women. The arrival of the three brothers-in-law, one German, one Austrian, and one Polish, adds to the vivacity, as does their sumptuous clothing and expensive jewelry: one is adorned with gem rings, a gold watch, diamond cuff-links, a diamond tie-pin and golden clips to hold down his tie, and another sports a garish chocolate-colored suit with stripes.

The sole member of the family to whom Harriet warms is Sasha Drucker, the adored son whose gentleness makes him seems like 'some nervous animal grown meek in captivity.' Educated at an English public school and destined by his father to learn the family business in the bank's New York branch, he seems to Harriet an anomaly in this driven, energetic, and animated family. The entrance of Drucker's wife completes the family tableau. Most definitely *not* Jewish, she is a moon-faced Romanian beauty, black-haired and black-eyed and wearing a fashionable dress of the moment—black, short, tight-fitting—with pearls, a large diamond brooch, and several diamond rings. Her husband is in thrall to her odalisque attractions and she barely disguises her distaste for the family into which she has married. The lunch features soup, sturgeon, braised steak, and a luxurious main dish: an enormous roast beef which the eldest Drucker sister has especially purveyed from Dragomir's, cut 'sirloin' in the English fashion. In the late afternoon the famous 'Five O'Clockul' arrives in the form of a trolley laden with 'sandwiches, iced cakes, cream buns, and several large flans made of sliced apples, pears, and plums' (pp. 112–13). Harriet almost faints under the surfeit of rich food, cloying perfumes, and hysterical attention.

Until the entrance of Sasha, the tone of this chapter can easily discomfort the reader. Why this rehearsal, verging on the anti-Semitic, of stereotypical images of vulgar Jewish life? Why this preoccupation with a preening display of wealth and the Druckers' impolite and undisguised disappointment in the wife of their beloved Guy? With the entry of Sasha, however, Olivia executes a subtle shift of tone: Harriet thinks to herself that Sasha's Semitic appearance means he will *always* be perceived as Jewish, and persecuted as such. To this moment, she has been vaguely appalled by the Druckers, but when she intuits the terrible vulnerability of the cherished son in a wealthy Jewish family soon to be torn apart, to the alarm of the Druckers and to the dismay of Guy, she begins to articulate her prescient sense of what is on the horizon. As one of Olivia's critics has observed, her authorial presence is never overt or intrusive; rather, through a restrained narrative voice (here channeled through Harriet) she imaginatively legitimates her authority as a historical witness: 'Historic occasions are deliberately rendered in terms personal, casual, very nearly unhistoric.'[25]

When the question of German invasion arises at the lunch table, Guy, somewhat sleepy from so much food, murmurs that there will probably be a financial collapse in Germany, which will put a halt to further territorial takeovers. Drucker, who believes that his vast investments in the German economy will protect him from persecution, testily dismisses this as a British rumor and asserts the country's financial structure is secure: 'We do not love the Germans any more than you, but we did not cause the war. We must live' (p. 107). At this moment, Drucker's eldest and most voluble sister declares that bankers uphold the existing order and that they will all be safe, whereupon Harriet, politely reserved since her arrival but now unable to suppress her irritation, loudly declares that such an order will 'cease to exist' should the Nazis arrive. She speaks the reality to which Guy remains blind and which the Druckers refuse to believe, or dare not believe. 'Roused by the talk,' Guy listens to his wife with a look of 'crumpled distress' and the Druckers all cry that it is the Romanians who ruin everything: they are lazy, content to do nothing but eat, sleep, and make love while the Jews run the country, do the work, and make the money. But despite this refusal to accept Harriet's hardheaded opinion that no political order is permanently stable, particularly when threatened by fascist military power, her remarks prompt a turn in

[25] Harry J. Mooney, Jr., 'Olivia Manning: Witness to history,' 41.

the family's talk from self-protective protest to revelation of persecution. In a sense, she begins to controls the chapter.

The German brother-in-law relates that at a German university
their son had been thrown from a window and his spine broken, and
that their daughter, a medical student, had been stripped and beaten by
young men with whom she was working in her laboratory. The son is
in a sanitarium in Switzerland and the daughter is in America. Guy's
feeble reaction to the revelation of these horrors is to say that when the
Russians arrive there will be an end to persecution; he is greeted with
appalled faces and Harriet struggles to control her derisive laughter at
his response. Sensing his wife's implicit contempt, he announces
briskly that 'She has nothing else to do' when the sisters insist she
stay behind as he leaves to return to the University. Forced to partake
of the famous Bucharest 'Five O'Clockul,' Harriet accepts a slice of
cake and looks out of the window: 'Rain was falling again. The wind
was blowing it in sheets from the soaked trees. Doamna Hassolel
watched her calmly as she returned to her chair' (p. 113). Within a
week of this lunch, the entire family vanishes from the novel, just as, in
the months to come, countless wealthy and not so wealthy Romanian
Jews vanished from Bucharest. The exception is Sasha, who, when his
father is arrested, disappears, manages to escape from conscription into
the Romanian army, and, when he returns to Bucharest, finds refuge
with Harriet and Guy, who hide him in a kind of servant's shed on the
roof of their building.

Harriet's prescience in this scene is borne out by events. Within
days, Drucker is arrested and paraded at a show trial to incite further
resentment of wealthy Romanian Jews. As she stands outside the
courthouse where he is to be tried, she witnesses his emergence from
the police van, 'an elderly stooping skeleton' wearing the suit of
English tweed he had been wearing when he entertained her at
lunch. Kicked by one of the guards, he sprawls upon the pavement
in front of Harriet, emitting 'a stench like the stench of a carrion bird'
(pp. 466–7). In 1944, Olivia recalled such scenes in her essay 'Poets
in Exile,' written in Cairo that year and published in *Horizon*. Including explicit reference to the fate of Jews as she recalls her time in
Bucharest, this was a time, she says, 'when Jews and later Englishmen,
disappeared from their homes to reappear, if they did reappear,
seriously crippled.' In her remarkable description of lunch at
the Druckers, Olivia seems to move beyond the boundaries of

autobiographical fiction, to enlarge her characteristically brilliant integration of historical narrative and personal memory, in order to produce a richly imbricated picture of her impressions of life in Bucharest and the tragic and understandable reluctance of the Druckers (and many Romanian Jews) to accept a terrifying inevitability.

Placing Harriet at the center of the chapter as a knowledgeable agent of her own unsentimental politics, Olivia Manning registers her remembered experience: sitting in Pavels café, say, and listening to Reggie and sundry deluded followers insist that the Germans will not invade Romania, that the Russians, should *they* invade, would prove a humane, even enlightened force of occupation, and that somehow, miraculously, British engagement in World War II will remain minimal. The anonymous reviewer of *The Great Fortune* in the *TLS* on 29 January 1960 praised Olivia's remarkable gift for an 'objective, analytical approach which displays the futility of so much conversation . . . Her direct and ironic sense of style, never "literary," but professional as a Mozart quartet, is what one expects from so unsentimental a writer.' Olivia had looked back to Bucharest and through Harriet Pringle offered a caustic, unsentimental analysis of the political situation as it seemed to her to exist in October 1939.

Stateless

By the summer of 1940, the British colony in Bucharest found itself permanently displaced from the English bar and exiled to the garden of the Athénée Palace Hotel, where it waited for news of a pending evacuation. As the situation worsened and the British Legation ordered its citizens to decamp, Reggie woke up from his fuzzy dreams of Russian rescue from German threat and began to see that Olivia needed to get out, although he fantasized he might remain as a vigorous representative of Western democracy. A few days before German and Romanian bombers flew over Bucharest and the Legation gave a final warning to all British citizens that they remained at their own peril, at Reggie's insistence, Olivia joined Adam Watson on board a Romanian plane bound for Athens. In *The Spoilt City*, the second novel in *The Balkan Trilogy*, before making exactly the same exit from Bucharest, Harriet Pringle visits the Golf Club out on the Chaussée that had been built in the 1920s by prosperous

English businessmen. Deserted, its dank garden paths smelling like a nineteenth-century English park, its principal sitting room is filled with chairs covered in faded chintz and tables covered with tattered copies of English journals. Harriet feels that she and Guy are 'like people left in an empty world. Everything was theirs. They could do what they liked, but there was nothing to do . . . On the walls were antlers, horns and many other second-hand trophies of the chase. There were also crossed spears and shields taken from some African tribe.' She asks Guy whether he thinks the Englishmen who founded the club believed this was what 'home was like' (p. 634). A world of golf clubs and relics of colonial conquest was definitely not Olivia Manning's idea of home: home was London, writing novels, drinking with friends, laughing, in fact, at anyone who might have put crossed spears from an African tribe on his sitting-room wall. Shortly after her arrival in Bucharest, she had written to Stevie Smith that she wished she were back in London, that she could experience once more 'the horrors of Bloomsbury,' and now she seemed to wish it even more, even if it meant enduring things much more horrible—sleeping in air-raid shelters, queuing for one's miserable meat ration, hearing the sound of German bombers overhead.

In *The Balkan Trilogy*, Harriet has gone to the golf club with Guy and David Boyd, a friend from the Legation who regularly appears and disappears from Bucharest throughout the trilogy (Harriet suspects he is on various spying missions): Boyd is going to meet Sir Brian Love, a Foreign Office advisor who has flown to Bucharest from Cairo in a last-ditch effort to arrange some sort of *modus operandi* to secure the release of British nationals accused of sabotage of the oil fields, and the safe departure from Romania of all other British citizens. Sir Brian talks 'in a leisurely way of a new sense of comradeship which he said was breaking down class-consciousness in England': after the war, he says, we shall see a new world, 'A classless world, I should like to think' (p. 636). What's interesting here, apart from the cleverly detailed sense of an ending that hangs over the whole scene (the moldy furniture, the old magazines, the deserted bar), is evidence of Olivia's well-researched or well-remembered (or, indeed, both) eye for historical detail. Even in the aftermath of the Blitz, the evacuation from Dunkirk, and fears of invasion, a Committee on Reconstruction Problems in Whitehall was working on a crucial document in British social history. Appearing in 1942 under the title *Social Insurance and Allied*

Services: The Beveridge Report in Brief, it was published by HM Stationery Office.

In his preamble to the Report, Sir William Beveridge spelled out the blueprint for what became known as the Welfare State. He began by saying that at a time when war was abolishing landmarks of every kind, Britain should make plans for a better world that could be built in a time of peace. 'Want, Disease, Ignorance, Squalor, Idleness' were the 'five giants' to be conquered in post-war Britain, indeed must be conquered if the nation were to recover from the devastation of war. The Report outlined the principal benefits to be provided to every citizen who pays a single security contribution: unemployment benefits, retirement pensions, national health services, children's allowances, and much more. Beveridge acknowledged that what he proposed was in some ways a revolution, but much more importantly, it was a natural development from the past since the social unrest of the 1930s clearly indicated the need for social change. In a sense, what was proposed developed organically from the pre-war years: it was a 'British revolution' (*Report*, 15). Interestingly, two of Olivia's least favorite novelists had something positive to say about the Report: Elizabeth Bowen wrote in the autumn of 1940 that 'the force of revolution' in Britain had 'already started and must accomplish itself.' As German bombs leveled the London streets, so too the war was leveling entrenched modes of behavior: 'subservience, smugness, habit-of-mind.' And Iris Murdoch in 1943 deemed the Report 'a good thing ... fine piece of work—thorough and equitable.'[26] In *The Great Fortune*, Sir Brian Love, chatting amiably with Guy and Harriet Pringle in Bucharest in autumn 1940, intimates the climate of political discourse taking place in Whitehall and he anticipates the Welfare State to which Olivia and Reggie returned in 1945. It's a small but telling incident, one that reveals Olivia's attention to the precise historical moment that characterizes so much of her writing and that corroborates her reputation as a conscientious historical novelist.

As she prepares to leave Bucharest, Harriet Pringle contemplates the 'involvement and disenchantment which was marriage,' a state of things into which one entered 'unsuspecting and, unsuspecting,

---

[26] 'Britain in autumn,' Elizabeth Bowen, *People, Places, Things*, 54. Iris Murdoch to Frank Thompson, 22 January 1943. *Iris Murdoch: A Writer at War*, 127.

found one was trapped in it' (p. 591). And if Harriet feels trapped in her marriage to Guy, so Olivia, when in Romania, felt trapped in her marriage to Reggie. Francis King believes that the marriage, 'delineated so unsparingly in so many of her novels, was decidedly odd,'[27] but judging from Olivia's letters, and, most tellingly, from her surrogate Harriet Pringle, the marriage was more than odd: it was downright dangerous. Olivia trusted Reggie so full-heartedly that she married him impetuously after only three weeks of living together and she left England with him shortly thereafter. In a kind of redemption of Reggie, however, *The Balkan Trilogy* indicates that Olivia's trust in him was justified, that he was not thickly indifferent to her vulnerability. At one point, for instance, Guy thinks to himself that Harriet 'must be protected from the distrust that had grown out of an unloved childhood,' and touched by the small, thin body that contained her spirit, he would say to himself, 'O, stand between her and her fighting soul.' He saw her as unfortunate because 'life, which he took easily, was to her so unnecessarily difficult' (p. 381). Guy recalls that before they married she had worked in an art gallery, had been the friend of artists and despite having come 'from the narrowest, most prejudiced class, she had nevertheless declassed herself.' Like her fictional surrogate, Olivia had rigorously set about becoming *declassée* for as long as she could remember.

What most prominently distinguishes Olivia Manning from Harriet Pringle, of course, is the fact that Harriet really has no serious profession nor, indeed, any kind of work at all when she is in Bucharest, whereas Olivia Manning when she met Reggie Smith, married him, and lived with him in Romania, was a working writer. Throughout the tumultuous time between her arrival on the Orient Express and her departure for Athens thirteen months later, she worked, often staying home to write while Reggie was out with his students or British Council pals. In her collection of short stories published in 1948, *Growing Up* (the eight stories were later included in *A Romantic Hero, and Other Stories* published in 1967), she appends at the end of each the date of composition. The fifth story in the collection, 'In a Winter Landscape', was begun in Bucharest and finished in Cairo in 1941.

---

[27] *Yesterday Came Suddenly,* 239.

The narrator of the story, her husband, and their friend Jake are on a ski trip in the Transylvanian mountains, where they encounter a refugee Polish soldier for whom they buy food and train tickets. Powerfully evoking the Transylvanian landscape, Olivia paints pewter-silver snow, piercing blue skies, and plum-colored sunsets: the narrator describes looking down on the roofs below her; they seem like 'folded slips of white velvet. Each chimney held up its collar of snow. A smoke gauze lay over the frigid glitter of the snow. As the path grew steeper it turned into steps beside which the sedate houses rose one above the other, painted terracotta, pink, lime-green, grey-blue, orange or cocoa-brown. Everywhere the snow, unbroken and brilliant on roofs and ledges, heightened the colours' (p. 101). In her critical study of Manning's war fiction, Eve Patten proposes that the Polish officer may be seen as an 'Other,' a troubling presence over-shadowing the skiing holiday in a Dracula landscape of Transylvanian mountains':[28] the tale, for Patten, 'illuminates the political nuances which inform Manning's writing, specially her willful destabilizaton of securities of belonging' (p. 103). The Drucker chapter in *The Great Fortune* illustrates Olivia's skeptical interrogation of the belief that belonging to something provides a sense of security, and as Harriet Pringle departs Bucharest for Athens, she has indeed become a refugee. The Romanian plane flies as far as Sofia and deposits its passengers at the gate for a Lufthansa flight for Greece. Fearful that the German aircraft will fly directly to Vienna, Harriet recognizes that she is unable to return to Romania and that it is by no means certain that she will be welcomed in Athens (if she makes it that far). As she fearfully prepares to board the plane in Sofia, Dobson (Adam Watson in real life) reminds her that she can neither stay where she is, nor return to where she has come from: 'She knew now what it was like to be a stateless person without a home' (p. 650).

That Olivia Manning did not publish 'In a Winter Landscape' and the other stories in *Growing Up* when they were written is not surprising. The material conditions of wartime Britain severely restricted publication of non-official texts, and even if Olivia, under considerable stress, had managed to send her work out for consider-ation, she would have faced obstacles: short stories, to be sure, were

[28] 'Olivia Manning, imperial refugee,' 103.

published but their venues were reduced in number, and novels, if they got published at all, were considerably shorter than their pre-war counterparts. After May 1940 it became illegal in Britain to start a new magazine, and Cyril Connolly just made it with the founding of *Horizon* in January of that year with backing from a rich patron; intending to ignore the war and focus on good writing, he announced in the first issue that 'Our standards are aesthetic, and our politics are in abeyance.'[29]

Much the same might be said of Olivia's feelings as the Romanian plane took off from Bucharest, or at least what she hoped her feelings might be when she landed in Athens. She was emotionally exhausted and physically depleted by the tremors of war—by the roars of green-shirted Iron Guardists marching around the main square, by the sight of Jews like her fictional character Drucker brutally beaten by the police, and by stories of British citizens being arrested and tortured. It was her ambition to become a successful writer that had sustained her from the time she arrived in Bucharest, as, like Cyril Connolly, she had aimed to keep politics in abeyance and her aims for aesthetic excellence always paramount. But involuntarily she was a woman at war, and as she researched her projected book on Stanley and Emin Pasha and worked on her short stories, the sights and sounds of violent conflict could not be kept at bay. In *The Great Fortune*, although Harriet Pringle is not a writer, she knows enough about the English novel to reprove one of Guy's colleagues when he declares scornfully that D. H. Lawrence's *Kangaroo* (a book on which Guy will soon be lecturing) is full of silly stuff about dark gods, phallic images, and packed with useless description—all 'just so many words strung together. Anyone could do it' (p. 203). 'Have you ever tried to write? Do you know how difficult it is?' cries Harriet. Has he no respect for the creative effort that goes into writing, she asks. Here, Harriet speaks for Olivia Manning without fictional mediation. It was writing that kept her going when she yearned to get out of Portsmouth, it was writing that kept her going through the most frightening days in Bucharest, and when she disembarked safely from the Lufthansa plane in Athens, it was still writing that sustained her.

---

[29] See Robert Hewison, *Under Siege: Literary Life in London 1939–1945*, 12.

4

Escaping the Barbarians

'We faced the sea,
Knowing until the day of our return, we would be exiles from a
Country not our own.'
              Olivia Manning, 'Written in the third year of the war.'[1]

The longed-for city

A foretaste of the Romanian winter, those chilly October winds that
blew down from the Transylvanian mountains and almost overnight
stripped the trees in the parks where Olivia and Reggie had walked
and lingered in lakeside cafés, were replaced on Olivia's arrival in
Athens with balmy breezes wafting from the Aegean. Where in
Bucharest the English colony had huddled in the garden of the Athénée Palace, desperate for news from the embassy about when and how
they were going to escape the city before the Germans arrived, in
Athens the English lounged happily in cafés, the autumn sun and
excellent ouzo lulling anxiety about the war. And where the English
in Romania had essentially constituted an insulated colony—oil company officials, bankers, journalists, many of whom were indifferent to
Balkan history and culture—in Athens Olivia discovered a group of
expatriate Hellenophiles, many of them happy pre-war exiles from
England's gloomy climate and delighted not to be working against

---

[1] Olivia wrote this poem soon after arriving in Alexandria in April 1941. Although it
celebrates the heroic yet futile struggle of the Greek resistance fighters, the poem's elegiac
evocation of exile resonates with Olivia's own continuing dislocation through war. It is
quoted in Jonathan Bolton, *Personal Landscapes*, 48.

newspaper deadlines or reporting to a managing director. Olivia's relief at landing safely after leaving Sofia was followed almost immediately by recognition of a difference between the English in Bucharest and the English in Athens: in the former city, they were there primarily to work, and in the latter, most seemed to have come to escape such a contingency, or, perhaps, to work at their own pace, like the novelist and poet Robert Liddell who lectured for the British Council in 1940 and who became Olivia's close friend during her time in Greece. In *Friends and Heroes* (the third novel in *The Balkan Trilogy*), Olivia modeled Harriet Pringle's English friend and ally Alan Frewen on Liddell and characterized him through his love of Greece and its culture. A sensitive and intelligent official in the British Information Office and the devoted owner of an aging dog named Diocletian, 'a Grecophil' like himself (p. 729), he proudly declares that he loves the country and that he loves the people. When Guy Pringle, with a good deal of pompous self-righteousness, charges him with wishing to keep the peasants living 'in picturesque poverty' while he enjoys the privileges of an education in Greek culture, Alan responds coolly that he wishes them to remain as they are—'courteous, generous, honourable and courageous' (p. 737).

Olivia also felt far more at ease with the British Council lecturers in Athens than with the group from whom she had felt alienated in Bucharest. When she and Reggie had arrived in Romania, Reggie had been embraced by a group of colleagues with whom he was already immensely popular and who misread Olivia's shyness and insecurity as unfriendly disdain. In Athens, she and Reggie shared an unsettling identity as refugees—Reggie was without a teaching assignment, having insisted on escaping to Greece rather than to Egypt (the British Council had posted him to Alexandria), and both were doubly exiled, first from England and now from Romania. Yet Olivia felt strangely at home, and when writing *Friends and Heroes* in the 1960s she relied on her memories of paradoxical liberation as she described Harriet Pringle, newly arrived in Greece, walking out into the 'fluid heat of the autumn afternoon' and thinking to herself, 'Athens . . . The longed-for city.'[2] In the previous months, as German invasion had become increasingly imminent, Bucharest had seemed to Olivia claustrophobically hemmed in by its proximity to Europe in the west and

---

[2] Harriet probably has in mind an exiled Aeneas's hasty desire to repair the wounds of Troy by building 'the longed-for city' in Crete.

Asia to the east: this sense of geographical enclosure and political menace had heightened her troubling thoughts about a hasty marriage and aggravated her alienation from a social world that adored Reggie and remained indifferent to herself. By delicious contrast, sunny Athens lay open to the sea and Olivia felt released from the numbing terrors of Bucharest and the worries about being a kind of camp follower in Reggie's social wake. The shimmering stone buildings, lush palm trees, and smiling people seemed to quiver with promise of a new life in her first weeks in 'the longed-for city.'

When Reggie arrived in Athens, one week after Olivia, the British Council was actually flourishing and his initial inability to obtain a lectureship (even though his salary was still being paid by London) was due more to an abundance of teachers than to a distrust of his quali-fications. In October 1940 (the month of his arrival), the Council was established by George VI as a permanent institution of the British realm, something that set 'a seal,' as *The Times* put it, 'upon the labours of the pioneers who have carried it from its small beginnings to its present wide sphere of influence.'[3] Existing to spread British ideas, to make known abroad the British way of life, and to encourage study of the English language, but never 'to ram propaganda down people's throats,' *The Times* announced that the Council was so phenomenally successful when established in Athens that an initial provision for four hundred students had been quickly enlarged to four thousand. Greece's enthusiastic acceptance of the Council was grounded in that country's long-standing hospitable reception of British visitors and expatriates, and appreciation of the British love of Greece embod-ied in Olivia's fictional character Alan Frewen. Even if Reggie ap-peared a somewhat scruffy, disheveled, and displaced figure when he stepped off the Lufthansa plane in Athens in October 1940, his only luggage a suitcase containing some pants, shirts, and socks and a rucksack containing lecture notes and his prized first-edition signed copies of D. H. Lawrence novels, he was not in alien territory. No menacing Iron Guard thugs patrolled Constitution Square and no Nazi flag covered the portico of the Grande Bretagne Hotel.

Olivia and Reggie's first refuge in Athens was a small room in a cheap hotel packed with a miscellany of displaced people who had

[3] *The Times*, 11 October 1940.

been arriving since late 1939: Poles, Smyrnan Greeks, White Russians. The hotel also housed a few English women, most of them scraping by on pitifully small pensions as the widows of British civil servants or 'Organization' men. Despite Olivia's relief at having escaped Romania and her enjoyment of the Greek sunshine, she did find the first few weeks unsettling, which is hardly surprising given the uncertainty of almost everything in her life. Since Reggie was unsure for how long London would pay his salary, she insisted they husband their money (throughout their marriage, she was always the canny keeper of their finances); some of their fellow-residents in the hotel were irritatingly nosy; and Reggie's characteristic exuberance began to flag without the stimulation of lively colleagues, pretty women, and the wherewithal to linger over coffee and ouzo in Zonar's, one of Athens' historic cafés. They were adrift, unable to do anything but wonder where they would find a home in a disordered world. But on 28 October 1940 their spirits were lifted, together with those of every Greek citizen, by the resounding defeat of an invading Italian army by Greek forces in battles at Elaia-Kalama and in the Pindus Mountains. Bulgaria having failed to attack Greece, as the Italians had hoped, the Greek High Command was able to transfer the mobilized divisions intended for the garrisoning of Macedonia to the Albanian frontier in the north and to repel an Italian incursion. For the moment, it seemed as if Greece would be safe.

With the encouraging entry of Greece into the war against the Axis powers, Britain began establishing bases on Greek soil, and *The Times* reported on 31 October that excited crowds in Athens were snatching newspapers from the hands of newsboys to read bulletins about British air and naval forces taking action against the Italians. News that the British navy was laying mines off the Greek coast spread 'like wildfire,' the newspaper reported, and almost every large shop window in the city's center mounted celebratory displays in honor of the British Navy. For Olivia, this was an uplifting contrast to the march of swastikas across Europe that she had viewed with horror in the window of the German Travel Bureau in Bucharest. She never forgot these scenes in Athens. Much later in life, in a negative review of a volume of Byron's letters and journals in which she vented her view that Byron was sadistic, vain, egotistical, and not a very good poet, she backtracked somewhat by saying, 'Still in Athens during the war I saw a young man carried shoulder-high in Constitution Square for no better reason than that his name was Byron. To be so remembered is no mean feat.'[4]

The Times concluded its 31 October report by paying homage to the Hellenic spirit that some twenty-five hundred years ago had vanquished invading Persian forces and by noting dryly that 'those who know Albania' will doubt the likelihood of an uprising on the part of that country against the Italians. The Italians refused to acknowledge the valor of Greek soldiers and attributed their thwarted invasion from the north almost entirely to torrential rains that had 'transformed roads into streams, streams into rivers, and plains into swamps and lake. Troops, horses, and mechanical equipment are advancing in rain and mud.'[5] With her customary attention to small but significant historical detail remembered years after the fact, Olivia notes in Friends and Heroes that while one could pick cyclamens in Athens in mid-November, in the mountains the Italians and their heavy gear were bogged down in the mire. On 14 November jubilant Greek forces crossed the border into Albania and took city after city despite a harsh winter, a lack of adequate supplies, and Italian military superiority. By mid-January of 1941, Greece had occupied a fourth of that country.

In 1940 celebration of the nation's defeat of the Italians and grateful recognition of British aid continued until the end of November. Back in London, Vere Hodgson noted in her wartime diary on 13 December that the 'better news' from Greece and Africa was cheering everyone up—'I am glad the stuffing is being taken out of Mussolini at last.'[6] From their hotel window, Olivia and Reggie heard the joyful noise of brass bands, church bells, cheers, and motor horns well into the still balmy Athenian nights. On 22 November, the Greeks took Koritza, the principal Italian military base in Albania, and after appropriating abandoned Italian tanks, they drove the Italians northward: this stunning victory was celebrated by processions of civilians (among them Reggie and Olivia) through the Athens streets bearing flowers and decorated pictures of King George II and the Prime Minister, General Metaxas. As The Times noted on 22 November, 'there were sufficient Union Jacks in evidence to make it clear that the Greeks in the moment of celebration had not forgotten the share played in the

[4] 'No tooth-powder!' The Spectator, 2 April 1976.
[5] The Italian Stefani Agency, quoted in The Times, 31 October 1940.
[6] Few Eggs and No Oranges: The Diaries of Vere Hodgson 1940–45.

victory by their Allies.' Mussolini, having failed to overcome his disappointment in Greek resistance to Italian occupation, immediately ordered a wholesale dismissal of all his naval and military commanders and staff officers.

Olivia begins Chapter 5 of *Friends and Heroes* with a pithy summary of the situation in Athens at the time the Italians were being routed on the Albanian border by unfriendly weather and by heroic Greek soldiers. She writes of what she witnessed. Young men were disappearing from the city, and each day 'lorry-loads of conscripts were driven through the streets to the station . . . Farmers came into Athens leading horses that were needed for the army.' In a wry voice, she recounts Italian complaints about Greek intransigence: the Duce, having offered to occupy Greece 'in a friendly, protective spirit,' was deeply disappointed by its resistance. Then, in a fluent narrative switch from the voice that registers immediate, eyewitness testimony of Athens in November 1940, she moves into the retrospective mode that is enabled by her distanced view of events when she was writing the third volume of her Balkan trilogy: 'It would take the Italians a day or two to get over the shock . . . the war was, in its way, comic, but no one imagined it would remain comic for long. The Italians had behind them the weight of the Axis armour. Beneath all the humour was the fear that the Greek line would break suddenly and the enemy arrive overnight' (p. 721). And, of course, eventually that Greek line did break in April 1941 with the fall of Kalamata in the Peloponnese and the complete occupation of the Greek mainland by Axis forces. Olivia's supple transition between recollection of immediate, eyewitness account and retrospective analysis enabled by historical distance is a distinguishing and sometimes easily overlooked sign of her novelistic skill. She was a deft controller of narrative time and historical event.

By the end of 1940, Reggie and Olivia had been in Athens for more than two months. Reggie had failed to obtain a lectureship with the British Council, and despite Olivia's frugality and her occasional freelance work writing handbooks for the military they were rapidly running out of money to sustain their already reduced mode of living. Reggie's continued lack of employment and a resurgence of pre-war anxiety generated by memories of surviving in London on a few pounds a week diminished the initial happiness Olivia had felt when she first arrived in Athens. Some of Reggie's colleagues believed she expressed her worries through an almost maniacal hatred of the organization. For example, R. A. Close, a teacher for the British Council and author of many textbooks dealing with English as a foreign language, reported that Olivia displayed 'an almost paranoiac fear that colleagues were doing Reggie down.' According to Close, she refused invitations to evening parties and weekend excursions and 'shrank into a shell out of which my wife and I tried to coax her.'[7] Whether Close exaggerates or not, in *Friends and Heroes* Olivia colors her depiction of several British Council types with the resentment and worry she felt in Athens in late 1940. Two particularly unappealing fellows, Lush and Dubedat, who had been given part-time work in Bucharest by Guy Pringle, have managed to get themselves out of Romania ahead of almost everyone else in the English colony.[8] They are now dancing attendance on Colin Gracey, the effete and lazy head of the Athens organization who, through a combination of fey charm and social connections, has managed to take over the directorship of the Council. When the Pringles are finally granted an interview with this elusive figure, Harriet is relegated to her familiar position as mere observer (her presence is barely acknowledged) and Guy, usually animated by a new acquaintance, sits silent, his glass of sherry 'held like a mask at the level of his lips. As was her custom, Harriet tried to accept the situation by detaching herself from it and watching the company as she would watch a play' (p. 714). The play she watches is a flirtatious game enacted by Gracey with one of his boyish hangers-on, Archie Callard, a creature possessed of 'auburn hair too long, mouth too full, eyes too large' and looks that are 'spoilt and entrancing' (p. 715), and a mysterious figure named Major Cookson, famous for his louche parties and squadron of influential friends.

The harsh description of Gracey and his unsavory pals, delivered to the reader from Harriet's astringent perspective, suggests Olivia's long-festering resentment of the British Council's clannish indifference to Reggie's plight in Athens and later in Cairo, and also of their

---

[7] Quoted in Braybrooke, *Olivia Manning: A Life*, 90.
[8] In his introduction to *Iris Murdoch: A Writer at War*, Peter J. Conradi asserts that one of Iris's lovers, David Hicks, 'would long claim to have been the model for the character of Dubedat in Olivia Manning's *Balkan Trilogy*. It is an odd boast, for the character is scarcely attractive. Dubedat, a scholarship boy from a provincial grammar-school, has been hitch-hiking in Europe equipped with inadequate clothing and an unpleasant voice. He is an eccentric elementary school-teacher with a sentimental view of the poor, reflecting David's then firm CP membership' (p. 166).

condescending indifference to her own situation. Olivia's unsympathetic depiction of Colin Gracey is thought to be based on
C. F. A. Dundas, the first Representative of the British Council in
Egypt, whom she suspected of deliberately neglecting Reggie. In *The
Levant Trilogy*, Gracey, having escaped from Athens along with Guy
and Harriet Pringle, manages to secure a plum job with the Council
and from his comfy perch continues to torment his underlings. By all
accounts, however, C. F. A. Dundas was a decent enough fellow, but
in a form of fictive revenge Olivia describes Colin Gracey as reclining
languidly on a chaise longue 'in an attitude of invalidism' (supposedly
suffering from a back injury of some sort), his 'desiccated youth' giving
him a deathly, 'mummified' pallor (p. 717). When Cookson arrives
bearing various 'prettily wrapped parcels,' Archie begins to sniff at
them. The Major squeals 'Naughty!' and slaps him so hard that he
jumps aside like a ballet dancer while Gracey giggles helplessly. Harriet
intuits 'a sense of union between the three who seemed to be hinting at
a game that was not played in public' (p. 718) and she asks Alan Frewen
if Cookson has ever been married: he replies laughingly, 'I really can't
say. He invited me once to "a ra-ther small and ra-ther curious party."
I'm afraid I left early; I could see it was going to get curiouser and
curiouser' (p. 729). The winsome posturing of Gracey's gang contrasts
significantly with Olivia's sensitive depiction of Alan Frewen's almost
certain homosexuality: scholarly and gentle where they are superficial
and malicious, Alan becomes Harriet's loyal friend and ally. He is but
one of the several intelligent male homosexuals depicted with great
sensitivity in Olivia's fiction.

A fourth member of the Gracey group, a journalist named Ben
Phipps, performs in this drama like an ingratiating puppy, his thick,
black-rimmed glasses misting over with excitement: Harriet scans him
from the side, here as elsewhere the vigilant observer, from where she
can see 'behind the pebbled lens, an observant eye that was black and
hard as coal' (p. 715). This observant eye is quickly trained on Guy,
and Phipps develops a manner towards him that suggests 'understanding and incipient intimacy.' Harriet, already disturbed by Guy's eagerness to be adored by all and sundry, feels that the 'atmosphere between
them was like the onset of a love-affair. She became more critical of
Phipps, suspecting that he was the sort of man who, though sexually
normal, prefers his own sex. He disliked her and probably disliked
women' (p. 797). As she and Alan Frewen watch Guy and Phipps

huddle in an atmosphere of scandalized conspiracy and dissect rumors that Gracey's pet Archie Callard is going to be appointed Director of the Council in Athens, she says, 'Look at them... They're like a couple of schoolgirls discovering sex' (p. 799). Just as Elizabeth in Olivia's first published novel *The Wind Changes* watches silently as two men (Arion and Sean) engage in a heated political debate so exclusive it prompts her to think they are like lovers, so in *The Balkan Trilogy* Harriet senses a homoerotic bond between Guy and Ben Phipps. None of this is to imply that Guy's real-life counterpart Reggie Smith was bisexual (at least, there is no evidence to support such a supposition): rather, what Olivia resented in Reggie's socially promis-cuous behavior, whether directed at men or women, was his neglect of herself. Reggie flirted with one and all.

If *The Balkan Trilogy* begins with a newly married woman's discom-fort with her husband's indiscriminate friendliness as they race through Europe on the Orient Express, then as it takes the Pringles from Bucharest to Athens, Olivia's fictive stand-in gains further unsettling insight into her husband's character. When Guy appears to her 'timid' in pressing his case for a lectureship, she considers 'how little they had known each other when they married, hurriedly, under the shadow of war' (p. 774). At the beginning, he had seemed 'all confidence'— good-humored, reliable, insouciant in the face of difficulty: now, in Athens, he seems 'a complex of unexpected follies, fears and irresolu-tions' (p. 774). As result, the bond born of dependence that Harriet had felt a year ago begins to weaken. In Olivia's actual life, the threatening German advance upon Greece was accompanied by her liberating recognition of an identity other than that of Mrs R. D. Smith, or, to put this another way, by a rediscovery of herself as Olivia Manning. In the trilogy, Harriet's friendship with Alan Frewen forms a catalyst for a similar enlightenment. Realizing that Alan is the first friend that she and Guy have made 'on equal terms' and that for Guy the 'world was his chief relationship,' she ruefully recollects that in Bucharest the only people she knew had been those known to Guy before his marriage: 'It had seemed to her then that she had left behind not only her own friends but her individuality. Now she began to feel the absurdity of this' (p. 726). In a revealing alignment of fiction and autobiography, Olivia describes her character's recuperation of a self apart from her husband, just as, at the same historical moment of Harriet Pringle's recovery of individuality, she began to detach herself from draining dependence on Reggie through the process of writing. Just as Harriet Pringle gains a degree of autonomy, so Olivia Manning in Athens in 1940–1 began to recover some of her pre-war independence through a renewed dedication to her work.

To others, however, Olivia's working habits signaled a certain distaste for their company: as R. A. Close recalls, Olivia preferred 'to stay in her room, writing and writing but not telling us what.'[9] What she chose not to tell him (and others) was that she was working on a non-fictional account of the expedition mounted by Henry Morton Stanley in 1886 to rescue Emin Pasha, the governor of Equatoria who had been stranded in the southern Sudan. She had begun to read about Emin Pasha immediately after publication of *The Wind Changes* in 1937. During the year in Bucharest the project had been lying fallow but in Athens, feeling that 'she wanted to be writing about something,' she had returned to it; in Reggie's view, Olivia was 'primarily a novelist and wrote non-fiction when she had no novel to write.'[10] One of the few things she had managed to carry from her London flat, keep with her in Bucharest, and now unpack in Athens, was the sheaf of notes she had taken in the British Museum Reading Room on Stanley's expedition, many culled from dispatches in *The Times* and others from the published letters and diaries of the expedition's officers and Emin Pasha's own diaries that were published in October 1898. Representing Olivia's continued commitment to writing, at least a form of writing more manageable at this particular moment than the development of a second novel, the notes tell a story of hubristic adventure, willful resistance, and sheer incompetence. When she had left London, writing fiction had seemed almost inappropriate in the grim face of approaching war, though she made sure to take typescript drafts of various short stories. Her feelings were close to those articulated by Elizabeth Bowen in 1942: in the *New Statesman*, Bowen asserted that the 'reflective writer' in wartime must feel 'an inability to obtain the focus necessary for art... These years rebuff the imagination as much by being fragmentary as by being violent. It is by dislocations, by recurrent checks to his desire for meaning, that the writer is most thrown out.'[11] Now, returning to her research on

---

[9] Quoted in Braybrooke, *Olivia Manning: A Life*, 90.
[10] Preface, *The Remarkable Expedition*, p. xi.
[11] Quoted in Hewison, *Under Siege: Literary Life in London 1939–1945*, 8.

perilous adventure, political abandonment, and sensational rescue seemed fitting to Olivia as she and Reggie began to fear that their Bucharest experience was about to be repeated. She wondered from where their very own Henry Morton Stanley would appear. Who would rescue them when German forces crossed into Greece?

Olivia's heart of darkness

It was only in 1949 that Olivia returned to the novel form and took up the subject of the recent war. Apart from tinkering with the short stories and a few poems, and writing book reviews for *The Palestine Post*, from 1939 to 1946 she was indeed 'thrown out,' as Bowen puts it, by the dislocations of her life. The creative effort and sustained focus needed for the novel seemed out of reach. She also had no desire to be known as one of those 'lady novelists' who deal only with a 'paper war,' as Cyril Connolly put it in *Horizon* in December 1941. Connolly assured its readers that *Horizon* would always publish 'stories of pure realism, but we take the line that experiences connected with the blitz, the shopping queues, the home front, deserted wives, deceived husbands, broken homes, dull jobs, bad schools, group squabbles, are so much a picture of our ordinary lives that unless they are outstanding we are prejudiced against them.'[12] Connolly, of course, is talking about the kind of domestic fiction conventionally associated with women novelists since Jane Austen. This is fiction that was being given a patriotic wartime twist by the politically conservative novelist Angela Thirkell in novels such as *Cheerfulness Breaks In* (1940), which features various Barsetshire country families saying farewell to their husbands and sons, and *Northbridge Rectory* (1941), which addresses the difficulties of a rector's wife in dealing with food rationing. Olivia aimed to write fiction that positioned those 'ordinary lives' to which Connolly refers in more intellectually sophisticated settings than the queue for sausages or jumble sales at the village hall: the writing of women's domestic fiction had never been her goal, and *The Wind Changes*, with its romantic drama played out against the political background of the Irish 'Troubles,' was of a different literary order.

[12] *Horizon*, no. 24, December 1941, 418.

In Bucharest, she felt she could manage the odd short story but a second novel would have to wait until peacetime, whenever that might be. In the meantime, the British Council libraries in Bucharest and in Athens proved an excellent resource when she returned to her London notes.

At first glance, why on earth Olivia Manning would have become so engaged by a narrative of late nineteenth-century imperial history and African adventure seems puzzling. Yet if we remember her enthusiasm for Rider Haggard's fiction and her boast to her bemused parents that she had become an expert in Zulu history, and if we recall that her father dearly loved Haggard's novels and had encouraged her to read them, it becomes clear that writing *The Remarkable Expedition* was, among other things, a form of homage to his influence. In its colorful detail and in its appropriation of many motifs found in the popular male adventure stories so common at the end of the nineteenth century (think of *King Solomon's Mines* for a start), Olivia's nonfictional narrative rivals much of Haggard's fiction.

Commander Manning was a strong admirer of Henry Morton Stanley and had read *In Darkest Africa* (Stanley's account of the expedition) whilst on one of his long voyages: in Portsmouth the two volumes of Stanley's book were on his bookshelves, together with the Haggard novels that Olivia had devoured as a young woman in her early twenties. Stanley's patriotism, his ruthlessness in dealing with those who threatened English civilization, that is to say barbaric Africans, and his bravery in undertaking perilous journeys into dangerous lands—all this appealed to a man whose naval career had been formed by colonial adventure. If Olivia Manning's short stories to that point in her writing career had emphasized a mother's sour nagging and had served, in part, as a displaced expression of her own resentment, now she crafted a tribute to her father and the qualities he most admired in his heroes: Stanley's keen will to vanquish the foes of European civilization and Emin's benevolent governance of barbaric natives. She dedicated *The Remarkable Expedition* to the memory of her brother, 'Lieutenant Oliver David George Manning, A.R.I.B.A., R.N.V.R., killed on active service October 7th, 1941. He had no grave but the sea.'[13]

---

[13] Olivia was grateful for Kay Dick's effort in persuading William Heinemann to publish the book in 1947: 'I do feel I have never thanked you properly for the good

By the mid-1880s, although not officially part of the Empire, Egypt had come under powerful British influence with the arrival of Sir Evelyn Baring (and his bank) to take over management of the country's tangled financial affairs. As a result, the English military hero General Charles Gordon had become a colonel in the Egyptian army, and when he subsequently headed Egypt's successful imperial advance south into the Sudan, he was rewarded with the governor-generalship of the entire area. Gordon's choice for lieutenant-governor of the Sudanese province Equatoria was a German physician and naturalist known as Emin Pasha, already serving as chief medical officer in Sudan. Born in Prussian Silesia as Eduard Schnitzer, he later acquired the honorary title of 'Emin Pasha' in recognition of his linguistic gifts—he was fluent in German, English, French, Italian, Turkish, and Arabic ('Emin,' roughly translated, means 'faithful one'). After settling in Khartoum, he established a medical practice and achieved considerable fame as a collector of plants and animals, which he shipped to European museums. Gordon's somewhat unusual choice of governor proved highly successful: Emin drove Nubian slave traders out of Equatoria, replaced Egyptian soldiers with native volunteers, built several badly needed roads, introduced new manufacturing, and generally improved the fortunes of the province. On 7 July 1886 he wrote to his friend Robert Felkin that 'the province is in complete safety and order . . . Since I last wrote to you, all the stations are busily employed in agricultural work, and, at each one, considerable cotton plantations are doing well. . . . I have also introduced the shoe-maker's art, and you would be surprised to see the progress we have made. We now make our own soap, and we have at last enough meat and grain.'[14] In 1878, when he became governor, the province was running a deficit of £32,000; by 1882, Emin Pasha had so transformed its economy that it showed a profit of £8,000.[15]

After the capture of Khartoum in 1885 by the forces of the Mahdi, the rebels against British/Egyptian rule pressed south and quickly besieged Emin Pasha, at which point Henry Morton Stanley entered the picture. Emin Pasha's perilous entrapment in darkest Africa,

work you did on my behalf about "Emin."' Olivia Manning to Kay Dick from Shepherd Market, 10 October 1946, OMP, UT, Series 1, Box 1, Folder 1.

[14] Quoted in 'The position of Emin Pasha,' *Science*, vol. 9, no. 225 (27 May 1887), 505–6.
[15] *The Times*, 25 February 1888.

threatened by the evil forces of the demonic Mahdi, quickly became the subject of sensational stories in the British popular press, and in November 1886 a Scottish businessman, William Mackinnon, approached Stanley about leading an expedition to relieve the besieged Emin with ammunition and other needed supplies. They cobbled together the 'Emin Pasha Relief Committee' and quickly raised £32,000. At a fund-raising dinner, Stanley prayed that 'the same impelling power which has hitherto guided and driven me in Africa would accompany me in my journey for relieving Gordon's faithful lieutenant.'[16]

Stanley's plan was to travel from Cairo around the Cape to the mouth of the Congo, and then proceed up the river, a route he adopted through striking a deal with King Leopold of Belgium: in exchange for the provision of steamers, he would persuade Emin to bring Equatoria into the Congo Free State, Leopold's essentially private corporation engaged in the export of rubber, copper, and other minerals from the area. Leaving the river at Leopoldville, he would then travel eastward overland through unknown territory to reach Lake Albert and Equatoria. On 21 April 1887, on arriving at Leopoldville, Stanley announced the division of the expedition into an 'Advance Column' and a 'Rear Column.' In a trek that could well have been led by that intrepid adventurer Alan Quartermain (from *King Solomon's Mines* and other Haggard novels), Stanley and his Advance Column took eight months to reach Lake Albert, and by then only one hundred and sixty-nine of the group initially composed of three hundred and eighty-nine men were still alive. And it was not until five months later, on 27 April 1888, that Stanley finally met Emin Pasha, who had traveled to the other end of Lake Albert unaware that relief was on the way. Moreover, he had no desire to be rescued since he wished to remain in Equatoria, in benevolent control of his native soldiers and also in charge of some seventy-five tons of valuable Sudanese ivory. Rather than rescue, he wanted ammunition and other vital supplies.

After a month of heated wrangling with Emin, Stanley gave up and retraced his steps in search of the Rear Column: the forest had cut off all communications and no word had been heard from them for several

---

[16] *The Times*, 21 December 1889.

months. Finally, on 17 August 1888, he found the sole European left in
charge of the Column, along with a handful of skeletal carriers; it had
been decimated by disease, desertions, and starvation. The aim in
creating the Rear Column had been to await the arrival of more
carriers to be supplied by a slippery Arab slave trader, Tippu-Tib,
but since no ammunition seemed to be on offer as barter for the
carriers, Tippu-Tib took off and left the Column to its tragic fate.[17]
In the meantime Emin Pasha still refused to leave Equatoria and
Stanley finally abandoned him, the ivory, and the relief expedition.
Traveling through Zanzibar, he took six months to make it back to
Cairo, whereupon he settled down and produced *In Darkest Africa* in a
mere sixty days. Returning to Europe in May 1890 to tremendous
acclaim, where his just-published book sold one hundred and fifty
thousand copies, on 4 September 1890 he washed his hands of the
whole debacle. In an interview with the *St Moritz Post* he characterized
Emin as follows, 'To a man of such exquisite and morbid sensibilities
and most inordinate self-esteem nothing can be right except slavish
adulation. He is continually in the sulks and it is useless to meddle with
him.'[18] Unperturbed by Stanley's opinion, Emin Pasha signed on with
the German East Africa Company and purportedly met his end at the
hands of an Arab slave trader, Seyd Bin Abed, who, according to a
report in *The Times*, 'took a large curved Arab knife from his belt and,
brandishing it aloft, struck off Emin's head.'[19]

In his Preface to the 1985 edition of Olivia's book, Reggie Smith
says that it was her love of 'a good yarn' and the early practice of
writing sensation serials for the Portsmouth newspaper that drew her
to a story about 'three sacred monsters'—by which I think he means
Stanley, Emin Pasha, and the dastardly Tippu-Tib, a character Olivia
paints in lurid colors. 'It was not for nothing that she loved Dickens,'
Reggie concludes (p. xii). All probably true enough, except for the bit
about Dickens: if *The Remarkable Expedition* resembles a Rider Haggard tale in its theme of perilous adventure and in its profusion of
exotic detail, then in style it owes a good deal to Joseph Conrad. There

---

[17] In 1978, Simon Ward dramatized the fate of those left behind by Stanley in his play
The Rear Column; it was directed by Harold Pinter and starred Jeremy Irons as Stanley's
chief officer, James S. Jameson, a big game hunter, artist, and traveler.

[18] *St Moritz Post*, 5 September 1890.

[19] *The Times*, 5 September 1893.

is little Dickensian about it, and parts read as if Olivia, in late summer 1939, had her head buried in *Heart of Darkness* rather than, say, *Nicholas Nickleby* while Reggie Smith, Louis MacNeice, and Walter Allen were strolling by her desk on their way to the Museum Tavern across Great Russell Street. She had chosen as her subject a quintessentially Victorian narrative of male adventure in darkest Africa and in writing it she revealed the influence of a writer she much admired for his meticulous and demanding style.

Allowing for the Haggard and Conrad influences (or perhaps even because of them), it does seem at times that Olivia's account of Stanley, Emin, and Tippu-Tib lapses into pedestrian narrative, as if she were stalled and entangled in various literary models; and she also seems buried in her research, only to surface with a concocted account woven from the considerable literature provoked by the expedition. Yet it's also possible that a scholarly immersion of this sort provided a distracting relief from the fears and uncertainty of war in the Balkans and Greece: nursing her notes and sketching her chapters helped to keep her reasonably calm. Devoting the first part of her book to the growth of the Egyptian empire, the history of Sudan, and the significance for the entire narrative of European profits derived from the ivory trade, Olivia provides a history of the Mahdi, the siege of Khartoum, the murder of Gordon, and the massacre of ten thousand people by Mahdist forces; she follows this with the story of Emin Pasha's travels through the Ottoman Empire, his arrival in Khartoum, and his appointment as governor of Equatoria. Despite a sense that she often slogged dutifully through her research, Olivia's keen eye for detail does enliven the narrative: for example, she tells us that Tippu-Tib, when traveling with Stanley from Zanzibar at the start of the expedition, was 'gorgeously clad in silks, a jeweled turban and jeweled kriss' and that he was accompanied by his ninety-six relatives. She also notes that the expedition steamer carried a comforting supply of Stanley's Madeira.

When Stanley's party begins its trek of fifteen months through the forest, beginning at Yambuya, Olivia enters Conrad's *Heart of Darkness* territory: 'Few of the Congo carriers would have been willing even to enter the forest. It was the last remnant of the primeval jungle that had once covered all dry land . . . here the trees were the direct descendants of the prehistoric trees that had stood on the same spot, and they grew with the same luxuriance . . . In the dense, misty, hot-house air the perfume of flowers and of stagnant waters was overpowering. The sun could scarcely penetrate the canopy of leaves, but the heavy, icy raindrops broke through like bullets' (pp. 75–6). It is as if Olivia assumes the voice of Conrad's Marlow as he describes his journey to Kurtz's station on the Congo: 'Going up that river was like travelling back to the earliest beginnings of the world, where vegetation rioted on the earth and the big trees were kings. An empty stream, a great silence, an impenetrable forest. The air was warm, thick, heavy sluggish. There was no joy in the brilliance of the sunshine.'[20] Given her admiration of Conrad and the influence of his style upon her prose in *The Wind Changes*, it's likely that in the mid-1930s, as she listened to her father's stories of Henry Morton Stanley, she recognized the obvious parallels between Conrad's powerful and enigmatic novella and Stanley's adventures in darkest Africa. One can certainly align Marlow and Stanley, both restless adventurers traveling up the Congo through a primeval landscape, allowing for the fact that Stanley possessed none of Marlow's quizzical introspection and that self-doubt was foreign to his blustering personality. The more provocative connections are between Kurtz and Emin: both are reclusive, well-educated, and mysterious Europeans who have created their own colonial empires through holding mysterious sway over the natives and controlling a vast store of ivory. And just as Kurtz resists Marlow's efforts to remove him from the Inner Station, so, too, Emin Pasha declined being budged from Equatoria: Kurtz's obsession with his ivory, his station, and his career could well be that of Emin. But whatever alignment one finds between the two narratives of male adventure, the clearest origin of *The Remarkable Expedition* must remain the influence of her father upon Olivia's reading.

As we know, she began serious investigation of the various accounts of Stanley and Emin Pasha in 1938, finding comfort after Hamish Miles's death in the serenity of the British Museum Reading Room with its soft blue leather desks and its hefty catalogues, difficult to lift and demanding to navigate. Everything about it was so much more appealing than the damp confines of the Portsmouth public library. And then, arriving in Bucharest as a woman at war, she had retreated from daily anxiety into more reading about Stanley and Emin, gone

---

[20] Joseph Conrad, *Youth, Heart of Darkness, The End of the Tether*, 92–3.

back fifty years to the heart of darkness, and there lost herself in yet more sifting through the copious notes she had brought with her on the Orient Express. In Athens, she continued her reading and her writing and by the time she and Reggie left in April 1941, she was about halfway through the project, having, in the process, found distraction from what Elizabeth Bowen termed the 'dislocations' of wartime and also having recovered the professional individuality that had seemed submerged in the alien world of Reggie's British Council circle. Quite simply, assembling all the bits and pieces of *The Remarkable Expedition* had kept her going for three years, and when she escaped from invaded Greece to Egypt it remained a comforting job of work, the ever-expanding sheaves of notes and drafts of chapters remaining by her side until she returned to England after the war.

The last civilian ship

During the night of Sunday 8 December and in the early morning hours of 9 December 1940, after a respite of some weeks, German bombers launched a heavy attack upon London. Seemingly without any military objective other than to kill and terrorize civilians, the onslaught was characterized by *The Times* as 'the lowest depth to which the art of war can fall.'[21] It was time now, the newspaper continued, for America to come to the aid of Europe, not only to repel attacks upon British civilians, but also to relieve Greek soldiers facing a bleak and bitter winter in the northern mountains. Having heroically fought off an Italian invasion, Greece was in desperate need of help if it was to repel an army re-supplied by German military power: the supply line must be strengthened, armaments brought up, and forces rearranged. Meanwhile, in Athens, Reggie was still without employment and feeling seriously demoralized, while Olivia continued working in the British Council library. Both were worried more than they cared to admit by news of the London bombings and by fears that Greece would be unable to hold out against a re-energized Axis assault. Exile and plans for escape had become the all-consuming preoccupations of their existence.

[21] *The Times*, 10 December 1940.

Early in January 1941, the times became leaner and the weather colder, and the warm lazy days of the previous October when they had sat outside in cafés enjoying pastisio and cheap retsina seemed far in the past. Just as food shortages in Bucharest had become more severe with every day of the encroaching German invasion, so now Athens restaurants began serving tired-looking tripe rather than gleaming fish fresh from the Piraeus harbor. In *Friends and Heroes*, Olivia records these lean times through her descriptions of food and what it means to various characters; it is a time when even the 'spectacle' of Italian prisoners being paraded through the streets does 'little to distract people in a hard winter when it was as cold indoors as out and food was disappearing from the shops.' Bystanders smile ironically, knowing that these prisoners on their way to Piraeus and shipment to camps in the western desert would eat better than the Greeks: 'a camp in the sun was more comfortable than the Albanian mountains where men bivouacked waist deep in snow' (p. 785). In her manuscript notes for *Friends and Heroes*, Olivia refers to these events: '10,000 amputations for frost bite in the Athens hospitals—peasant women toiling up mountains with supplies for their men.'[22]

In *The Balkan Trilogy*, at the flat of Mrs Brett (the widow of a Legation official) on the slopes of Lycabettos, the hill that rises above Athens, various English expatriates assemble hopefully for a hot-pot dinner. In the BBC memorial program for Olivia aired in July 1981, 'Never a Day Without a Line,' Roy Foster pointed to the sadly querulous Englishwomen in Athens trying to maintain English customs in the face of short rations and impending German invasion: clearly, he had in mind the scene in which Olivia writes that Mrs Brett's sitting room was 'full of middle-aged and elderly guests, mostly women who had remained in Athens because they had no reason to go anywhere else' (p. 810). One, a very large bossy character named Miss Jay, is showing the effect of 'lean times'—'her monstrous face had drooped into the sad, dew-lapped muzzle of a blood-hound' (p. 812). Mrs Brett, a Lancashire woman determined to produce a real Lancashire hot-pot, has miraculously secured a whole leg of kid from a farmer in Kifissia, just outside the city. Warmly fortified by the taste of a dish from home, even if the meat was a trifle tough and the gravy a

---

[22] OMC, HRC.

little greasy, Guy and Harriet leave Mrs Brett's flat and cling to each
other in 'the wet wind blast of the main street ... knowing they might
never see the end of hostility and confusion. The war could devour
their lives' (p. 814). Quite literally, they begin to go hungry, and in
depicting their hunger Olivia vividly sets out the bleak situation as she
and Reggie confronted it in the Greek winter of 1940–1.

Perhaps because the trilogies' superb dissection of a wartime marriage tends to impress itself more deeply in the mind of critics and
readers than the horrors of war, one forgets the terror and deprivation
that Olivia suffered during these years. For example, in writing about
novels dealing with World War II, Adam Piette suggests that the epics
produced by Evelyn Waugh, Anthony Burgess, and Olivia Manning
tend to be 'products of manners that dissolve ... the enormity of the
war.' In particular, he believes that Manning's 'self-pitying dogged
focus' on the Pringle marriage trivializes widespread suffering.[23] Quite
the opposite would seem to be true. In the weeks before escaping
Athens just ahead of the Axis arrival, Reggie and Olivia dodged
nightly bombing by German Junkers and endured deafening sounds
of anti-aircraft gunfire—and all this is vividly registered in *Friends and
Heroes* through Olivia's fluid fusion of historical event and autobiography. Although never physically wounded, Olivia carried with her for
the rest of her life the trauma of wartime survival. The physical
restlessness often noticed by her friends—at parties she constantly
collected glasses, patted cushions, popped in and out of the
kitchen—and the irritable sense of injury for which she was criticized
after the war, I believe originate in her experience of foraging for food
in Athens' empty grocery shops, shuddering with fear as German
bombers zoomed overhead, and plotting yet one more escape from a
Nazi invasion.

As a consequence of the enlarged presence of British servicemen in
Greece, in *Friends and Heroes* Guy and Harriet volunteer as dishwasher
and waitress at a NAAFI canteen; work is organized by the wives of
the English diplomats, who decree that the food should be for the
servicemen, and only for them, and the volunteers are 'honour bound
not to touch a mouthful themselves. In the first throes of unaccustomed hunger, the women fried bacon, sausages, eggs and tomatoes

---

[23] 'World War II: contested Europe,' *The Cambridge History of Twentieth-Century
Literature*, 432.

and served men who accepted their plates casually and took it for granted that the civilians ate as much as they did' (p. 786). Unable to contain her misery in the face of food prohibited to her and Guy, Harriet nearly bursts into tears when serving slap-up breakfasts to the soldiers; gruffly touched by her plight, the next day they present her with a leg of lamb, which is promptly appropriated by Mrs Brett as repayment for another hot-pot and also on the sensible grounds that Harriet has no kitchen. On Christmas Day 1940, hoping if not for a leg of lamb then at least some fried fish, Alan Frewen, Guy and Harriet, and Yakimov (who has also managed to get himself to Athens from Bucharest) take the bus down to the sea-front for a stroll along the beach, long promised to Alan's now almost skeletal dog Diocletian. Hoping to eat in one of the seaside restaurants that before the war had been noted for crayfish and mullet, they discover that all are shut, 'not from a shortage of fish but a shortage of fishermen.' Hungry with a hunger 'that had not yet touched starvation but caused an habitual unease' (p. 800), luckily they spot a fisherman with a basket of mullet, which he generously fries for their Christmas Day dinner. The graphic effectiveness of these scenes of hunger causing 'habitual unease' originates in Olivia's wartime experience.

For Olivia and Reggie, the winter of 1940–1 was more than one of discontent: news of the London bombings aggravated their sense of homelessness and exile and German reinforcements in the north precipitated fears of imminent invasion. They lived in a city where, Olivia remembered, people were eating intestines from unidentified animals: inserting this memory into *Friends and Heroes*, she describes them as 'Grey, slippery and bound up like shoelaces' and the cause of an epidemic of dysentery. Never blessed with a cast-iron stomach, in Athens Olivia began to suffer from gastrointestinal problems that were exacerbated by contracting amoebic dysentery in Egypt and that plagued her for many years. Her fictional surrogate, Harriet Pringle, faced with 'some sort of lung hash,' feels her disordered stomach turn over at the sight of the inedible dish. In the final weeks of their time in Athens, Olivia and Reggie subsisted almost entirely on wine and potatoes.

In early January 1941, the Prime Minister of Greece, General Metaxas, and the British Minister in Athens, Sir Michael Palairet, signed a treaty signifying the desire, as *The Times* put it, 'to continue in peace that cooperation which has proved so happy in time of war.'[24] Optimistically looking forward to a time when the people of Athens would again eat legs of lamb, fresh fish, and juicy figs, the treaty committed the Greek government to providing full support to the British Council, which even in early 1941 had over three thousand students enrolled in its classes: the Council was thereby authorized to open ten new institutes in addition to those in Athens and Salonika and to establish a secondary school for British subjects in Athens. For Reggie, the treaty meant a job after kicking his heels for three months, and for Olivia it meant some relief from the anxiety of scraping by on meager funds, even if there was virtually nothing on which to spend one's money. Cultural cooperation between Greece and Britain was accompanied in early 1941 by a renewed promise from the British to provide further aid to Greece in its efforts to contain the Italian threat in the north. To this point, asserted Field Marshal Sir Archibald Wavell, British Commander-in-Chief in the Middle East, British aid had taken the form of airmen, machines, and supplies. Needed now were anti-aircraft guns, lorries, and warm clothing for the Greek soldiers.

As she traced the experiences of the Pringles in Athens, hanging on as long as they can but knowing they must leave for who knows where, in *Friends and Heroes*, Olivia followed a meticulous timeline of the events in Greece from January to April 1941. Following this carefully plotted sequence, assisted by Reggie's memory of events, and calling upon her own searing recollections of terrifying air-raid sirens and the sight of lorries full of wounded troops (Greek, British, Australian) being brought back to Athens from the north, she devotes the last chapters of *The Balkan Trilogy* to a vivid unfolding of Greek collapse in the face of Axis forces after their defiant and amazing defeat of the Italians (her manuscript notes for this novel, for example, sketch details of the battle of the Pindus gorges where the third Alpine Division of fourteen thousand fully equipped Italian mountaineers was met and routed by eight thousand Greeks). Had she not been writing fiction, the chapters could well have functioned as a brilliant long essay about Athens in wartime. But she was also writing the story of the Pringle marriage (and her own) and these chapters weave a dazzling tapestry of brutal history and private story.

---

[24] *The Times*, 10 January 1941.

As the Germans close upon Greece, Harriet Pringle comes to accept her marriage for what it is: hastily entered into, marred by temperamental incompatibility, but cemented now by a shared experience of being at war. When she watches British tanks arriving in Athens, 'the young Englishmen . . . came out of the past. They all looked alike: not tall, as she remembered the English, but strongly built, with sun-reddened faces and hair bleached blond' (p. 887). The sight of these familiar yet unfamiliar English soldiers, their bodies and faces altered by war, imaginatively suggests the altered state of the Pringle marriage: grounded in the familiar story of frenzied love affair and impetuous wedding, its 'face,' so to speak, has been altered by the harrowing history of its brief existence. Writing in the 1960s, Olivia fashioned her character's recognition of personal and historical change from her own memory of memories, as it were: in Athens in early 1941, she had remembered her English past—Portsmouth, London, Hamish—and felt it being crowded out by the tumult of recent experience. The journey on the Orient Express, the initial strangely calm days in Bucharest, the menace of the Iron Guard, the perilous escape on Lufthansa, and even the very recent lean and terrifying times in Athens were being overtaken at a rapid and disorienting pace by the press of rapidly unfolding history.

With the death of Metaxas at the end of January 1941 (from a probable combination of diabetes, heart problems, and overwork), Alexandros Korizis, the governor of the National Bank of Greece, became Prime Minister, and in mid-February he formally accepted Britain's offer of troops, with the proviso that the troops could arrive only if the Germans crossed the Danube into Bulgaria, which they did. Within a month British and Commonwealth expeditionary forces landed in Greece (Olivia's manuscript notes show detailed outlines of these events). On 22 February, Anthony Eden flew to Athens for discussions with the Prime Minister and Greek and British expatriate spirits were lifted by a reinforced sense of unity between the two countries: the Anglo-Greek alliance was hailed by the Greek newspaper *Proia*, 'No new difficulty that may arrive can find us spiritually unprepared or take us by surprise. . . . we have on our side a powerful ally with common ideals.'[25] Eden declared that like all Englishmen he

---

[25] Quoted in *The Times*, 5 March 1941.

had watched with admiration the heroic resistance of the Greek people
and that he was moved to have seen for himself the 'spirit and resolution which animate every man and woman in the country.'[26] But by
early April, German forces were threatening on three fronts—Greek,
Yugoslavian, and Turkish—and when Belgrade surrendered to the
Germans in mid-April the Greek and British forces fell back to the
Mount Olympus line in Greece. With a German attack upon the new
front line, the Greek army withdrew, allowing Axis forces to move
south and to break through British positions at Thermopylae. Fierce
dogfights over Athens between British Hurricane planes and the
Luftwaffe continued until late April and by the 30th Axis forces had
occupied the entire Greek mainland and Commonwealth Expeditionary Forces had begun evacuation, a withdrawal described by the
German News Agency in this way: 'The remnants of the fleeing
British troops are now trying to escape from Greece in barges, fish-
ing-boats, and all sorts of vessels, leaving behind arms, war material,
and equipment of all kinds.'[27] German troops entered Athens on 27
April just days after Reggie and Olivia managed to get on a boat for
Cairo—the last civilian ship to leave the Piraeus harbor.

Until it became clear that the government was withholding news of
the German advance upon Athens from the north, Olivia had hoped
for a reprieve. She remembers that people shouted rumors across cafés
at one another—for instance, that there were no ships and that the
Piraeus harbor had been destroyed by a munitions ship explosion. On
Good Friday morning, however, she and Reggie were ordered to
leave their house and proceed to the harbor with one suitcase each
and enough food to last for three days. The shops were shut for Good
Friday (not that there was much to sell) and she and Reggie had only
three tins of bully beef in the house, which they shared with six people
who had nothing. Packed into a coal lorry with their luggage, they
were driven down a hot road, past their little bungalow where they
had left most of their belongings, out of Athens and into the bombed
area. The buildings around the harbor were burnt out, the water was
black with oil and charred wreckage, and one of the few vessels
standing upright in a watery wasteland littered with the masts and
funnels of sunken ships was a rusty old boat: the *Erebus*. Having

---

[26] Quoted in *The Times*, 5 March 1941.
[27] Quoted in *The Times*, 30 April 1941.

chartered the ship for the exclusive use of his own commercial company and friends, the English businessman standing at the top of the gangway was not happy about accommodating a crowd of strangers. He delivered a volley of insulting remarks as the intruders filed on board. When the *Erebus* set creaky and overloaded sail, the passengers watched the Peloponnese sunset and the Acropolis glimmering white and slowly fading from sight. In accord with the chilling appropriateness of its name (Erebus in Greek mythology is associated with deep darkness and shadow), the ship set sail into the night and into the unknown. As Olivia described this scene in *Friends and Heroes*, Piraeus seemed already like 'an ancient ruin, reaching again towards the desolation that covered it for eighteen hundred years after the Peloponnesian Wars' (p. 1023). When reconstructing this moment for the end of *The Balkan Trilogy*, Olivia came across a first-person account that appeared in *The Times* on 1 May 1941 of an Australian correspondent's escape from Greece under conditions virtually identical with her own (the historical verisimilitude of the trilogies derives almost always from her meticulous integration of private memory and public record). This correspondent writes that he boarded a three-thousand-ton steamer with no proper passenger accommodations and packed with civilian refugees carrying blankets, bedrolls, and suitcases stuffed with whatever could be salvaged. Many of the passengers were Englishwomen, for the writer 'magnificent' in their display of 'courage and endurance.' A good deal of courage and endurance was required to survive the three-day voyage of the *Erebus* to the coast of Africa.

Conditions on the ship, which had previously been deployed in taking Italian prisoners to the Middle East, were appalling: rusty, filthy, and dangerously crammed. Reggie and Olivia were assigned to the lowest deck, where they shared a two-berth cabin with six friends: Ettie and Harold Edwards, R. A. Close and his wife, Robert Liddell, and an unidentified sixth person (probably a friend of Robert Liddell). The bunk beds lacked mattresses or covers, were sticky to the touch, and spattered with the bloody remains of bugs. These miserably cramped conditions were not helped, at least as far as Olivia was concerned, by the selfishness of Ettie Edwards, who had brought on board an impossibly large hat box; almost hourly, Olivia placed the hat box in the passageway outside the cabin, whereupon Ettie would promptly retrieve it. At the end of three days, the two women barely spoke to one another, Liddell had retreated to another part of the ship, and Reggie continued preparation for teaching Shakespeare's sonnets. To whom he would hold forth, and where, remained uncertain, but with his unquenchable good spirits in the face of bedbugs, German bombers, and short rations, he kept his chin up while Olivia fretted about Ettie's hat box, their friends left behind in Greece, and their uncertain future in the Middle East. When the ship had pulled slowly out of Piraeus, an air-raid warning had sounded and bombs began falling on the harbor; now, as the ship lumbered on to Crete, they heard Junkers dive-bombing a troop ship steaming in the wake of the *Erebus*. Olivia had managed to buy three oranges when the ship stopped in Crete and the fruit, along with the one tin of bully beef, sustained them until they reached Alexandria.

Now triply exiled—from England, Romania, and Greece—and on her way to Egypt, Olivia Manning arrived at a bittersweet acceptance of her difficult marriage. Eighteen months of dislocation and fear led to recognition of a hitherto unacknowledged truth: that these eighteen months had bound her to Reggie and that in all likelihood she was going to stay married, despite her resentment of his profligate need to expend himself on every social occasion and despite the fact that she was not the exclusive object of his affection. In those heady three weeks in August 1939, before they married, she had thought he might change, but now, steaming to Egypt, she realized that he was unchangeable. Regardless of whether he was in Birmingham or Bucharest, he would remain maddeningly indiscriminate in his affections. But she also realized that in his own distracted fashion he admired and loved her, that he genuinely admired her work, and that he wholeheartedly supported her literary ambitions. In Athens, Olivia had spent a good deal of time with Terence Spencer, a lecturer for the British Council (the original for Charles Warden, with whom Harriet almost goes to bed in *Friends and Heroes*): he was serious and scholarly (in 1954 he published a study of literary philhellenism from Shakespeare to Byron), and she may or may not have found his romantic and protective attitude persuasive enough to begin an affair. But he was posted from Athens in March 1941, and as she and Reggie scrambled to survive the voyage on the *Erebus*, she put Terence Spencer out of her mind and realized that Reggie was suffering as she had suffered, that despite the bravado, the gung-ho determination to carry on, he was frightened. His robust physique thinned by hunger and his face tired and gray, he bore the marks of their shared trauma.

With virtually no possessions (all they had was one suitcase and a rucksack full of books), Olivia and Reggie, like Harriet and Guy, know that they are refugees: 'Still, they had life—a depleted fortune, but a fortune. They were together and they would remain together, and that was the only certainty left to them' (p. 1033). Olivia always insisted that although most people seemed to consider the Romanian books of *The Balkan Trilogy* better than the last, for her, 'the Greek one, as a summing-up, is a better book.'[28] In addition to summing up the first eighteen months of World War II in the Balkans, it also summed up, I think, the pros and cons of her marriage.

As the *Erebus* miraculously continued its journey, Olivia thought to herself that it was not so much the danger of being dive-bombed that pained her so much (the troop-ship following the *Erebus* was the main target) as the fact, she wrote in an autobiographical fragment, that 'we had lived in the country we were abandoning.'[29] During the frantic embarkation, Reggie had recited, repeatedly and doggedly, lines from the opening lines of Cavafy's 'Waiting for the Barbarians': 'What are we waiting for, assembled in the forum? | The barbarians are due here today.' In early May, Axis forces completely occupied the country whose abandonment Olivia felt so strongly and Athenian residents who had suffered through months of bombing, food shortages, and threats of invasion, were forced to witness a 'victory parade' laid on by the barbarians. The Germans dismissed large numbers of Greek soldiers and sent them home but, as a correspondent for a Stockholm newspaper reported on 7 May, 'There is no organization to help them and each must journey as he can. Their footwear is often tattered, but they wander past in old uniforms with an overcoat strapped on the back to serve them as pillow during the night, which is generally spent in the open air.'[30] Forty-three thousand Commonwealth forces were evacuated from Greece; five hundred British servicemen died during the evacuation; and between three thousand and four thousand Australian troops perished on the mainland. More than ever a woman at war, when Olivia went on deck as the *Erebus* neared Egypt, she saw the coast of Africa and wondered what fresh theater of conflict awaited them. They were refugees without money, with few possessions, and with no guarantee that they would ever return to England.

[28] Kay Dick, *Friends and Friendship*, 39.
[29] 'Soon to be forgotten,' OMC, HRC.
[30] Quoted in *The Times*, 7 May 1941.

5

The Dark Side of the World

'Exile, nostalgia and uncertainty produced in poets a variety of responses.'

Olivia Manning, 'Poets in exile' (1944).

Writing in exile

When Olivia and Reggie reached Alexandria they had eaten virtually nothing for three days, and for weeks before that they had lived on 'little but wine and exaltation, oranges and flowers.'[1] They were anxious, hungry, and exhausted, but the welcome sight of English soldiers throwing bananas up to the ship led Olivia to jump up and catch one. Never again did she taste a banana quite like it—green outside, pink inside, and smelling of honey. After being vetted by the military, the refugees were allowed ashore with their hand luggage and useless money (if they had any), taken to a canteen where they were fed bacon and eggs and tea so sweet, Olivia remembered, that flies could walk on it, and then told to wait in the canteen, which they did for the entire afternoon. At dusk they were herded on to the Cairo train, and during the three-hour journey Olivia shuttled between watching the delta on one side of the tracks and the desert on the other: strangely flattened by a brilliant

---

[1] Olivia Manning, typescript 'Cairo in those days,' OMC, HRC. Together with a manuscript draft titled 'Soon to be forgotten,' Olivia used this typescript for an essay on Cairo that appeared in the *Transatlantic Review* in 1964 titled 'The dark side of the world.' An expanded version of 'The dark side of the world' appeared in the *Sunday Times Magazine*, on 17 September 1968 under the title 'Cairo: Back from the blue.' Citations of 'Cairo' in this chapter refer to 'Cairo in those days.'

white light, the landscape was unlike 'any other country we had ever lived in and yet it was suffocatingly familiar ('Cairo').' It seemed to her that while Romania and Greece presented a reality different from their popular images, Egypt from the train looked exactly like the Middle East depicted in the Bible illustrations from her childhood. She and Reggie had come from a city of marble and now were gazing at a great, flat, irrigated plain that was lush with beans, flax, tobacco, cotton, and palms; the biblical scene was completed by camels whose stately progress across the plains reminded Olivia of the 'oily rich Victorian oleographs of the Land of the Pharaohs.' From the train windows, the air smelled like an 'an old, old cupboard, a long time shut up ('Cairo').'

Arriving in the late evening at the half blacked-out Cairo railway station—'possessionless, moneyless, homeless'[2]—they could smell the heat in the spicy, humid night, and as they were led to their hotel 'white robed men, unfamiliar and unnerving, flickered through the blue darkness.' The so-called hotel turned out to be an insalubrious former brothel converted into a sort of doss-house divided into male and female dormitories with a single shower to be shared by both sexes. It did not take long for Olivia to realize that the 'tattered exaltation' she had shared with the heroic Greeks and that she had trailed in her wake as the *Erebus* crossed the Mediterranean was fast becoming vexation: 'The Egyptian with his philosophy of *ma'alesh* can bear with equanimity the heat, dirt, flies, and smells of Cairo. The European has nothing but irritation to keep him going' ('Cairo'). The next morning, as they huddled in a café with other refugees, she and Reggie wondered how soon they could get away and where they could go. Cairo having become the final bolt-hole for privileged Europeans, the city was thronged with kings, princes, courtiers, and all the hangers-on of royalty, 'trying to maintain, amid rivalries, squabbles, hurt feelings, scandals, and aggressive self-importance, some real or imagined status from the past' ('Cairo'). King Peter of Yugoslavia and King George of Greece had both evacuated from Crete to Cairo with private entourages, and George's long-time mistress Joyce Britten-Jones, the English wife of a captain in the Black Watch who had been ADC to the Viceroy when King George visited India in the early 1930s, flew from London to Cairo to be with him.

---

[2] Olivia Manning, 'The dark side of the world,' *Transatlantic Review* (Spring 1964), 100.

Socially insignificant newcomers like Olivia and Reggie felt stranded, as if they were attending an 'international fair' but had no money to visit the exhibits. For Olivia, the crowded streets, the noise, the uncertainty of everything, the prices that varied according to whether you were Egyptian, European, or English, and the rumors of German advances upon Cairo, convinced her this was a war even more frantic and disorienting for civilians than that experienced in Romania and Greece.

When it became clear that no transportation from Egypt was to be provided for British citizens and that they would need to see the country 'not as a junction but as a terminus,' Olivia urged Reggie to get some tide-over funds from the British Embassy. This allowed them to leave the brothel turned doss-house and move to a small and dismal pension, a stuffily-furnished and gloomily-shuttered establishment presided over by the Coptic wife of a British officer who specialized in serving miserable breakfasts composed of a few dates and an ancient egg and in shouting a barrage of rules at her guests before they were allowed to leave the table. The pension was immensely better than the doss-house, but as they coped with the daily press of Cairene life, Olivia and Reggie both realized they needed to find jobs, secure a decent place to live, and accept the city as their wartime refuge. Things took a turn for the better, however, when after six weeks in the back-street pension, Adam Watson, the diplomat with whom they had shared quarters in Bucharest and now one of the Third Secretaries at the British Embassy, invited them to take a room in his spacious flat at 13 Sharia Ibrahim Pasha Nagib in the Garden City neighborhood. And Olivia finally found a job as assistant press officer at the American Embassy, although Reggie still wrestled with the bureaucracy of the British Council and remained unemployed.

Olivia spent her early days in Cairo exploring the dusty boulevards, dodging her way through swarms of British Army privates as she had dodged her way through throngs of fashionably dressed women on the Calea Victorei in Bucharest. To her eyes, all the British soldiers looked much alike: 'not tall, burnt pink, hair, shirts and shorts all bleached to the same yellowish white...gross in their consciousness of their superiority and in their nervousness of their surroundings.' Permanently 'browned-off,' they were set on edge, as was Olivia, by the glare, the pestering flies, the beggars, the petty cheating, the street salesmen who called out 'Hi, George' and pushed fruit and sweat into their faces, their only relief found in the air-conditioned cinemas and in the night clubs 'where belly dancers rolled white velvet flesh ('Cairo').' In the evenings, if not seeking relief from the enervating heat in the chilly cinemas, she and Reggie attended many disorganized, 'anyone-welcome-if-he-brings-a-bottle' parties, where it seemed to her the English lost all their sexual aplomb in the Egyptian heat and where the shortage of women led to a great time for 'plain girls,' sought after in a manner to which they were unaccustomed ('Cairo'). Occasionally, they were invited to grander affairs, usually given in Embassy circles, where one met young men fresh from a raid on Rommel's headquarters, or notable figures who had been flown over occupied territory above gun range, or King Farouk, 'fat playboy who treated the throne of Egypt as a day-bed' ('Cairo'). But they were never part of the Cairo world described by Alan Moorhead in *African Trilogy* (1944): 'We had French wines, grapes, melons, steaks, cigarettes, beer, whisky, and abundance of all things that belonged to rich, idle peace.'[3] For Olivia, the only thing in abundance was the stupefying heat.

But she was delighted to leave 'the polyglot refugee crew' and join the British colony when she and Reggie moved into Adam Watson's flat overlooking the lush gardens of the British embassy.[4] Relieved as she had been to get out of Greece in one piece when she boarded the *Erebus* in the Piraeus harbor, Olivia had been sad to leave the parks and gardens massed with cyclamens and anemones: most of the city's green spaces remained undamaged by the bombing, and she remembered that in the olive groves in Athens the flowers had stood as high as her waist. The sight of Cairo's dry lawns and withered flowerbeds had increased her misery when she stepped off the train from Alexandria, but the breezy comfort of Watson's flat and the views of the embassy gardens thick with myrtle, mango, and a purple-blossomed banana tree lifted her spirits. Watson had been posted to Cairo in 1940 and his particular assignment was to handle the surrender of Egypt in the event that Britain lost the desert war. Having penetrated Olivia's frosty manner when they were together in Athens, and also having understood its provision as a cover for her insecurities and desire to be left

[3] Quoted in Roger Bowen, '"Monologue for a Cairo evening": A cultural landscape in wartime,' 53.

[4] 'Cairo: Back from the blue,' *Sunday Times*, 17 September 1967.

alone to do her writing, Watson was happy to have her as a lodger. Olivia's admiration of his decency, learning, and common sense is evident from her characterization in *The Levant Trilogy* of the British diplomat Dobbie Dobson, who remains a wise advisor for Guy and supportive friend for Harriet throughout the three novels, even if he offers that friendship and support in a deceptively laconic manner. In *The Danger Tree*, Dobson, seeing the Pringles 'displaced, homeless, moneyless and futureless' when they arrive in Cairo, tides them over with cash until Guy can draw funds from the British Council. In actuality, Watson was similarly helpful to Reggie and Olivia and the three of them remained friends for the rest of their lives.

On New Year's Day 1941, just over three months before they escaped from Greece to Egypt, Reggie and Olivia had listened to a broadcast message by General Sir Archibald Wavell, Commander-in-Chief, Middle East, in which he declared that the events of the past year—1940—revealed 'the faults and virtues of the British race at war.'[5] With a complacent lack of foresight in preparing for her own defense, Britain had coasted throughout the first part of the year on a 'lazy and careless optimism.' Looking back in the 1950s, Field Marshal Montgomery concurred in Wavell's judgment that Britain had been derelict in preparing for war: in his memoirs he declares that 'It must be said to our shame that we sent our Army into that most modern war with weapons and equipment which were quite inadequate, and we had only ourselves to blame for the disasters which early overtook us in the field when fighting began in 1940.'[6] But, Wavell went on to say on New Year's Day in 1941, with the disastrous retreat from Dunkirk,[7] the fall of France, and the German domination of the coastline of Norway and the Low Countries, in June 1940 the real strength of the nation flashed like 'a sword from its sheath at the sudden challenge of imminent, deadly peril.' Britain's 'virtues' began to overcome her 'faults.' She had defeated Napoleon in the early nineteenth century and now, Wavell concluded triumphantly, with 'the unity of the Empire' behind her, she would smash the exultant armies of the Axis

---

[5] *The Times*, 4 January 1941.

[6] *The Memoirs of Field-Marshal Montgomery*, 50.

[7] Montgomery was scornful of those who wore embroidered flashes on their military uniforms after having escaped from Dunkirk; it was not understood by the civilian public that 'the British Army had suffered a crashing defeat at Dunkirk and that our island home was in grave danger. There was no sense of urgency.' *Memoirs*, 68.

powers, particularly General Rommel's elite Afrika Korps which was readying itself on the Libyan border to make a push into Egypt. Shuddering in Greece, Olivia and Reggie had taken heart from Wavell's message.

At the time of Napoleon's defeat at Waterloo in 1815, Britain was at the beginning of a century-long acquisition of territory and the creation of an immense empire dependent on native consensus and collaboration, both civil and military. By January 1941, therefore, Wavell could rally his listeners with a roll call of Commonwealth troops fighting for the British cause in the Middle East. Moreover, Arab and Jewish units from the Mandated Territory of Palestine and Transjordan were fighting side by side with forces of the Free French, the Poles, and the Czechs, and British garrisons in Egypt, the Sudan, East Africa, and British Somaliland were being fortified with troops from Australia and New Zealand. And Egypt had long been teeming with British troops, civilian businessmen, and colonial officials. Although Britain had recognized Egyptian independence in 1922, after forty years of occupation and the virtual inclusion of Egypt within the empire, British influence continued to dominate Egyptian political, military, and administrative structures. So when Olivia and Reggie disembarked from the *Erebus*, they not only set foot in a country that had to all intents and purposes been a part of the British Empire since the 1880s, they were also surrounded by cadres of its colonial troops, some newly arrived and others long-time defenders of British interests in the Middle East. The Cairo streets were thronged with soldiers in uniforms from all reaches of the empire.

In Bucharest and Athens, when not worrying about German invasion, food shortages, and aerial bombardment, Olivia had found those cities fascinating by virtue of their dramatic difference from England. Romania's exotic proximity to the Orient and Greece's cultural magnificence engaged her bright intelligence, and at those moments when she had felt ignored by Reggie's boisterous colleagues, she had taken solitary walks through the tangled side streets of Bucharest and Athens, relishing the architecture, the cafés, the teeming life of cities radically unlike any other she had visited. But the throngs of English-speaking soldiers in Alexandria and Cairo, the English sporting clubs, and the flocks of schoolchildren in English-style uniforms created an ambiguous recognition of cultural influence not experienced in Romania and Greece. After recovering from the shock to her frail nerves and fragile body experienced with the onslaught of Cairo's heat, noise, and dirt, and realizing that there was more to the Middle East than conveyed by the Bible pictures that had decorated the classroom walls of her Portsmouth grammar school, Olivia developed a divided attitude towards Egyptian life: she was repelled by what she saw as a crass 'Levantine' society and reassured by pervasive evidence of a long-standing British presence. To be sure, the British in Egypt clustered in colonies, as they had in Bucharest and Athens, but outside that sphere she also encountered a world that had long been subject to British political and cultural influence.

As a consequence of Olivia's eyewitness recognition of Britain's pervasive sway in Egypt, she began to question the stories of imperial superiority that were crucial in construction of British national identity and that were regularly articulated in the world of the English colony in Cairo. In Portsmouth, influenced by her father's fierce loyalty to the empire, she had acquiesced unthinkingly in the powerful national narratives that supported British power: that imperialism brought immeasurable benefits to its colonized subjects and that those subjects happily welcomed subjugation to the colonizer's culture. And in marrying Reggie Smith, Olivia had also become an adjunct participant in the propagation of British cultural superiority, whether she realized it or not. The undisguised mission of the British Council, after all, was to advance such beliefs through education in British art, literature, and political thought, even if its lecturers were sometimes suspected of being agents of British Military Intelligence (in Reggie's case, some have also speculated that he was an agent of the Communist Party whilst in Bucharest).[8] But freshly arrived in the Middle East, despite the reassuring sense of familiarity that she felt in Cairo after barely escaping from Athens, Olivia began to develop a somewhat jaundiced view of British governance that may be seen, in part, to shape her writing of The Levant Trilogy some thirty years later. As Jonathan Bolton notes in his study of the literary journal Personal Landscape that was published in Egypt from 1942 to 1945 under the joint editorship of Lawrence Durrell, Bernard Spencer, and Robin Fedden, 'writers from a colonizing nation who reside for extended periods abroad

---

[8] Reggie's autobiographical notes for a book to be titled 'Party Card' contain a mention of 'Undercover C.P. contacts' in the section dealing with his time in Romania.

are likely to be altered by the culture of the colonized.'[9] Olivia's view of Empire was definitively altered by her experience in Egypt. She moved from unthinking validation to skeptical critique.

Just as *The Balkan Trilogy* both evokes wartime survival and anatomizes the Pringle marriage, so *The Levant Trilogy* performs a similar double evocation by querying the glories of British imperialism while continuing to dissect the emotional dissonance between Guy and Harriet. Harriet, in particular, identifies the commercial foundation of British rule and queries its self-justifying narratives of cultural superiority and magnanimous governance of the colonized. In *The Danger Tree*, chatting with Simon Boulderstone (the young British officer to whom Olivia devotes roughly half of the Levant novels), Harriet realizes that in the two years of her marriage, a whole new group of young people had entered the war, young people who mistakenly believe that the British Empire is 'the greatest force for good the world had ever known' (p. 24). In a familiar alignment of non-fictional prose and fiction, in her typescript 'Cairo in Those Days' Olivia describes the British soldiers as puzzled by the unfriendliness of the Egyptian natives—having been taught that the Empire brought justice and civilization to those who dwelt in darkness, they had expected gratitude not hostility: in the first novel of *The Levant Trilogy*, Harriet demands of Simon, 'What have we done here, except make money? . . . the real people of the country, the peasants and the backstreet poor, are just as diseased, underfed and wretched as they ever were' (p. 24). Articulating the hardheaded grasp of political reality that she displayed in *The Balkan Trilogy* when having lunch with the Druckers, Harriet goes on to insist that the British are only in Egypt to protect the Suez Canal, its shipping routes to India, and the interests of the oil companies. In Bucharest, she shocked the Drucker family into painful acknowledgment of a doomed and brutal future and she shamed Guy into embarrassed recognition of his sentimental politics. In Cairo, Harriet Pringle expresses a sharp questioning of British motives that stems, in part, from Olivia's caustic responses to the chauvinistic optimism articulated by the crowd who socialized at the Anglo-Egyptian Union, however understandable that hopeful

---

[9] *Personal Landscapes: British Poets in Egypt during the Second World War*, p. xvi.

optimism might have been in the face of what seemed imminent German attack.[10]

As is clear from Olivia's non-fictional writings about Cairo, the move to Watson's flat had been preceded by weeks of horrified reaction to Egypt, which she struggled to temper by writing it all down. Initially, it was the dazzling light and blistering heat that infected her 'like an itch,' dulling all perceptions until she could only register such things as the smell of her hair frying and the stench from the waste lots and rubbish dumps, 'sweetish and acrid, that came from urine, dried ordure and vegetable decay' ('Cairo'). For her first few weeks in Cairo, despondently conscious of her exilic condition, she saw only the worst of things, although she acknowledged later that she turned her back in panicky disgust on whatever good might be found in Egyptian culture. For almost all visitors, its curiosities and beauties revealed a country like no other in the world, yet for Olivia that strangeness and ancient magnificence was obscured by the filth and opulence of its cities. Writing to 'Darling Mummy and Dumps' on 10 May 1941, on the positive side she reported that Adam Watson's flat was beautiful, that Reggie had managed to snare temporary employment cataloging the library of the Anglo-Egyptian Union, and that there was 'an extremely interesting crowd of people' in Cairo. But on the negative side, she added, everyone hates the city, is wiped out by the stupendous heat, and appalled by the sight of 'diseased' and 'partially blind' poorer Egyptians.[11]

It seemed to her that the Cairo middle class was consumed in 'narrowness and tedium . . . endless, silly intrigues' and she disparagingly declared that there was 'less mystery in the orient than in the occident—less crime, less genuine passion, evil, corruption, depth of any kind, because less imagination' ('The Dark Side of the World,' 101–2). The only thing that matters to Egyptians, she writes scornfully, is money—to the extent that her European homosexual friends complained the 'boys' refused to put up even a pretence of reciprocal desire: they wanted only to be paid for their services, and quickly.

---

[10] In this connection, Eve Patten sees Olivia Manning's work as 'a product not of exile or expatriation but of an informed literary refugee-ship, which moved beyond the binary of home and elsewhere towards a more radical examination of the empire's collapsing cultural and political geography.' 'Olivia Manning, imperial refugee,' 103.

[11] OMC, HRC.

The Egyptian 'peasants' she dismisses as having lost all self-respect: sprawling over the public gardens and pavements and polluting every side street and waste patch with their own urine, kicked aside by clerks described in *The Danger Tree* as 'rising in the world, leaving behind the peasants and the back street balani from whom they derived' (p. 81), to Olivia they presented a daily trial and evidence of Oriental indifference to suffering. Offering a sympathetic reading of Olivia's appalled response to Egypt, Artemis Cooper points to the unsettling experience of being a British refugee in Cairo, despite that city's pervasive evidence of British influence. Emphasizing the unhappy fact that Olivia and Reggie were, at that point in their lives, exiles thrice over, Cooper notes that Olivia's health had never been robust, and that, further enfeebled by the Cairo heat, she 'felt constantly ill and run down.'[12] She spent a lot of time on the sofa in Adam Watson's flat with cold compresses on her head and suffering from what everyone called 'gyppy tummy,' while Reggie, unemployed by the British Council but given a meager stipend, took up drinking Stella beer with the British colony in the cool garden of the Anglo-Egyptian Union. Reluctant to give Reggie a job, C. F. A. Dundas, the head of the Council in Egypt who was transformed by Olivia into the corrupt and despicable Colin Gracey in the last novel of *The Balkan Trilogy*, was suspicious of staff who had come out of the Balkans and Greece and he dismissed most of them as long-haired, woolly-minded Communist sympathizers. In Reggie's case, there was some truth to Dundas's assessment.

Revolted by the squalor, the smell, and the materialism, Olivia existed, as she puts it, 'in a state of recoil.' What's more, she was terrified of becoming ill, as Artemis Cooper points out: she lived in daily fear of coming down with smallpox, catching bilharzia from contaminated water, or being bitten by mosquitoes. In her essay on the English poets living in Cairo and Alexandria, 'Poets in Exile,' which she began writing in 1942 and which was published in *Horizon* in October 1944, she tries to explain this initial recoil and declares that she had not been alone in her revulsion since 'the first shocking impact of the Middle East numbed everyone. It took months to get over it, and longer to become reconciled to it': she writes that the British

[12] *Cairo in the War, 1939–1945*, 154.

refugees from Athens were shattered by an onslaught of squalor, dirt, disease, beggary, and luxury, overwhelmed by nostalgia for Greece. Some who had lost everything lived for months in extreme poverty.[13] Recalling the despair of these refugees in *The Danger Tree*, Olivia writes that they wept as they heard the final broadcast from the Greek radio station: 'Closing down for the last time, hoping for happier days. God be with you and for you.' The silence that followed was, for them the silence of the civilized world' (p. 66).

Yet Cairo also inspired in Olivia some of her most spontaneously poetic and vivid writing. In her typescript draft for 'Cairo in Those Days' and in the published essays based on that draft, she describes in sensuous detail the magical evening hours when Cairo awoke from its siesta, released from the oppressive heat and eager for the night. After sunset, the twilight filled the streets with a gray-green mist and poorer Cairenes came out on their balconies or put chairs on the pavement or just squatted down to eat their little saucers of beans. She and Reggie would walk in the gardens of Gezira, the river island, where the trees grew to an immense height, and where they would watch the feluccas pass like petals on the gray-green water of the Nile. Small boys, 'as thin as spiders,' would jump on to the steps of their garry and swing jasmine necklaces in her face, selling tuberoses and lilies as big as soup plates. In a moment, the twilight would be over, and the sky would deepen 'through violet to indigo, a pure and brilliant colour, and put out amazing stars.' Then, it would be off to the famous café Groppi's, passing through the bead curtain to gaze at the finest display of cakes in Cairo and then to take a seat in the garden, a sanded area planted with striped umbrellas and patrolled by waiters wearing red fezzes and red sashes around their galabiahs. Olivia remembers marveling at the colored lights strung around Groppi's garden and at the lighted windows of apartments that overlooked the garden, but also feeling terrified that the blazing splendor would prove a target for German bombers. Groppi's 'was a place for incipient romance, meetings, gossip and the latest funny story' ('Cairo'). And, she writes, 'there was the desert.' Having grown up on a wet, fertile, and small island, she found the desert spacious without being monotonous; she loved the way the

---

[13] 'Poets in exile,' 273.

sand became colored by winter clouds, ebony, indigo, and white, and how it looked sculptured like a still sea after a rainstorm.

The Levant Trilogy is, of course, no less transparently autobiographical than the Balkan novels, and as we know Olivia always admitted that the tumult of her own life inspired and shaped her writing. Every reader of the trilogies recognizes Harriet Pringle as Olivia's fictional surrogate, yet what many readers tend to overlook is that it is a male character in The Levant Trilogy, the young British soldier Simon Boulderstone, who also mirrors her traumatic experiences, particularly when she was living in Egypt and Palestine from April 1941 to late 1945. She projects onto this male character much of her memory of the Middle East when she was writing the trilogy in the mid- to late 1970s (thirty years after the fact). This projection suggests a number of things: first, that she might have exhaustively mined a projection on to Harriet of her resentment at being assigned the role of female spectator; second, that in these last three novels she aimed to perfect her already impressive ability to enter the mind of a male protagonist; and, third, that through Simon Boulderstone, whether she realized it or not, she could create a male character who, in the actuality of the wartime Middle East, would have been welcomed gladly into Reggie's world of chummy fellows. Through Simon, she enrolls herself, in a sense, into a fraternity that in Cairo tended to ignore or dismiss her as resentful, unfriendly, and too ironic for her own good.

In a crystalline instance of calling up memories of traumatic experience and then giving them fictional form through her male protagonist, Olivia begins The Levant Trilogy with images of disorientation and loneliness. After two months on the Queen Mary, Simon has arrived in Egypt in June 1942 with the draft and on a mission: he is in search of his brother Hugh, who has been fighting in the desert for eighteen months, sending letters home about 'brew-ups, desert chicken, bully splodge and flies' (p. 12). Detached almost immediately from his convoy, Simon is stranded in Suez, 'the most desolate and arid place on earth' (p. 9), then shunted to Cairo, where he finds himself posted to a column camped at Helwan in the desert, a place whose miserable conditions clearly show Olivia's reliance upon Montgomery's memoirs: arriving at the desert headquarters of the Eighth Army in mid-August 1942, Montgomery writes that he encountered a sight 'enough to lower one's morale. It was a desolate scene; a few trucks, no mess tents, work done mostly in trucks or in the open air in the hot sun, flies everywhere . . . The whole atmosphere of the Army Headquarters was dismal and dreary.'[14] Simon sleeps on the sand in a sleeping bag (there are no tents), endures the unrelenting buzz of mosquitoes and sand flies, and receives orders from superior officers who run things from a truck HQ.

Simon has arrived in Cairo just after the fall of Tobruk to Rommel's Afrika Korps in January 1941, and, waiting for a taxi at the railway station, he breathes in 'the spicy, flaccid atmosphere of the city,' sees 'figures in white robes, like night-shirts' flickering through the gloom, smells a city 'foetid with heat and human smells' (p. 10), a dislocating experience described in language virtually identical with that deployed by Olivia in her typescript draft for 'Cairo in Those Days,' written in the early 1960s. With a few days to spare before he must report to the Helwan camp, he decides to go in search of Hugo's 'girl'—Edwina Little, who is also a lodger with Guy and Harriet in Dobson's flat in Garden City—and leaving 'the shabby purlieus of the Cairo station,' he wanders through the main streets, impressed and unnerved by the experience: 'everywhere there were British troops who had nothing to do but wander the streets, shuffling and grumbling, with no money and nowhere to go' (p. 15), an image again strikingly similar to that found in Olivia's typescript draft of soldiers parading through the Cairo streets. Simon becomes increasingly disoriented as desperate women press babies with fly-ringed eyes in his face, old men thrust swagger sticks, flywhisks, and fountain pens into his hands, and a hot and gritty wind sends sweat running down his chest. Not only committed to Marie Belloc-Lowndes's imperative 'Never a Day Without a Line,' Olivia also believed strongly in never wasting a 'line': she grounds her conjuring of Simon Boulderstone's unsettling experience in vivid memories of her own 'nightmare' arrival in Cairo.

Cosmopolitan Cairo

Long a cultural junction of European, Middle Eastern, North African, and Asian societies, Cairo in the spring of 1941 became a cosmopolitan center for exiled writers and artists. The city was thronged with

---

[14] *Memoirs*, 99.

refugees from the Balkans, Armenia, Palestine, French North Africa, and Russia. Two well-known Greek poets, for example, George Seferis and Elie Papadimitriou, had arrived on the *Erebus* with Reggie and Olivia. Elie's behavior on board ship had appalled Robert Liddell and in his view she had behaved little better when they all arrived in Alexandria; writing to Olivia, he recalled 'those awful hot days of our first arrival . . . Elie Papadimitriou was so strident, rude and overbearing and silly that had she been Sappho and Miss Austen rolled into one, one would nevertheless have avoided meeting her again if possible.'[15] Cairo also attracted journalists and photographers on official assignments. The stage designer and photographer Cecil Beaton, for instance, came in March 1942 designated by the Ministry of Information as an 'official photographer' (he recorded his impressions in *Near East*, published in 1943). Stunned by the noise of hurdy-gurdies, bicycle bells, newsvendors, trams, bagpipes, loudspeakers, and the braying of donkeys, he never really recovered from the shock to the senses with which Cairo seemed to greet its visitors. At first sight, he thought Cairo rather like Nice, but then a dust storm started blowing in swirling eddies on the pavements, on to the slices of water melon, into the cafés, laundries, and postcard shops, and Cairo no longer evoked the French Riviera. Like Olivia and her character Simon Boulderstone, Beaton was amazed by the troops in their thousands thronging the streets, fighting off hawkers attempting to sell sunglasses, fly-whisks, and 'hopelessly out-of date American magazines.'[16]

With a seasoned eye for colorful scenery, Beaton takes his reader on a fascinating tour of the Arab Quarter. Driving through the narrow lanes, he notes the pretty iron balconies of the harems almost meeting above the jostling crowds, the colored turbans of the various sects, dynasties, and families that form 'a bobbing sea' of Cairenes out shopping. He passes streets dedicated individually to butchers' shops, to jewelers selling gold necklaces arrayed in glittering splendor against a black background, to craftsmen working on engraved brass, and to artisans fashioning pearl inlay bracelets: 'The most romantic is the spice quarter, with its fragrance of the Arabian nights. In bulging, buff-coloured sacks, the cedar wood, rose, mint, sandalwood and innumerable varieties of curry powder are equally seductive in scent

---

[15] Robert Liddell to Olivia Manning, 28 April 1944, OMC/C, HRC.
[16] *Near East*, 22.

and beauty.'[17] But like Olivia and countless other British people in Cairo, he realizes that the climate eventually reduces Europeans to inertia: the heat is 'frightful,' even when one is protected by shut windows in a coolish room with drinks to hand: 'It was as threatening as if something on a large scale was out of control.'[18]

One refuge from the heat was the cool garden of the Anglo-Egyptian Union, a social mecca in 1941 for the British business colony in Cairo. Also, many members of the Union were teachers, lecturers, and professors employed by the Egyptian government or by the British Council. In this milieu Olivia was less popular than Reggie. Her frosty demeanor and occasional malice cracked the veneer of witty banter that masked unease about the success of Rommel's Afrika Korps. Olivia also looked somewhat peculiar. Unlike the British wives and girlfriends who dressed carefully in silk dresses and pearls, and, if it was chilly, a demure cashmere twin-set, she wore turbans and strangely patterned frocks, her slim body and sharp features marking her as both eccentrically attractive and also unwilling to perform the role of pliant middle-class wife. The Scottish poet and critic G. S. Fraser (1915–80) who was serving in the British Army in Cairo, described her at the time as 'slim and tubular, with a face at once oval and birdlike . . . so that an artist of the school of Wyndham Lewis might have drawn her as a swathed, beaked egg balanced on a cylinder,'[19] and Hamish Henderson (1919–2002), the poet who was working as an intelligence officer in Cairo, wrote in his journal that Olivia was 'a languid, alert woman.'[20] Thinking back to the time when she, too, stayed in Adam Watson's flat, the wife of a British Legation official (Priscilla Esslen) recalled Olivia's 'white face, great angry eyes and hands so thin they seemed like half hands.' Sarcastic, cutting people in half with her remarks, she was also 'outrageously funny' as she told 'wicked, sometimes malicious stories about absolutely everyone.' Particularly notable about Priscilla Esslen's memories of Reggie and Olivia is that as far as she could tell they never displayed any affection towards one another, never, in fact, 'laid hands on each other.'[21] It seems likely that the

---

[17] *Near East*, 32–3.
[18] *Near East*, 92. For a useful survey of nineteenth- and twentieth-century travel writing about Egypt, see Fayza Hassan, 'A betrayal of history.'
[19] Quoted in Artemis Cooper, *Cairo in the War, 1939–1945*, 155.
[20] Quoted in Braybrooke, *Olivia Manning: A Life*, 109.
[21] Letter from Priscilla Esslen to Neville Braybrooke, November 1990. OMC, HRC.

behavior documented by those who knew Olivia in Cairo may well have been prompted by her belief that the intellectual and literary community, presided over by the accomplished painter and wealthy hostess Amy Smart, failed to recognize her talent. Everyone loved Reggie; few appreciated Olivia's cutting wit.

The daughter of an English mother and a socially prominent Arab newspaper mogul, Faris Nimr, Amy Nimr had traveled to England, studied fine arts at the Slade in London, and visited Paris and Rome. In 1932 she married an Englishman, Walter Smart, then Oriental Secretary at the British Residency and a respected scholar of Persian and Arabic, and they set up house in the Zamalek district in a villa reserved for high-ranking British officials, where they became celebrated for their hospitality and patronage of artists and writers. According to Keith Ovenden, the biographer of Dan Davin, the New Zealand-born author and long-time editor at the Clarendon Press division of Oxford University Press who served as an Intelligence Officer in Cairo from August 1942 until September 1943, the Smarts entertained people from all over the Middle East and Europe, 'from Romanian princesses to Palestinian doctors and Coptic lawyers. And writers were plentiful. Here he [Dan Davin] met Lawrence and Nancy Durrell, the Greek poet Papadimitriou and the expatriate British poets Bernard Spencer, Robin Fedden, Terence Tiller, Roger Bowen, and G. S. Fraser.'[22] Davin also met Reggie and Olivia on the sole occasion that they were invited to a Smart dinner party. The absence of any further invitation Davin's biographer attributes to Olivia's 'carping and vindictive personality,' whereas Reggie apparently endeared himself to everyone with his cheerful personality, his great talents as a drinker and a talker, and his penchant for English and Irish folk songs—'He and Dan enjoyed each other's company, and any evening on which he might be brought together with Paddy offered the certainty of great talk and wondrous singing.'[23]

Ovenden's deeply critical view of Olivia's personality and behavior is grounded for the most part in an excerpt from Dan Davin's diary, which he quotes as follows: '...and no doubt once again [I will] shudder at his [Reggie's] shrewish wife. At our last encounter we conversed: "I should think you must be one of the happiest of

[22] Keith Ovenden, *A Fighting Withdrawal: The Life of Dan Davin, Writer, Soldier, Publisher*, 157.

[23] *A Fighting Withdrawal*, 157.

women." "Why?" Bridling. "Because you do most successfully that which you set out to do." "And what is that?" "Be as unpleasant as possible to as many people as possible." '[24] Certainly, this general dislike of Olivia is confirmed by the recollections of David Abercrombie, who was also a lodger in Adam Watson's flat; he declares that 'Olivia soon established herself as the most unpopular person in Cairo,' which would seem to be quite an achievement on her part given the dense, polyglot population of the city in 1941. But although he concedes Olivia's rocky health might have partially created the 'carping and vindictive personality,' Keith Ovenden insists she resented 'a social world which she was, by personality, incapable of sharing': he finds it difficult to understand why Reggie had ever married her—'She was incurably middle class in the English manner, the daughter of a naval officer, narrow-minded, spiteful. He was a working-class intellectual, generous, amusing, and thoughtful. She was six years older than he was.'

Few who knew Olivia in Cairo would deny that she was difficult, that she complained a lot, that she had none of Reggie's magnetic charisma (she neither sang Irish folk songs at the drop of a hat nor proved herself a great drinker and talker), but Ovenden's stinging views of Olivia seem based on only one source—Dan Davin's diaries and interviews with his family. And according to Priscilla Esslen, Olivia actually participated happily in numerous social activities: picnics in the desert, a political discussion group led by Adam Watson, and a play-reading circle that met on the island of Gezeria. It seems to me that Ovenden's views of Olivia's behavior smack of snobbish condescension: that she was 'incurably middle class' and that she was six years older than Reggie seem mean-spirited judgments of a woman who had worked tremendously hard to get herself out of middle-class Portsmouth, who could hardly help the fact that she was six years older than her husband, who had survived two years of German threat in Romania and Greece, and who, throughout it all, kept on with her writing as a way of keeping herself sane in wartime. Ovenden patronizes the ambitious middle-class woman and romanticizes the working-class male intellectual.[25]

---

[24] *A Fighting Withdrawal*, 157.

[25] Olivia's review of a Dan Davin novel, *For the Rest of Our Lives*, which appeared in *The Palestine Post* on 4 July 1947, would not have endeared her to him: 'no clear picture of anything or anyone emerges' and the main character is seen through his own 'glower of

Never slow to recognize or to imagine social exclusion, Olivia was convinced the Smarts had blackballed Reggie and herself, and it would seem she was correct. But there is no evidence the Smarts shunned her solely on the grounds of what Ovenden terms her 'disagreeable' personality: perhaps they disliked Reggie's egregious volubility or did not appreciate 'wondrous singing' at the dinner table. To be sure, many of Olivia's friends and critics believe that the grim scene in *The Danger Tree* in which the eight-year-old son of Sir Desmond and Lady Hooper is killed when he picks up a stick bomb is based on the death of the Smarts' son on 17 January 1943 through a similar tragic accident, and that it was cruel and tasteless for her to include this in the novel, especially to depict the Hoopers trying to feed the dead boy through a hole in his cheek.[26] In Ovenden's view, Olivia took revenge on the wartime Cairo that she felt had snubbed her by re-inventing herself as Harriet Pringle, 'a thoughtful, acute, and wronged woman,' and by making Amy Smart responsible for her son's death. Dan Davin was enraged by what he saw as a literary act of malice and, according to Ovenden, when he heard of Olivia's death, commented, 'poisoned, no doubt, by her own venom.'[27] Taking a rather less rancorous view, Paul Gotch, who was with the British Council in Cairo at the same time as Reggie, recalls that he was actually present on the occasion of the tragic accident: in his words, 'went for tea, terrible fracas, dying child,' and he believes that Olivia merely used the story, as do all writers in creating their novels.[28] Olivia actually had the last word in this matter in her response to a letter from solicitors retained on behalf of the Smarts' surviving relatives; they had demanded she make no further reference to this tragedy in her writing, arguing that her characterization of Lady Hooper 'does grave harm to the memory of Lady Smart, whose conduct was beyond question.' Olivia replied:

---

self-righteous indignation rather than with a writer's comprehension.' Davin, Olivia declares, 'could with profit have cut out about ten thousand words of superficial dialogue and a number of incidents that at this distance in time and space have lost their significance': he is 'a romantic trying not very successfully to see life as it really is . . . using his art as a weapon in a lot of old squabbles now forgotten and unimportant to anyone but himself.'

[26] For an account of Amy Nimr's life and career as a painter, see Fayza Hassan, 'In search of Amy.'

[27] *A Fighting Withdrawal*, 159.

[28] Paul Gotch interviewed by David Marler, Oral History of the British Council, 14 May 2003, British Library Sound Archives, F18092.

'The real woman and the imaginary character bear no resemblance to each other. Lady Smart was a Syrian or Egyptian of subdued temperament. Angela Hooper is an ebullient English gentlewoman. I find it impossible to believe that anyone who knew Amy Smart could possibly imagine she was portrayed in the character of Angela Hooper.'[29]

A more fortunate member of the British colony in that he was regularly welcomed by the Smarts was Gwyn Williams, who in 1942 became the head of the English department at the newly founded Farouk I University in Alexandria; Williams recalls that he saw a great deal of Reggie 'but not so much of his wife Olivia Manning, who stayed at home writing the novels that were to make her famous,'[30] which is not quite the case since Olivia did not really begin writing those particular novels until the mid-1950s. Williams is correct, though, in saying that Olivia tended to stay home while Reggie boozed it up in the gardens of the Anglo-Egyptian Union: in addition to working on her study of the Henry Morton Stanley/Emin Pasha expedition, she was developing ideas for an essay dealing with the literary community in Egypt. In the approximately four and a half years that she lived in the Middle East, Olivia was constantly at work: she drafted two novels set in Cairo, Alexandria, and Jerusalem that were published after the war; she produced many book reviews for *The Palestine Post*; and she wrote the important essay on writing in exile that appeared in *Horizon* in 1944. That she worked steadily from the time she arrived in Egypt in April 1941, and that she and Stevie Smith remained close friends throughout the war, is attested to by a letter from Stevie to Louis MacNeice, written on 10 May 1943: 'Olivia sent me some stories of hers and two novels more than a year ago and asked me to do something with them. I have in a way but I don't seem to have had much luck so far. I feel awfully guilty about them as a matter of fact and keep getting letters from Jerusalem asking for news.'[31]

On 23 June 1942, Olivia had written to Stevie from Cairo, begging her to 'keep on writing'; she and Reggie are homesick and keen for news of their London friends and she longs for one of her long gossipy

[29] Blacket Gill and Swain to Olivia Manning, 15 January 1979; Olivia Manning to Blacket Gill and Swain, 22 January 1979. OMC, HRC.

[30] Gwyn Williams, 'Durrell in Egypt,' 298.

[31] BBC Written Archives Centre, Caversham. Olivia Manning, Scriptwriter 1943–1982. On 16 November 1944, in a letter to Kay Dick, Olivia wrote, 'If you see Stevie, tell her to write at once and not be so disgustingly lazy.' OMP, UT, Series 1, Box 1, Folder 1.

letters full of wit and information. She also writes that she has sent some stories and wonders if they have arrived safely since she has been very unlucky with all the manuscripts she has sent from Cairo: more than half have been lost. But she is still working on a novel 'which has passed through the fire and brimstone of two evacuations, innumerable fears and rumours and awful changes of climate, and suffered accordingly.' She dreams of settling down somewhere and really getting to work, and ends her letter on the sad note that Reggie's two brothers have been reported missing in Singapore, adding, 'Mine, my only one, killed perhaps you heard, on active service in the navy.'[32] Writing again on 15 September 1942 to convey her delight that a manuscript version of the Stanley/Emin narrative (to her mind 'the most mature thing I've done') had reached her, she ends affectionately by saying, 'Stevie darling, if you get Emin published, then I really think you should make a fortune as a literary agent.' It's very clear from these letters that Olivia remained fond of Stevie, telling her, for instance, that she always asks people if they know her, and when they say yes, they are all admiration. And she looks forward to receiving her new book of poems, adding, though, that books are very expensive in the Middle East and arrive very late. One letter ends with the sad admission that Reggie has had no news of his brothers, and his mother is heartbroken, and that her parents in their letters 'talk of nothing but my poor brother. None of us will ever really be the same again.'[33]

Olivia's resigned realization that no one would ever be the same again was not voiced, of course, for the first time in September 1942. When she stepped off the train in Bucharest she knew that the war would irrevocably change everyone and all things. By the time she and Reggie arrived in Egypt in late April 1941, the war had lasted for roughly eighteen months, and just over a year later German forces under the leadership of General Erwin Rommel took Tobruk in Libya and drove the British back into Egypt. Cecil Beaton writes that Cairo at this moment was full of rumors and that 'There was a great deal of talk as to who would be punished for the fiasco in the desert': restless queues formed outside banks, shops selling luggage were jammed, and in offices everyone was burning papers. As Beaton describes it, the effect was 'horrible': 'black charred pieces of paper drifted down from

[32] Olivia Manning to Stevie Smith, SSP, UT.
[33] Olivia Manning to Stevie Smith, SSP, UT.

the chimneys—a storm of black cinders, a hail of funereal confetti; the air was thick with the pungent smell of burning.'[34] This day became known in wartime Middle East lore as 'Ash Wednesday' because of the huge burning of official papers.

Rommel's eastward offensive (with an eye on taking the Suez Canal) was eventually halted at the small railway stop of El Alamein, just 150 miles from Cairo, in July 1942. This was the first battle of El Alamein. The second battle of El Alamein, three months later, under the leadership of Montgomery, was preceded by a victory at Alam Halfa in early September in a set-to which, had it been lost, in Montgomery's opinion would have led to a devastating British defeat in Egypt.[35] After Alam Halfa, the Eighth Army pressed on once more to El Alamein, where it routed the Afrika Korps and, between 23 October and 3 November 1942, drove the Germans westwards back to Libya and Tunisia—or, as Montgomery liked to say, batted the Germans for a six out of Egypt. During these momentous eighteen months in the war in North Africa, between the fall of Tobruk and Montgomery's victory at El Alamein, in an effort to find some settled refuge in their exile, Reggie and Olivia shunted between Cairo and Alexandria, until, in July 1942 with Rommel 'supposedly at the gates' of Cairo and the British Embassy making bonfires of its files, they left Egypt and settled in Jerusalem, where Reggie took up the post of Controller of English and Arabic Broadcasting. They stayed in Jerusalem until the end of the war.

Before finally leaving Egypt for Palestine, with help from Gwyn Williams, Reggie and Robert Liddell in October 1941 obtained jobs teaching English at the new Farouk I University (housed in a newly built nunnery on the sea-front). Reggie and Olivia moved to Alexandria, where they shared a flat with Liddell. Despite its cooler temperature and the fact that it was considered not an exclusively Egyptian city but rather a cosmopolitan enclave of Italians, Greeks, Lebanese, and European Jews and thus more to Olivia's sophisticated liking (she never really got over her dislike of Cairo, although she protested otherwise), Alexandria proved more devastating to her fragile nervous system and delicate stomach than the noise and dirt of Cairo. Closer to

---

the desert war, Alexandria was under constant bombardment as part of the German build-up to a planned winter offensive. Just as Olivia had cowered under the sound of anti-aircraft guns in Athens, in Alexandria she trembled at the whine of air-raid warnings for enemy planes on their way to Port Said and then on their way back as they dumped left-over bombs on Alexandria. Robert Liddell found her fragility particularly trying and he quickly tired of a nightly troop down to the basement, which Olivia insisted was essential for their survival. Her already rocky state of mind received a further jolt when, in early November, she received the letter from her parents bringing the news that her brother's plane had disappeared into the sea off the Dorset coast.

At this moment, Olivia was preparing a final draft of *The Remarkable Expedition* to send to Stevie Smith, and she decided that if and when it were to be published, she would dedicate it to her brother's memory. She also composed a commemorative poem, 'Dying in Kind,' found in her papers after her death and never published. The speaker describes her father as having 'fallen into long silence' and her mother as 'distracted': 'both too old now ever to recover.' She then remembers her brother as 'secretive, in emotion | Violent, ambitious in long studentship, | Or brilliant for companion's sake, | Feigning, in reck-lessness, indifference.'[36] In the last stanza of the four-stanza poem, she evokes their shared misery as children in an unhappy household:

> In childhood's desolation, adding
> By our impatience to the anchor's weight,
> In listing needed miracles, he'd accuse me
> Of charming fortune. Who has gained her now?
> Dying in kind—he once, I with him endlessly in mind?

Dragged down by the weight of their parents' miserable marriage, Oliver accuses his sister of 'charming fortune'—an image that suggests both attempting to soothe or allay through blandishment or to bewitch or enchant through magic. Either way, the fortune or fate that had Olivia and Oliver Manning imprisoned by their parents' unhappiness remains potently destructive: two of a 'kind' (as siblings) they suffer different fates, his in the sea off the Dorset coast and hers in the unending memory of that ending.

---

[36] Typescript, OMC, HRC.

After three months in Alexandria, jangly from the bombing, depressed by Oliver's death, and saddened by being unable to comfort her father, Olivia decided to leave Reggie to his teaching and return to Cairo and her job as an assistant press attaché at the American Embassy. The enervating heat of the city seemed more manageable than the sound of German bombers. Her principal assignment was to keep current a map showing troop movements in the western desert. The experience of working with brash Americans fostered her already well-developed skepticism about British imperial superiority. Surrounded by young men who displayed the confident braggadocio of their vigorous nation, Olivia began to feel that she was a citizen of a country fast losing its vaunted authority to its transatlantic ally. In *The Levant Trilogy*, she projects her remembered feelings on to Harriet Pringle, who understands the fragility of thinking she 'had grown up in the belief that Britain was supreme in the world and the British the most fortunate of people' (*The Danger Tree*, 71).

For the first six months of 1942, Reggie returned to Cairo from Alexandria every weekend, where for the radio station he produced *Juno and the Paycock* and ran a fortnightly program about the state of the arts in Egypt. At the beginning of 1942 he started editing *Citadel* (a small arts magazine) for the British Council and towards the end of that year Olivia began work on her essay about a group of writers she had met in Greece and in the Middle East. In a spirited defense against charges made by English critics that poets 'exiled' in Cairo and Alexandria had lost touch with English literary culture, Olivia emphasized that when Italian entry into the war closed the Mediterranean, manuscripts, if not lost on the way, could take three months to reach England (this had been her own experience); writers consequently 'ceased to look homeward' and turned to artistic and intellectual inspiration from fellow-exiles. Meeting refugee writers of other countries, learning foreign languages, absorbing new literatures, they are troubled only by thoughts of what has been left behind in their exile: 'The sense of a missed experience, that no alternative experience can dispel, haunts most of us. Seferis should have suffered in Athens; we should have gone through the London blitz' (p. 275).[37]

---

[37] 'Seferis' refers to the Greek poet and diplomat George Seferis who traveled to Egypt with Reggie and Olivia on the *Erebus*. As Adam Piette notes, the 'Landscape' poets (those who wrote for the journal *Personal Landscape*) 'structured their Cairo and Alexandria

Given Olivia's supposed reputation in Cairo for having a 'carping and vindictive personality' and her more easily verifiable post-war tendency to resent her fellow-writers (especially women), 'Poets in Exile' is remarkable for the affectionate and well-measured praise of many poets residing in Egypt in 1942. To be sure, with the exception of Elie Papadimitriou, all these poets are male, but Olivia does offer high praise for Papadimitriou: lauded as a 'gifted' and 'important' figure, she deserves greater recognition than hitherto received for her translation of her own poem 'Anatolia' into vivid and powerful English. Among the male poets, Olivia points to Bernard Spencer (1909–63), who, she declares, has long deserved a wider public: 'His poems are in the direct tradition of English poetry, and are marked by sincerity, exact observation, and a deep feeling for nature. They are patient, honest, individual, and always come out of the life he is living' (p. 277). Spencer served, in part, as a model for the doomed poet Bill Castlebar, the lover of Angela Hooper, in *The Levant Trilogy*. The verse of Keith Douglas, who was born in 1920 and met his death on the Normandy beaches on 9 June 1944 after serving as a tank officer in the Middle East, Olivia believes to be on a par with the very best poets of World War I. She particularly admired the fact that in his tank he kept a small shelf of books, including *Alice in Wonderland* and David Gascoyne's *Short Survey of Surrealism* (until her death, Olivia much admired the poems of David Gascoyne, for her someone she would place 'before that august trio—MacNeice, Auden and Spender. I read his poems again and again and am always entranced by them').[38] As she admits in her essay, there is always an undoubted danger for the writer in exile, that of being 'out of touch,' but she concludes that this danger is offset by the possibility that writing in England 'has been suffering from inbreeding' and that the new work being done in exile 'may take home a strain that will prove of real value to the stock' (p. 279).[39]

poems around a bitter contrast between the free mobility of pre-war travel and the enforced stasis of wartime exile' ('World War II: contested Europe,' 425).

[38] Olivia Manning to June Braybrooke, 19 January 1979, OMC/C, HRC.

[39] In a 'Letter from London' dated 8 May 1949, V. S. Pritchett describes Olivia's novel *Artist Among the Missing* as 'a new, clever book' and adds that 'those English writers who were obliged to wear themselves out in the busy, wretched island fortress during the war have suffered from it.' *New York Times*, 8 May 1949.

Much of this new work appeared in *Personal Landscape*,[40] the journal edited by Lawrence Durrell, Robin Fedden, and Bernard Spencer. About Durrell Olivia has nothing positive to say in her essay, other than to remark that Spencer's poems are unlike those of Durrell in that 'they never pretend to be more than they are' (p. 277). In this regard, she was clearly at odds with Reggie, who was enthusiastic about Durrell's work and published his poem 'In Europe' in the *Citadel* in October 1942. It was Reggie who nicknamed Durrell 'the magician' during the Cairo years.[41] There was no love lost between Olivia and Durrell: she considered him a pretentious and vain misogynist, in his life and in his work preening himself in Byronic poses, and she sided sympathetically with his wife Nancy when Lawrence left her for Eva Cohen (to Robert Liddell, Nancy seemed to 'flourish' after having been cast aside[42]). Durrell, after the publication of 'Poets in Exile,' wrote to the editor of *Poetry* in London, 'I see that the hook-nosed condor of the Middle East Olivia Manning has been writing about us in *Horizon*. She's determined to be *dans le mouvement*.'[43] Whether or not she aimed to be accepted by Durrell's predominantly male poetic fraternity, she was strongly determined to get 'Poets in Exile' published in London. Circumventing the long delays described in her essay, Olivia managed to get the manuscript of 'Poets in Exile' placed in a diplomatic bag and conveyed to Cyril Connolly, the editor of *Horizon*. It appeared in October 1944.

When Reggie received the offer to become Controller of the English and Arabic programs of the Palestine Broadcasting Service, despite the fact that he was not scheduled to begin his new job until the autumn, Olivia decided to move immediately to Jerusalem. She was glad to leave Egypt: to put behind her the hot, gritty wind, the sight of raw British troops sweating profusely into their uniforms as they wandered through the Cairo streets, and the annoyance of small-minded gossip. As she put it in 'Poets in Exile,' to those who 'had

---

[40] Jonathan Bolton asserts that this magazine 'remains a historical document of great importance—a record of group experience, a collection of responses to, among other things, world war, exile, and the Levantine landscape, culture, and art.' *Personal Landscapes*, p. xi.

[41] Roger Bowen, '"The artist at his papers": Durrell, Egypt, and the poetry of exile,' 483.

[42] Robert Liddell to Olivia Manning, 18 April 1943, OMC/C, HRC.

[43] Quoted in Braybrooke, *Olivia Manning: A Life*, 113.

been exhilarated by the Greek fight for freedom, the indifference, waste and dishonesty of the vast, profiteering Levantine population of Cairo was an unending nightmare' (p. 276). Coincidentally, she left Cairo at almost the same moment as Montgomery's arrival in that city (on 12 August) and it was in Jerusalem that she learned of his tremendous victory at El Alamein on 12 November. For the first time since she left Victoria Station on the Orient Express in late August 1939, she was free of the threat of German invasion, and on the chilly night of Rommel's retreat from Africa she sat in the poor light of a hotel dining room reading poetry aloud with half a dozen other writers. This was her milieu, not the small-minded British colony world of Cairo. In 'Poets in Exile,' she describes George Seferis exclaiming from his dark corner, 'Think of it . . . exiles reading poetry to each other' (p. 275).[44] In Jerusalem, Olivia's writing life gained fresh vitality, even if she remained an exile, and even if, as Robert Liddell paraphrased her sentiments, 'no one will, anyhow, publish one's work just now.'[45] Despite her enduring identity as a woman at war and as a refugee, and despite the fact that wartime conditions made publication erratic and unpredictable, Olivia never stopped writing.

Jerusalem

Jerusalem in late 1942 may have been free of the threat of German bombardment but it was hardly free of violent conflict. Earlier in the year, in April, the Intelligence arm of the British Police Force in Palestine reported that a gelignite bomb attached to the underside of a car owned by an assistant inspector-general in the Force had fallen off as he left his house in the German colony. Later in the day, children at the British community school in the German colony reported to the police the discovery of a suspicious-looking object in the road near their school: this object proved to be a huge bomb filled with 70 sticks of gelignite and 6 lbs of rivets attached to a long wire by means of which the bomb could be activated from an adjacent field. *The Times* reported on 23 April that the bomb was of the same type as that deployed 'by the Stern gang of terrorists.' Olivia had escaped German

---

[44] Seferis received the Nobel Prize for Literature in 1963.
[45] Robert Liddell to Olivia Manning, 30 September 1942, OMC/C, HRC.

bombing and threats of invasion to find herself in the epicenter of a
territorial conflict that continues to plague the Middle East to this day.
Rather than being strafed from the skies over Alexandria, she now
scurried through the Jerusalem streets fearful of being blown up by a
gelignite bomb or caught in the crossfire between British Police Forces
and Jewish resistance fighters bent on breaking the League of Nations
Mandate of June 1922 that formalized British rule in Palestine. As
respite from strife in the streets, she holed up in the boarding-house
room she had taken until Reggie could join her and they could find a
flat, where she devoured *War and Peace*, telling Robert Liddell that she
read it non-stop, hardly pausing to eat. Such absorption in Tolstoy's
novel struck Robert Liddell as exactly right and he wrote to her from
Alexandria: 'It is nice that you can read *War and Peace* because there is
so much of it.'[46]

On 4 November 1942, *The Times* reported that the twenty-fifth
anniversary of the Balfour Declaration[47] found Palestine so 'deeply
engrossed' in the war effort—recruiting drives, food rationing,
stepped-up war production—that there was little room 'for either
celebration or recrimination' on the part of its residents. This assessment, however, was distinctly at odds with the newspaper's recounting
in the same story of a commemorative meeting of the Declaration held
in the Jewish Agency hall in Jerusalem addressed by Chief Rabbi
Herzog and 'Mr. Bengurion [*sic*].' The Chief Rabbi declared that
Jewish claims and hopes for Jerusalem 'date back to declarations far
older than that made by that eminent British statesman Lord Balfour,
declarations embodied in chapter after chapter of the Holy Book,' and
David Ben-Gurion described the Declaration as the first sovereign
document that recognized the Jews as a nation. He emphasized that
although the Declaration stated Palestine could be claimed exclusively
neither by Jews nor by native Palestinians, it opened the way for Jewish

---

[46] 26 February 1943, OMC/C, HRC.

[47] The Balfour Declaration of 2 November 1917 was a formal statement of policy by
the British government that 'His majesty's government view with favour the establishment in Palestine of a national home for the Jewish people, and will use their best
endeavours to facilitate the achievement of this object, it being clearly understood that
nothing shall be done which may prejudice the civil and religious rights of existing non-
Jewish communities in Palestine, or the rights and political status enjoyed by Jews in any
other country.' The declaration was made in a letter from Foreign Secretary Arthur James
Balfour to Baron Rothschild, a leader of the British Jewish community.

immigration. After reviewing the 'benefits' conferred on the Arab inhabitants by 'Jewish progress,' Ben-Gurion lamented the fact that the Balfour Declaration had been replaced by the White Paper of 1939, which limited Jewish immigration.[48] He declared that it was 'the duty of Jewish Palestine to come, proud and erect, before the victorious United Nations to claim its rights for the sake of the persecuted millions of Jews in the prison that Europe had become.' *The Times* concluded by noting that 'the silence of the Arabs at a time when Zionists, abroad and here, are resuming active discussion of the Palestine problem with its inevitable political implications' should not be read as complacent acceptance of Jewish claims to Arab lands. Olivia had arrived in Jerusalem in the midst of a battle between those who believed the 'Jewish question' could be settled through establishment of a state on Arab territory and those who believed that the 'Arab cause' demanded the creation of a Palestinian state and the protection of Palestinian lands, although for the major part of her residence in Jerusalem (between August 1942 and late 1945) the 'Yishuv'[49] curtailed its resistance in the face of German advances upon the Middle East.

Living, then, in relative serenity after Monty had knocked Rommel for a six out of Africa and yet also inescapably aware of guerrilla readiness on the part of the 'Yishuv' to disrupt the eerie wartime calm of Jerusalem, Olivia continued her writing life. First, she obtained a job as press assistant at the British Council; next, she contacted *The Palestine Post* and secured regular assignments as book reviewer (John Connell, the newspaper's editor at the time, saw her as a 'formidable figure'); and, finally, she began making notes for a novel that is at least as autobiographical as the Balkan or Levant trilogies that were to

---

[48] The White Paper came out of a conference of Arabs and Jews held in London in 1939 under the auspices of the British government. In the wake of a lack of agreement between the participants about the future of Palestine, the British government issued a White Paper that severely compromised the promise of the establishment of a Jewish homeland spelled out in the Balfour Declaration of 1917. Jewish immigration to Palestine was limited to 75,000 persons over a five-year period; any further increase required the agreement of various Arab states. The White Paper also foresaw the establishment within ten years of an independent Palestinian state in which Arabs and Jews would share governance. The White Paper remained the basis of British policy in Palestine until the end of the Mandate with the establishment of the State of Israel on 15 May 1948.

[49] A term meaning literally 'settlement' and deployed to refer to a Jewish population already settled in Palestine before the establishment of the State of Israel in 1948.

follow: *Artist Among the Missing*, which she finished after the war and published with William Heinemann in 1949. She later declared that this novel was 'the first book in which I dealt with reality as I had discovered it for myself.'[50]

Set mostly in Cairo and vivified with detail culled from Olivia's experiences in 1941–2, *Artist Among the Missing* relates the story of Major Geoffrey Lynd. As Stevie Smith noted in her review, the background for Lynd's story is the 'hot and smelly Middle East, the terror and beauty of the desert.' She added, 'This book stands out.'[51] Married to an Englishwoman named Viola who enjoys the relaxed sexual mores of wartime, Lynd descends into paralyzing neurosis after having been touched by a rabid dog on a trip to Petra in Jordan. Lynd is the English 'artist' of the title, a painter who has resided in Greece before the war and who is identified as among the 'missing' when he joins the army and is posted to Cairo. His geographical journey mirrors that of Olivia. Lynd has gone 'missing' from a community of Greek artists where he was immensely at ease, and Olivia has gone 'missing' from the happy bohemianism of her pre-war London life. What's more, *Artist Among the Missing* is not only remarkable for parallels between Olivia's actual life and the experiences of her fictional character, it is also fearsomely graphic in its depiction of the horrors of war. When working as a stretcher-bearer in Jerusalem, for example, Lynd's job is to lift bodies from a train full of military casualties: leaning over a stretcher to warn a soldier he is about to be moved, he meets 'only the gaze of empty eye-sockets. A fragile beak of bone stood up, the only feature on a skinless face' (p. 34). Jeremy Treglown notes that this novel 'contains touches of realism that wouldn't have been out of place in Norman Mailer's once shocking-seeming *The Naked and the Dead*': in particular, he points to the scene in which an exhausted woman ambulance driver, just back from Syria, describes the practical business of transporting corpses in the desert heat; by the time her lorry reaches base, the corpses are running all over the floor.[52]

In a notably self-aware decision, Olivia projects onto this male character her enduring sense of being an outsider. Set apart from the crowd by his implied homosexuality and artistic vulnerability, Lynd is

[50] John Wakeman (ed.), *World Authors*, 937.
[51] 'Stevie Smith's guide to new books,' *Modern Woman*, 19 June 1949, 113.
[52] Jeremy Treglown, 'Olivia Manning and her masculine outfit,' 149.

an androgynous surrogate created from a fusion of autobiographical narrative and imaginative creation. 'I used to be a painter; now I'm nothing' he announces, an admission that suggests Olivia's sense of diminished autonomy in marriage to Reggie, of being engulfed by his generous presence and absorbed into the world of the British Council, her work as a writer un-noticed and unappreciated. Only at art school, Lynd feels, has he felt at home in the world—there, 'where talent was everything,' he found comfort in being with people who had 'intelligence, vitality, wit, and importance' (p. 109), a sentiment that evokes not only Olivia's pleasure in attending art school in Portsmouth but also her heady days in pre-war London with Hamish Miles and his Bloomsbury friends. In many suggestive ways, Geoffrey Lynd is as compelling a fictive surrogate for Olivia Manning as Harriet Pringle and Simon Boulderstone.[53]

In a scene that recalls Olivia sitting with a group of fellow-writers in a Jerusalem café and reciting poetry as Monty bats the Afrika Korps out of Egypt, Geoffrey Lynd sits in a Jerusalem café with Greek friends listening to a Greek poet read in Greek: the verse leads him to remember a party in a taverna where he sensed the warmth of the sun on his hands, the sparkle of crystal-clear running water, the sharp taste of retsina, and the smell of pine-trees that grow in distorted shapes over a windy hillside above Athens. Brilliant cyclamen flowers dot the ground, tortoises of all sizes and beautiful design move across the paths in the pine woods: 'Far below, the salt-white city sparkled under the mist of heat' (p. 50). As he walks down the Jaffa Road in Jerusalem, as did Olivia many times during the three years she spent in that city, he smells 'wafting about in the air a smell of sweat, paraffin, oranges, latrines and spice.' And 'swaggering in their nervousness of alien surroundings and in the long-ingrained consciousness of British superiority' (p. 65), British soldiers jostle him out of the way, their bragging attitude reminiscent of the soldiers Olivia evokes in her first

---

[53] Jenny Hartley considers Olivia's first novel with a war setting to be 'an interesting false start. Apparently in the belief that war novels should have male protagonists, Manning has moved women to the periphery.' *Millions Like Us: British Women's Fiction of the Second World War*, 182. This strikes me as an unsubtle reading since the principal fascination of Lynd as a character is his homosexuality, or if not that, his androgynous qualities. The *TLS* reviewer of *Artist Among the Missing* judged Lynd to be an unconvincing character but one who works well as 'a medium' for Olivia's ideas. *TLS*, 16 April 1949.

impressions of Cairo. But it is Lynd's obsession with the memory of his dead mother that summons forth Olivia's unresolved conflict with her own parent.

As is apparent from many of her writings, Olivia felt deeply injured by the withdrawal of her mother's affection after the birth of her brother Oliver in 1913. In a pattern suggestive of meting out punishment for maternal neglect and scorn, Olivia returns with a compulsive regularity in her fiction to the figure of a cold and resentful mother. Unlike Virginia Woolf, she never freed herself from this fixation. Woolf confessed that until she was in her forties she was 'obsessed' by the presence of her mother; she remained an 'invisible presence' in her life until one day, when walking around Tavistock Square, 'in a great, apparently involuntary rush' she made up *To the Lighthouse* in her head. When she had finished writing, Woolf discovered that she had ceased to be obsessed by Julia Stephen. She had, somehow, explained to herself the neurotic attachment and thus 'laid it to rest.'[54] Olivia reached no such understanding or release.

In *Artist Among the Missing*, rather than creating a demonic mother, she imagines an ideal figure, romantically different from her own parent, a figure who haunts Geoffrey Lynd's waking imagination and nightly dreams. Brought up by an aunt in England, he is consumed by his only memory of his dead mother (who was probably unmarried): 'a winter's night with snow on the window-ledge and she no more than a shadow in the dark nursery, bending to kiss him so that he smelt the perfume of the Parma violets in her muff' (p. 84). On a visit to Petra (the well-preserved ancient city in the Jordanian desert whose buildings are carved into the mountainside and which Olivia visited in the spring of 1943), he undergoes the uncanny experience of seeing something that returns him to the image of his mother bending over him in the nursery. Clambering over the Petra rocks, he confronts a stairway cut roughly in a narrow pass between two rock faces which, seen in silhouette, seems to him to have the appearance of a woman holding a child in the crook of her arm. Devastated by the trauma of imagining his lost mother, Lynd is almost immediately confronted by a rabid scavenger dog, which although it does not bite him, grazes his hand with its muzzle. Involuntarily, he submerges the image and

---

[54] Virginia Woolf, 'A sketch of the past,' *Moments of Being*, 80–1.

memory of the lost mother into an obsessive belief that he has been infected with rabies. It is not until he enters psychoanalysis with a German Jewish doctor in Jerusalem that he understands his obsession covers the grief about being a motherless outsider. In tracing this process, Olivia constructs a romanticized memory (the perfume of Parma violets on the muff); describes the image of a mother seen in the Petra rock face; submerges this image into a morbid fear of rabid infection (in actuality, Olivia was terrified of being bitten by a rabid animal); and through description of Lynd's psychoanalysis, discloses his neurotic longing for the idealized mother figure.[55]

Lynd's neurosis is compounded further by his unrecognized homosexuality. Never directly characterized as homosexual, at several moments in the novel he betrays his unrecognized and unfulfilled homoerotic desires. For example, in a café outside Cairo, drinking with a fellow-officer, Lister, and Arab friends, he is transported not so much by an Arab male singer but by the sight of the rapt male listeners: 'With no women to impose restraint, the men leant forward, eyes glazed, mouths open in abandonment to their sensuality. The atmosphere quivered with excitement and Geoffrey felt himself drawn into it as into a sort of opium state of exaltation and wisdom. He watched the hand of the boy in front of him tighten round the wrist of a friend. Deprived of women, they had learnt all the compensation of symbols. No reality could give them more satisfaction' (p. 90). On his return to his Cairo flat, he finds himself thinking not of Viola, his absent and unfaithful wife, but of his friend Lister: 'The vacancy at his side was the absence of Lister. His return to Viola was like a journey to a stranger' (p. 129). In Amman, on his way to Petra, Olivia describes him as fascinated by groups of young nomad Arabs in from the country: 'They were still and quiet, yet seemed on the alert like wild animals; all small, elegantly made, like delicate girls in their white robes. They had slender hands, painted eyelids and long curls' (p. 104). Lister, an unembarrassed anti-Semite, compares them favorably with the 'gross Jews with their backsides bulging out of khaki shorts' one sees in Palestine' (p. 105).

At the beginning of the novel, at the border of Egypt and Jordan and shortly after the fall of Tobruk to the Germans, Lynd's job is to

---

[55] In her review of the novel in *The Observer*, 20 March 1949, Angela Milne praised it as a 'rather frighteningly clever study of a mental breakdown.'

shepherd European refugees out of Cairo on their way to Jerusalem. A huddled group of women—an Italian, a Romanian, two Yugoslavs, and two German Jews—cluster around him, attracted by his good looks but distanced 'not so much by a lack of response as an emptiness. Whatever it was they expected to find in him was not there' (p. 17). Unmoved by female charms, Lynd is, however, fascinated by women's lives, especially those women living in Cairo: to him they seem happier than men, full of a confident gaiety, chattering with an endless vitality, assured by the knowledge that 'they were the creators. Without them the world would come to an end ... Only their miserable men had to go about excusing themselves with a show of bravery, arrogance, vanity, wealth or talent' (pp. 131–2). Lynd envies these women: their carelessness, their comfort, their confident sense of being at home in the world. Tormented by fractured memories of his dead mother, unsettled by his homoerotic attraction to his fellow officers, he wishes to be like them, to *be* them: union with a mother figure would efface her loss and reclaim him from those among the 'missing.' Towards the end of the novel, Lynd suffers a complete nervous breakdown, but as he recovers in a rest home set into the cliffs above Alexandria, he feels the world seeming to solidify around him and he sublimates his neurosis in a return to painting. That Olivia's obsession with *her* mother never triggered a nervous breakdown may, perhaps, be traced to the displacement of feeling angry and abandoned onto the creation of fictional characters such as Lynd, an artist who surmounts neurosis through creative work.

After the final battle of El Alamein, Olivia began conducting informal interviews with cooperative participants in the battle and also with people who had worked behind the scenes in British army headquarters in Cairo. At this point, she wasn't sure what she was going to do with this material but she knew that one day she would write about the battle and the African war. Squirreled away in the British Library doing research for her Stanley and Emin Pasha book had been exhilarating and thrilling, but here, obviously not a participant in the battle but close enough to smell it, to sense it, and to witness its effect on those who fought, she felt an imperative to record as much as she could for the future. She had finished *The Remarkable Expedition*, dispatched 'Poets in Exile' via the diplomatic pouch to London, and was continuing to review for *The Palestine Post*. What's more, during her three and a half years in Jerusalem, she regularly sent poems and short stories to Stevie Smith in London. In his letters to Olivia when she was in Jerusalem, Robert Liddell referred regularly to her writing, congratulating her, for example, in October 1942 on 'nearing the end of the Romanian book' and giving her the New York address of the literary agents Curtis Brown. Although Liddell mentions no specific title, it is safe to assume, I think, that he refers to Olivia's unpublished short novel 'Guests at a Marriage', which anticipates the six-novel dissection of the Pringle marriage that we find in the trilogies.

In February 1943, Liddell also wrote sympathetically to Olivia in Jerusalem about her difficulties in being confined by guerrilla action on the part of Jewish resistance to British rule: 'How enclosed your life sounds, and how sad—I hope you get out on Sunday...I am really very sorry for you indeed: neither Emily Bronte nor George Eliot ever had to live cheek by jowl with a wireless set...I do hope at least you keep a notebook.'[56] When she could get out, Olivia loved to walk through the narrow streets of the city, past the most famous religious and ancient shrines—the Mosque of El Aksa, the Dome of the Rock, the Church of the Holy Sepulchre, and the Western Wall of Solomon's Temple—and then up into the hills past newer building such as a Franciscan basilica near the Garden of Gethsemane and the Hebrew University built around the country house of an English lawyer on a lower spur of the Mount of Olives. Olivia had also long wanted to travel to Petra and Robert Liddell wrote from Alexandria that he hoped her planned 'excursion to Petra will come off...I wonder how you will manage to get Reggie there?'[57] As things turned out, Reggie did not travel to the extraordinary place Olivia described in great detail in the notebook Liddell hoped she was keeping: as she reported to her friends, Reggie would disappear into the nearest underground bar while she traveled in the Middle East. Insisting he could not afford to travel, he would, Olivia insisted, 'spend more on drink than I spent on my trip.' Petra figures prominently, of course, in *Artist Among the Missing* and it is also the subject of a long poem Olivia composed when she returned to Jerusalem.

Richly embroidered with a remarkable eye for color, the poem sometimes borders on the 'beauty-conscious' language of the unpublished novel Olivia began when she was eighteen: clumps of iris are

[56] 26 February 1943, OMC/C, HRC.
[57] 18 April 1943, OMC/C, HRC.

'black and beast glossy,' grazing camels are seen through a 'silver mirage,' hills 'plum velvet in their folds' float like islands in the haze. The 'dream-monstrous' Treasury building floats deceptively 'pink' in the distance. The poem concludes on a strange note that in all likelihood refers to Reggie and her feelings for him:

I find behind the façade of my acts and thoughts
The troubling, combated will that this long-sought arrival should prelude
only return to you.

Having long wished to visit Petra, once there she feels not exhilaration at having achieved her goal but a desire, a 'will,' that she return to Jerusalem, and to Reggie. The poem is signed 'Olivia Manning, c/o R.D. Smith, Controller of English and Hebrew Programmes, Palestine Broadcasting Service, Jerusalem, Palestine.' For reasons to do with postal efficiency, it is understandable that she would need to sign herself as care of her husband and the Palestine Broadcasting Service, but in actuality Olivia Manning had, at this point in her marriage, achieved a notable independence from Reggie. Yet she was still in love with him and it is perhaps for that reason that the 'will' to return to him she evokes in the Petra poem is 'troubling' and 'combated.'

6

Going Home

'I have been crying as I write. It has been strange to find that I still have so many tears left.'

Olivia Manning, mid-1970s.[1]

'I expect you find, as I do, the end of the war in Europe filling you with relief and melancholy—because one has no longer any motives for excessive joy.'

Robert Liddell to Olivia Manning, 12 May 1945.[2]

Great stress and strain

In the time between her Petra trip and her departure from the Middle East (from spring 1943 to summer 1945), Olivia made notes for the novel that became *Artist Among the Missing*, produced many reviews of new fiction for *The Palestine Post*, started putting together an anthology of verse culled from the poets she discussed in 'Poets in Exile,' and polished some of the short stories that appeared in the collection *Growing Up* (1948).[3] She remained a woman at war and a disciplined and prolific writer, although she felt that novel-writing and

[1] It is difficult to provide an exact date for this handwritten note found folded into typescript fragments of *The Danger Tree*, published in 1977. The note is headed 'The Levant Trilogy' and I am speculating that Olivia wrote it while she was drafting this novel. OMC, HRC.

[2] OMC/C, HRC.

[3] Writing from Alexandria in March 1944, Robert Liddell enquired about Olivia's 'anthology' and asked that she let him know of any Cafavy poems she did not plan to include. He was probably planning his own anthology of Cairo poets. As far as I can tell, neither anthology reached the publication stage. OMC/C, HRC.

novel-reading had become virtually impossible 'in a time of great stress and strain.'[4] At the beginning of the war, a reviewer in the *New Statesman* had declared that there was no moment 'since the invention of novels, when fewer people wish to read them' and Cyril Connolly announced in 1944 that 'The reading public panicked with the fall of France; their literary curiosity, which is a luxury emotion, dependent on a background of security and order, vanished overnight.'[5] Also in 1944, from the perspective of the writer, Pamela Hansford Johnson chimed in to agree with Connolly: 'It is possible that no novel of major importance will be written during the present war. The impact of external events, the constant fluctuations in social and moral temperature, must affect the flow of the artist's creation.' How can it be expected, she goes on to ask, that a writer who had begun a book in the summer of 1942 with Tobruk fallen and the Eighth Army in retreat and tries to finish it at the beginning of the first Soviet counter-offensive and Monty's great victory at El Alamein, that he or she 'will retain the tenor of its conception?'[6]

When Olivia wrote in February 1945 of the 'great stress and strain' that continued to inhibit novel-writing, she had in mind, of course, the last months of the war in Europe and the increasingly volatile situation in Palestine. Glued to the news of Allied victories and worried by the inflammatory rhetoric of a Zionist insurgency, Olivia felt that the relatively brief writing of a short story was more manageable than the long-term commitment required for completion of a novel. What she could not mention in her 1945 review was that her own work on a novel to be published at the end of the war (she hoped) had come to a calamitous stop in July 1944. In the middle of that month she suffered the traumatic death in utero of a seven-month-old fetus. At a moment in the history of the war when it seemed feasible to hope for victory (the Allied invasion of Normandy took place on 6 June), rather than joyfully anticipating the birth of their child and an end to their exile, Olivia and Reggie mourned its death and thought little about their return to England.

Not only did Olivia lose the child at seven months (clinically termed 'a missed abortion'), in accordance with gynecological practice in the

---

[4] 'The short story today,' *The Palestine Post*, 16 February 1945.

[5] Brian Howard, *New Statesman*, 7 September 1940, quoted in Robert Hewison, *Under Siege: Literary Life in London, 1939–1945*, 27; Cyril Connolly, quoted in *Under Siege*, 31.

[6] *The Windmill*, 1.9.

Middle East at the time, she carried the dead fetus to term for fear of abnormal, even fatal bleeding should labor be induced or the fetus surgically removed. In July 1944, there was a lack of really good antibiotics (the newly invented penicillin was not widely available) and blood transfusions had not been perfected; and although it is possible a drug might have induced labor, which would then have permitted extraction of the fetus, this assumes such a drug would have been available in wartime conditions in Jerusalem in 1944.[7] Before the development of ultrasonography, the term 'missed abortion' referred to a clinical situation in which an intrauterine pregnancy is present but is no longer developing normally. The causes are generally considered identical with those that precipitate spontaneous abortion, most commonly fetal chromosomal abnormalities, placental abnormalities, and uterine abnormality. In Olivia's case, to this list might be added five years of wartime 'great stress and strain.' What precisely precipitated the death of the fetus remains unknown, and even assuming she had been told the cause, she revealed this information to no one. In fact, Olivia spoke very rarely about this tragedy and she almost never referred to it in her letters, even to her closest friends. In the immediate aftermath, it was only to Kay Dick that she mentioned the matter, and, later, to her close friends June Braybrooke and Francis King: in connection with her obsessive fear of rabies, she wrote to King in 1969, 'My neuroses started years ago when we were staying in Famagusta with the medical officer of health—I was very near a complete breakdown at the time as I had what is known as a missed abortion, and had to go around for nearly two months with the dead baby inside me.'[8] Reggie had arranged the stay in Famagusta in Cyprus in the hope that Olivia would recover some of her physical and emotional health if he took her away from Jerusalem. It was a holiday neither planned nor eagerly awaited.

When Olivia discovered early in 1944 that she was pregnant, she and Reggie were delighted. She was almost thirty-six years old and had begun to worry that she might never have a child. But now, her customary anxiety tranquillized by the prospect of motherhood, her

---

[7] I am grateful to Bruce Young, MD for background information about details of a missed abortion and of how in 2011 Olivia would have had labor induced and the fetus would have been extracted by dilation and curettage or by caesarean section.

[8] FKC/OM, HRC, 28 August 1969.

slim body assuming an unaccustomed plumpness, and her writing for the moment put in abeyance, she took up knitting, painting water-colors of the principal Jerusalem landmarks, and napping in the warmth of the Jerusalem sunshine. In a jocular letter that he later deeply regretted, Robert Liddell wrote from Alexandria in late April begging her not to name the child Christopher: 'such an unlucky name. I associate Christopher with early and painful death, or worse . . . Oliver is so much nicer and more suitable.' Neither did he like the name Victoria since it would rather date the poor child, 'due,' he noted, in September.[9] In mid-July, however, he learned from Reggie details of the missed abortion and on 25 July wrote to Jerusalem, 'I am terribly sorry for your disappointment, and hope the complications which ensue will not be too foul or painful. It is such an anticlimax for you after all this time of expectation . . . I hope you will have better luck next time.'[10] There was, of course, no next time and the complications were indeed foul and painful. For eight weeks, Olivia had felt like a walking cemetery (as she put it to Robert Liddell), at the time of delivery she went through a long labor doomed to end in tragedy, and as a consequence of the missed abortion, she could never again conceive because of irreparable gynecological damage. For the rest of her life she suffered from irregular uterine hemorrhaging.

The month in Famagusta was horrendous. Boarding the Cyprus boat, Olivia was on the verge of a nervous collapse, which was aggravated by the day-and-a-half trip under stifling conditions. Plagued by oppressive heat and swarms of flies that triggered memories of her tense and terrible three-day journey from Athens to Alexandria, and hysterically unmanageable by the time she arrived at the home of the Chief British Medical Officer, for her first few days in Famagusta she sequestered herself in virtual isolation. That her beloved Athens had been liberated by Allied forces on 14 October scarcely registered and she was indifferent to the charms of Famagusta. Cyprus had been a British Crown Colony since 1925 and Famagusta was a pleasant and favored resort for British travelers. But nothing pleased her. Suspicious about the motives of everyone who tried to help, from Arab porters to her kindly host, she complained incessantly—about the intense heat, the insanitary bathrooms, the dismal nightclubs, the rancid olive oil in

---

[9] Robert Liddell to Olivia Manning, 28 April 1944, OMC/C, HRC.
[10] Robert Liddell to Olivia Manning, 25 July 1944, OMC/C, HRC.

her salad, and the dull Cypriots who presented a pathetic contrast to her noble Greeks. Reggie's pained and heroic struggle to lift her spirits was met only with sarcastic rebuff and cruel refusal to recognize that he, too, had been devastated by the loss of the child.

Perhaps because of his inherently cheerful nature, Reggie somehow managed to tolerate Olivia's bitter despair during the terrible month in Cyprus, while at the same time hiding as best he could his own very real sorrow about the loss of the baby. From the moment he learned of the pregnancy he had been exuberantly happy, writing to all his friends back home with the news and disciplining his customary fondness for sitting around in cafés while Olivia worked at home, in order to be with her as they awaited the birth. When she stepped out of the bath that fateful day in mid-July 1944 and noticed a curious crease across her stomach and a strange shrinking of her belly, and from the time he had driven her to the doctor and seen her stricken face when she received confirmation of what she had already sensed, he never really left her side. Eventually, with the lessening of grief brought about by time and their return to England after six years of tumultuous exile, the shared memory of what happened in Jerusalem in July 1944 bound them in sorrowful acceptance of loss, rarely spoken of but always there. When Olivia died on 23 July 1980 in a hospital on the Isle of Wight after suffering a stroke three weeks earlier, Reggie was in London, staying at the Islington home of their old friend and neighbor from St John's Wood days, Johnny Slattery: she remembers vividly that when Reggie was told of Olivia's death he cried out, 'Oh the baby, the baby.'[11] It's impossible to know what this cry might have signaled: most plausibly, perhaps, a simple association of one death with another.

On their return to Jerusalem from Cyprus, hoping that a change of residence would lift their spirits, Olivia and Reggie moved out of the rented house in the German Colony where they had joyfully antici-pated the birth of their child, and took rooms at the Jerusalem YMCA. Directly opposite the King David Hotel and opened by Field Marshal Allenby in 1928, the building is a combination of Byzantine, Romanesque, and Gothic design, deliberately arranged to symbolize a fusion of the architectural traditions of Judaism, Christian-ity, and Islam. The foundation contains stones from quarries used in

---

[11] Author's conversation with Johnny Slattery, 4 April 2009.

the construction of the Second Temple and forty columns in the forecourt arcade represent forty years of Jewish wandering in the desert and the forty days of the temptation of Jesus. Olivia loved the colorful and intricate mosaics to be found throughout the building and spent many hours in a deckchair enjoying the panoramic view over the Old City from the roof garden of the YMCA's one-hundred-and-fifty-foot tower. Unlike Cecil Beaton, who when he visited Jerusalem in the summer of 1942 was disappointed to find the city 'so new,' filled with 'overhead telephone wires, frosted glass lamps, and cubist architecture' (not to his delicate taste), Olivia found fascinating the mix of religions, architecture, and cultures that made Jerusalem unlike any other Middle Eastern city.[12]

During the awful two months between the death of her child and its delivery, Olivia had been indifferent to momentous wartime events. After the invasion of Normandy on 6 June, Allied forces had pressed forward in Europe and on 31 August news had reached Jerusalem of the Soviet capture of Bucharest. Olivia's marriage had been framed by the European war that had begun on that September day when she arrived in Romania, but from July to September 1944 she had cared little for the unfolding European conflict that would end with the unconditional surrender of Germany to the Allies of 7 May 1945. But with the return to Jerusalem after the awful month in Cyprus, residence in appealing new quarters, and the resumption of work, she managed to pull herself out of a depression that was technically post-partum, and yet not. Working in the YMCA's comfortable and well-stocked library, she resumed book reviewing for *The Palestine Post*, drafting chapters for *Artist Among the Missing*, and, when she could bear it, wondered whether she would—or, indeed, could—ever translate the actual trauma of the loss of the child into a work of fiction. Even though she had published only one novel, by late 1944 she was strongly convinced that her best writing had—and would in the future—come out of her own life. Olivia knew she wrote most powerfully when writing from her own experience and her own passions, and, in general, she believed that the most gripping and brilliant prose drew its inspiration from the writer's life. In a review in *The Palestine Post* of Joyce Cary's *The Horse's Mouth*, published in 1944, she declared it

---

[12] *Near East*, 110.

could only have derived its dazzling clarity from Cary's own experience as a struggling artist.[13] Her praise of Cary coincided with that set forth by Pamela Hansford Johnson in the first number of *The Windmill* that appeared in 1944; she declared *The Horse's Mouth* to be 'splendid and sensuous, unmoral and wildly comic, and perfectly serious in intent.'[14]

The Windmill was edited by Reginald Moore and 'Edward Lane,' the pseudonym for Kay Dick, the editor, critic, and novelist with whom Olivia first formed an epistolary friendship in November 1944. Writing to 'Edward Lane' from Jerusalem, she thanks her for a letter received on her return from Cyprus, 'the one ray of light in a gloomy homecoming.' She begins this revealing letter by saying that writers in England are mistaken in believing that writers in exile are 'more alive' than those at home: 'a glamour of distance' creates this false impression. All of her fellow-writers in the Middle East are 'miserably homesick,' and she and Reggie, she declares, are dying to get home again after being chased all about Europe and finally trapped into this 'cul-de-sac' of Palestine. She apologizes for not having written sooner and then confesses that she has been going through 'rather a bad phase and have had what I suppose was (and still is) some sort of a nervous breakdown—anxiety neurosis, terror and depression,' attributable, she admits, to 'making too rapid a recovery after losing the baby, and partly five years of almost continual anxiety followed by more troubles in this wretched, unhappy country.' Only she can make herself better, she believes, and she must, if only for the sake of her 'poor husband' who has been suffering from dysentery for months and needs a rest from caring for his fragile wife.[15] She concludes by saying that she would be delighted if *The Windmill* took her short story, 'The Children': 'it is good and felt so when writing it' (in August 1946 she accepted £20 for it, an amount she assured Kay Dick was 'quite satisfactory').

In January 1945, Olivia had a chance to take her ideas about fiction from the printed review to the public podium when, as one of a group

---

[13] 'A painter's world,' *The Palestine Post*, 17 November 1944.

[14] *The Windmill*'s first number declared that it was 'a selection of essays, papers, stories and verses which, by reason of their varied opinions and styles, make especial claim to the attention of the thoughtful reader in search of entertainment and the stimulation of original ideas.'

[15] OMP, UT, Series 1, Box 1, Folder 1.

of seven lecturers in a series on 'Aspects of the English Novel' sponsored by the British Council in Jerusalem, she expounded on the
literary genre to which she was most seriously committed and in
which she continued to work until the end of her life. One of the
novelists she discussed at some length in her lecture was Virginia
Woolf, an inspiration from the time she had been typing away in
Portsmouth and devising schemes to get herself to Bloomsbury. The
lecture proved useful when she reviewed a short critical study of
Woolf, published in *The Palestine Post* on 4 May 1945; Olivia salutes
Woolf as 'one of the two greatest women novelists and one of the half
dozen best novelists that the century has yet produced in England.'
Coyly declining to name the other great woman novelist, she praises
Woolf's mastery of 'the very high art form which she evolved for the
expression of her thoughts and feelings' and for her rejection of the
work of 'long-story' novelists such as Arnold Bennett, John Gals-
worthy, and H. G. Wells. Olivia deeply admired Woolf's novels for
their refusal to impose formal order on social chaos, 'as did the
Edwardian novelists,' and it is a testament to her unflinching assessment of her own skills as a writer, I think, that she never attempted to
mimic Woolf's luminous style, that she recognized her own talent as a
writer rested less in a lyrical evocation of time passing than in the sharp
delineation of a particular historical moment. For her introduction
into literature of 'qualities of subtility, descriptive beauty and almost
clairvoyant perception of mood and emotion,' Olivia offered a further
tribute to Woolf in a *Palestine Post* review of 28 September 1945.
Although later in her life Olivia was sometimes less than generous in
evaluating her female contemporaries, she admired Virginia Woolf
from the time she first read *Jacob's Room* in the mid-1920s and took
the name 'Jacob' for her pseudonymous writing of sensation serials and
linked it to her mother's maiden name to become 'Jacob Morrow.'[16]

---

[16] The adoration of Woolf tended to waver, however, as we can see from a letter
written to Francis King in 1968: Olivia's own literary recognition seemed to bring about
disillusionment with what she saw as a pampered Bloomsbury set. She inveighed against
them all—'what a vicious lot—the whole group, saying one thing to a friend's face and
another behind his back. Virginia quite the worst of them—wrecking people's relationships with venomous half-truths, jealous, and seeing rivals everywhere.' When one reads
'her cloudy, poetic prose, so full of Beauty,' she goes on to say, 'one can scarcely believe
she was what she was.' FKC/OM, HRC, 1 February 1968.

By the spring of 1945, with the Germans close to unconditional surrender in Europe, Olivia and Reggie realized they would soon return to England, but despite their longing to get away from the Middle East, they were apprehensive about going home. Olivia had written to Kay Dick back in December 1944 indicating they hoped to return at the end of April 1945, but she was worried about what they would find when they arrived: 'Everyone gives us the most desolating pictures of England so we almost feel we are setting out for Siberia.' She was anxious about their dim chances of finding somewhere to live in London, about having to stay with her parents in Portsmouth while Reggie camped out on the floors of friends' flats, and about arriving in Liverpool in a downpour of rain and icy winds, 'fighting to get one's baggage ashore, no taxis and no beds and not much food.' But, she added, she must get home since her parents had been 'completely broken' by Oliver's death; what's more, Reggie's father had died while they were in Bucharest, his two brothers had been taken prisoner in Singapore, and his mother was 'completely alone and broken-hearted.'[17] To top it off, Reggie's future was highly uncertain: having left the British Council to take the job in Palestine, he had no idea what he was going to do when he got back to England.

Before facing the family unhappiness that awaited them in England, Olivia decided to travel to Lebanon and Syria prior to leaving the Middle East. Early in May she visited Damascus, and after exploring the ancient walled city she did a fair amount of shopping—textiles, rugs, and painted glass panels that she planned to ship to London. When exactly she and Reggie would leave Jerusalem remained unclear and where they would live when they arrived in London was even murkier, but Olivia was determined to furnish her first real home with as many of the beautiful objects that were on offer to European buyers as she and Reggie could afford. From Asfar and Sarkis in Damascus, the dealers from whom Doris Duke purchased inlaid furniture and an entire historic interior from a private home that she installed in the Damascus Room of 'Shangri La,' her estate in Honolulu, Olivia purchased a particularly beautiful painted glass panel. The salesman at Asfar and Sarkis was sufficiently impressed by Olivia's taste and per-sonality, or, at least, so fulsome in his gratitude for her patronage, that

[17] OMP, UT, Series 1, Box 1, Folder 1.

in writing to confirm the shipment of the panel to the British Legation in Beirut (from where Olivia planned to have it shipped to England), he noted his 'very respectful appreciation for the company and valuable souvenir of the high culture, and the rich intelligence which I touched in your goodself.'[18] All her life, Olivia loved beautiful things, and when she and Reggie began to have some money to spend she liked nothing better than to poke around antique shops along the King's Road. A wicked bargainer, she carried home many nice pictures, beautiful rugs, and fine silver, and when she and Reggie settled into a spacious house at 26 Queen's Grove, St John's Wood, in 1951, after living in various poky London flats, the painted glass panel from Damascus became a souvenir of their time in the Middle East and a splendid decoration for their dining-room wall.

In its August 1945 issue, British *Vogue* published a brief essay by Elizabeth Bowen about the peacetime return to houses requisitioned by the Army during the war years. 'All over Europe, people are going home,' Bowen begins. 'Gates, or doors in walls, are being pushed back on their rusty hinges, paths hacked through overgrown courts or gardens.' Shutters are being taken down, fires lit, and rusty water begins to trickle out of the taps: 'As an organism, the house comes back to life slowly: like the people returning to it, it seems dazed.'[19] Houses that had to be left when war came and were thereupon occupied by unknown people will confront returning owners 'with their own complex mystery.' Neglected gardens, the smell of unfamiliar cigarettes, rings left by glasses, books displaced or upside-down—all these signs of alien occupation confront the returning owner and create dismay, until, that is, the linen cupboard is filled with freshly laundered sheets and towels, the furniture shunted back into place, and the Aga once again gives out its comforting warmth. Bowen imagines, of course, that the neglected house belongs to a privileged family and there's a note of class-tinged nostalgia in her essay that recalls Cyril Connolly's 1944 elegy for a pre-war England where village fêtes took place under striped marquees and the local gentry pronounced judgment on the best marrows and finest rose bushes.

[18] George Owayshek from Damascus, Syria to Olivia Manning, c/o YMCA Jerusalem, 17 May 1945. OMC/C, HRC.

[19] *People, Places, Things*, 131.

When Olivia arrived at Liverpool in mid-summer 1945, she entered no such romanticized house as that imagined by Elizabeth Bowen, but proceeded directly to her parents' modest villa in Portsmouth. She was, essentially, homeless. From the time she had left Laburnum Grove in the mid-1930s until her return to England, she had lived in a series of rented accommodations: London bed-sitting rooms, flats in Bucharest, Athens, Cairo, and Alexandria, and, for the two years in Jerusalem, in various houses and, finally, in the YMCA. Eager to have at last a home of her own, she anxiously awaited Reggie's arrival, scheduled for a month after her own return after his completion of wrap-up responsibilities with the Palestine Broadcasting Service. Almost the first thing she did on arrival was to send him a lengthy account of her journey. On board the troop ship crowded with returning soldiers, the civilian passengers, mostly women and children, had barely found a place to sit on deck. Frustrated by having to spend twenty-four hours at the mouth of the Mersey and then another twenty-four on board while the ship docked, Olivia, with five pieces of luggage, two coats, and a typewriter, barely wrestled herself on to the St Pancras train. Crossing London to Waterloo station was a 'desolating experience—everything looked so dingy, confined and deserted and strange.'[20]

Half a turkey

Olivia found her father irreparably shattered by his son's death: 'He has become really old—worn, pale, his eyes sunken and red-rimmed, round-shouldered, thin'; exhausted by the war and making do, her mother also seemed 'much older and her nerves are, if anything, worse.'[21] Appalled by the 'discomfort and privation' that greeted her, in particular her mother's incessant desire to talk about Oliver's death, Olivia felt she could not bear it: she recalled this time for June Braybrooke some years later, 'Sometimes I walked away, it was so painful...Perhaps it was cruel not to let her talk. One is always wishing one had been different when it is too late.' Given the fraught nature of Olivia's relationship with her mother, it is not surprising

[20] 23 July 1945, OMC/C, HRC.
[21] 23 July 1945, OMC/C, HRC.

she was unable to offer the small comfort of listening to an outpouring of grief; if, on the other hand, her father had been willing to accept her consolation, Olivia would not have walked away from him. The news of Oliver's death plunged him into months of silent mourning.[22]

Along with millions of English people, Olivia's parents had endured almost six years of grim rationing, devastating bombing, and, given their location on the south coast of England, a persistent fear of direct German invasion. Almost all the main streets of Portsmouth were covered in grass with few buildings still standing, great gaps yawned in almost every side street, and, as Olivia wrote to Reggie, 'poorer people' were feeling the desolation of deprivation of post-war life much more severely than those who 'have come home to hotels and restaurants, or to affluent country houses.' Olivia seems to have been remarkably prescient here in regard to Elizabeth Bowen's August 1945 article in *Vogue*. Ironically, post-war strictures upon the simplest of ordinary pleasures were even more severe than those imposed during the war and Olivia returned to a diet that irritated her already delicate digestive system weakened by bouts of amoebic dysentery (when she arrived in Portsmouth she weighed eighty-four pounds). Draconian food cuts had so radically reduced the already pitiful meat ration that the Sunday joint became a comical fragment of what it once was; clothing coupons were so restricted that women were constantly darning socks, mending children's knickers, and re-knitting unraveled jumpers. By the end of the war, people had become accustomed to having almost everything 'on the ration.' Starting in July 1940, sugar, butter, and bacon had required coupons; meat followed in March, and tea, margarine, and cooking fats became rationed in July of that year. During the war, bread was never rationed, but, in a move ridiculed when it was not being bemoaned by a hard-pressed populace, in 1946 Attlee's new-broom Labour government was forced to restrict the supply of bread due to shortages of flour. As Susan Cooper observes in writing about 'Snoek Piquante,' an especially nasty concoction of tarted-up canned South African fish being pushed by the Ministry of Food after the war, 'For those who remembered the years between the wars, the gradual

[22] Olivia Manning to June Braybrooke, 16 May 1970, OMC/C, HRC.

climb back to prosperity was a long dispiriting haul, echoing with pre-war memories of better days.'[23]

The dismal severity of post-war daily life led to puzzled discontent and resentment among ordinary British people, as a participant in the Mass Observation diaries collected between May 1945 and July 1948 attested: 'Edie Rutherford' (pseudonym of a Sheffield housewife) noted on 27 September 1945, 'I find folk are grumbling more now than they ever did in the war years. It is easy to see why. Whilst the war was on we realised the need for economy and going short, and we grimly did it with the belief that the end of the war would see some let-up ... As peace has so far brought us less than we had in the war, and we realise how well off USA and others are, folk are getting restive.'[24] The sight of bombed-out streets and little sign of rebuilding fed that restive resentment. As Olivia wrote to Reggie, Laburnum Grove had escaped a direct hit but German bombs had gutted the area around the Portsmouth Docks, and the brightly painted houses on the sea-front where Commander Manning had walked with his children before taking them to visit Whale Island had been demolished, as had the architectural offices where Olivia's brother had worked in the early 1930s. Essentially, Portsmouth was one big bombsite by the sea and Olivia could do little to brighten the bleak atmosphere of Laburnum Grove. Done in by wartime rules and regulations that dictated no waste of bread or fuel, no journeys to be taken unless really necessary, and no careless talk that might endanger the lives of others, her parents were a helpless mess.[25] By Christmas 1945, the national mood sank even further after a request from the Minister of Food to butchers that they spread a curtailed supply of the traditional Christmas bird by cutting it in two: 'Half a turkey,' *The Times* reported, 'will supply a good meal for most families.'[26]

---

[23] Susan Cooper, 'Snoek piquante,' Michael Sissons and Philip French (eds.), *The Age of Austerity*, 56.

[24] Simon Garfield, *Our Hidden Lives: The Remarkable Diaries of Post-War Britain*, 103.

[25] Patrick Hamilton's chilling novel, *Slaves of Solitude* (1947), grimly captures the wartime atmosphere of constant denial of even the smallest pleasures. The principal female character laments the following restrictions: 'She was not to waste bread, she was not to use unnecessary fuel, she was not to leave litter about, she was not to telephone otherwise than briefly, she was not to take the journey she was taking unless it was really necessary, she was not to keep the money she earned through taking such journeys where she could spend it, but to put it into savings, and keep putting it into savings. She was not to talk carelessly, lest she endangered the lives of others' (p. 100).

[26] *The Times*, 15 December 1945.

Resisting her parents' pleas that she and Reggie (when he got back to England) remain in Portsmouth, Olivia was determined they would live in London. Ten years earlier, it had been difficult enough to get away from provincial gloom and her mother's nagging: now, knowing the good-natured susceptibility to family blandishments that resulted from Reggie's essentially happy childhood, she took pre-emptive action and managed to rent a one-bedroom flat in Knightsbridge at £5 per week. He arrived back in England in late August, shortly after the momentous General Election in July 1945. After a generally lackluster campaign by the Conservative Party and some tactless remarks by Churchill about his Labour Party opponents—'No Socialist Government conducting the entire life and industry of the country could afford to allow free, sharp or violently-worded expression of public discontent. They would have to fall back on some form of Gestapo, no doubt very humanely directed in the first instance'[27]—by 393 votes against the Conservatives' 213, the Labour Party came into power. As Peter Hennessy observes, however, the Labour victory cannot be attributed entirely to Churchill's inflammatory rhetoric: the electorate was fatigued by war and receptive to change, and, most of all, it hoped that peace would bring social justice—housing, full employment, and social security were the matters most on people's minds.[28] Both Reggie and Olivia arrived back in England too late to vote but, had they been able to do so, almost certainly Reggie would have voted Labour given his open membership of the Communist Party, and Olivia probably Conservative given the Tory sympathies inherited from Commander Manning.

Marooned in Portsmouth and awaiting Reggie's return, Olivia kept herself occupied with book reviewing, revising her short stories, and polishing the Stanley/Emin Pasha manuscript. She escaped her parents' unhappiness by trudging for miles through Portsmouth's bombed-out streets and going through the books she had left in her Laburnum Grove bedroom when she went to London. A brief essay titled 'Old Friends' that appeared in The Palestine Post in September 1945 describes poignantly her feelings as she awaited Reggie's return. She sets the scene by locating herself propped up in bed by six pillows,

---

[27] Conservative Party Political Broadcast, 4 June 1945. Quoted in Peter Hennessy, Never Again: Britain, 1945–1951, 82.

[28] Peter Hennessy, Never Again 1945–1951, 82.

cough medicine and throat pastilles on the table beside her, the electric
fire burning full blast, and the window framing trees bent by the cold,
gray wind of an English summer (she had written to Kay Dick from
Jerusalem that she had become 'the most frail little object that curls up
at a hint of a draught'[29]). She settles down to re-acclimatize herself to
the native weather, at home 'in a badly blitzed town where all the
bookshops seem to have disappeared.'[30] Nothing for it, she says, but to
return to the books of her adolescence, still arranged in her bookcase as
she had left them ten years before, and as she takes them out and re-
reads she discovers how much she has forgotten and how much new
pleasure may be found in re-reading. If one wishes to keep any book
'as a permanent part of one's mental furniture,' then it must be read
again at least every five years. Her first choice was Wilde's *The Portrait
of Dorian Gray*, as dazzling in 1945 as it was when she devoured it as a
precocious young woman in 'the brilliant secure, well-fed, atom-
bomb-less world of the 30s.' Jane Austen, she declares, should be re-
read at least every two years, and even more frequently as one ages,
since she gives 'a truer picture of human nature than the wicked Mr.
Wilde could ever do.' Propped up by her pillows in the bedroom
where she had fled from her family to make notes about her readings in
Havelock Ellis and Sigmund Freud, and suffering from head colds as
she had twenty years before, she waited for Reggie's return and wrote
more reviews for *The Palestine Post*.

Considered together, the reviews published mainly during the last
three months of 1945 outline Olivia's assessment of the immediate
post-war literary scene. On 17 August, in her piece 'New Periodicals'
in which she delivers high praise for Cyril Connolly's *Horizon*, in a
world 'given over to destruction,' she declares, the magazine has 'held
ground for the intellectual and held it well.' Even with the appearance
of new periodicals or the revival of those put to bed during the war,
Horizon will, she predicts, remain supreme, just as, she announces,
Connolly remains 'an essayist of high order—and one of the few
reviewers whose reviews are worth preserving between stiff covers.'[31]
Olivia, though, did not share the deep despair about the cultural life of
post-war Britain that Connolly expressed in the December 1944 issue

[29] OMP, UT, Series 1, Box 1, Folder 1.
[30] 'Old friends,' *The Palestine Post*, 14 September 1945.
[31] *The Palestine Post*, 8 February 1946.

of *Horizon*; he scathingly announced that books were becoming as bad as they were ugly, that reviewing had sunk to polite blurb-quoting, and that the BBC was pumping religion and patriotism into all its programs: in sum, he concluded, 'Mediocrity triumphs.'[32] For Olivia, there was nothing mediocre about *The Windmill*: in her piece praising *Horizon*, she also congratulates Reginald Moore and 'Edward Lane' for an innovative move in publishing the first chapters of about-to-be-published novels—a clever means of whetting the appetite, she observes, and at the close of her review she makes a modest mention of her own piece about escaping Greece on the *Erebus*, 'The Last Civilian Ship,' that appeared in this same issue.'[33] In a review of Henry Green's *Loving*, she pays tribute to a novelist who may or may not have been her lover before the war; Olivia certainly boasted to Francis King about her various amorous conquests and she included Green in her list of literary lovers, although it is difficult to verify her claims beyond these confidences. In her review, she judges Green to be 'one of the few serious fiction writers at work in England today,' a novelist not to be confused, she adds, with Graham Greene (a writer to whom she never warmed) whose 'inflated reputation is beginning to show the first fine pin-pricks of critical commonsense.'[34] Although she rates *Loving* below *Caught*, Green's 1943 novel set in the throes of the Blitz, she hails it as splendidly distinct from 'dreary library novels turned out as alike as turnips,' on offer not just in the local libraries but also in the High Street booksellers such as W. H. Smith whose sales were picking up with a more robust publication of popular fiction than that which had appeared during the war.

When Reggie finally arrived in Portsmouth, he faced the pressing question of what he was going to do with himself. He felt that returning to the British Council might prove difficult and he was not even sure this was something he wished. Restless and adrift, he now joined the ranks of thousands of men returning from the war and looking for a job. Highly intelligent, cheerfully robust, and an inveterate performer, he had much to offer, but it was not until he was

---

[32] Quoted in *Under Siege*, 172.

[33] When reviewing Kay Dick's *By the Lake*, Olivia mourned the fact that *The Windmill* had recently ceased publication, a casualty of 'the present slump.' 'First novel,' *The Palestine Post*, 16 December 1949.

[34] *The Palestine Post*, 21 September 1945.

reunited with his old friend and tutor Louis MacNeice that he found the perfect job that kept him happily engaged for the next twenty-seven years. With an introduction from MacNeice to the Head of Radio Features at the BBC, Laurence Gilliam, he began his career as a producer, until, in the early 1950s, he was shifted to the Drama Department after MI5 became nosy about Reggie's membership of the Communist Party. While remaining genially tolerant of Reggie's politics, Gilliam realized that a less controversial assignment than Features would be best both for the Corporation and for Reggie. As things turned out, with his generous confidence in everyone he worked with, he was an ideal person to head up the revitalization of features and radio drama after the war.

This was a golden time for the BBC, a period in which the Director-General from 1944 to 1952, William Haley, believed that programming needed to forge a strong connection with a rapidly changing audience. The Labour government was preparing to enact a number of the prescriptions for a just post-war society that had been spelled out in the Beveridge Report of 1942—among other things, old-age pensions, a national health service 'designed to secure improvement in the physical and mental health of the people of England and Wales,' and a school-leaving age raised from fourteen to fifteen—and Haley believed broadcasting should participate in the renovation of British society by elevating public taste. Looking back on his ambitious plan to move listeners from one stratum of programming to another, he admitted that he had always believed that 'every civilized nation, culturally and educationally, is a pyramid with a lamentably broad base and a lamentably narrow tip.'[35] Convinced that this pyramid would probably remain in place, given the entrenched nature of English class divisions, he devised programs that he hoped would transcend social class and entice listeners into taking the cultural initiative by switching their wireless dials from, say, the Light to the Home Programme, and then, perhaps, ambitiously to the Third. When the Third began broadcasting on 29 September 1946, Haley promised that 'Its whole content will be directed to an audience that is not of one class, but that is perceptive and intelligent.'[36] 'B. Charles,' a participant in the Mass Observation Project, noted in his diary on 10

---

[35] Hennessy, *Never Again*, 111.
[36] Quoted in David Kynaston, *Austerity Britain*, 176.

February 1948, 'I have just listened to the Eighth Mahler symphony and enjoyed it. I consider the Third Programme one of the greatest cultural events of the century. It is, probably, right to describe it as being THE cultural event of the century. It will be a national calamity if it falls through.'[37]

The new Light Programme, which aired first on 29 July 1945, followed the wartime success of the Forces Programme by offering music, comedy shows, and serialized domestic dramas: among its offerings were *The Archers*, originally billed as 'an everyday story of country folk' and now the world's longest-running soap opera; *Housewives' Choice*, a musical request program; and *Music While You Work*, which speaks for itself. The Home Service, which began airing on the same day as the Light Programme, concentrated on news, drama, and discussion programs, whilst the Third Programme, which aired first on 29 September 1946, aimed to appeal to the 'high-brow' listener through a wide range of serious classical music and live concerts and specially commissioned plays, poetry readings, talks, and documentaries. Reggie produced drama for the Home Service and the Third Programme and supported the work of many playwrights, actors, and poets: figures such as Samuel Beckett, Harold Pinter, Joe Orton, and Dylan Thomas, whose *Under Milk Wood* was written specially for the Third, got their start with his enthusiastic encouragement. In this connection, Beryl Bainbridge, reminiscing about Reggie's BBC reputation, declared that he was 'touched with greatness . . . a man who soared far beyond' the margins of the Corporation and 'encouraged poets and playwrights others would have rejected.'[38] Walter Allen remembers being asked by Reggie, sometime in 1946, to come to the BBC and watch a play he was producing. The play was not especially interesting but its principal actor commanded attention through his sweet and resonant delivery: Dylan Thomas, who at the time, Allen recalls, 'got most of his living from radio-acting, and very impressive he was, even in the hammiest parts, just as he could make the most tawdry verse sound wonderful.'[39] Reggie and Dylan Thomas became firm friends and regular drinkers at 'The George' around the corner from the BBC.

---

[37] Simon Garfield, *Our Hidden Lives*, 489.
[38] 'My week: Beryl Bainbridge,' *The Observer*, 6 July 2008.
[39] *As I Walked Down New Grub Street*, 152.

Reggie's BBC employment provided welcome justification for leaving Portsmouth, and in early October 1945 he and Olivia moved to a rented flat at 48 Rochester Row, SW1, close to a convivial pub, 'The Cardinal.' Almost immediately, however, a physically and emotionally drained Olivia, exhausted by the war and depressed by the plight of her parents, experienced a total breakdown and was placed in a nursing home for observation. She wrote to Kay Dick and Kathleen Farrell early in January 1946 that she had 'escaped to go home for Christmas,' had refused to return, and was 'heartily sick' of doctors who seem to have decided there was nothing very seriously wrong but also want 'to go on trying to find out.'[40] Conditions in the Rochester Row flat did not help her recovery: the gas fire in the sitting room gave out, no one would come to mend it, and for weeks she and Reggie lived entirely in the one small bedroom and went out every night to escape (usually to 'The Cardinal').

Despite her fragile health and rocky state of mind, during the winter of 1945–6, Olivia continued to write for *The Palestine Post* and began submitting ideas to the BBC for adaptations of Victorian and Edwardian fiction: writing from Laburnum Grove, for example (just before she and Reggie left for London), she acknowledged receipt of an agreement to adapt Arnold Bennett's *Clayhanger* novels (four in all, published between 1910 and 1918), and in a stroke of professional independence hastened to add that in future correspondence she did not wish to be addressed as 'Mrs R. D. Smith'—although married to R. D. Smith, she assured the BBC, she retained the name of 'Olivia Manning' for professional purposes. The adaptation of *Clayhanger* was her first BBC commission, secured through her connection with Reggie, and understandably they had addressed her by her married name. She also proposed a program about Thomas More, set almost entirely in conversations with a minimum of narrative; it failed to appeal, perhaps because Olivia insisted More be presented not as a gloomy martyr, but as 'a man of humour, spirit and brilliant intellect!' But rather than being grateful for the BBC commissions (when she got them), she complained to Kay Dick and Kathleen Farrell that she was being 'harried' by the Corporation to do endless work of the same sort for them—all 'very profitable but a terrible waste of time.' However,

---

[40] OMP, UT, Series 1, Box 1, Folder 1.

in a rapid change of attitude (this time in accord with her characteristic willingness to admit pressing realities), she ended the letter with a wry acknowledgment that she simply had 'to get some money from somewhere. Reggie's salary is miserably inadequate.'[41] Seeking to supplement that miserable salary with a series of articles about war-torn Europe, Reggie took off for Paris in early 1947 and rang Olivia in February from Budapest to say that the trip had been 'wonderful': he traveled through France, Belgium, Switzerland, Yugoslavia, and Romania and then back through Vienna and Paris to London.[42]

Under the name 'Olivia Manning' (not Mrs R. D. Smith), in her book reviewing Olivia continued to offer a fascinating glimpse of the cultural and political climate in post-war England. In a November 1945 review of Storm Jameson's *The Journal of Mary Hervey Russell*, an unusual autobiographical novel that rejects 'straight autobiography' in favor of what Jameson's biographer describes as 'studies of thoughts and feelings, the projections of subjectivity, for which the historical account of her [Jameson's] life could provide the necessary supporting frames,'[43] Olivia finds particularly memorable the elegiac nature and pessimistic intimations of Jameson's book. Clearly distracted by the horrific aftermath of the atomic bomb attacks on Hiroshima on 6 August and on Nagasaki on 9 August 1945, Olivia declared that Jameson's work is not only a record of a life but of 'the emotions of a generation that has known more anxiety and suffering than any past generation': she predicts that in the immediate future—provided, that is, 'the atomic bomb permits us a future'—the world will be so 'acutely horrible' that people will look back on the time between the two world wars 'as a calm stretch between two storms.' According to Olivia, Jameson 'has seen, felt and understood' much of her own traumatic life as a woman at war, now, in post-war England, battling fears of atomic annihilation.[44]

In a November 1945 review of a collection of short stories edited by Reginald Moore and Woodrow Wyatt, Olivia does not disguise her political disdain for writers who fail to engage with the pressing social

---

[41] Olivia Manning, BBC Scriptwriter 1943–1982. BBC Written Archives, Caversham, OMP, UT, Series 1, Box 1, Folder 1.

[42] Postcard from Olivia Manning to Kay Dick from Shepherd Market. OMP, UT, Series 1, Box 1, Folder 1.

[43] Jennifer Birkett, *Margaret Storm Jameson: A Life*, 249.

[44] *The Palestine Post*, 9 November 1945.

problems of post-war Britain, to say nothing of those who devote themselves to precious social satire (she has in mind the Sitwells) and ignore such momentous events as, say, the Nuremberg Trials that commenced in late November 1945. She singles out for particular praise a story by Alun Lewis for his concern with 'the great theme' of the present historical moment: that of coming home, returning to post-war England. To Olivia's mind, Lewis, an Anglo-Welsh writer actually best known for his poetry who died in Burma in 1944, has written 'probably the most important war story' that has appeared to date, a tale of a young soldier returning to the civilian war of the Blitz to discover that his wife has been killed: 'Its simplicity does not detract from the tremendous implications of this new horror come into war.'[45] Alongside Lewis's writing, Sir Osbert Sitwell's short story 'Staggered Holiday', dealing with eccentric old ladies dithering around at the onset of the Blitz, 'seems tinny and unimportant,' and even worse is Elizabeth Bowen's short story 'Summer Night,' 'typical of the sort of washed-out prose that this writer is now producing.'[46] In a big critical about-face, however, two years later Olivia reviewed a re-issued edition of Bowen's 1932 novel *To The North* and, in remarking upon an indebtedness to Virginia Woolf, adds that in this novel 'we may also see the unusual sensitivity, perception and power of expression that has brought Miss Bowen to her position of foremost woman writer in England today.'[47] Bowen, though, could not bring herself to return the compliment: in an interview with the *New York Times* that appeared in March 1949, Olivia's name was not on the list of favorite modern writers she was asked to name.[48] Olivia ends her 1945 review of collected short stories with a devastating swipe at Elizabeth Smart's novel *By Grand Central Station I Sat Down and Wept*. Beginning by quoting the following fragment, 'A wet wing brushes away the

[45] *The Palestine Post*, 23 November 1945.

[46] Olivia's harsh judgment of Elizabeth Bowen's short fiction would, perhaps, have been revised had she read at a later date some of her fine stories about the effect of the Blitz on London—for example, 'Oh Madam,' 'In the Square,' and 'Mysterious Kor.' See *The Collected Stories of Elizabeth Bowen*.

[47] *The Palestine Post*, 28 November 1947.

[48] Bowen's list is as follows: Henry Green, Graham Greene, Mauriac, Montherlant, Sartre, Colette, Evelyn Waugh, Camus, Eudora Welty, Rosamond Lehmann, Bemelmans, I. Compton-Burnett, Faulkner, Elizabeth Taylor, Elizabeth Jenkins, E. M. Forster, Frank O'Connor, Seán Ó'Faoláin, Rumer Godden, P. H. Newby, Dorothy Parker. 'Miss Bowen on Bowen,' *New York Times*, 6 March 1949.

trembling night, and morning breathes cold analysis into my spectre-waiting mind,' she then announces, 'If you like this sort of thing, Miss Smart's prose-poem—one cannot call it a novel—will give you all you want.' In the early 1950s, Smart arrived 'blind drunk' at one of Olivia's drinks parties, collapsed on the floor, and howled for more whiskey.[49]

From November 1945 until November 1946, Olivia continued her reviewing and witnessed a year of worsening conditions on the British labor front: by mid-October 1945, over forty thousand dock workers were out on strike and six thousand troops were called in to unload food; in February 1946, British rationing was tightened to release supplies for the British Zone in Germany; and in December coal shortages led to a total shut down of cotton mills in Lancashire. This was also a year of increasing turmoil in Palestine, and it seemed to Olivia that even with the coming of the peace, wartime experiences continued to shadow her daily life. Her three years in Jerusalem were still fresh in her mind, and once she and Reggie had accommodated themselves to the inconveniences of the Rochester Row flat, she began work on a novel set in that troubled city (*School for Love*, published in 1951). During the year of post-war reviewing for *The Palestine Post* (1945–6), she had followed closely news of volatile conflict in the Middle East as details of bomb throwing in Palestine replaced accounts of V2 attacks on London in street-corner conversation.

Throughout the war, Palestine had certainly presented a challenge to the British government, whether in terms of Zionist demands that more Jewish immigrants than the number specified in the White Paper of 1939 be allowed to enter the British controlled territory or whether in terms of Arab resistance to any further incursion into their lands by Jewish refugees. But after the war the situation presented an even stiffer challenge to the British. On 14 November 1945 British troops in Tel Aviv had engaged in a nightlong battle with Jewish fighters; fifty civilians, ten Palestinian police officers, and five British soldiers were seriously injured. Government offices in the Allenby Road were attacked by bombs and flame-throwers and the offices of *The Palestine Post* where Olivia had often worked were destroyed. The British authorities imposed curfews in Jerusalem, Tel Aviv, and Jaffa, and

---

[49] To June Braybooke, 16 July 1976. In this letter Olivia reminisces about her early days in St John's Wood.

the Zionist leader David Ben-Gurion voiced 'disappointment and shock' at the actions of a Labour government in continuing the policy of the White Paper of 1939 that limited Jewish immigration to Palestine since it had previously 'unreservedly condemned the White Paper as a breach of faith.'[50] On 22 July 1946 Jewish terrorists blew up the King David Hotel (across from the Jerusalem YMCA where Olivia and Reggie had lived for many months) and on 12 July 1947 two British sergeants were kidnapped by Jewish terrorists and found hanged at the end of that month. On 14 May 1948 the British Mandate ended in Palestine and Chaim Weizmann was named the first President of Israel. Olivia was both relieved by an end to violence and saddened by what had happened to Jerusalem, the city where she had initially been very happy after leaving Egypt and where she had mourned the loss of her child.

As Reggie settled into his exciting new job at the BBC and Olivia accustomed herself to living in a bombed-out London and to scrounging around for anything off the ration, she continued to propose projects for serialization to the BBC, writing to Felix Fenton in the Drama Department that since *Clayhanger* seemed to have been a success, would it not be a good idea to serialize *The Idiot*, and 'If you think Doestoievsky [*sic*] more than the British public could take, would you be interested in *Vanity Fair*?'[51] When the BBC declined, Olivia pressed on with her reviewing, never abandoning her commitment to writing despite the dismal rationing, lack of clothing coupons, and difficulty of finding a nice house to rent. Keenly interested in the struggles of novelists and poets in post-war London, she assessed the work that had appeared in *New Writing* over the last few years and concluded that the 'devastation of six years of war is still as clearly marked among our writers as our townscape': proclaiming the achievement of established figures such as Louis MacNeice as so far beyond 'the promises of the postwar men,' she wonders if the war has actually wiped out a younger generation of poets. The most woeful

---

[50] *The Times*, 15 November 1945. On 3 December 1946, Edie Rutherford, one of the participants in the Mass Observation Project, noted in her diary, 'So Monty leaves Palestine. I had hoped he'd stay a bit and do something definite, as it seems we just go on and on there without doing a thing to get matters straight.' Simon Garfield, *Our Hidden Lives*, 321.

[51] Olivia Manning, BBC Scriptwriter, 1943–1982. BBC Written Archives, Caversham.

representative of this 'younger generation' is her old Cairo nemesis Lawrence Durrell. His two poems in the collection under review 'scarcely merit their titles.'[52]

Early in January 1946, at a time when she was contemplating possible publication of her short stories and when recurrent paper shortages still led publishers to favor narrative concision over novelistic length, Olivia reviewed a collection by V. S. Pritchett, *It May Never Happen*. She writes that Pritchett, always memorable, more than any other English short story writer, 'understands as Chekov did the stuff of which a short story is made.' Writing with a sensitive acuteness about the human situation 'which would be significant in any age,' Pritchett possesses a 'brilliance unsurpassed by any other living writer.'[53] Full of admiration, then, for Pritchett and having been encouraged by a friend, Jim Phelan, to approach William Heinemann with a book of short stories, Olivia set to work revising those she had already written or published and mulling over some fresh ideas. Her collection, *Growing Up*, was published by Heinemann in 1948 and contained four written before the war, one during the war, and the final three after she returned to England. Whether she regarded them as approaching Pritchett in possessing unsurpassed brilliance is uncertain, but she knew, at least, that some were artistically successful depictions of childhood unhappiness. The three post-war stories are notably different from each other: 'A Spot of Leave' draws upon Olivia's time in Cairo and tells a familiar wartime tale of unconsummated flirtation between an English officer and the Greek wife of an English banker; 'The Man Who Stole a Tiger' relates the experience of a working-class former Borstal boy who, when rescued from a torpedoed British ship, steals a tiger from a Jerusalem zoo and decides to free the animal. The narrator of the story, a prison chaplain, listens amazed to the tale of how the boy steals a lorry, a typewriter to write fake passes, and tins of bully beef for the tiger, and proceeds to drive down through the Sudan to the Congo, where he releases the animal: at this point in the story the narrator interrupts the boy to tell him that there are no tigers in Africa and that he has condemned the animal to a life of solitude.[54]

---

[52] *The Palestine Post*, 8 November 1946.

[53] *The Palestine Post*, 11 January 1946.

[54] Tony Richardson, the film and theater producer and Olivia's lodger in the 1960s, adapted and produced a televised version of the story that was aired on the BBC in 1954.

The final story in the collection, 'Twilight of the Gods,' written in London in 1946, is in many ways the most arresting of the eight for its delineation of post-war austerity. The principal character, Elizabeth Jackson, desperate to escape the dreariness of post-war London, goes on holiday to Dublin where she gazes astonished at the food in the shops—'at hams, tongues, bacon, sausages, baskets of eggs and bottles of whisky.'[55] Arriving at her boarding-house, she thinks to herself that in England 'we're all becoming invalids. We're all suffering from obsessional neurosis. We're all persecuted because we've come down in the world' (p. 143). On a whim she decides to visit an old friend from pre-war bed-sitting room days, now a raddled peroxide blonde pathetically attached to a boozy old actor. After witnessing half an hour of their abusive exchanges, Elizabeth retreats to her boarding-house room, 'thankful to have a refuge' (p. 159). Investing this brief narrative with symptoms of a national malaise such as exhaustion, suspicion, and resentment, Olivia implicitly gives thanks for the 'refuge' she has found in London—with Reggie, with work, and away from her parents. When *Growing Up* was published, she was also grateful for the *TLS* review that praised the stories as 'distinguished for both their clarity and their good writing,' for their sharp dialogue and excellent psychological analysis, even if she wasn't too happy with the remark that they disclosed a certain 'hardness and intellectual inhumanity.'[56]

Frozen Britain, balmy Ireland

Olivia Manning worked on revising the eight stories for *Growing Up* during one of the worst winters ever recorded in British meteorological history. By now she and Reggie had moved to 50a Shepherd Market, W1, and judging from her letters to Kay Dick, their new flat provided little relief from the miserable weather: the difficulties of getting gas and electricity connected, the irregular appearances of house-painters, and the place being 'indescribably dirty and broken up' left them feeling cold, irritated, and wondering whether it might not have been better to remain in Palestine.[57] But Shepherd Market

---

[55] *Growing Up*, 141.
[56] 'Collected short stories,' *TLS*, 1 May 1948.
[57] Undated letter from Olivia Manning to Kay Dick from 50 Shepherd Market, Curzon St., W1, OMP, UT, Series 1, Box 1, Folder 1.

was a raffish area well stocked with convivial pubs (which suited
Reggie) and notorious for housing up-market prostitutes (which
Olivia found fascinating) and they tried to make the best of it.
Conditions worsened, however, in mid-January 1947 when icy
winds from the east ushered in snowstorms; by the end of the month
virtually the whole of the British Isles was covered in white. The bitter
wind blew for the entire month of February without cessation and the
Kew Observatory recorded no sunshine at all from the second to the
twenty-second. The Thames iced over, coal was frozen at the pits, fuel
boats bound for London were icebound in the north-east ports, and
bitterly cold Londoners scrabbled for fuel in local coal yards. As Peter
Hennessy notes, 'Big Ben, the sound of the nation throughout the war
as it "bonged" listeners into the *Nine O'Clock News* on the Home
Service, was silenced, its mechanics frozen solid.'[58] It was not until
the second week of March that the great thaw began, setting off
record-breaking spring floods, although there was no cessation of the
intermittent electricity cuts that the government had imposed
throughout the first three freezing months of 1947: people hoarded
candles and oil lamps, and huddled in their kitchens wrapped in over-
coats, scarves, and blankets. 'The news grows worse, and the
re-imposition of the blackout is the final blow. We seem infinitely
worse off than at any time during war,' wrote George Taylor in his
Mass Observation diary, and Maggie Joy Blunt, another participant,
noted that there was 'wartime gloom on every face.'[59] On 2 April, she
wrote despairingly, 'The battle against the cold this long winter, the
continual Government crises and blunders, the cold, wet, delayed
spring and everlasting austerity has exhausted us all to the bone. Our
nerves are on edge, our anxieties and depressions enormous.'[60] It
hardly seems plausible that the government could have risked worsening the domestic mood with further restrictions but it did: on 22
January the meat ration was reduced, coal and gas fires were
banned until the autumn, the petrol ration for pleasure motoring was
eliminated, the bacon ration was halved on 19 October, and on 5
November potatoes, the staple of working-class diets for generations,

[58] Hennessy, *Never Again*, 282.
[59] Garfield, *Our Hidden Lives*, 352.
[60] *Our Hidden Lives*, 374.

went on the ration. It was not until 25 July 1948 that bread rationing was abolished.

While Olivia and Reggie shivered in Shepherd Market, Reggie became the subject of inquiry by MI5 by virtue of his open membership of the Communist Party: starting in October 1947, their telephone number—Grosvenor 2714—was regularly tapped, the request for telephone checking having been submitted to the appropriate authorities on 30 September with a note that Reggie's activities had become suspicious: 'from secret sources . . . He is in touch with a number of active communists and is apparently hoping to organize a small communist study group.'[61] A memorandum dated 17 November 1947 indicates that Reggie was 'a very active' member of the Communist Party, that his current project as a features assistant at the BBC was a program titled *Youth Trial*, and that he hoped 'to become a member of the National Cultural Committee of the C.P.' The memorandum concludes with the observation, 'His wife is a writer of some distinction under the name of Olivia MANNING; she does not appear to be a Party member.' Had she read this document at the time Olivia would have been delighted to find herself described as possessing 'some distinction.' Both she and Reggie were well aware of the surveillance and regularly joked about it when on the phone with friends, wishing both to advertise their awareness and to ridicule the whole business.

Depressing as the bitter cold, the fuel cuts, and the wartime gloom on every face might have appeared to her during the winter of 1947, Olivia never stopped working, even if she sat at her typewriter wearing several jumpers and swathed in a woolly scarf. She cut back on her book reviewing, finished *The Remarkable Expedition*, and set to work on *Artist Among the Missing*, both published by William Heinemann, the former in 1947 and the latter in 1949. But when some negative reviews of the novel came in, she turned her disappointment upon her publishers and, feeling that they patronized her work and failed to promote her emerging visibility, she griped to her friends about

---

[61] The National Archives KV2/2533. In reporting details of how MI5 kept watch over Reggie and Olivia, *The Times* mistakenly stated that 'secretly' Reggie was part of a Communist cell within the BBC, having been recruited into the party in 1938 by Anthony Blunt, later exposed as a Soviet spy. From his Birmingham University days, Reggie's membership in the party had been widely known, hardly secret. See *The Times*, 3 March 2007.

Heinemann. John St John, in his history of the house, recalls, 'From the outset Olivia Manning was clearly very competent but it took some time before it was realized that the firm had acquired a major talent.'[62] So, discouraged by Heinemann's neglect (imagined or not), in spring 1948, Olivia decided to travel to Ireland a year before Eire declared itself a republic and left the Commonwealth. She was becoming increasingly pessimistic about almost everything, as Stevie Smith indicated in a letter to Kay Dick written in March 1948: 'I have just lunched with Olivia who gives such a gloomy reading of the *News* that I feel I must sell all my investments and retire to the most outer of the Hebrides clad in pure wool combinations ("wool will be impossible to get").'[63] No longer the vibrant companion with whom she had explored London before the war, to Stevie Olivia now seemed almost pathologically depressed by the gloom and deprivation of post-war British society as she dwelt at length on a struggling economy being kept afloat with American loans, the dispiriting business of clothes-rationing, and the grimness of bomb-ravaged London streets.

Armed with a contract from Evans Brothers, publishers known for their textbooks, children's literature, and travel books, Olivia hoped for a pick-me-up in a journey to Ireland. The result was *The Dreaming Shore* (the title evokes Yeats's poem 'His Dream'),[64] dedicated to her mother and organized as a travel diary with potted histories of notable places visited along the way. At times, the book reads remarkably like unedited journal entries made at the end of the day (which was very often the case), but at others the writing pays heartfelt tribute to Irish resistance to English oppression and to the Irish landscape: for example, in a passage shaped by the feeling for color and form Olivia developed as a student at the Municipal Art School in Portsmouth, she writes about County Donegal on one of 'those exquisitely still, mild days that are so becoming to Ireland. The hills were dark blue but with a grape-bloom on them that gave them a tinge of violet. The colour

---

[62] *William Heinemann: A Century of Publishing 1890–1990*, 344.
[63] Stevie Smith to Kay Dick, 3 March 1948, Kay Dick Collection/Washington University Libraries.
[64] The first stanza of 'His dream' reads:
I swayed upon the gaudy stern
The butt-end of a steering oar,
And saw wherever I could turn,
A crowd upon the shore.

varied from hill to hill and on the nearest it was as richly deep as the blue
of the sea. A cloud, very white in contrast, had drifted down and lay like
a fleece around the peak.'[65] On a more prosaic level, the book also
attempts some comic relief with stories about the arrival of a new bacon-
slicer constituting the principal entertainment in many small villages.

Since her travels to Ireland with Hamish Miles in the mid-1930s,
and despite the critique of political insurgency expressed in *The Wind
Changes*, Olivia had long admired the Irish people for what she saw as a
brave refusal to bemoan their subjugated condition. Wondering how it
is that during 'centuries of injustice and oppression, when the qualities
of enterprise and efficiency were being systematically destroyed in
them by the invaders, the Irish, instead of developing that whining
self-pity and bullying rudeness characteristic of oppressed peoples,
preserved in themselves the manners of natural aristocrats,' she attributes this feeling and behavior to an innate self-esteem.[66] Particularly
fascinated by the behavior of English visitors, 'the taciturnity of years
covering them like an encrustation,' she notes how their traditional
reserve dissolves in the presence of gregarious Irish hosts—here they
are, she says, with 'no ration books, no queues, nothing to worry
about, all the food they can eat,' in some ways behaving very much like
herself, liberated from the grim bombed-out London landscape and the
grim tired faces of a worn-out population.[67] Always alert to nuances of
social class, she dismisses very handily two women dressed dowdily in
tweeds; 'giving off a manner of calculated aloofness, and speaking with
an English accent,' they represent the snobbish Irish 'gentry' whom she
satirized in some of the short stories published in *Growing Up*.

Despite the bittersweet pleasure of a return to Ireland and the
chance to eat 'off the ration,' Olivia found her advance woefully
inadequate and the actual writing of *The Dreaming Shore* a dreadful
chore. In an letter to Stevie Smith written from Hanratty's Hotel in
Limerick on 18 May 1948, which among other things confirms a
continuation of their friendship in the immediately post-war years,
Olivia begins by saying, 'Stevie darling, thinking nostalgically of
England, home and beauty, I decided to write to you.' What she
writes about is a weariness of traveling around in a heat wave sporting

[65] *The Dreaming Shore*, 65.
[66] *The Dreaming Shore*, 53.
[67] *The Dreaming Shore*, 99.

a thick tweed suit, heavy brogues, and two woolen jumpers—not, she adds, that she would want to buy any of the 'dowdy' clothes on offer in the Irish shops; she also complains that she has already spent much more than the advance and that she still had 'to write the bloody book before I get the other half of the advance. No more commissions, never again. I simply hate writing to order and as to travelling to order—God save me from it!'[68] She signs off with a note that she can get no news from Reggie: 'He has sent two post-cards of the vaguest scribbles—typical, of course.'

In June 1949, still struggling with what she called her 'awful Irish book,' Olivia felt so bored with it she believed it would never get finished. For the most part, her boredom infects the narrative, although she does liven things up with a fascinating anecdote about a white flannel bush jacket that had belonged to her brother and that she had taken away with her when she left Portsmouth to return to London after the war. Now so shrunk from frequent dry cleaning that it fits her perfectly, she treasures it as a memento of her brother— besides which it is very warm. She wears it to read in bed, both at home and here in Ireland. One day she leaves it in a café in Letter-kenny, County Donegal, and when she returns to retrieve it, it is missing: the old woman who runs the café suggests that one of the girls who works there must have purloined it to wear to a local dance— Olivia departs feeling 'wretched' that people could be so poor that 'my old jacket could seem to them finery for a dance.'[69] When she returns to Letterkenny on her way home to catch the ferry, her jacket is waiting for her. Here in Donegal, she writes, are people of the purest Gaelic blood with ancient qualities of simplicity, chivalry, and uncor-rupted honesty. Olivia may have dedicated the book to her mother and she may have drawn the endpapers showing a map of Ireland without frontiers, but its celebration of Irish history, resilience, wit, and decency really pays tribute to the Ireland Olivia visited in the mid-1930s with Hamish Miles, not to the stony landscape of Bangor and the stony heart of her mother.[70]

[68] Olivia Manning to Stevie Smith, 18 May 1948, SSP, UT.

[69] *The Dreaming Shore*, 193.

[70] In general, *The Dreaming Shore* was not well reviewed on the grounds that it trod already well-covered territory and was little more than the usual travel diary livened up here and there with local anecdote. The *TLS* reviewer deemed it 'a pleasant if superficial addition to the unending catalogue of Irish travel-books,' 25 August 1950. Louis

After the abundance of Irish butter in contrast to a skimpy two ounces per week and after a balmy Irish summer, it was a shock to return to the English autumn. London's notorious smog—a polluting, yellow fog—often made it impossible to see the next lamppost even in daylight, and Olivia, as was everyone, was depressed by the sight of people with scarves over their faces, groping and choking their way down the street. Olivia wrote to Kay Dick from Shepherd Market, 'It is very gloomy coming back to England nowadays. I felt so well and energetic in Ireland because I was properly fed. I expect you felt the same. Here I get more and more tired and oppressed by household difficulties. It makes writing almost impossible.'[71] But writing was never entirely impossible for Olivia and she soon came up with the idea of dramatizing eighteenth-century novels for the BBC and asked whether they might consider either Fanny Burney's *Evelina* or *Camilla* for the Sunday evening serial. She promises to do a 'good job' and her correspondence indicates that she was trying hard to establish herself as a working writer in London, if only for the moment as a scriptwriter for the BBC and even if they said no to the eighteenth century. But Olivia was also entering what she described to her friend Rupert Croft-Cooke as 'a dismal non-creative period,' depressed by a political situation 'so desolating that one has no sense of the future at all.' International developments were certainly pretty grim: in June 1948, the Soviets had instituted the Berlin Blockade; in September 1949 they tested an atomic bomb and Mao proclaimed a People's Republic of China; and North Korean troops invaded South Korea in June 1950. As a result of the General Election held in February 1950, Attlee's Labour government remained in power but with a very slim majority: Labour 315 seats, Conservatives 298; Liberals 9. By now, she and Reggie had moved out of their flat in Shepherd Market to slightly larger quarters at number 101 Baker Street, where she acquired the first of her Siamese cats; the flat was a definite improvement, but, as she

---

MacNeice did his best to be kind in a review for *The Observer* by noting that 'Miss Manning has a mind with fingertips' and that she was 'intelligent and sensitive.' But the book remains 'second-best... brittle and bitty' and not representative of her best writing, 17 September 1950.

[71] Olivia Manning to Kay Dick, OMP, UT, Series 1, Box 1, Folder 1. Stef Pixner, one of the contributors to Liz Heron, *Truth, Dare, or Promise: Girls Growing Up in the Fifties*, declared that the smog 'makes you feel trapped and closed in and think of the nineteenth century when the streets were hardly lit at all.' See 'The oyster and the shadow,' 92.

wrote to Rupert Croft-Cooke, the previous summer she had begun to feel claustrophobic and lonely: with Reggie out every Saturday and Sunday playing cricket, she had been alone from morning to night 'going through a bad non-writing spell' and feeling suicidal.[72]

And yet at the time she indicated she was feeling suicidal and unable to work, she was actually finishing *School for Love*, a novel set in Jerusalem in which she managed to touch upon the death of her unborn child. Also mulling over new projects, she wrote to Laurence Gilliam, Reggie's boss and Head of Features at the BBC, that Arthur Koestler, whom she had first met in Jerusalem in early 1945 when he was there on a freelance assignment from *The Times*, had suggested she write the story of the *Struma*, the ship that had been chartered to carry Jewish refugees from Romania to Palestine early in 1942. On 23 February, its engine inoperable, the ship was towed from Istanbul out to the Black Sea, where it was left adrift. Within hours, it was torpedoed and sunk by a Soviet submarine and seven hundred and sixty-seven Romanian Jewish refugees bound for Haifa perished: there was a sole survivor, a fifteen-year-old boy.[73] In a detailed letter to Gilliam, she recounts her research at the Jewish Agency, her accumulation of official documents and letters, and ends by saying that the story is 'dramatic, heartbreaking and terrible . . . a pretty fair example of man's inhumanity to man.' Gilliam agreed wholeheartedly but turned it down as far 'too horrific' for a BBC listenership.[74] Determined, one day, to write about the *Struma*, Olivia put the project aside and accommodated herself to the many alterations in social and cultural life that occurred in the late 1940s and early 1950s.

In June 1948, the *Empire Windrush* arrived at Tilbury with some four hundred and ninety-two male Jamaican immigrants on board, an event that signaled the beginning of a transformation of British life through the wide settlement of immigrants from the West Indies and from India and Pakistan: as Mike Phillips and Trevor Phillips note, 'the *Windrush* sailed through a gateway in history, on the other side of which was the end of Empire and a wholesale reassessment of what it

[72] Olivia Manning to Rupert Croft-Cooke, 18 December 1950. OMC/C, HRC.

[73] Olivia eventually wrote about this episode for the *Observer Magazine* in March 1970. I discuss her article in Chapter 10.

[74] Olivia Manning to Laurence Gilliam, BBC Scriptwriter 1943–1982, BBC Written Archives, Caversham.

meant to be British.'[75] In 1949, Christian Dior in Paris unveiled 'The New Look,' an intensely feminized mode of dressing that emphasized the waist and featured full skirts whose yards and yards of material stunned British women accustomed to six years of drab dressing. And in 1951 the Festival of Britain opened on the South Bank of the Thames, a combination of trade show and fun fair designed to broadcast to the world that post-war Britain was not only on the mend but striding forward into a peaceful and productive future. Olivia Manning published *School for Love* in 1951 and *A Different Face* in 1953 and between those years truly began to resettle herself into British life and to become noticed in the literary marketplace as an accomplished post-war novelist. In writing *School for Love*, she also came to terms with what happened in Jerusalem in July 1944.

[75] *Windrush: The Irresistible Rise of Multi-Racial Britain*, 6.

7

Writing in Austerity

'I am beginning to wonder if I can write novels at all. Short stories, or descriptive pieces, yes—but the novel with a sound plot etc., I don't know. Reggie says this is the result of living such a bitty life at present and somewhere when we are settled again I will feel differently.'

Olivia Manning to Kathleen Farrell, 19 December 1944.

Making do

In 1950, feeling more settled into post-war society some six years after writing to Kathleen Farrell in 1944 about her 'bitty life,' Olivia Manning could feel differently about her work. As she had told Kay Dick in 1947, notices of *The Remarkable Expedition* had been 'plentiful and good,' with the exception of 'a very smartie review in last week's N.S. & N. [*The New Statesman and Nation*[1]] which you will probably see was signed Edward Beaver.' Olivia was pretty sure that 'Edward Beaver' was Graham Greene since she had heard 'he had it in for me for my review of his stories in "The Spectator" but I did not think he would use a pseudonym. He is, of course, a notoriously weak and rather mean-spirited character.'[2] In her withering *Spectator* review, Olivia had described Greene as 'an established writer who knows he can sell anything he writes,' a novelist who had made his reputation 'by adding to crime and adventure stories the spice of high purpose,'

---

[1] Founded as a socialist journal in 1933, *The New Statesman* acquired *The Nation* in 1931, and in 1957 reverted to being simply *The New Statesman*.
[2] Olivia Manning to Kay Dick, 11 November 1947, OMP, UT.

someone who goes in for intellectual camouflage to 'stifle the creak of his invention.'[3]

In *his* review, Greene (or Edward Beaver) admits Olivia has told the story of Stanley and Emin Pasha 'coolly, collectedly, and more or less correctly,' but then charges her with ignoring the atrocities perpetrated by the abandoned Rear Column on some of its members and its bearers: she has 'tidied up the story, but at the cost of the darker shades'—where are details of the rumored cannibalism, the hysterical sadism, the brutal floggings?[4] Olivia, however, did not let this bother her, and by the late 1940s, with Reggie off at the BBC during the day, she was happily settled into a writing life in the Baker Street flat, Graham Greene with his literary pretensions dispatched to creaky invention. Her first and last stab at travel narrative out of the way, she relished getting back to fiction and began accustoming herself, along with almost everyone else in England, to a make-do-and-mend society. Rather like one of the housewives who participated in the Mass Observation project and declared in the late 1940s that 'making-do' was now just a 'tiresome necessity' rather than a national duty, she coped as best she could, delighted to be back in London.[5]

Despite the facts that rationing for many essential food items remained in effect, that housing was still a desperate need for many bombed-out citizens (particularly in London), and that most English people presented the same drab, down-at-heel appearance as they had during the war,[6] the popular mood was not quite as grim as it had been in the dreadful winter of 1947. To be sure, those men who for reasons mostly to do with age and medical fitness had contributed to the war effort through government work or filling the ranks of the Home Guard were still wearing the same shiny suits that had taken them through the war, and women were still dressed in the short skirts, square jackets, and heavy shoes that had served them well, if not fashionably, from 1939 to 1945. A 'New Look' concocted in Paris by Christian Dior, however, appeared in the High Street shops and it was quickly embraced by fashion-starved women like Olivia, who happily

---

[3] Olivia Manning, 'Short stories,' *The Spectator*, 8 August 1947.

[4] Edward Beaver, 'The filibuster,' *The New Statesman and Nation*, 18 October 1947.

[5] David Kynaston, *Austerity Britain*, 297.

[6] As David Kynaston notes, approximately three-quarters of a million British houses were destroyed or severely damaged during the war, *Austerity Britain*, 20.

ignored the stern warning about full skirts billowing over padded hips expressed by Mrs Mabel Ridealgh MP in the *Daily Herald* on 22 February 1949: she thundered that the 'New Look' was an 'utterly ridiculous, stupidly exaggerated waste of material and manpower, foisted on the average woman to the detriment of other, more normal clothing.'[7] But the 'average woman' was sick and tired of 'normal clothing' and was eager to buy a 'Ballerina' coat advertised by Richards Shops that boasted a Victorian bodice accentuating the waist and a skirt that came almost to the ankles. This 'Ballerina' number required fifteen coupons.[8] What's more, flashily dressed 'spivs,' tricked out in colorful striped suits with exaggerated shoulders, were livening up the drab streets with their swaggering braggadocio.[9]

By 1950, London itself did not look quite as grim as it had in early 1947 when Christopher Isherwood, freshly arrived from America, had been appalled by peeling house fronts in the most fashionable squares and crescents, and by the sight of once stylish restaurants reduced to drabness and squalor: 'London remembered the past and was ashamed of its present appearance. Several Londoners I talked to at that time believed it would never recover. "This is a dying city," one of them told me.'[10] London, of course, did not die, those squares gradually got a fresh coat of paint, and the restaurants recovered some of their pre-war glory. And by 1950 London was not as grim as it had seemed to Doris Lessing when she had arrived from Rhodesia in the early summer of 1949: 'No cafés. No good restaurants. Clothes were still "austerity" from the war, dismal and ugly. Everyone was indoors by ten, and the streets were empty.... The war still lingered, not only in the bombed places but in people's minds and behaviour.'[11] One year later, Londoners were going out in the evening to restaurants, to cinemas, and to the theater—and staying out well beyond 10 p.m. Back in 1945, the theatrical producer Basil Dean had hailed with patriotic fanfare the reopening of the Royal Opera House: the British theater would soon be restored to its pre-war glory, he declared, and the Opera House itself was 'a cultural centre for the British

---

[7] Pearson Phillips, 'The New Look,' Michael Sissons and Philip French (eds.), *Age of Austerity*, 148.

[8] Clothes rationing did not end completely until late 1949.

[9] See David Hughes, 'The spivs,' Sissons and French (eds.), *Age of Austerity*, 93.

[10] Quoted in Kynaston, *Austerity Britain*, 191.

[11] *Walking in the Shade*, 122.

Empire:...a noble conception, an Empire and Commonwealth memorial worthy of the achievements of the recent struggle, and of lasting benefit to the British race.'[12] Six years later, London theater did indeed display brilliant signs of a post-war recovery: in 1951, one could see Alec Guinness in *Hamlet*, Laurence Olivier and Vivien Leigh in *Antony and Cleopatra* and *Caesar and Cleopatra* on alternate nights, Celia Johnson and Ralph Richardson in *Three Sisters*, and John Gielgud and Flora Robson in *The Winter's Tale*.

On the food front, rationing eased a little and things were about to look up in the sophisticated English kitchen with the publication of Elizabeth David's *Mediterranean Food* (1950), even if sausages were still more full of bread than pork and the local Kardomah café was about as fancy a place as one could find a cup of not very good coffee.[13] Eating in England, sad to say, compared miserably with eating in America. A bountiful American table at Thanksgiving set alongside an English Christmas dinner in the late 1940s was a pretty dispiriting sight, as Olivia noted in a review of an American novel in *The Spectator* in 1948: the English reader, 'with his courageous poverty' and 'seven austerity Christmas dinners in mind,' will find it difficult to sympathize with the plight of the novel's characters as they sit down to a twenty-pound turkey stuffed with oysters, two kinds of potatoes, asparagus in Dutch sauce, and pumpkin pie.[14] Although never much of a cook, Olivia had been exposed to stylish cuisine from the time of her Soho dining with Hamish Miles in the late 1930s, and the cafés of Bucharest and Athens had continued her education in sophisticated eating. She liked going to restaurants and, despite suffering intermittent bouts of dysentery when in the Middle East and being forced at times to eat mysterious intestines when in Athens, she developed a liking for Mediterranean food. Back in London, she enjoyed sailing out to Marylebone High Street from the Baker Street flat, string-bag in hand, to stock up on the olive oils and French cheeses that were beginning to make an appearance in London grocery shop windows. Buoyed by a celebratory post-war climate, she and Reggie initiated what was to become

---

[12] Quoted in Dan Rebellato, *1956 And All That*, 60.

[13] Overcoming a British resistance to such things as rice, olive oil, and garlic Elizabeth David continued her introduction to Continental cooking for the English middle classes with the publication of *French Country Cooking* in 1951 and *Italian Food* in 1954.

[14] Olivia Manning, 'Fiction,' *The Spectator*, 27 August 1948.

a long-standing tradition in their household: lively drinks parties with plenty of wine and cheese and a crowd of BBC types, journalists, actors, and writers. It felt good no longer to go without.

Going without, a common trope of daily life in wartime Britain, figures prominently in the two novels that Olivia published in the early 1950s: *School for Love* and *A Different Face*. In the former, she draws upon her years in Jerusalem to narrate the story of an orphaned sixteen-year-old boy, Felix Latimer, and his residence as a lodger in the house of a distant relative, Miss Bohun. Awaiting passage to England in the frantic atmosphere of Jerusalem right at the end of the war, he is forced to go without on several fronts: his father has been killed in Baghdad and his mother has died of typhoid; Miss Bohun keeps her house by Herod's Gate miserably cold in the chilly Jerusalem winter, and she serves the most frugal of meals (a small grilled sardine is the fanciest dish on offer). Hugo Fletcher, the protagonist of *A Different Face*, Olivia's second novel of the early 1950s, seems to have gone without for most of his life. The son of a cheese-paring and financially improvident naval officer who conspicuously lacks the generous bon-homie of Olivia's beloved father, he has suffered a grim and nasty childhood in Coldmouth (a barely disguised Portsmouth whose deso-lation Olivia describes with bitter distaste). His sole consolation has been the adoration of his pitiable, dim-witted mother. After a war spent teaching secondary school students in Upper Egypt, he returns to England to become the co-proprietor of a small prep school mired in serious financial difficulty. Like poor Felix in *School for Love*, Hugo Fletcher spends a lot of time trying to keep warm and when not doing that masochistically rehearsing his miserable past as a resentful social misfit in a world of middle-class smugness and petty snobbery.

In the months between publishing these two novels of austerity, isolation, and eventual violence (one ends in the death of an unborn child and the other in the death of a homeless homosexual), Olivia continued to propose possible serializations to the BBC and to review her position as a self-supporting woman writer at a historical moment when the more conservative elements in society aimed at restoring women to domesticity. During the years that have since become known as the Age of Austerity (roughly from the late 1940s to the early 1950s) Olivia not only traced physical and emotional austerity as a determinant of her characters' existence in *School for Love* and *A Different Face*, she also sought recognition in a literary culture invigorated by a resumption of plentiful publication and robust read-ership. But as a woman long accustomed to earning a living, she had returned to a society that popularly promoted a return of women to the kitchen, a place where she had never spent much time in the first place. Yet it was also a society that in its implementation of the Welfare State paradoxically opened up many opportunities for women in positions of political power, however local and however restricted to the traditionally female roles such as social workers, care-givers, or leaders in voluntary organizations.[15] A firm believer in equality between the sexes yet refusing the label of feminist in this conflicted cultural climate, Olivia maintained her firm belief in the importance of forging a strong identity for professional women.

As a working woman writer without children, in many ways, of course, Olivia obviously had little interest in Welfare State employ-ment and consequently had a small stake in the debate about woman's role in society that was re-introduced at the end of World War II, yet her fiction in the 1950s often engages obliquely in the fraught debate about woman's place in post-war Britain. And this debate was re-introduced, I emphasize, because what was known as the Woman Question in the nineteenth century merely got sidelined after 1939 by the exigencies of war. In surveying the woman's movement from Victoria to Elizabeth II, Vera Brittain argues that the Welfare State brought about an ambiguous transformation of the Woman Question: the roles traditionally associated with women such as moral gover-nance and child-rearing were given fresh means of expression in the realization of many recommendations contained in the Beveridge Report of 1942.[16] In other words, woman's role remained essentially

---

[15] In assessing the contribution of women workers to the origins of the Welfare State, Seth Koven points out that 'While British historians have exhaustively argued the causes and nature of the so-called Victorian Revolution in Government, these same scholars have been much less attentive to the roles women played as policy makers, care providers, and clients in the construction of British welfare policies and programs . . . These studies have failed to look closely at those places where women were most influential: in their localities as elected and appointed officials and as leaders and rank-and-file members of voluntary societies that addressed every conceivable social problem.' 'Borderlands: Women, voluntary action, and child welfare in Britain, 1840–1914,' 94–5. Pat Thane similarly argues that women in local government and voluntary organizations made a positive contribution to state formation. See 'Women in the British Labour Party and the construction of state welfare, 1906–1939,' 372.

[16] See *Lady into Woman*, 29.

unchanged, although the venues of its enactment shifted somewhat from the private to the public sphere. Many others argued that the freedom afforded women during the war—to work in the factories, farm the land, manage governmental departments—would (and must) eventually further political and social equality between the sexes.

During the war, as regularly and as often as she could, and frequently at the cost of earning a reputation of being unpleasantly standoffish, Olivia had maintained a disciplined working schedule, whether developing short stories, mulling over research for the Stanley/Emin Pasha book, sending essays back to London, or drafting ideas for the novels she was determined to publish on a return to England. To be sure, in post-war London, as a working writer and as a member of a kind of raffish intelligentsia composed of producers and actors who worked with Reggie at the BBC and publishing types and writers with whom she was becoming friendly, she was in many ways inoculated against popular pressures for women to recover a femininity eroded by war work in the factories or on the land. Olivia, Reggie, and their friends greeted with amused derision warnings such as those issued by *The Lady* magazine in January 1946 that 'If men and women fail to take their traditional positions in the dance of life, only a great dullness is achieved.'[17] The anything but dull position Olivia wished to assume in post-war literary London was that of acclaimed and well-paid novelist.

The literary 1950s, of course, soon became a decade dominated by sustained overturning of tradition, whether to be found in Kingsley Amis's comic abhorrence of madrigal-singing in *Lucky Jim* (1954), John Osborne's ridicule of 'chinless wonders from Sandhurst' in *Look Back in Anger* (1956), or Harold Pinter's brilliant demolition of English drawing-room comedy, *The Birthday Party* (1957). Notably, though, male writers dominated fiction and drama in the exciting 1950s, a sovereignty that forced Olivia to examine the often marginal position of the woman writer. Refusing to be pigeonholed as a woman novelist, she preferred to think of herself as a novelist who happened to be a woman, a preference confirmed by Margaret Drabble in recalling her warm friendship with Olivia in the 1960s: for Drabble, Olivia possessed a kind of 'fearless quality' that fueled her ambition to succeed in a man's world.[18] Olivia, for instance, found it both gratifying and

---

[17] Quoted in Kynaston, *Austerity Britain*, 98.
[18] Author's conversation with Margaret Drabble, 29 April 2010.

disconcerting to find herself congratulated on the dust-jacket of the American edition *A Different Face* when it appeared in 1957 in the following way: 'Miss Manning is one of the few women novelists who can tell a story through masculine eyes without leaving trace of lipstick on the cup.' More to her critical liking was Elizabeth Bowen's comment in the *Tatler* when reviewing *Artist Among the Missing* in 1949 that she displayed 'a masculine impersonality in the work.' Earlier that year, in reviewing Bowen's *The Heat of the Day*, Olivia had praised Bowen as having entered 'the ranks of those rare writers . . . to whom nothing is impossible,' and she was gratified by Bowen's critical reciprocity.[19] But, characteristically unable to accept unquestioned even the most favorable reviews, Olivia managed to dilute the praise: Elizabeth Bowen, she wrote to Kay Dick, 'is so generous to everyone that it does not mean as much as one would like. I believe she was just as enthusiastic about Elizabeth Taylor who has, I am glad to see, rather faded out.'[20] The Home Counties domesticity so delicately etched in Taylor's novels contrasted sharply with the cosmopolitanism characteristic of Olivia's dry, often sardonic fiction: what Olivia called an 'unbearably smug' tone in Taylor's novels grated against her own wry view of an imperfect world and Taylor's fiction was a favorite target in her war on male reviewers (or male-identified female reviewers) who favored domestic lyricism over worldly irony.[21]

The beams of love

Olivia dedicated *School for Love* to Robert Liddell, her close friend from the Athens days of spring 1940 and someone she had hailed in 1947 as keeping alive through his gift for comic narrative 'the tradition of Jane Austen and Mrs. Gaskell.'[22] He was also one of the few people who knew the sad details of what happened in July 1944. Writing a strangely moving and sometimes frightening novel, Olivia embellishes a conventional coming-of-age narrative with a brilliant command of

---

[19] Olivia Manning, 'Miss Bowen's new novel,' *The Spectator*, 25 February 1949.

[20] OMP, UT, Series 1, Box 1, Folder 2.

[21] OMP, UT, Series 1, Box 1, Folder 4.

[22] Olivia Manning, 'Fiction,' *The Spectator*, 16 July 1948.

setting and characterization.[23] *School for Love* opens as Felix Latimer arrives on a winter afternoon at the house by Herod's Gate in Jerusalem of Miss Bohun, and rather than finding a tiled courtyard filled with the jasmine and roses of his Baghdad childhood, he discovers a barren space covered in glassy snow where the only living thing appears to be a large mulberry tree. The barren frostiness of the courtyard metaphorically registers the bleak aridity of Miss Bohun's treatment of her new lodger. Arguably the most chillingly peculiar and sadistic character in Olivia's fiction and possibly modeled on Robert Graves's sister, with whom Olivia lodged for a few months when she was first in Jerusalem, she is a member of the Ever-Readies, a sect waiting for the Second Coming[24] She keeps one immaculate room in the house ready for the messiah; in the attic lives a Mr Jewel, an elderly, impoverished excolonial official; and in a rickety sort of guest house in the courtyard live a Polish/German refugee woman named Frau Leszno and her disaffected son Nikky, who possesses a moth-eaten fur-trimmed overcoat not unlike that sported by Yakimov in *The Balkan Trilogy*. This refugee hodgepodge, a gathering of dislocated exiles—Felix from a home with his mother, the Lesznos from German persecution, and Mr Jewel from the fragile security of a job in the passport office at the British Consulate—is completed by the arrival of Jane Ellis, the world-weary, pregnant, and very attractive widow of an English army officer. (See Figure 3.)

As the daughter of a high-level officer in the regular army, she has lived in India and Alexandria and her cynicism quickly replaces the delicate niceness memorialized in Felix's mother. When he secretly shows Jane Mr Jewel's paintings (thinking them rather good), she says crisply that she is sure he enjoyed doing them; Felix suspects his mother would have said they were 'wonderful' and that her judgment would not have been 'true': 'It would have belonged to the story-book world which his mother always somehow produced around her and which he knew he must leave now he was growing up. Venturing into reality, Mrs. Ellis was the guide for him. Almost every time he was

---

[23] In praising *School for Love* on 16 September 1951, *The Observer*'s reviewer singled out the 'delicate and incisive' manner in which Olivia Manning draws her characters.

[24] Francis King, for example, is confident that Graves's sister was the model for Miss Bohun: an 'acid portrait' in 'one of the best' of Manning's novels. *Yesterday Came Suddenly*, 239.

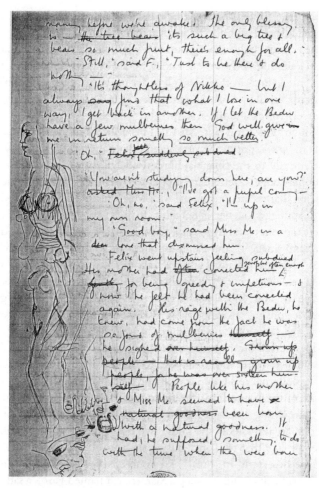

Figure 3. Olivia Manning, manuscript page from *School for Love*. The sketches of a woman's voluptuous body suggest Manning's characterization of the pregnant Jane Ellis in this novel. With permission of Victoria Orr-Ewing.

with her some incident widened his understanding of life, or of himself.'[25] In keeping with the coming-of-age trope that shapes this work, Jane Ellis educates Felix in the frightening but also exciting ways of the world and consoles him for the terrible loneliness he had felt

[25] *School for Love*, 162–3.

when he first walked along the Jaffa Road: 'He, out in the cold, dark street, felt lost and without destination in the world' (p. 63). In a raffish café, she introduces him to a group of Jewish and Arab men who rarely speak of Palestine's private war; rather, as one of them announces, they mix in 'intellectual amity. Were all to act in such a way, the problems of Palestine would be solved' (p. 157). Their conversation is devoted 'exclusively to sex and the arts' (p. 157).

Although, as it turns out, Miss Bohun does more than think occasionally of 'sex' if not of the 'arts,' her conversation at meals is devoted almost entirely to the financial burden of maintaining her house and feeding her lodgers: Jerusalem shopkeepers are all conniving thieves, electricity charges are exorbitant, and Mrs Leszno and her son Nikky are lazy spongers on her generosity. In her acute depiction of Miss Bohun's meanness and hypocrisy, Olivia creates a withering parody of the cultural image of the Englishwoman in Arabia, women such as Harriet Martineau, Lady Hester Stanhope, and Gertrude Bell, who traveled widely, wrote extensively, and in general were respected by Arab friends and colleagues. Fluent in Arabic, Miss Bohun gives English lessons to sweating and bemused Levantine businessmen while at the same time urging them to help with the gardening, and she prides herself on the respect she thinks she receives from the Arab elders when she goes to the mosque to pay her rent (in a complicated set of exploitative real estate transactions, Miss Bohun has taken over the lease of the house from the rightful tenants, Mrs Leszno and her son). Declaiming loudly to Felix that English women are 'highly respected' in Jerusalem, she adds, 'we have Lady Hester Stanhope and people like that to thank, but, apart from that, I think the Arabs appreciate our spirit' (p. 110).[26] Her one charitable gesture in Felix's direction is to allow him to keep a Siamese cat named Faro, 'a sad little cat, as lost as himself.' Through his passionate love for Faro, Felix comes to understand what Jane Ellis has tried to tell him when she murmurs some lines from Blake's 'The Little Black Boy': 'And we are put on earth a little space | That we may learn to bear the beams of

---

[26] Phyllis Lassner argues that Miss Bohun may be read as 'a female agent of colonial ideology whose traditional role of making an English home in alien space has come to a perverse end.' *Colonial Strangers*, 21. This seems fair enough, but her claims that the house resembles 'a punitive concentration camp' and that when Felix witnesses Arab servants burning rats, he resembles 'the British soldiers who in April 1945 will accidentally come upon Bergen-Belsen' (p. 25) strike me as far-fetched.

love.' Shocked that he doesn't know the poem and by his admission that his mother thought all poetry was 'nonsense,' she explains that the poem means 'life is a sort of school for love.'

Writing to Kay Dick on 2 August 1950, Olivia summarized *School for Love* by saying that war is kept 'well in the background, that the boy does fall in love with a grown woman (in a sort of way), has a miserable time at the hands of a mean old woman (who is really the chief character) and finds his chief comfort in a Siamese cat.'[27] In several scenes that disclose Olivia's skill as attentive commentator on contemporary political events, she writes as an eyewitness to the way few English people in Jerusalem appear elated about the end of World War II; rather than engaging in joyful celebrations of the arrival of peace, most are worried about 'the really important war,' the war that will break out immediately over control of Palestine and Jerusalem. This is a war whose early rumblings Olivia heard while living in Jerusalem and that had gained alarming immediacy just before she sailed for England in 1945. *School for Love* concludes with two momentous events, the first immediately evocative of Olivia's tragic experience in Jerusalem in July 1944 and the second freighted with memories of her departure from the Middle East: the death of Jane Ellis's unborn child and the sailing of Felix Latimer for England. After a boyhood filled with loss and deprivation but also an education in the 'beams' of love, he will go home, Faro in his arms.

Smelling the chance of getting more rent from wealthier lodgers as Jerusalem becomes increasingly unsettled, Miss Bohun suggests that Jane Ellis move to the King David Hotel, adding that when she had taken her in, as she puts it, she had no idea how 'unsuitable' an influence she would be upon Felix—dragging him 'to low drinking dens where he listens to the most improper conversations.' Heating up what quickly becomes a calamitous physical altercation, Jane responds by announcing she intends to have her baby in the house and that she has hired a nurse: Miss Bohun labels her 'vulgar and immoral.' In return, Jane calls her a 'hypocrite, a liar, a cheat, a dirty-minded old maid.' At the foot of a staircase (this exchange takes place on a landing), Felix hears the sound of a slap and then sees Jane half fall, half totter down the stairs, and eventually crumple into a heap. At the English

---

[27] OMP, UT, Series 1, Box 1, Folder 2.

Hospital (in all probability, the hospital where Olivia gave birth to her dead child) she survives. But the child dies. Olivia takes great care to show that Felix never discovers who slapped who, but it is as a result of Miss Bohun's neurotic hatred and fear of Jane's youth, sexuality, and fertility that the child dies—or, to put this bluntly, is killed. Berating Jane as she does triggers the ugly contretemps, and if we allow for the possibility that it is she who slaps Jane, then Miss Bohun could be seen as responsible for the death, or, if we wish to read Miss Bohun as an emblem of English hypocrisy and vengeful narrow-mindedness, one could argue it is those forces that imaginatively terminate Jane's pregnancy.

Finally, given the fact that *School for Love* is the first piece of fiction dealing with the death of an unborn child published after Olivia's devastating experience in 1944, it is also possible to construct an imaginative and determinative alignment between Miss Bohun, English hypocrisy, and the 'missed abortion.' In other words, the strain of living under sometimes unsympathetic and judgmental English eyes might have contributed to Olivia's psychological and physical vulnerability. But one needs to tread carefully here since the cause of Olivia's loss remains unknowable: it is over-determined—traceable, perhaps, to a blighted ovum, uterine weakness, fetal malformation, or, to add to that list, the toll taken on Olivia's physical and emotional health by the stress of her wartime travails. In my view, it is enough to say that in writing *School for Love* she resumed the transformation of remembered experience into fiction that had begun with *The Wind Changes* and that came to define almost all the writing that followed her first novel.

After Jane is taken to hospital, Felix never sees her again. Given two days by the British authorities in which to pack and catch the boat at Port Said that will take him to Liverpool, he buys a litter-box and carrier for Faro, and throughout the transactions behaves 'with deliberation and complete confidence of success.' It only remains for him to say good-bye to Mr Jewel, for whom he has lost all respect having learned that he plans to marry Miss Bohun after discovering she has received a small inheritance: it seems to him that Mr Jewel 'was little better than a child, while he, knowing all he knew—would never be a child again.' Schooled in love by Jane Ellis, Felix has come to know about sex, about Palestinian politics, about Blake's poetry, and about what a trickle of blood on a pregnant woman's leg might mean after she has fallen downstairs. It is as if in building the blocks of Felix's

Bildungsroman, in telling the story of exile and return for a sixteen-year-old boy, Olivia expresses and releases some of her own sorrow. The primary agent of that boy's coming-of-age is a woman in some ways not unlike herself: savvy about the world, unafraid to speak her mind, and disdainful of the sanctimonious fanaticism embodied in Miss Bohun.

Cathartic as it may have been, finishing *School for Love* also precipitated one of Olivia's by now familiar bouts of depression, which, exacerbated by a nasty attack of influenza, prompted her to write to Kay Dick that, during this period, she had 'felt that life was not worth living and what was the good of writing when no one cared anyway and I simply could not raise a finger to do anything. Thank goodness it is passing somewhat.'[28] In the same letter, she also declared she was not pleased with the dust-jacket for *School for Love*—she felt it lacked 'panache,' that it was badly drawn in purple and yellow, and that it was adorned 'with a very unlikely cat's head.' However, by the time the novel was published in September 1951, she had recovered some of her energy and was able to write to Rupert Croft-Cooke that she had been going through 'a dismal non-creative period' since finishing the novel, but that she was writing again.[29] Also, some good reviews lifted her spirits, particularly those that appeared in the *TLS* on 12 October and in the *World Review*, also in October. The first was written by Anthony Powell (writing anonymously, of course, since the *TLS* did not abandon anonymous reviewing until June 1974—Olivia, though, quickly learned the identity of her reviewer). He praises the novel for its 'remarkable qualities of force and originality,' for its vivid sense of place, particularly in Jerusalem cafés and souks, and for telling 'a story distinctly out of the ordinary.' Olivia had much admired *A Question of Upbringing*, the first of Powell's twelve-novel saga, *A Dance to the Music of Time*, which also appeared in 1951, and that Powell, an established figure in English literary circles, had praised her work signaled a long-desired acceptance into that world. Her battle for recognition seemed almost won.

In *World Review*, an always supportive Stevie Smith offered Olivia a string of generous compliments. Terming her a 'scrupulous and gifted writer who will admit no compromise [for whom] the novel is a work

---

[28] Olivia Manning to Kay Dick, 20 March 1951, OMP, UT, Series 1, Box 1, Folder 3.
[29] Olivia Manning to Rupert Croft-Cooke, 18 December 1950, OMC/C, HRC.

of art or it is nothing,' she praises what she terms 'the ferocity' of her writing. Unlike Olivia's earlier novel, *Artist Among the Missing*, *School for Love*, says Smith, displays no 'pettishness' and its author is to be congratulated for the 'great advance' she is making as 'a professional writer in the highest sense, a conscious artist.'[30] Olivia was also highly pleased by C. P. Snow's review in the *Sunday Times*, particularly by his characterization of her writing as 'deep, sharp, and narrow...never distracted and never sentimental': for him, *School for Love* was 'a remarkable book.'[31] And when William Gerhardie telephoned 'to speak with extreme enthusiasm' about her novel, she was delighted, although, as she told Kay Dick, 'It is always so maddening that these things are not said in print.'[32]

Gerhardie, however, did wish to say enthusiastic things in print about Olivia's work and he wrote to her in September 1951 proposing an appreciative article in the *TLS*. Delighted by the prospect, she sent him a brief summary of her life but added pessimistically that she feared no one at the *TLS* would allow him to write such an article, despite the fact that Anthony Powell was the fiction editor (in this regard, she was correct since Gerhardie's article did not appear until 1953). When Gerhardie wrote to her, she had heard that Powell liked her work but did not know that a positive review of *School for Love* was to appear in the 12 October issue. She ended the letter (the first of many she wrote to Gerhardie) by thanking him 'for the enormous encouragement of your good opinion and the kindness of your intentions. I cannot tell you how much both mean to me.'[33] The Gerhardie/Manning correspondence in the Cambridge University archives ends in 1973 and I can find no evidence that they corresponded again from that year until his death in 1977, nor can I find evidence that Gerhardie may have been Olivia's lover, despite Jeremy Treglown's claim that 'Gerhardie had tried to persuade Powell to let him write for the *TLS* about Olivia Manning, with whom he was having, or had had, an affair' (implying Gerhardie would only have wanted to write in the *TLS* about Olivia if he had been sleeping with her).[34] What is certain is

---

[30] Quoted in Frances Spalding, *Stevie Smith: A Critical Biography*, 1985.

[31] C. P. Snow, 'A memorable story,' *The Sunday Times*, 9 September 1951.

[32] OMP, UT, n.d., Series 1, Box 1, Folder 3.

[33] Correspondence of William Gerhardie, Cambridge University Library. Letter from Olivia Manning dated 19 September 1951.

[34] Jeremy Treglown, 'Anthony Powell at the *TLS*,' *The Times*, 25 January 2006.

that they were deeply fond of one another, that as he grew increasingly infirm and sequestered in his squalid Portland Place flat she regularly worried about his health, and that she complained loudly to all who would listen about his neglect by academic critics.

Praise from Anthony Powell, Stevie Smith, C. P. Snow, and William Gerhardie did not lessen her dissatisfaction with her publishers, William Heinemann. Mostly, she complained of their failure to acknowledge her growing reputation; for example, in 1949 she received the Tom-Gallon biennial prize for best short story for 'The Children,' originally written in 1938 and revised for the publication of *Growing Up* in 1948. Heinemann sent no congratulations. Her injured feelings are justified to some extent by John St John in his history of Heinemann when he concedes that the press took too long to treat her as a major talent.[35] On 26 February 1952 (five months after the publication of *School for Love*) Olivia wrote abjectly to Louisa Callender at Heinemann asking if her sales have been 'so terrible that Heinemann's have lost all faith in me? I feel I have been a disappointment... I really don't know what to do to make myself sell. I don't know at all. I often feel like giving up writing altogether.'[36] But even if Olivia felt like giving up writing 'altogether,' she never did and she always managed to pull herself out of the self-pitying moods that dictated querulous letters to publishers and newspaper editors. Writing also kept her on a reasonably even keel when facing unavoidable personal unhappiness. Just as in November 1944, four months after the loss of her child, she had managed to drag herself into the YMCA library in Jerusalem to resume work on her Stanley/Emin Pasha book, so in April 1949 after a wrenching visit to her 'her poor, darling old father (90 today)... in pain all the time' (she wrote to Kay Dick), she tackled final revisions for *School for Love*. Commander Manning died a few months later: in Olivia's words, 'after two years of pain and helplessness.... He was so patient and sweet and things seemed hopeful until near the end but he had suffered so much, it seemed cruel to wish him to drag on as he was.'[37]

Encouraged by Reggie, in December 1951 Olivia wrote to Charles Lefeaux in the Drama Script Unit at the BBC to propose a serial

[35] *William Heinemann: A Century of Publishing 1890–1990*, 344.
[36] Quoted by St John, from the Heinemann archive, 345.
[37] Olivia Manning to Kay Dick, OMP, UT, Series 1, Box 1, Folder 2.

adaptation of *Middlemarch*, to her mind George Eliot's 'best book.' Agreeing with Francis King that Jane Austen 'really had no conception of what men talked about when they were away from women,' she greatly admired Eliot's facility in creating male characters (something she knew she herself did extremely well). For Olivia, Eliot's depiction of Casaubon's pitiful sterility, Lydgate's fatal susceptibility to Rosamond Vincy's serpentine charm, and Bulstrode's tormented religiosity make Eliot 'as good as any man' in the pantheon of nineteenth-century novelists.[38] When the BBC agreed to pay twenty-two guineas for a trial script and a synopsis of succeeding episodes in half-hour installments, Olivia put aside her one minor criticism of the novel—that Eliot grinds her axe on behalf of Victorian womanhood and gives Dorothea far too much narrative space at the expense of the more entertaining story of Rosamond and Lydgate—and set to work. From the evidence of a typescript fragment of her synopsis, she did a serviceable, if not brilliant job, concluding, along with most of Eliot's readers and critics, that Dorothea 'gladly sinks her personality in that of her husband who becomes a successful public man and member of parliament.'[39] Her workmanlike synopsis, however, did not please a Mrs Helena Wood, who reviewed it for the BBC and judged the script for the first episode of *Middlemarch* a 'competent rather than a discriminating piece of work.' She found the synopsis clear enough but the first installment 'undramatic and confusing' and none of the characters revealed 'with anything like the subtlety or life of the originals.'[40]

Responding quickly, Olivia conceded that she had tried to be 'too clever the first time' and she now offered a simpler plan that followed more nearly the construction of the book. In March, Mrs Wood reported that the script for the first installment was still far from satisfactory but she agreed to read two more installments. On 28 July she delivered another crisply damning report announcing that Olivia's style of writing 'stands out in unfortunate contrast with that of George Eliot' and that she avoids vivid detail 'with unerring instinct.' Still

---

[38] Francis King in conversation with Kay Dick, *Friends and Friendship*, 123. Olivia Manning: typescript review of *Weymouth Sands* by John Cowper Powys; *The Sparrow* by Mary Hocking; *Shadow of a Sun* by A. S. Byatt. OMC, HRC.

[39] OMC, HRC.

[40] Olivia Manning Scriptwriter 1943–1982. BBC Written Archives Centre, Caversham.

determined to get some BBC work (as Olivia regularly announced to her friends, Reggie's salary was pitifully inadequate and she needed to make money), she next suggested an adaptation of Elizabeth Gaskell's *Wives and Daughters*, and although her ideas didn't go down too well with another stern BBC reader, Miss Mollie Greenhalgh, the BBC did broadcast the adaptation in the autumn of 1953.[41] When her next proposal, an adaptation of Arnold Bennett's *Riceyman Steps*, received a frosty reception from Miss Greenhalgh, Olivia agreed to substitute for Pamela Hansford Johnson on a BBC Talks program. But she insisted she be paid competitively even if she were only subbing. Since Hansford Johnson regularly received seven guineas and the BBC offered her five, she returned the contract unsigned with a note stating she would be pleased to accept the same as her colleague and friend: a new contract in the sum of seven guineas was sent by return post.[42] In December 1952, after almost a year of back and forth with producers at Portland Place (and with Mrs Helena Wood), Olivia threw in the script-writing towel in terms of nineteenth-century novels and asked if she could write a few episodes of *Mrs Dale's Diary*, the wildly popular radio serial. The answer was an amused no. Her last-gasp effort to get BBC work was a proposal in October 1953 that she do something for the Talks Programme on the old Madame Tussaud's; despite touting various selling-points as having been taken there with her brother before a fire destroyed many of the old waxworks and her possession of the original catalogue, Olivia received a polite rejection.[43]

To put things mildly, Olivia's experiences with the BBC were not successful: too much the 'deep, sharp, and narrow' narrator admired by C. P. Snow, she seemed to lack the skills required for adaptation. But responding to Reggie's favorite words of encouragement, 'Rally the troops,' she continued to review for *The Palestine Post*, from time to time sending them 'A Letter from London.' In a 1952 'Letter,' for instance, she reviewed Terence Rattigan's new play *The Deep Blue Sea*

---

[41] Mollie Greenhalgh wrote that Olivia's sample script for *Wives and Daughters* was 'strangely reminiscent of a story for the tinies.' A recurring theme in all the BBC readers' reports on Olivia's proposals is that she relies too much on dialogue and provides insufficient characterization.

[42] Olivia Manning to the BBC, 21 February 1952. Olivia Manning, Talks 1951–1982, BBC Written Archives Centre, Caversham.

[43] Olivia Manning Scriptwriter 1943–1982, BBC Written Archives Centre, Caversham.

and a film version of Stephen Crane's *The Red Badge of Courage*, both of which she and Reggie much admired.

Festive Britain

School for Love, Olivia's novel about an end to exile, published in September 1951, and *A Different Face*, her novel about the brutal reality that awaits a character when he *does* return home, published in August 1953, form an imaginative frame for the creation and ending of a celebratory event designed to mark the centenary of the Great Exhibition of 1851: the Festival of Britain. The two radically different moods of these novels mirror the oscillating spirits of elation and disappointment that mark the historical moment of Britain's cultural effort to end the Age of Austerity and each registers Olivia's skill in transforming eyewitness recollection of a particular historical moment into persuasive, riveting fiction. And, consistently with the familiar autobiographical nature of Olivia's fiction, if *School for Love* imaginatively transforms her return home after the desolation of July 1944, then *A Different Face* reveals her preoccupation with a post-war grimness disfiguring the social landscape, rather like the prefab houses that had gone up right after the war and that in the early 1950s seemed permanently settled in place. Despite her own pleasure in no longer having to go without and the comfort that she and Reggie enjoyed as cosmopolitan intellectuals surrounded by talented, interesting, and lively friends, Olivia felt strongly the dispiriting nature of aspects of English life after the war. And she wrote about it: always the eyewitness to contemporary history, the novelist committed to social realism and political criticism.

With a slim majority, the Labour Party returned to power in the General Election of February 1950 (Labour 315 seats, Conservative 298, Liberal 9, Irish Nationalist 2, Communist 0). The National Health Service under way and the major part of the nationalization of industry having been completed, the government decided to implement plans for a Festival of Britain that had originally been proposed by the Royal Society of Arts in 1943. In the House of Commons on 7 December 1947, the Leader of the House of Commons, Herbert Morrison, had announced that Britain would mark the centenary of the Great Exhibition of 1851 by mounting 'a national display illustrating the British

1. Olivia Morrow Manning, with baby Olivia, aged three months. With permission of Victoria Orr-Ewing.

2. Lieutenant-Commander Oliver Manning. With permission of Victoria Orr-Ewing.

3. Olivia Manning, with doll, aged five years. With permission of Diana Hogarth.

4. Olivia Manning (seated) at Portsmouth Municipal School of Art, *c*.1934. With permission of Diana Hogarth.

5. Olivia Manning, studio portrait, just before leaving Portsmouth for London in 1936. With permission of Victoria Orr-Ewing.

6. Hamish Miles, editor at Jonathan Cape, and Olivia's lover until his death in December 1937. With permission of Victoria Orr-Ewing.

7. Stevie Smith, *c.*1950. Mary Evans Picture Library/Robin Adler.

8. Reggie Smith, in Bucharest, 1939, shortly after his marriage to Olivia Manning. With permission of Diana Hogarth.

9. Louis MacNeice, 1946, Reggie Smith's mentor at the University of Birmingham in the mid-1930s. Getty Images.

10. Athénée Palace Hotel, Bucharest, February 1940. Getty Images/Margaret Bourke-White.

11. Calea Victoriei, Bucharest, February 1940. Getty Images/Margaret Bourke-White.

12. Romanian Iron Guard, December 1940. Getty Images/Hulton Archive.

13. Reggie Smith, broadcasting from Jerusalem, 1942. With permission of Victoria Orr-Ewing.

14. Olivia Manning's brother, Oliver, 1941, who died in an airplane accident in the same year. With permission of Victoria Orr-Ewing.

15. Olivia Manning, studio portrait, Cairo, *c.*1942. With permission of Diana Hogarth.

16. Olivia Manning, studio portrait, on her return to England in 1946. With permission of Victoria Orr-Ewing.

17. Olivia Manning and Kay Dick at a William Heinemann garden party, c.1947. Olivia Manning Papers, Special Collections and University Archives, McFarlin Library, University of Tulsa.

18. Reggie Smith in his office at the BBC, after his return to England in 1946. With permission of Diana Hogarth.

19. PEN Party, Pamela Hansford Johnson and Olivia Manning, December 1948. Getty Images.

20. Olivia Manning at 'her beautiful home in St. John's Wood' photographed for *The Tatler*, 5 October 1955. Mary Evans Picture Library.

21. Olivia Manning in her study, 1960, by Ida Kar. National Portrait Gallery, London.

22. Christmas 1968 in St John's Wood. From left to right, June Braybrooke, Olivia Manning, Jerry Slattery, and Neville Braybrooke. With permission of Victoria Orr-Ewing.

23. Olivia Manning, 1969, by Mark Gerson. National Portrait Gallery, London.

24. 'Bookish Line-Up'—Olivia Manning with Margaret Drabble (right) and others, July 1972. Hulton Archive/Getty Images.

25. Olivia Manning and Reggie Smith at home in St John's Wood, late 1970s. With permission of Victoria Orr-Ewing.

contribution to civilization, past, present and future, in arts, in science and technology, and in industrial design.'[44] Politically, the Festival was designed to provide uplifting images of recovery from war and reinvigoration for the second half of the twentieth century. As David Kynaston observes, 'A meat shortage, a fuel crisis, a flu' epidemic, a hastily conceived and overambitious rearmament programme having a sharp impact on the consumer' did not make for a happy picture in early 1951.[45] Britain needed a pick-me-up. Despite strong Tory opposition grounded in dire warnings about foreign currency imbalances, shortages of coal, steel, and skilled labor, a twenty-seven-acre site in a derelict, low-lying, and marshy area between Waterloo Station, the Thames, and London County Hall (a lot of it rat-infested bomb-sites) was cleared for the building of pavilions with names such as 'Land of Britain,' 'Minerals of the Island,' 'Power and Production,' and 'British Tradition.' In addition, the plans called for the construction of desperately needed blocks of flats and shopping centers. The official guide spelled out very clearly the aims of the Festival: 'The South Bank Exhibition is neither a museum of British culture nor a trade show of British wares; it tells the story of British contributions to world future.'[46]

The Festival was not just an event restricted to the South Bank. Pageants, galas, and performances of patriotic productions of Shakespeare and Gilbert and Sullivan were planned for major cities throughout Britain; small theater companies such as the Cambridge Arts Theatre presented *The Mayor of Casterbridge* from 30 July to 4 August 1951 and offered *The Tempest* when they had finished with Thomas Hardy; Whitchurch Town Hall offered a concert version of *Tom Jones* that same summer. According to the art historian Roy Strong, the design mood of the Festival aimed to match what its proponents imagined hopefully was the national mood of 1951, and if not that, then to jog people to feel brightly cheerful about being British in the middle of the twentieth century: 'It was the age of a lick of red, white and blue paint over anything to give it a quick face-lift, most of all over anything Victorian.' As Michael Frayn notes, the tone of the Festival

---

[44] Quoted in Adrian Forty, 'Festival politics,' Mary Banham and Bevis Hillier (eds.), *A Tonic to the Nation*, 27.

[45] David Kynaston, *Austerity Britain*, 580.

[46] Banham and Hillier (eds.), *A Tonic to the Nation*, 74.

was 'philanthropic, kindly, whimsical, cosy, optimistic, middle-brow.'[47] In other words, this was not a festival for the masses but rather something designed to appeal to people like those middle-class listeners to radio dramas being produced by Reggie Smith at the BBC in the early 1950s. Overall, it was a knockout success, Adrian Forty observes, because for the first time in ten years people 'saw freshly applied coloured paint, saw new furniture that was not utility, saw buildings that were both new and also very different to anything constructed on these shores before, and had fun that was, in austerity jargon, "off the ration" . . . It was an image of what Britain might be like with full employment and a welfare state.'[48]

The cheery 'off the ration' national mood, however, dimmed somewhat after the opening of the Festival on 3 May 1951. The disappearance of Burgess and Maclean into the dark espionage world of the USSR on 25 May created worries about Britain's vulnerability in the Cold War and also fed homophobic fears that Britain was being sold out by 'pansy' spies. The Korean conflict that had broken out in June 1950 prompted dark thoughts about the possibility of nuclear conflict (immediately after the tanks of North Korea crossed the 38th parallel on 25 June Britain placed the British Pacific Fleet under American command, following President Truman's offer of military aid to the South Koreans), and in the autumn of 1951, the Conservatives returned to power. Their victory in itself did not necessarily dampen the Festival mood after its closing on 30 September (except, of course, for Labour voters), but virtually the first order issued by the new Minister of Works David Eccles was for demolition of the Festival pavilions and clearing of the grounds for planned coronation celebrations for Elizabeth II in 1953. The only building left untouched was the Royal Festival Hall.

During the year of the Festival, Olivia felt buoyed by the splashes of color in the South Bank pavilions and also by the fact that she and Reggie finally found an almost ideal place to live. Until then they had lived in rented flats too small to accommodate their rapidly mounting piles of books and pictures (Baker Street was a particular trial) but in March 1951 they began negotiations for a six-year lease on a small

---

[47] Roy Strong, Prologue, *A Tonic to the Nation*, 9; Michael Frayn, 'Festival,' Sissons and French (eds.), *Age of Austerity*, 335.

[48] 'Festival politics,' Banham and Hillier (eds.), *A Tonic to the Nation*, 38.

house in St John's Wood—not, she confessed, her favorite part of London, but 26 Queen's Grove was to her mind a pleasant little house. Even if it lacked architectural distinction, it had a light self-contained basement and a studio in the garden already rented out. All they needed to do was sell the lease on the Baker Street flat, learn to live with an overdraft going 'up by leaps and bounds,' and cope with builders talking about damp, faulty drains, and leaking ceilings. Since Olivia had long known that Reggie was hopeless about managing money, she had become the business manager in their household; consequently, she signed the lease for 26 Queen's Grove and thus became responsible for the rent, the rates, gas and electric bills, and so on. Reggie's contribution to the budget was to hand over a monthly allowance for food and general household expenses.

Unfortunately, the escalating overdraft accelerated rapidly in 1951 when Reggie discovered he had been assessed by the Income Tax authorities as a single man for the previous six years; for Olivia this was a costly and vexing consequence of his inattention to their financial situation. As she wrote to her friend Rupert Croft-Cooke, they were being hit by the 'most desolating tax demands.' Reggie, she announced despairingly, was 'hopeless about money matters' and it was left to her to clear up the mess—a process that required production of 'an elaborate statement with claims for everything I could think of—but they seem not be impressed and heaven only knows what they hope to squeeze out of us now.'[49] Fed up with the tax authorities and eager to celebrate the forthcoming move into their first real home, in the late summer of 1951 Olivia and Reggie took a brief holiday in Paris, from where Olivia sent an affectionate postcard to William Gerhardie sending love from them both and noting that the trees are already 'golden and tan.'[50]

On her return to London and a house invaded by builders, Olivia set to work finishing A Different Face, a novel whose preoccupation with class resentment, financial disaster, and a bombed-out seaside town hardly alleviated her recurrent bouts of depression. If School for Love in its jaunty description of Felix Latimer preparing to board a Liverpool-bound ship, Faro on his shoulder, cat-carrier and litter-box in his hand, suggested a sweet relief from his bleak yet instructive exile, then A

[49] From 101 Baker Street, n.d. OMC/C, HRC.
[50] Correspondence of William Gerhardie, Cambridge University Library.

Different Face registers a somber recognition of the devastation wreacked upon England by the dislocations of war. Apart from an ambiguously hopeful ending, this novel describes a world sunk in cultural stasis, social malaise, and political prejudice. Moreover, in its depiction of the violent consequences of furtive homosexuality, *A Different Face* affiliates itself with a political critique of early 1950s homophobia, an association that reveals once more Olivia's sustained commitment to imaginative representation of contemporary culture and society. Overall, *A Different Face* may be read as an imaginative demolition of popular post-war myths, fed by the Festival of Britain in 1951, about a cheery, chin-up spirit in the face of lingering austerity.

At the opening of the novel, Hugo Fletcher returns to his birthplace, Coldmouth, the scantily disguised ghastly Portsmouth of Olivia's childhood. In the context of post-war fiction about young men seething with class resentment, Hugo Fletcher is a kind of humorless Lucky Jim, a picaresque hero in a distinctly unfunny novel: like Jim Dixon, he lusts after women he can't have, feels humiliated by a pompous and provincial middle class, and wears the wrong outfit at the wrong time. But whereas Jim Dixon defeats provincial smugness with a subversive wit, Hugo Fletcher sinks under its snobbish hand. Olivia dedicated the novel to Reggie and her handwritten manuscript shows that originally she planned to name her main character Guy, not Hugo, a name she kept in reserve for Guy Pringle when she began *The Balkan Trilogy* some ten years later. Hugo Fletcher's social unease bears little resemblance, of course, to Guy Pringle's exuberant openness to the world: similarly, Guy's real-life counterpart, Reggie Smith, has absolutely nothing in common with Hugo Fletcher, perhaps the least appealing of Olivia's male characters.[51]

Fletcher has returned to Coldmouth to become the co-proprietor of a small prep school, Ridley House, run by Charles Martyn. Martyn's son by his first wife having absconded with the school's funds (funds formed in part by Hugo having invested his entire savings in the enterprise), Hugo's arrival is not exactly a joyful occasion. Embracing the opportunity to humiliate Charles Martyn and entirely without financial resources, Hugo has no choice but to move in with Martyn and his ex-actress second wife Kyra and a knowingly nasty housekeeper, Mrs Prosser, who was Kyra's theater dresser. He embarks on a

---

[51] Manuscript fragments of *A Different Face*, OMC, HRC.

dispiriting journey through memories of his childhood triggered by wandering through 'a murderous city' (p. 4) under cold grey skies and buffeted by a bitter east wind. In this traverse through remembered rejection and injury, by revisiting what Olivia evokes as a kind of English seaside hell—the 'hideous' esplanade, cheap cafés, and poorly lit hotel bars—he also recurs obsessively to memories of his struggle to win the attention of Coldmouth's smug bourgeoisie and the affection of a girl named Tilly. Always the shunned outsider, he had been scorned by the rugby-playing sons of Coldmouth's shop-owners and ridiculed by a stone-faced ex-naval officer father. His only comfort as a child was the adoration of his mother.

Two houses are centrally important in *A Different Face*: Ridley School itself, rapidly decaying due to damp and lack of maintenance, and the once-grand house next door that Hugo believes still belongs to Cyril Webley, the son of the owner of Coldmouth's most prominent department store (as things turn out, it has been long abandoned). Through a series of retrospective narratives, we learn that Hugo's compulsive interest in Cyril Webley and the house is grounded in a grotesquely self-destructive action: having found some comfort with Tilly, a not very bright but affectionate girl who works at Webley's department store, he impulsively and literally pushes her into Cyril Webley's arms, in essence handing her over to his most despised class rival. Shortly thereafter, he offers to drive a drunken acquaintance home and outside the local cinema his passenger suddenly lurches, grabs the wheel of the sports car, and sends it crashing into a crowd leaving the cinema. A teenage girl is killed but Hugo is acquitted of manslaughter: a social pariah, he leaves England and finds work in Upper Egypt where he sits out the war. In a chilling instance of Olivia's navigation between creating sympathy and distaste in her reader, she clinically describes his mother's despair as he sails from Coldmouth: 'she, who had been a darling only child, an heiress in a small way and a notable beauty in Coldmouth, had married a man no one liked, and borne a son no one liked, and now, shabby as a charwoman, had become a stout, bun-faced, featureless woman with little, wet, faded eyes, who had to make her way back to the empty flat: deserted, friendless.'[52] Olivia causes us to be both moved and repelled by this humiliated woman with her 'little, wet, faded eyes.'

---

[52] *A Different Face*, 137.

Olivia worked on *A Different Face* at the start of almost twenty years of British homophobic persecution of homosexuality, which abated only in 1967 when the House of Commons passed crucial recommendations of the Wolfenden Committee. Named for its chair, Sir John Wolfenden, the Committee was charged with investigating British laws on homosexuality after a series of highly publicized prosecutions of well-known individuals for homosexual acts. The Committee began meeting on 15 September 1954, published its Report in 1957, and saw its recommendation that 'homosexual behaviour between consenting adults in private should no longer be a criminal offence' incorporated into the Sexual Offences Act of 1967. As David Kynaston notes, shortly after the flight in May 1951 of the openly homosexual Guy Burgess and Donald Maclean, the new Tory Home Secretary, Sir David Maxwell Fyfe, had vowed to purge the Civil Service of those with 'serious character weaknesses' and he embarked on the active prosecution of homosexuals: cases of sodomy and bestiality rose from one hundred and thirty-four in 1938 to six hundred and seventy in 1952 and offences of gross indecency between males rose from three hundred and twenty in 1938 to three thousand and eighty-seven in the same time span.[53] Olivia Manning, then, wrote and published *A Different Face* at a historical moment when homosexuals were being actively prosecuted and when homosexuality became a byword for deviant and dangerous behavior. In the words of Dan Rebellato, 'homosexuality seemed to be everywhere.'[54] Olivia's novel is part of that 'everywhere.'

With a succession of high-profile prosecutions, 1953 turned out to be a banner year in David Maxwell Fyfe's campaign to stamp out sexual deviancy in Britain. In January, Bill Field, a Labour Member of Parliament, was found guilty of 'persistently importuning men for an immoral purpose in Piccadilly Circus and Leicester Square': Field resigned his seat and disappeared from politics, smarting from what he believed had been a politically engineered police trap to catch Labour MPs. Alan Turing, the brilliant mathematician who cracked the German Enigma code during World War II, was insufficiently alert

---

[53] Kynaston, *Family Britain*, 97–8.

[54] *1956 And All That*, 192. On 5 September 2007, BBC Four aired a dramatic play, *Consenting Adults*, by Julian Mitchell (Olivia's lodger in the early 1960s) dealing with the relationship between John Wolfenden and his gay son, Jeremy.

to prevent his arrest on 7 February following a brief liaison with a Manchester youth. He was charged with 'Gross Indecency contrary to Section 11 of the Criminal Law Amendment Act 1885,' tried at the Quarter Sessions in Knutsford, Cheshire, seven weeks after his arrest, and sentenced to a course of hormone therapy at Manchester Royal Infirmary that rendered him impotent and caused him to develop breasts. Shortly thereafter, John Gielgud was arrested for 'persistent importuning' in Chelsea public lavatories and sentenced to a fine of £10 after pleading guilty and apologizing to the court.

The distaste of Reggie and Olivia and their theatrical and literary friends for the government's obsession with sexual 'deviancy'—Sir David Maxwell Fyfe announced in the House of Commons in December 1953 that 'Homosexuals, in general, are exhibitionists and proselytizers and a danger to others, especially the young. So long as I hold the office of Home Secretary I shall give no countenance to the view that they should not be prevented from being such a danger'[55]— intensified for Olivia with the arrest of her friend the novelist and travel-writer Rupert Croft-Cooke at two o'clock in the morning on a Sunday in September 1953. He was accused of 'indecent offences against sailors,' two Royal Navy cooks who had spent a weekend with him and his partner Joseph Alexander. Despite the evidence of such witnesses as Sir Compton Mackenzie, who swore to Croft-Cooke's high moral standards, and Lord Kinross, who added that his reputation 'for decency and cleanness of living was very high,'[56] he was sentenced to nine months in prison and Joseph Alexander to three. In his memoir recounting the experience, Croft-Cooke wrote that he was not greatly disturbed by being linked with Shakespeare and Michelangelo and with 'about a third of the writers and artists and musicians who have embellished human life, and with a rather greater proportion of the world's heroes in war, exploration, politics, and sport,' but he *was* bothered by being characterized as 'a homosexual of the inverted, effeminate type... because it reflected on my manhood, not because it reflected on my morals.'[57] After his release from prison, he and Joseph Alexander left Britain and settled in Tangier where, over the next twenty years, he wrote and published sixty

[55] Kynaston, *Austerity Britain*, 332.
[56] *The Times*, 10 October 1953.
[57] *The Verdict of You All*, 29; 68.

books, among them a biography of Oscar Wilde's lover: *Bosie, the Story of Lord Alfred Douglas, his Friends and Enemies* (1963). Rupert Croft-Cooke and Olivia remained close friends through his period of Moroccan exile.

The most politically significant of high-profile arrests for male homosexuality in the 1950s came in January 1954: Lord Montagu of Beaulieu was accused along with his cousin Michael Pitt-Rivers and the *Daily Mail*'s diplomatic correspondent Peter Wildeblood of gross indecency with two airmen who were granted immunity from prosecution despite their involvement in twenty-four other homosexual affairs. The case was freighted with class-fueled suspicions about exploitation by the aristocracy of their social inferiors; for example, the prosecuting counsel asked Wildeblood whether it was true that 'inverts or perverts seek their love associates in a different walk of life than their own,' to which Wildeblood responded that during the war it had never occurred to him that he was 'associating with people who were infinitely my social inferiors.'[58] All three accused were given prison sentences of between twelve and eighteen months, and the *Sunday Times* declared that 'The case for the reform of the law as to acts committed in private between adults is very strong . . . The case for an authoritative enquiry into it is overwhelming.'[59] That authoritative enquiry came with the almost immediate establishment of the Wolfenden Committee.

Homosexuality as a significant subtext in *A Different Face* appears first when Hugo enters one of the dusty classrooms at Ridley House and sees that on a large blackboard someone has scribbled two male figures: 'Hugo's glance passed over them, then, startled, returned. Unable to believe what he had seen, he stepped up to the dais to see the drawing more closely. He stared at it for several moments before jumping down and hurrying from the room' (p. 39). The scribbled drawing depicts a homosexual embrace (never described explicitly but Hugo's reaction supplies the omitted graphic details) between Pippin, Kyra's brother, and Brian, Martyn's son. When Hugo asks Martyn about an official enquiry by Ministry of Education officials into a scandal and the running of the school, Martyn replies, 'There had been an unfortunate friendship . . . a bit of talk among the boys . . . some gossip in Coldmouth' (p. 46). Pippin appears in the novel in

58 Kynaston, *Family Britain*, 373.   59 Kynaston, *Family Britain*, 374.

scenes in local hotel bars where his sister sits nursing a gin and water, waiting for him to turn up; Olivia describes him as a slight and small man 'with a delicate, pale face and cloud of very fair hair. At first glance he looked like a youth of twenty, but as he approached his hair showed less gold than white, and his face was netted with fine lines. His youthful look dissolved until, as he paused beneath the central light, his face, corpse-pale, and deeply hollowed, was the face of a man in late middle age' (p. 123). After Brian's disappearance, Pippin takes up cruising for sailors, and plenty are available in Coldmouth (1950s homophobic zealots regarded Portsmouth as a particularly vicious center of homosexual deviance).

Sitting with Kyra in one of Coldmouth's bleakest hotel bars, Hugo sees Pippin make a slight but meaningful signal to a sailor, who then follows him out of the door. Shortly thereafter Pippin is found dead, spreadeagled in the well of the old Coldmouth courthouse, now shabbily converted to housing for the homeless. A sailor has been seen hastily leaving the building but the police decline to pursue the investigation and Olivia leaves the situation unresolved (Pippin may have fallen, may have been pushed); this lack of resolution is, I think, a political gesture on her part designed to indicate the homophobic indifference of the local authorities to sordid matters such as aging 'pansies' and cruising sailors, to the fate of a figure described by Richard Hornsey in his discussion of the 'deviant' spiv and homosexual as the 'painted boy menace' (in the case of Pippin, an aging 'painted boy').[60] Olivia writes that the ground around Pippin's broken body reeks of disinfectant seeping from a broken bottle that he carried in his pocket: Kyra explains, 'He always carried a bottle. He was afraid of . . . of infection' (p. 191).[61] At the end of the novel, Hugo discovers Brian's decomposed body in the abandoned Webley House, an open suitcase with the stolen money lying nearby. Perversely, he leaves the money in place, reports the situation to the police, buys a one-way ticket to London, and sets off to begin a new life. The reader is left with a disquieting uncertainty about his ability to liberate himself from a masochistic obsession with his past.

---

[60] *The Spiv and the Architect*, 6.

[61] The *New York Times*, reviewing the novel when it was published in the United States, argued that the 'shockingly macabre climax . . . is not in keeping with the novel's carefully controlled tone and pattern,' although the reviewer, Nancie Matthews, did praise Manning's 'relentlessly honest mind.' *New York Times*, 1 December 1957.

In August 1953, Olivia and Reggie traveled to Stratford-upon-Avon, where Reggie was scheduled to record the Old Vic for the BBC. Knowing that reviews for *A Different Face* were about to appear made Olivia somewhat jumpy, and the anxious anticipation was not alleviated by discovery on their return to London that their house in Queen's Grove had been burgled while they were away. It was a desolate homecoming. Already disappointed by a review in *The Times* that appeared on 2 September which declared the 'fault' of the 'dispiriting' and 'disquieting' *A Different Face* was the absence of a single character 'sufficiently normal to act as a yardstick by which to measure the peculiarity of the others,' her shaky state of mind received a further blow when next day she opened the *Sunday Times*. There, she read John Lambert's scathing review of her new novel: she wrote to Kay Dick, 'It was a case of opening the papers, feeling quite secure, and getting slapped full in the eye.'[62] Kay hastened to write a reassuring response, for which Olivia was immensely grateful: 'Your letter has been some compensation for all the brutal attacks which have been made on me by women reviewers—two attacks I should say. Both Violet Garvin in 'Telegraph' and Nancy Spain [this was in the *Daily Mail*] say almost exactly the same thing. Do you think they agreed upon it together?'[63] Writing to William Gerhardie about these 'attacks' on her by women writers, Olivia attributed their animosity to a desire to outdo men in condemning other women, 'a sign of the slave mind in woman, the result of years of oppression.' A sad thing, she adds, but probably to be 'expected in some sort of lesbians whose wish is to identify themselves with the male,'[64] an inclination she clearly did not ascribe to her close lesbian friends, Kay Dick and Kathleen Farrell, who remained on-and-off partners for many years.

After the shattering reviews from Violet Garvin and Nancy Spain,[65] Olivia was consoled by Stevie Smith's piece in *The Spectator* review.

---

[62] OMP, UT, Series 1, Box 1, Folder 5.

[63] OMP, UT, Series 1, Box 1, Folder 5.

[64] Olivia Manning to William Gerhardie, 12 September 1953. Correspondence of William Gerhardie, Cambridge University Library.

[65] In reviewing Victoria Glendinning's edition of letters exchanged between Elizabeth Bowen and Charles Ritchie (*Love's Civil War: Elizabeth Bowen and Charlest Ritchie: Letters and Diaries*) Peter Lewis in the *Daily Mail* on 9 February 2009 highlights Bowen's reference in a letter to her 'new girlfriend Nancy Spain.' As Lewis puts it rather dramatically, 'Nancy Spain made no secret of her rampant lesbianism.'

Stevie saluted Olivia's 'outstanding gifts—a consistent and somber vision, a use of words most elegant and strict,' all in the service of describing a man who 'lusts after insult and injury' surrounded by characters moving as if they are in 'hell in icy drifts.' For Stevie, this novel is a 'book of great beauty and interest.'[66] But Olivia, always obsessively fearful of rejection, was convinced that Heinemann would withdraw as her publishers; eventually, through buck-up conversations with her friends, she rallied and rejected with spirit such charges as that made against her by Violet Garvin that all her subsidiary characters were as flat as pancakes. The most comforting and exhilarating rejoinder to all her critics, however, came from William Gerhardie in a lengthy article in the *TLS* that appeared on 4 September 1953.

Gerhardie begins by demolishing the critical narrative of artistic development treasured by academic critics: rather than fueling such a narrative, Olivia Manning's fiction encourages readers to 'set out roaming happily in her domain. They jump from one pert instance to another, in this book or that, as their fancy takes them.' How then to judge her writing? Must the critic lament an absence of development, progress, evolution? Is there, he asks, 'no moral standard of excellence in literature' against which we might judge Olivia Manning's fiction? Most decidedly there is, and the judgment rests in the reader's discovery of 'the extent to which she has genius.' The genius comes from a certain mystical quality in her writing, a quality that infuses *A Different Face*, particularly in depiction of the 'despair of one but half alive, no longer able to go on living in a half-world,' that is to say in Hugo Fletcher's last-minute 'transvaluation of lost cash into securities of an imperishable order.' For Gerhardie, *A Different Face* superbly displays 'gifts . . . bestowed on this born writer, now elbowing her way, with the abashed consent of more popular if lesser writers, to a position in contemporary English letters she cannot be denied.'

Recalling for the *TLS* reader *The Remarkable Expedition*, Gerhardie likens Olivia, the writer, to Stanley the explorer, fighting his way through darkest Africa to rescue Emin Pasha, the reader, who is 'in danger of being, according to immemorial native custom, lingeringly disparaged.' *A Different Face* may be read as 'an allegory of a born writer setting out in the teeth of every difficulty to reach her ideal reader

---

[66] Stevie Smith, 'New novels,' *The Spectator*, 18 September 1953.

who, being reached, refused to be rescued' (as, of course, did Emin Pasha). Preferring the customary, the known, the already-traveled routes through demanding literary terrain, the reader 'slinks' back to a metaphorical Africa, or into the comfort of an armchair, and refuses the rescue offered through the genius of Olivia's writing. The ordinary and lazy reader, says Gerhardie, wants pre-digested situations, not scenes like those in *A Different Face* that give us the smell of the port, the crepuscular gloom, the incredible snobbery penetrating even a bar (for whatever reason, he omits mention of homosexuality). This difficult, demanding, even frightening novel is a 'devastating social indictment' of post-war England, which is exactly what Olivia intended it to be.

'Delighted, exhilarated and encouraged,' on the day the review appeared, Olivia sent a postcard from Birmingham, where she and Reggie were visiting his mother: 'It will, I am sure, set my reputation—and it is such a profound piece of literary criticism that even my worst enemy will be compelled to read on, though he gnaw his finger nails to the quick as he does so.' Eager to return to London and begin at once a new novel, Olivia wrote that they would be back within a few days.[67] If she was like Stanley, as Gerhardie speculated in his allegory of the writer of genius in pursuit of the reluctant reader, then she was spurred by this review to continue 'elbowing' her way to the top (as Gerhardie would have it). Her working habits now well established—she wrote her first drafts in longhand on paper supplied by Reggie from the BBC as she had scribbled her first drawings in account books brought home by her father from naval stores, and typed the final version with a speed learned in Portsmouth offices— she plotted her next move in the battle to conquer completely 'even her worst enemy.' Drawing upon a long-cherished memory of being freshly in love, she began work on her next novel, *The Doves of Venus*.

---

[67] Postcard posted from Birmingham with 26 Queen's Grove, NW8 as the address. Correspondence of William Gerhardie, Cambridge University Library.

8

The 'Booksey Boys' and the Woman Writer

'I think anyone who wants to return to Britain in the Fifties is on to an insane project. The society was so oppressive and so false, particularly sexually. Neighbours had this prurience and primness and this awful kind of policing of each other's lives... Nobody could now imagine how dull things were and how respectful people were and how dead they were from the neck up.'

David Hare, 1999.[1]

Angry Young Men

A few weeks after arriving in Bucharest in August 1939, Olivia Manning had written to Stevie Smith begging for news of what might be happening back in London. An exchange of gossip about mutual friends had long shaped their friendship and in her letter Olivia offered the latest about a group she termed 'the booksey boys,' men such as Walter Allen, Reggie's friend from Birmingham days and her pal when they both worked as script readers for MGM, and John Mair, the detective-fiction author who might have been her lover when she met Reggie Smith (according to Neville and June Braybrooke, Reggie told friends that when he first met Olivia, 'she was living with a young chap called Mair').[2] She passed along the news that Louis MacNeice

---

[1] Quoted in David Kynaston, *Family Britain*, 529–30.
[2] Olivia Manning to Stevie Smith, 11 October 1939, OMP, UT, Series 1, Box 1, Folder 1; Braybrooke, *Olivia Manning: A Life*, 137.

was still in Ireland, waiting for clearance to travel to the United States, that every letter from mutual friends was full of hatred of the war, and that 'all the booksey boys seem to be having a bloody time.' Some fifteen years later, in that decade to which no one in his right mind would wish to return, says David Hare, a different crowd of 'booksey boys' was having anything but 'a bloody time' in England. They were the 'Angry Young Men,' riding a celebrity crest of critical and popular acclaim.

Olivia's attitude towards this new literary crowd in the 1950s differed substantially from her friendships with her male chums back in the late 1930s; then, she had felt no rivalry, only an ambition to join the club, not smash it to smithereens. But in the early 1950s, despite the critical praise for *School for Love*, she felt sidelined by young male novelists whose alienated protagonists, ironically, bore some resemblance to a number of her male characters. Had Hugo Fletcher in *A Different Face*, for example, possessed the cheeky confidence and cold determination to advance himself displayed by Joe Lampton in John Braine's *Room at the Top* (1957), in all likelihood he would not have ended up as broke and friendless as he does. Olivia regarded *A Different Face* as her most successful novel to date, designed, she said, as 'a novel of shock—the shock of discovering postwar England,' and despite reviewers dismissing it as dismal and depressing she always regarded it as one of her best books.[3] In creating characters such as Hugo Fletcher, Olivia had worked outside the conventions generally associated with British women novelists, since these writers had been drawn more frequently (and still were) to tracing romance and domestic life from the perspective of female characters, rather than focusing in detail on the lives of their male relatives, friends, or lovers. To be sure, George Eliot and Virginia Woolf in their superb delineations of male feeling (think of Lydgate and Casaubon in *Middlemarch*, Septimus Smith in *Mrs Dalloway*) may be said to have enlarged the familiar boundaries of British women's writing, but Olivia chose to make the thoughts and feelings of Geoffrey Lynd, Felix Latimer, and Hugo Fletcher the pivot of her three immediately post-war novels.

Rather, then, than fashioning mid-twentieth-century versions of, say, Emma Woodhouse, Dorothea Brooke, or Clarissa Dalloway, Olivia had focused on male protagonists. But in 1953 she began

---

[3] Typescript notes for BBC talk 'The novel,' January 1960. OMC, HRC.

work on a novel devoted almost entirely to women's lives in post-war London, a city where women survive through trading on their good looks or on their social privilege. In recounting the adventures of an artistically ambitious young woman (notably like herself before the war), Olivia rehearses what one might call the master narrative of her life: embattled escape from stifling provincialism to a challenging freedom in the metropolis. *The Doves of Venus* (published in 1955) opens with an exhilarating release from depressing small-mindedness as the heroine departs a dismal seaside town for London, where her experiences mirror those of Olivia when she arrived there in the mid-1930s: Ellie Parsons works as a furniture-painter in a posh studio similar to that run by Peter Jones department store, has her heart broken by an older man portrayed by Olivia as a vain and heartless version of Hamish Miles, and watches a sophisticated young woman thought by many critics to resemble Stevie Smith practice feminine wiles as a means to social survival.

In writing *The Doves of Venus*, however, Olivia was not exactly breaking new ground, as much as this novel initiates a new turn in her career. Since women novelists by the mid-1950s had securely established the genre as a powerful means of exploring female experience, a novel by a female writer that described the joys and difficulties of a young woman's life was hardly remarkable. Moreover, Olivia's female contemporaries, writers such as Elizabeth Bowen, Ivy Compton-Burnett, Pamela Hansford Johnson, and Elizabeth Taylor, were respected presences in Britain's post-war literary landscape, even if they did not enjoy the knockout commercial success of the politically conservative Angela Thirkell: speaking to a worried Tory gentry, Thirkell's *Peace Breaks Out* (1946) direfully declares that the Labour government has ushered in a 'Brave and Revolting New World' and *Love Among the Ruins* (1947) laments a leveling of class differences that has led to 'the horrors of war' being succeeded by 'the tyrannies of peace' and to an enfeebled population 'too listless to resist petty tyranny.'[4] Thirkell, of course, was not the only writer to wonder (at the very least) about the leveling effects of the Welfare State: for example, the freshly acclaimed novelist Angus Wilson chimed in on the BBC's Third Programme (quite possibly in a program produced by

---

[4] *Peace Breaks Out*, 281; *Love Among the Ruins*, 378; 385.

Reggie Smith) to argue that the future of the English novel in the context of the Welfare State lay with a new generation of novelists coming from a 'new ruling class—that strange mixture of business experts, bureaucrats, social scientists, and the rest of the Welfare set-up.'[5] Uncomfortably aware that she did not enjoy the critical admiration accorded Elizabeth Bowen and certain she was not one of Angus Wilson's 'Welfare State' novelists, Olivia decided it was time to return more explicitly to writing from her own experience as she had done in *The Wind Changes*.

Ironically, however, she made this choice at a cultural moment when that group of writers collectively and popularly labeled the Angry Young Men began to dominate the literary marketplace and to fascinate the popular imagination. With the exception of Iris Murdoch, who after publication of her first novel *Under the Net* in 1954 was grouped with the Angry Young Men and hailed as a brilliant example of that rare thing, an accessible philosophical novelist, all these writers were, of course, male.[6] Novelists such as John Wain, Kingsley Amis, and John Braine and the playwright John Osborne, whose *Look Back in Anger* Kenneth Tynan welcomed as a fresh and accurate portrait of post-war youth, were the post-war 'booksey boys' with whom Olivia found herself in competition for readers and for popular recognition, despite critically unacknowledged similarities between their experience and her own. She, too, had come from a lower-middle-class background (but in the south of England, not, she noted sarcastically, from 'fashionable Salford' in Yorkshire);[7] she, too, had made her determined way out of provincial despond; and although she was neither a man nor at the age of forty-six young in comparison, say, to Amis, who was thirty-two when he published *Lucky Jim*, she, too, was angry. Taking encouragement from J. B. Priestley, who wrote in the *New Statesman* on 26 June 1954 that the central characters in the Angry Young Men novels were 'artful dodgers rather than open rebels...such bumbling nitwits that it is hard to sympathise with them in their misfortunes,' she began work on *The Doves of Venus*,

---

[5] Kynaston, *Family Britain*, 382.

[6] The considerable commercial success of *Under the Net* launched Olivia Manning's lifelong envy of Iris Murdoch. As Liz Heron points out, the protagonists in working-class fiction of the 1950s were almost exclusively male, 'their conflicts and dilemmas assumed as masculine by their very nature.' Introduction, *Truth, Dare or Promise*, 7.

[7] Olivia Manning, 'Too late generation,' *Sunday Times*, 3 June 1962.

hoping to dislodge them from their popular supremacy with a narrative she believed would garner sympathy for its revelation of female 'misfortune.'

The explosive emergence and rapid rise in critical popularity of the Angry Young Men, fed by a good deal of media hype about the smashing of tradition, also prompted Olivia to think about the general status of the woman novelist in the 1950s. Brooding over her own small reputation compared to the avid coverage accorded these writers (particularly Amis), she re-examined her long-standing reluctance to be labeled a woman writer. Until she began *The Doves of Venus* she insisted that she be considered a novelist who happened to be a woman and she disliked the classification of novelists into schools (regional, philosophical, Angry Young Men, etc.): for example, she greeted a reporter from the *Guardian* with the tart comment that she suspected she was being interviewed for the 'Woman's Page'—abolish it, she advised, or else start another called the 'Man's Page.'[8] Yet the seeming preference of the literary editor of the *Sunday Times* for male reviewers in the early 1950s prompted her to write in sympathetic anger to Kay Dick: 'I know just how you feel about prejudice against women. You will not get a man to admit it exists and lots of women pretend to be unaware of it because it is unfashionable to be any sort of feminist, but I know it is there all the time. It is simply sex jealousy . . . There is always the excuse that the male has to keep a wife and children and so is more deserving.' As an instance of the annoying favoritism enjoyed by male writers and reviewers, she added that Walter Allen had told her he liked *A Different Face* very much but he couldn't 'do it on the air' in his radio book review program since he felt he should promote a man's novel as 'they need the publicity more,'[9] which is somewhat ironic since *A Different Face* is very much 'a man's novel' in its sharp analysis of Hugo Fletcher's destructive masochism. So brilliantly does Olivia penetrate the interior life of this troubled character that most readers would believe only a male writer could have fashioned such insights.

Kingsley Amis's Jim Dixon is generally thought to fire the opening shot in the storming of English snobbery, self-satisfaction, and hypocrisy

---

[8] Isobel English (pseudonym of June Braybrooke), Introduction to the Virago edition of *The Doves of Venus*, 615–16.

[9] Olivia Manning to Kay Dick, 11 February 1954, OMP, UT, Series 1, Box 1, Folder 6.

by lower-class male heroes. However, John Wain's *Hurry On Down*, published in October 1953, preceded Amis's riotous novel in an assault upon academic pomposity. Wain himself was solidly middle-class—the son of a Potteries dentist and a lecturer in English at Reading University—but the hero of his novel was, in the words of the *TLS*, 'in flight from his parents, from academic culture and gentility, from a manner of speech and a way of living.'[10] Walter Allen wrote in the *New Statesman* that Wain was very funny indeed, 'in his grim and gritty and tough-minded way.' Following the success of *Hurry On Down*, *Lucky Jim* swept cultural critics off their tired post-war feet and the *New Statesman* hailed Amis as 'a novelist of formidable and uncomfortable talent.' A few days later Anthony Powell in *Punch* saluted him 'as the first promising novelist who has turned up for a long time.' Olivia wondered about the talented and promising cluster of women novelists who had been around for 'a long time,' their fiction seemingly buried under the formidable force of *Lucky Jim*.

Much to her disgust, the *TLS* tribute to Amis's picaresque hero that appeared on 12 February mentioned only male novelists and failed to acknowledge the contribution of women writers in shaping post-war English fiction. Agreeing it was fair enough to say Jim Dixon 'is the anti- or rather sub-hero who is beginning to figure increasingly as the protagonist of the most promising novels written by young men since the war,' she wondered why there was no mention, however incidental, of the contributions by women writers to a post-war resuscitation of the English novel. Where did Olivia Manning, a writer who shared their attacks upon provincial cultural tyranny, fit in? Without question, an absence of higher education for intelligent women in the 1930s and even in the 1950s was not remarkable, yet Olivia obsessed about what she perceived as her crippling cultural limitations. Where was her place in what seemed to be shaping up as an exclusive male club? Not long after asking herself these questions and finding few satisfactory answers, she decided to enter a world elsewhere of women's writing and to address the plight of young women made vulnerable to male exploitation through a lack of money and social connections.[11]

---

[10] Kynaston, *Family Britain*, 357.

[11] It's worth noting that in *The Times* 1955 list of Books of the Year, the reading public voted for Nicholas Monsarrat's *The Cruel Sea*, Paul Brickhill's *Reach for the Sky*, and

Yet she continued to marvel at Kingsley Amis's 'astonishing press.' For her, he was a 'Lucky Jim' and always would be. To be sure, by this time Olivia's resentment of other writers had become familiar, often tiresomely so, and more often than not it was aimed at female rather than male novelists. Despite her success, she felt she was forever pressing her nose against the glass of an indifferent literary culture that favored female authors younger and more attractive than she (Edna O'Brien became a particular target), or those who had gone to university (who else but Iris Murdoch?). Although Olivia established an intimate correspondence with Anthony Burgess in the early 1970s (almost always addressing him as 'John darling'—his middle name) his 1965 comment that she was 'among the most accomplished of our women novelists' struck her as grudging, even condescending. She wished to be regarded as *the* most accomplished, to dislodge Iris Murdoch from her perch as 'the glamour girl' of the *Sunday Times* (which was how Olivia characterized her). Perhaps because she felt certain similarities between them, Olivia particularly disliked Iris Murdoch: both identified themselves as Anglo-Irish (neither of them officially quite the ticket), both spent long holidays in Ireland as girls, both had fathers who were keen readers, and both dealt with the 'Troubles' in their fiction: Olivia in *The Wind Changes* and Iris Murdoch in *The Red and the Green* (1965). In a snide remark to Francis King, for example, Olivia declared that she was 'not in a position to judge Miss M's scholastic attainments, my own education was sketchy.'[12] She never got over the lack of university credentials.

Olivia also complained loudly to editors that other women writers received more per review than she: why should Pamela Hansford Johnson get eight guineas from *The Spectator* and she only seven? And her letters to Francis King are rife with attacks on her female contemporaries: for example, Doris Lessing's work was 'humourless and heavy-going,' *The Golden Notebook* 'tedious beyond belief,' and the diatribes 'from her left-wing admirers who have, about four times, used me as an example of how much better she is,' inexcusable.[13] Yet Olivia's feminist sympathies occasionally trumped her jealousy of other

Alistair MacLean's *HMS Ulysses* as the three top choices. No woman novelist made the list.

[12] FKC/OM, HRC, 2 January 1965.
[13] FKC/OM, HRC, 15 April 1971.

women writers. After the war, she was delighted to see that women had come into their own. Young women friends whom she left clinging 'with their teeth to junior jobs in which they did all the work while some lazy, self-satisfied male got all the credit,' were now holding down well-paid senior administrative positions in publishing houses and at the BBC.[14] Still, it was galling to see that Muriel Spark was 'the *Observer*'s girl because she began by winning their short story prize; and Iris is the *Observer*'s girl because Jack Lambert [the newspaper's literary editor at the time] thinks he discovered her.'[15] Muriel Spark in a television interview, Olivia added, appeared 'terribly silly and affected and looking very raddled.' It seems to me important, though, to distinguish between, say, Olivia's remark (again to Francis King) that it was hardly believable Muriel Spark could receive £2,000 'for a light 2 ½ page piece about the Brontës in the "New Yorker" . . . the sort of thing which would have come back by return of post if I had sent it in'[16] and her not unreasonable belief that male literary editors tended to sideline women writers and reviewers.

To be fair, throughout her career Olivia received a goodly share of reviewing assignments from *The Spectator* and the *Sunday Times* (roughly just over a hundred), yet in the early to mid-1950s she complained of discrimination by editors and reviewers who to her mind favored, first, male writers, and, second, female writers other than herself. Olivia was neither a member of the 'booksey boys' club nor the literary pin-up girl of the *Sunday Times*. I imagine she would have been delighted by the tart comments of A. S. Byatt delivered at the Edinburgh book festival on 20 August 2010: Byatt told her audience that 'Women who write smart, demanding novels are perceived by critics as strange and unnatural, "like a dog standing on its hind legs."' Byatt also lambasted the Orange prize, which is limited to women novelists: 'The Orange prize is a sexist prize . . . You couldn't found a prize for male writers.'[17] A smart and demanding novelist

---

[14] 'Against the past,' *The Palestine Post*, 14 December 1945.

[15] FKC/OM, HRC, 23 June 1970.

[16] FKC/OM, HRC, 25 March 1966.

[17] *The Guardian*, 20 August 2010. Ian Rankin, the Scottish crime writer, disagreed with Byatt, saying 'I don't think it's a gender thing. I think Byatt should stop reading the critics and start enjoying the sales.' John Carey, professor emeritus of English at the University of Oxford, denied that intellectual novels by women writers were not taken seriously by his fellow critics and declared that when Byatt was 'on about ideas,' she was

if ever there was one, Olivia would probably have rejected the Orange prize (had it been on offer in her lifetime) despite her ardent need of professional recognition.

In his biography of Kingsley Amis, Zachary Leader anatomizes the male literary world in which Amis felt very much at home, noting that he had 'a lifelong attraction to groups, gangs, circles, cliques, clubs, clubs within clubs, cabals, collaborations.'[18] The Garrick Club, Bertorelli's restaurant in Soho, and, much later in the 1970s, Friday lunches at the Bursa Kebab House off Theobald's Road, near the offices of the *New Statesman*: these were the gathering places for Amis and his pals, and his son Martin's gang—writers such as Christopher Hitchens and Ian McEwan. As Leader notes, 'Women came infrequently; the atmosphere was masculine and competitive... even the most accomplished writers could find the lunches intimidating.'[19] When asked in 1975 whether he had found it difficult as a young writer to break into the literary establishment, Amis did acknowledge that having heard 'there was a thing called the London literary racket' he was worried about being an outsider, but with his good degree from Oxford (an asset conspicuously absent from Olivia's résumé) he found his progress 'unimpeded by any matters of that sort.'[20] Characterizing the Angry Young Men as a group of three or four writers, none of whom was from ruling-class backgrounds yet had gone to elite public schools, Amis attributes their critical and commercial success to 'a feeling of exhaustion after the war. The older writers were still writing, but for some reason no new writer of any fame, any note, had appeared for seven or eight years.'[21] Certainly, Amis is correct in that novelists whose careers spanned the 1930s, 1940s, and 1950s were the most visible figures on the post-war literary landscape, a pattern traceable in large part to the difficulty faced by new writers in getting published in the immediate post-1945 period: publishing, in general, took a while to return to a robust level of activity and 1945 was not a good year for fiction—only just over a thousand novels were published that year

---

astonishing. 'If one looks at nineteenth-century literature and intellectual scope, it's George Eliot... and Elizabeth Gaskell.'

[18] *The Life of Kingsley Amis*, 284.

[19] *The Life of Kingsley Amis*, 648.

[20] Dale Salwak and Kingsley Amis, 'An interview with Kingsley Amis', 1–2.

[21] Dale Salwak and Kingsley Amis, 'An interview with Kingsley Amis', 2.

compared with more than four thousand in 1939.[22] Olivia was not alone when she identified the turbulence of wartime and reduced opportunities for publication as impediments to settling down to a stable writing life after 1945.

Braemar Mansions

In telling contrast in the 1950s to that male enclave the Garrick Club, number 5 Braemar Mansions, Cornwall Gardens, South Kensington, became the gathering place of another group of London writers, artists, and critics. Braemar Mansions housed the spacious flat of Ivy Compton-Burnett and her partner Margaret Jourdain. As we know, it was here in 1954 (the year of publication of *Lucky Jim*) that Olivia Manning became a member of Compton-Burnett's circle, composed principally of female and gay male writers. Olivia had written to Compton-Burnett in September of that year to suggest she propose an adaptation of her novel *Pastors and Masters* (1925) to the BBC and Compton-Burnett had replied that the BBC already had it 'in hand,'[23] but an invitation to come to tea along with Kay Dick quickly followed. A Saturday tea party was the principal mode of entertaining at Braemar Mansions and invitations went out on postcards in Ivy's large handwriting (Francis King's correspondence at the Harry Ransom Center contains a slew of postcards ordering him to tea). Within a few months, Olivia became a regular visitor, very much at home not only with Compton-Burnett and Margaret Jourdain but also with her fellow-guests, some of whom she had known for a long time, such as Robert Liddell (who came when he was not in Greece, where he had moved after the war) and Kay Dick and her partner Kathleen Farrell, and some who became lifelong friends, such as the playwright and screenwriter Julian Mitchell, who lived in Reggie and Olivia's basement flat in the early 1960s, and, of course, Francis King, whom she introduced to Ivy in 1957. King recalls that he was on leave from

[22] Bernard Bergonzi, 'The British novel in 1960,' Marina MacKay and Lyndsey Stonebridge (eds.), *British Fiction After Modernism: The Novel at Mid-Century*, 203. As the editors of this volume note, 'The war was the major turning point of the century in Britain: a domestic and geopolitical watershed that profoundly affected cultural life from 1945 until well into the 1950s' (p. 6).

[23] Ivy Compton-Burnett to Olivia Manning, 5 October 1954, OMC/C, HRC.

Greece where he was working for the British Council and that he met Reggie and Olivia in a pub opposite Gloucester Road tube station, from where he was led to Cornwall Gardens: '"You'll find her rather a bore," Reggie warned. But I can truthfully say that, unlike dear old Reggie, Ivy never bored me.'[24] Literary gossip was the principal means of entertainment at Ivy's tea parties and Olivia was not exempt from her cutting commentary: Ivy announced to Francis King that Olivia seemed to specialize in travel books and that in contrast to his facility in 'building' a novel, 'poor Olivia has no idea of *building*. The materials are good but they're all over the place, just all over the place.' Ivy also slyly lamented Iris Murdoch's 'involvement in philosophy. If she had studied domestic science...I'm sure her books would have been much better.'[25] Ivy's guests, in turn, brought her entertaining tattle from the theater, the BBC, and publishing.

Towards the end of Ivy's life (she died in 1969), the tea parties tended to become somewhat grim affairs and the atmosphere was not helped by the dimly lit dining room. Olivia found the gatherings oppressive and wrote to Francis King, 'How dreadful tea is at Ivy's now! I am always in trouble for not eating anything. When I had got down a piece of ancient cake, Ivy pressed me to have some white pre-sliced bread. I said I could eat no more. She looked at me narrowly and said in a very sharp tone, "People are giving up all this slimming. They are tired of looking old and ugly."'[26] Pamela Hansford Johnson recalls the horrified expression on Ivy's face if you happened to put the wrong spoon back in the wrong jam pot at one of these teas, and also being invited to dinner, arriving half an hour late (she had misread the time on Ivy's postcard), and being completely ignored for the entire meal. She admitted that while Olivia may have been on Ivy's 'wavelength,' she was not.[27]

Attuned as she was to Ivy's idiosyncrasies, the tea parties with other women writers made Olivia feel part of a community happily unlike that cozy male-dominated world of the 'booksey boys' and, with Ivy's gatherings in mind, she began to have regular parties of her own at her elegant house in Queen's Grove, lunches rather than teas, where,

[24] *Yesterday Came Suddenly*, 222.
[25] *Yesterday Came Suddenly*, 227.
[26] FKC/OM, HRC, 17 April 1969.
[27] Pamela Hansford Johnson, 'A visit to Dame Ivy,' *The Times*, 2 February 1974.

Elizabeth Jane Howard recalls in her memoir, she met 'such luminaries as Stevie Smith and Ivy Compton-Burnett... Olivia introduced me to old-fashioned roses, and she had a Siamese cat called Faro whom she adored.'[28] Faro, of course, was named for Felix Latimer's beloved pet in *School for Love* and was just one of Olivia's many cherished Siamese; the first was acquired when she and Reggie were living in the Baker Street flat in 1946 and until her death she would stay with friends only if she could bring her cat, its special food (carefully poached turkey breast was always on the feline menu), and litter for its box. And not only did Olivia establish her own lunch parties in a kind of imaginative defiance of the 1950s 'booksey boys,' she vigorously combatted their cultural hegemony: when Stevie Smith gloomily predicted, 'We're all finished now. The Angry Young Men are going to take our place,' Olivia sharply responded, 'Don't be absurd, Stevie. These people will never take our place. What will happen is that they will develop as we develop.'[29]

Although the Compton-Burnett flat in Braemar Mansions seemed uncomfortably stuffed with antiques (most of them selected by Margaret Jourdain, who was an accomplished historian of Regency furniture), it contained many valuable pieces, not least of which were seven antique looking-glasses. In her will, Compton-Burnett bequeathed them to the seven stalwarts of her tea-party circle: Lettice Cooper (British novelist and biographer), Kay Dick, Robert Liddell, Kathleen Farrell, Francis King, Julian Mitchell, and Olivia Manning. Olivia received a heavy Jacobean looking-glass and she was not pleased: Julian Mitchell recalls that when the mirrors were taken down from the walls after a reading of the will, she looked thoroughly miffed.[30] That very evening Olivia telephoned Francis King to say she was sure there had been a mix-up: Ivy had assured her that she was to have the Regency looking-glass that had gone to Francis—could they not switch? After declining firmly and dismissing Olivia's claim that the Jacobean mirror was a man's mirror and the Regency one more properly belonged in her sitting room, King learned that Olivia had taken her bequest to be valued at Christie's and had been astonished to learn that it was worth

[28] *Slipstream*, 286.
[29] Isobel English (June Braybrooke), Introduction to the Virago edition of *The Doves of Venus*, 612–13.
[30] Conversation with author, 6 May 2010.

far more than his, or, indeed, anyone else's. Mischievously, he called to say he had thought it over and was happy to do a swap, to which she responded that she had come to treasure her Jacobean mirror since it was so much a 'Compton-Burnett' object, that is to say somewhat intimidating. The mirrors remained in place and Francis King's still hangs in the sitting room of his London house (or at least, it did until his death in July 2011). What happened to Olivia's mirror remains a mystery, although it's possible it might be found in the possessions of Diana Hogarth, whom Reggie married after Olivia died in 1980.

In late 1952, just after she had finished *A Different Face*, Olivia wrote to Kay Dick that she wished she could feel a 'real urge' to write again: 'One is only at peace when really inside a novel—at least so it seems when one is outside one. I suppose the most satisfying period is a few hours after the satisfactory conclusion of a novel—after that a great emptiness descends.'[31] This feeling of great emptiness persisted for a few stressful months while Olivia continued to write reviews for *The Spectator* and resumed her campaign to find work with the BBC. Wondering what might have happened to her *Middlemarch* proposal after it had been so savagely dismantled by Mrs Helena Wood, she wrote to Charles Lefeaux, in charge of the Drama Script Unit at the BBC, suggesting an adaptation of George Eliot's *Daniel Deronda*. Her idea was to omit all the Jewish characters ('put in for idealistic reasons . . . completely wooden and unreal'). Clearly ignorant of Eliot's serious study of Jewish history and religion in preparation for writing *Daniel Deronda*, Olivia declared, 'George Eliot seems to have known nothing about Jews and the Jewish world, but her country and working-class characters are, as ever, magnificent.'[32] This uninformed criticism of George Eliot did not go down too well and Charles Lefeaux declined. Still doggedly persistent, after reading D. H. Lawrence's short stories at the urging of Reggie, Olivia next proposed an adaptation of 'Fanny and Annie.' Unfortunately for her, the proposal was sent to the

---

[31] Olivia Manning to Kay Dick, October 1952, OMP, UT, Series 1, Box 1, Folder 4.
[32] Olivia Manning to Charles Lefeaux, 28 May 1954, Olivia Manning Scriptwriter 1943–1982. BBC Written Archives Centre, Caversham. In the spring of 1955, however, the Midland Regional BBC ran a ten-week adaptation of *Middlemarch*, based loosely on Olivia's proposal but with every episode rewritten by the director of BBC Drama, Birmingham. Memorandum from Victor Menzies, Drama Birmingham, to Donald McWhinnie, 5 April 1955. Olivia Manning Scriptwriter 1943–1982. BBC Written Archives Centre, Caversham.

stern Mrs Helena Wood, who declared it to be inadequate on all counts: Olivia fails to establish atmosphere and characters, all is crammed into dialogue with the result that conversation is unconvincing and clumsy, and the adaptation shows no understanding of the brilliant technique of the original.[33]

Compounding the depressing disappointment that resulted from her dealings with the BBC, she and Reggie, along with many of their friends, were becoming increasingly worried about the Cold War, particularly the development of nuclear weapons by all the major powers. A governmental committee, whose findings were leaked to Reggie and other BBC producers, estimated that ten ten-megaton Soviet H-bombs dropped on the United Kingdom would kill twelve million people and seriously injure a further four million (nearly a third of the population) even before the poisonous effects of radioactive fall-out spread across the country.[34] Such frightening predictions prompted Churchill to confide to his doctor, Lord Moran, in the spring of 1954, 'I am more worried by the hydrogen bomb than by all the rest of my troubles put together'[35] and also prompted Olivia and Reggie to become members of the Society for Cultural Relations with the USSR, an organization obviously political in its aim to foster cultural exchange with the unofficial enemy, yet principally involved in projects such as sending selections of newly published British books to the Soviet Union. Founded in 1924, the Society had among its original members such key intellectuals and writers as E. M. Forster, John Maynard Keynes, Bertrand Russell, and Virginia Woolf. Shortly before his death in 1991, the poet Roy Fuller recalled that in the mid-1950s the threat of a third world war became so acute that small groups of writers began meeting in each others' houses; at one such meeting 'came one night Reggie Smith and his wife Olivia Manning, between them a half comatose individual who, dormouselike, sat but added nothing to the proceedings, and was later discovered to be Dylan Thomas.'[36] Long a friend of Reggie's, who had first given him much-needed work in the BBC Drama Department in the late

[33] Report on Olivia Manning's proposal by Mrs Helena Wood, 1 March 1955, BBC Written Archives Centre, Caversham.

[34] Peter Hennessy, Having It So Good, 320.

[35] Quoted in Having It So Good, 319.

[36] Roy Fuller, 'The end of the forties,' 276.

1940s, Thomas died in New York a few months after his 'dormouse-like' appearance (on 9 November 1953) and two months later the BBC Third Programme broadcast his *Under Milk Wood*. Deeply saddened by the death of their old friend, Reggie and Olivia also struggled at this time with a nagging domestic difficulty: finding a satisfactory tenant for the basement flat in Queen's Grove. The first occupant was Tony Richardson.

After moving in in early January 1953, Richardson quickly acquired several cats and parrots (shamefully neglected, accordingly to Olivia) and proceeded to sublet the flat to various unsavory friends, the most troublesome 'a frightful girl' accompanied by a small child and several lovers who kept the place in 'an uproar.' The 'frightful girl' remained for six weeks and then cleared off leaving unpaid bills for milk, news-papers, and groceries at the local shop in St John's Wood High Street. Claiming that since Richardson had sublet the flat to this wanton person he should pay her debts, Olivia demanded compensation. He refused.[37] By the end of 1953, Olivia began scouting around for a new tenant and Kay Dick came up with someone Olivia referred to as 'your S. American friend,' but when she mentioned this to Richardson, Olivia wrote to Kay, he 'refused to believe he exists and takes a rather high-handed view of the whole matter.'[38] Thoroughly fed up, Olivia ordered Richardson to leave the flat, and he, in turn, declared he had 'new friends' who had a place for him and who were more than delighted to take care of his cats and parrots. But he stayed put and, according to Olivia, persisted in complaining that the flat was damp and badly in need of a paint job and new curtains and chair covers. In January 1954, he finally moved out, Olivia redecorated the flat for a new tenant, and thus ended her relationship with the then aspiring theater and film director who went on to direct the first production of John Osborne's *Look Back in Anger* in 1956, and to marry Vanessa Redgrave in 1962. Alluding to Richardson's bisexuality, Francis King asserts that the fractious relationship between Olivia and Richardson was probably caused by his refusal to respond to her sexual advances: Olivia was in the habit of making passes at her male lodgers, says King,

---

[37] Olivia Manning to Kay Dick, 3 December 1953, OMP, UT, Series 1, Box 1, Folder 5.

[38] Olivia Manning to Kay Dick, 25 November 1953, OMP, UT, Series 1, Box 1, Folder 5.

'I know that in the case of both Julian Mitchell [a tenant in the house to which Olivia and Reggie moved in December 1962] and Tony Richardson, this proved, not surprisingly, futile.'[39] King may be correct, although I have discovered no evidence that Olivia was sexually attracted to either Richardson or Julian Mitchell, or that they repulsed her overtures.

Compounding the distracting need to deal with her tenant, Olivia also had to cope with a visit from Reggie's mother. In the December 1953 letter to Kay Dick that recounted her testy dealings with Richardson, she added that she was having 'a dreary, exhausting time' due to the lingering presence of Mrs Smith, a woman, she confided, who is 'without any exception at all the most wearisome bore I have ever come up against. Reggie leaves the brunt of it to me and is, of course, able to get away from the house. She was supposed to leave today about 12 and now, after a lot of silly dithering, cannot go until after 2—that, somehow, seems the last straw. I am pounding away on this typewriter, scarcely knowing what I am writing, just to keep her from driveling.'[40] After the war years in which she and Reggie had lived a refugee's existence with no settled home, Olivia had taken great pleasure in decorating the Queen's Grove house. The living room contained leather buttoned sofas and chairs, satinwood furniture meticulously decorated by Olivia in gold leaf, Persian miniatures picked up in Jerusalem, and some quite valuable modern pictures (publication of a novel was marked with a new purchase). This elegantly appointed space was also sometimes Olivia's workroom and the big leather sofa was often piled high with loose sheets of paper covered in a big looped handwriting. The last straw when she was close to completing *The Doves of Venus*, pounding away on the typewriter that she would roll into the living room from her study when she felt like working elsewhere in the house, was the 'dithering' Mrs Smith, who lingered beyond 2 o'clock, refusing to recognize that Olivia worked in the afternoons (Olivia's working habits were to make at least three drafts in longhand on paper and then type the final manuscript herself). A reward for finishing this novel (and also some respite from Reggie's tiresome mother) came with a trip to

---

[39] *Yesterday Came Suddenly*, 240.

[40] Olivia Manning to Kay Dick, 3 December 1953, OMP, UT, Series 1, Box 1, Folder 5.

Venice in June 1955: Olivia wrote to Stevie Smith that she thought it 'the loveliest and most exciting place I have ever seen... I have finished the novel but have not yet had Heinemann's final word on it. I had to work continuously on it to get it finished before leaving. It is longer than my usual.'[41]

Despite Olivia's well-earned reputation as an envious belittler of her female contemporaries, becoming a member of Ivy Compton-Burnett's circle led both to forming new friendships and to maintaining old ties. In the letter to Kay Dick complaining about the wretched Tony Richardson and the tiresome Mrs Smith, she adds that she is looking forward to having her come to dinner with Ivy, Elizabeth Jane Howard, and Cecil Woodham-Smith, whose 1950 biography of Florence Nightingale had been a great success and whose study of the Charge of the Light Brigade in the Crimean War (*The Reason Why*) had been published to critical and popular acclaim in 1953. Strangely, given her considerable success, Woodham-Smith, Olivia reported, was feeling 'very nervous at the prospect of meeting THE GREAT WOMAN NOVELIST: I told her to make a few damning remarks about Elizabeth Taylor as that could not fail to please.' In the gossiping circle that gathered around Ivy in Braemar Mansions, Elizabeth Taylor was a favored topic of ridicule by virtue of what its members regarded as her dreary, sentimental writing. A few weeks later, Olivia wrote to Kay Dick that she had received 'a horrid lecturing letter from Robert Liddell' because she had gossiped enviously about Taylor selling 40,000 copies of *The Sleeping Beauty* (1953), a delicate novel of middle-aged love. Olivia thought Liddell 'too virtuous and modest for the world' and pointed out that Compton-Burnett did not exactly admire Elizabeth Taylor, to which he responded by asking whether she was certain that Ivy thought any more highly of *her* work.[42]

Olivia and Kay Dick, of course, had become friends back in 1947 when *The Windmill* published one of Olivia's short stories. And Kay Dick and Stevie Smith had been friends before the war and saw each other regularly, most often when Stevie would visit Kay Dick and Kathleen Farrell at their house in the country. In January 1947, Dick teasingly asked Stevie for a story for *The Windmill*—'It's about time

---

[41] Postcard from Venice from Olivia Manning to Stevie Smith, 23 June 1955, SSP, UT, Series 1, Book 3, Folder 1.

[42] Olivia Manning to Kay Dick, 16 January 1954, OMP, UT, Series 1, Box 1, Folder 6.

you remembered that Windmill is there to print Madame Smith'—and also thanked her for sending along the manuscript of Olivia's book on Stanley and Emin Pasha.[43] It's clear from the correspondence between Kay Dick and Stevie Smith that they were both deeply fond of Olivia, understood her insecurities, and did all they could to get her work published and favorably reviewed. For example, Kay wrote in 1953 that if Stevie were to see 'our beloved Olivia (beloved in our fashion) tell her I hope she is still writing to me and that I want to see her soon. Après tout I am picking her as my example of best novelist of generation younger than the celebrated Bowen, Lehmann etc. in my Personality and Purpose scripts on contemporary novelists.'[44] A few months later, Kay wrote to Stevie saying how delighted she was to see the strongly appreciative piece by William Gerhardie in the *TLS*: 'I love Olivia dearly and do hope she gets all the success she deserves and more.'

Several days afterwards she confided to Stevie that an attack of nerves triggered by the impending publication of her novel *An Affair of Love* had been alleviated by Olivia's reactions to the book: 'that girl is certainly wonderfully encouraging even in her criticisms which I take *absolutely* from her . . . how I love that creature. She is really superb: we wouldn't have her changed would we?' Certainly, beneath Kay Dick's comments lurks an occasional exasperation with Olivia's demanding personality—never enough attention, never enough love—yet her pals clearly admired her intelligence and her writing, and she was always a loyal friend. When Kay Dick was having problems in her relationship with Kathleen Farrell, Olivia offered sensible advice—stay with her and reconcile yourself to her difficult personality, or make a clean break—and when June Braybrooke felt some trepidation at the prospect of going to a publisher's party because 'All the nobs will be there,' Olivia bracingly replied, 'Don't be ridiculous . . . We are the nobs.'[45] In a literary marketplace dominated in the mid-1950s by the Angry Young Men, Olivia's friends constituted a counter-group of highly intelligent and charming women writers who admired her work, loved her wit, and promoted her reputation.

---

[43] Kay Dick to Stevie Smith, 14 January 1947, SSP, UT, Series 1, Box 1, Folder 9.
[44] Kay Dick to Stevie Smith, 27 January 1953, SSP, UT, Series 1, Box 1, Folder 9.
[45] Isobel English (June Braybrooke), Introduction to *The Doves of Venus*, 617.

A man's world

The social oppression and hypocrisy of the 1950s that David Hare found so detestable is certainly present in *The Doves of Venus* as Olivia describes 'the darkest rim of provincial ignorance' where Ellie Parsons has grown up, the daughter of a rough and ready mother who runs a restaurant in Portsea, an old-time English café serving egg and chips and strong cups of tea. In Portsea, as Ellie's mother announces darkly, 'people talk.' Like Fanny Price in Jane Austen's *Mansfield Park* (a novel much admired by Olivia), who is transported from the crowded conditions of her Portsmouth home to the spacious grandeur of her cousins' country house, Ellie Parsons moves from 'the smallness and discomfort of her own home' to a world that makes her wonder how 'people could live out their lives in rooms as small as that.'[46] But the London world to which Ellie escapes from Portsea is notably free in matters of sexual behavior: for instance, Olivia describes in graphic terms the attraction felt by Ellie's lover and his estranged wife (when they first meet)—shut together in a car, rain blinding the windscreen, 'their senses heightened by nearness and a constant consciousness of one another,' they drive at maniac speed to the nearest hotel, take a room, and stay in bed for days (p. 265). The two major themes of *The Doves of Venus*, for Jeremy Treglown 'the best' of Olivia's novels outside the trilogies,[47] are female initiation into the sexual ways of the world and a preoccupation shared by both men and women with growing old. In 1954, at the age of forty-six, in the openly autobiographical pattern that characterizes so much of her fiction, Olivia recurred to her heady London days before the war and bravely dissected her fears of aging and death.

Gratefully dedicated to William Gerhardie in acknowledgment of his laudatory essay in the *TLS* that had appeared in September 1953, *The Doves of Venus* was published on 24 October 1955 (Gerhardie's Cambridge archives contain an invitation from Heinemann to a book party at 90 Oakley Street in Chelsea). Several reviewers speculated that Olivia had taken the title from the opening lines of Ben Jonson's

---

[46] *The Doves of Venus*, 160.
[47] Jeremy Treglown, 'Olivia Manning's masculine outfit,' 148.

'A Celebration of Charis: IV. Her Triumph'—'See the chariot here at hand of Love, | Wherein my lady rideth! | Each that draws is a swan or a dove, | And well the car Love guideth.' Jonson's poem directs the reader to look upon Venus's bright hair, smooth forehead, and soft complexion, attributes that emphasize her untouched, youthful beauty. The title, then, prepares us for the caustic critique of male preoccupation with virginity that follows, particularly since the sole reference in the novel to the doves of Venus comes from the least attractive male character in a work notable for its descriptions of male vanity and failure: the decrepit roué Tom Claypole, pressing the fingertips of his left hand into Ellie's 'deep, soft, pink palm,' declares, 'Girls... They are the doves of Venus... little soft white doves... silver doves that carry our thoughts—where?' (p. 159).

As Jeremy Treglown cogently observes, *The Doves of Venus* treats 'with feeling irony aspects of the life of a single woman of the time... not least at moments where it displays a feminist dimension of the 1950s anger more often associated—in British writing at least—with young men.'[48] In a sense, then, this is Olivia's Angry Woman's novel, her feminist writing back to the 'booksey boys' at the top of the best-seller lists, and, despite a lifelong resistance to labeling novels either women's or men's fiction, she aimed this at her women readers. *The Doves of Venus* depicts without mercy the patronizing patriarchal attitudes encountered by Ellie Parsons, Petta, the runaway wife of Ellie's lover Quintin Bellot, and Nancy Claypole, Ellie's friend and fellow furniture-painter in the Sloane Square studio (Ellie sounds somewhat like 'Ollie,' the nickname for Olivia devised by her brother Oliver).

Like Olivia in the mid-1930s, Ellie lives in a top-floor bed-sitting room on Margaretta Terrace in Chelsea, and like Olivia celebrating her similarity to Madame Bovary when Hamish Miles becomes her lover, Ellie, after sleeping with Quintin Bellot, dances around her room in celebration of the loss of her virginity. A practiced seducer and former lover of a Mrs Primrose who runs the Sloane Square studio where Ellie finds a job antiquing reproductions of Regency furniture, Bellot lives very comfortably on a private income. Like Tom Claypole, but less repellently perhaps because he is not quite as

---

[48] 'Olivia Manning's masculine outfit,' 148.

decrepit as Tom, he is on a constant lookout for fresh young things. Ellie catches his eye one day when he visits Mrs Primrose's studio. Soon, he is introducing her to French food, as did Hamish Miles when he took Olivia to Soho restaurants: '*Langue de Boeuf en Paupiettes*—that's ox-tongue done with a sort of meat stuffing and bacon; in *paupiettes*, in . . . oh, you know! . . . in slices. *Côtes de veau foyer*—veal cutlets done in white wine with grated cheese and breadcrumbs. Very nice. Would you like that? Or some sort of chicken?' (pp. 2–3). To Ellie, accustomed to egg and chips, these fancy French names are just a lot of folderol: why not just put veal cutlets on the menu and leave it at that? For a while, Quintin is captured by her naïveté, by her fresh openness to life, by her sheer joy in being alive: even if she has no money and suffers the dire warnings of her sour mother that she will come to no good in London, she is, quite simply, living in an enchanted present. In her autobiographical fragment, Olivia writes, 'It seemed to me that I did not start living until I came to London. Before that, I existed in a limbo of loneliness, longing for someone I never seemed to meet.'[49] The joy of being young, of becoming truly alive in London, and of meeting a longed-for someone animates the plot of *The Doves of Venus*.

Yet this novel also recurs persistently to a fear of aging and death. In an unsettling description of an old woman's wrinkled body, Olivia describes Ellie's repulsion at the sight of an elderly fellow-lodger in the Chelsea boarding-house where she has a room that had been 'advertised on a postcard in a sweet-shop,' just as Olivia found her first bed-sitting room in the mid-1930s. Deprived of hot water for her weekly bath by the monopolization of the bathroom by this old woman, Ellie feels 'so menaced' by the incident that 'even at the distance of her youth, she felt the threat of lonely, maniac old age' (p. 59). Petta, Quintin's estranged wife, is a middle-aged beauty depressed by the loss of her pre-war looks and a post-war preoccupation with the Bomb, food shortages, and squalid bombsites. She has no patience with a rowdy lower-class world of queues, crowds, and noise. Life is no more fun, especially when one's social capital has been invested in a glamorous, delicate beauty: and the dividends have, as it were, dried up. Quintin, in turn, has inherited from his father a distaste for extreme elegance in middle-aged women since that elegance invariably turns

---

[49] 'Let me tell you before I forget,' OMC, HRC.

his thoughts to 'the mortal end of the flesh beneath' (p. 76). His lingering fascination with Petta's beauty suddenly turns to repulsion when he notices the crepe-like quality of her neck: gazing into 'the white flesh of her bosom,' he sees it 'crinkle slightly where it had lost elasticity' (p. 74). And walking behind Tom Claypole as they leave a restaurant, he notices a 'strut, masculine, self-sufficient yet defiant,' and thinks to himself, 'To grow old! There is no greater tragedy!' (p. 257).

In terms of Olivia's by now customary appropriation of autobiography for fiction, she executes some fascinating and revealing transformations of actual individuals into fictional characters: Hamish Miles becomes a vain and cruel seducer, interested solely in gratifying his male ego through the infatuation of young impressionable women and living as well as possible on a limited private income; Olivia's plaintive, nagging mother becomes a masculine, strong, square woman who wears tweeds in all seasons (her clothes are spotted with grease from the café fryer, her cheeks stand out like red rubber balls, and her chin is a third ball stuck on below her mouth)—brave and good-natured when serving her customers, she is belligerent and peevish with Ellie; and Olivia herself is both Ellie and Petta, the deliriously happy girl in London in the mid-1930s and the middle-aged woman worried about her fading attractions in the mid-1950s. These transformations suggest that Olivia extrapolates and exaggerates negative aspects of the most important figures in her life and, of course, in herself: as much as she adored Hamish Miles, she also suffered from his neglect; her mother is figured in almost all her short stories as a whining nag but here she is made almost clownish, a grotesque physical figure; and Olivia's worry about her loss of sexual appeal is expressed darkly through the pitiful Petta.

Predictably, Quintin quickly tires of Ellie, promising to telephone her but never doing so, making excuses: 'He had not said he was going to a party, but she supposed he must be. A cocktail party. She had never herself been to one, but she had heard of cocktail parties. She knew all about them. She was well-read in fiction borrowed from public libraries. At cocktail parties witty persons, gorgeously dressed, talked to one another in the manner of Aldous Huxley characters' (p. 68). Abandoned by Quintin, Ellie feels she has been injured by people 'much more powerful than herself. They had knowledge and power' (p. 242), and her education in male indifference to women's feelings continues when she visits the country house of Tom Claypole, uncle of Nancy Claypole, a character whom Isobel English (June Braybrooke) believes 'has much of Stevie in her. There has been some obvious attempt at disguise. Nancy is portrayed as a tall, plain girl who went to the Slade [a well-known London art school], whereas Stevie was small and attractive and went to a secretarial college.'[50]

Possibly, some of Stevie's practiced knowingness about the ways of the world might have gone into Nancy Claypole, and some believe that Stevie Smith's review of *The Doves of Venus* that appeared in *The Observer* on 23 October 1955 soured her friendship with Olivia. Olivia certainly confirmed how distressed she was by the review. Admitting that she included a detail in *The Doves of Venus* based on Stevie's supposed 'love of death,' she regarded it as unfortunate that the novel 'came to her to review and she was able to get her own back. The review was so bitchy that I was amazed when she turned up for a party which Heinemanns gave on publication . . . It was at this time that I began to feel I had had enough of Stevie.'[51] Yet they continued to see each other at literary parties, even if certain tensions strained their long friendship. Olivia, for example, in describing a book party in mid-November 1955 to Kay Dick, noted that Stevie was present in a 'curious dress of yellow and white striped furnishing material which she had made herself. She said I should be thankful not to be published this month and have to face the rivalry of Elizabeth Jane Howard who is very good.'[52] Stevie, she added 'was still very much Stevie.'

Stevie begins her 'bitchy' *Observer* review by saying that nobody in the novel 'seems a tolerable human being' except Ellie . . . Miss Manning writes always with a poet's care for words and it is her usual distinction of style and construction that sets this novel, for all its faults of moral naivety, far, far, above the average run. It is balance of thought that one misses.'[53] 'Moral naivety' seems strangely inappropriate for a novel that forthrightly shows the multiple ways in which men subordinate women through condescension and exploitation, and the ways in which women in return denigrate men. The 'balance' very

[50] Introduction to *The Doves of Venus*, 613.
[51] Manuscript notes for memoir of Stevie Smith, OMC, HRC.
[52] Olivia Manning to Kay Dick, 17 November 1955, OMP, UT, Series 1, Box 1, Folder 7.
[53] Stevie Smith, 'Youth and age,' *The Observer*, 23 October 1955.

much present in this novel is that between male and female weaponry in a war between the sexes. Petta, for instance, feels that few men understand 'passion' and none has ever been able to 'draw her from the prison of herself'; her first husband Henry, whom she left for Quintin, during sex would look down at her blank face and ask what she thought about at such a time; her response, 'I design clothes for myself' (p. 201). Visiting Clopals, Tom Claypole's country house, Ellie marvels at Nancy's boldness in raising the topic of inequality between the sexes. When Nancy voices disgust that the furniture studio has one wage scale for men and another for women, Tom nods approvingly and says quite right since men need more money: she responds that they don't need more, they just get more. She stands her ground, asking how women who lack charm are to live, but Tom remains indifferent, 'imbued with so complete a sense of masculine ascendancy' that the two women know 'themselves a penniless feminine combine in no position to quarrel with benefits received' (p. 157).

Tom Claypole describes perfectly the milieu that Olivia exposes so incisively in this undeniably feminist novel: 'Surely, my dear girl,' he says to Ellie, 'you've discovered by now that you're living in a man's world. You must try to gain things by your charms' (p. 156). If *The Doves of Venus* recalls George Gissing's admittedly far more depressing novel *The Odd Women* (1893) in its representation of the miseries of being female and virtually penniless in London, then it also anticipates Doris Lessing's *The Golden Notebook* (1962) in its examination of how women compete with and support one another in a patriarchal society. At a later moment, Nancy Claypole articulates a prevalent 1950s discriminatory attitude towards women: when her mother becomes ill and she is called by family members to return home, she says to Ellie, 'If I were a man they wouldn't think of dragging me back. They'd have to find someone else—but because I'm a girl, I must give up everything and go' (p. 173).

What Stevie Smith neglected to discuss in her review of *The Doves of Venus* is Olivia's always wonderful talent in describing landscape, in making us feel, for example, Ellie's discomfort and unhappiness as she walks in Regent's Park on a cold, wintry, and miserable day. The weather matches Quintin's coldness in dispensing with her, his selfish belief that if he buys her a present she will get over his rejection of her (the present is a cheap powder compact bought on Camden High Street after leaving Regent's Park). Olivia describes the ice on the lake, 'the colour of a fish's eye. In its thickness were held plane leaves and twigs, with here and there a bullet-star of cracks or a white cockle-shaped air-pocket. On the surface walked gulls and mallards and ducks with flame-golden breasts. Among these smaller fowl, awkwardly, like overgrown adolescents at a children's party, were swans that kept peering down, beak-tip to ice, as though puzzling over the disappearance of the water' (p. 61). The frozen lake suggests Quintin's icy demeanor when he decides to send Ellie packing, and the puzzled swans peering down into the icy surface suggest Ellie as one of the 'swans' that draw Venus's chariot in Jonson's poem, here bewildered by her lover's icy rejection.

Abandoning both the plaintive Ellie and the troublesome Petta, Quintin leaves for Switzerland with a wealthy widow and Petta maliciously spreads gossip that he has died on arrival in Geneva, news that sends Ellie into paroxysms of weeping similar to that described by Olivia in her autobiographical fragment when she heard of the death of Hamish Miles. Unlike Hamish, however, Quintin is not dead and returns to London, where, at the end of the novel, he attempts a resumption of the sexual affair. Ellie, however, has married a decent young man and remains indifferent to his advances: as he touches her chin, narrows his eyes, and draws down his lips in a smile 'that would once have enthralled her,' she becomes 'acutely aware of the marks of age on him' and thinks happily of her husband's strong young body. The novel ends as she boards a bus that passes 'in spectral quiet through the twilight of Kentish Town and Camden Town, journeying westwards into the transformed city where Ellie had her home' (p. 313). London has been transformed through her rough education in male vanity, exploitation, and marriage to someone not unlike Reggie Smith: supportive, loving, and generous—but without Reggie's annoying social promiscuity.

Reviews of *The Doves of Venus* were mixed. After lauding Olivia for the 'outstanding quality' of her earlier novels—a detachment that until now has enabled her 'to present objectively precisely those situations which usually provoke from the feminine writer sentimentality and personal involvement'—the anonymous reviewer of the *TLS* declared that Olivia seems to have decided to 'charm rather than to disturb.' Petta, 'a desperate woman left over from the jazz age and unable to grow old, it must be frankly said, is an awful bore'; none of Ellie's responses to her education in male shallowness and selfishness are 'real' and, like Oliver Twist, her story 'has an implausibly happy ending.'[54] It would seem a sharply intelligent female novelist admired for her lack of sentimentality who constructs a feminist narrative of exploitation and survival in a male-dominated world can only be seen as succumbing to the dangers lurking in women's writing. For the *New York Times* reviewer William Du Bois, Olivia is 'a Bloomsbury-come-lately' who has written a novel that 'oozes gloom from every comma,' but, he adds, this is a novel that is 'an astringent tour de force, guaranteed to send chills up every sensitive spine.' Chilling as he may have thought it, however, nowhere does Du Bois remark upon the feminist implications of *The Doves of Venus*: the struggles of young women in what the reviewer terms 'the hand-me-down literary and artistic fringes of a London' that Olivia knew by heart.[55]

Kay Dick wrote to express her admiration of *The Doves of Venus* and in response Olivia said how very pleased she was by the letter: 'You have really understood what I was trying to do, and have appreciated those points I most hoped someone—the ideal Reader which you have proved to be—would appreciate. I do not need to tell you how much that means to a writer.'[56] So, Olivia was consoled for a few negative reviews of her first feminist novel by affectionate letters from her friends and, as always, by the support of Reggie, who never wavered throughout Olivia's career in his admiration of her talent. She was also consoled by the admiration of someone who bore a striking resemblance to Reggie: her general practitioner and St John's Wood neighbor, Jerry Slattery. By the mid-1950s, she and Reggie and Jerry and his wife Johnny had become close friends.

Jerry

In April 2010, Elizabeth Jane Howard amplified for me the views of Olivia Manning she had set out in her memoir, *Slipstream*. She declared forthrightly that Olivia was a neurotic, treacherous woman—excessively keen on sex and obsessively jealous of other

---

[54] *TLS*, 4 November 1955.

[55] *New York Times*, 16 November 1956.

[56] Olivia Manning to Kay Dick, 1 November 1955, OMP, UT, Series 1, Box 1, Folder 7.

writers. Her first memory of Olivia was of an evening party at Queen's Grove where she had gone with a barrister friend who was Olivia's neighbor, and, Howard suspected, also her lover. She sensed immediately that Olivia liked to collect famous people, that she could be very charming, and that she always wanted to be the center of attention. Contrary to my belief that Olivia was physically attractive, albeit in an offbeat fashion, Howard disagreed: her pop eyes, poor complexion, beaky nose, and unremarkable figure did not make for an attractive woman, an impression distinctly different to that remembered by June Braybrooke, Olivia's close friend, who declared that right up until her death Olivia never looked old—'her eyes were brilliant and beautiful and her skin was smooth and unlined.'[57] Olivia's principal appeal, according to Elizabeth Jane Howard, was a strong interest in sex: men sensed this and were drawn to her, eager to become one of her many lovers. In all this, Howard believes, Reggie was compliant, untroubled by his wife's promiscuity and close relationship with Jerry Slattery. Most of all, he was genuinely fond of her, supportive of her work, and a firm believer in her genius.[58] The relevance of Olivia's extracurricular love life in a biography whose primary focus is upon her writing might strike some readers as questionable, yet it seems to me a writer's life is not just to be found in the figure at the typewriter, especially in a writing life so deeply rooted in a fusion of autobiography and fiction.

In their biography of Olivia Manning, Neville and June Braybrooke discuss a letter discovered after her death, resting on top of a pile of manuscripts, typescripts, letters, bank statements, and press cuttings, all filling a large metal trunk. They believe that the letter, reproduced in its entirety, was addressed to Jerry Slattery, typed in Athens in the summer of 1949, and never posted. To know the letter was addressed to Slattery would be helpful for anyone writing about Olivia, but examination of the typed original discloses no evidence to this effect. Undated, lacking a heading (a hotel, perhaps?), and addressed to 'My dearest love,' the writer remembers that 'in April. . . . became my

---

[57] Introduction to *The Doves of Venus*, 612.

[58] Untangling different accounts of the relationship between Olivia and Jerry presented a challenge as I wrote about Olivia's life and work, and I have aimed to present the truth as disclosed by the evidence to hand, or, as best one can, to sort out the facts from the gossip.

lover.' If addressed to Jerry Slattery, why the ellipses? In fact, there are no clues that identify with certainty the writer or the recipient; the language is all generalized sentiment about being truly in love for the first time, about feeling 'the most delicious flesh' of one's lover, and about how they are part of one another. Most tellingly, I think, on the back of the letter Olivia has written in longhand, 'Is there an outside

+   3 copies   P 1

My dearest love,

I miss you more than I can say. At first you seemed still to be with me and the journey passed like a dream. The only reality was my life with you. Then, in the middle of the night, I woke up alone, and felt the train rushing forward into darkness and the distance growing between us. I remembered the lonliness and the long periods of desolation before I met you. I wanted you unbearably.

Darling, I love you. I love you. I love you. I have been wandering about this city - which is delightful, full of flowers and sunshine - and I have thought of nothing but you.   (Amen>)

I can only think that in April .... became my lover. You asked me once if I would give up everything for you and I replied 'Everything' and I meant everything. You may think I have not, after all, so much to give up. You have much more - and yet all my life I have only wanted to be an artist. All the affirs of which you made me tell you, were secondary to that one ambition - they were all a background to the thing I felt I must do. Now, for the first time in my life, I am in love in such a way that it comes before anything. I cannot tell you why.

You have often asked me why I love you and I have tried to think of reasons I could tell you. I have already told you most of them - ...use for me you are a man, and have been from my first awareness of you; but, alas, because part of your nature is feminine, and part of ⬛⬛⬛ masculine, and these parts fit so perfectly, it seems at times we must be one person. And because physically and mentally and spiritually we belong, and are in sympathy, and understand each other.

I have never felt any need to deceive you. I tell you the truth about everything because there is no need to do anything else.

I thought of other reasons for loving you, but they don't seem to matter now. Surely I do not need to give you reasons when we have come together so closely, we are almost part of one another. When we lie wrapped around each other, my arms about your shoulders, feeling the movements of your muscles, and your flesh - the most delicious flesh in the world - your breast to my bosom, your mouth to my mouth - then it is as though we had loved each other from the beginning of time.

You accuse me of having been unaware of you the first time you took my hand. It is true. I had tried to cut myself off from people and emotional relationships. I did not want to be aware of anyone. I tried to shut myself away and say 'It doesn't matter' and 'I don't care', and expect nothing, and tell myself I wanted nothing.

Only something I could not resist, could break in one there When I did become aware of you, I felt our relationship inevitible. There must be intercourse. And complete intercourse. Indeed, I feel now if we withheld ourselves from each other in any way, it would be more of a sin against ourselves and each other than anything we could do together.

What else can I say? If I read this through I shall probably not send it. so it must go unread. That is all. My beloved is mine and I am his. Saying that, I have said everything.

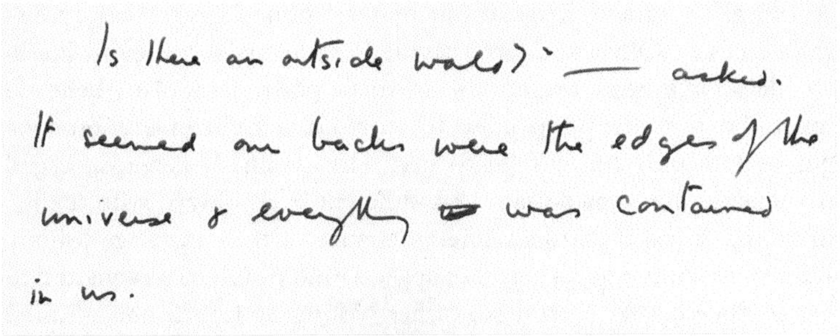

Is there an outside world? — asked.
It seemed our backs were the edges of the
universe & everything was contained
in us.

Figure 4. Typescript of letter, perhaps from Olivia Manning to Jerry Slattery. With permission of Victoria Orr-Ewing.

world?.... asked. It seemed our backs were the edges of the universe and everything was contained in us.' (See Figure 4.)

This strikes me as remarkably like the many notes Olivia wrote to herself when plotting a novel or short story. In sum, the sentimental tone of the letter is radically at odds with Olivia's ironic voice and suggests, perhaps, a drafted document to be included in a work of fiction, not a love letter written to Jerry Slattery. Finally, the Braybrookes believe that Olivia was 'highly sexed,' and point to accounts in her fiction of orgies, sexual exhibitions in brothels, and tales of men who suffer from premature ejaculation. It seems to me not necessarily true that if a novelist writes about sex, she or he is 'highly sexed.' However, Olivia's letters suggest she enjoyed a robust sex life and persuasive evidence would seem to affirm that Jerry Slattery was her lover.

Jeremiah Slattery was nine years younger than Olivia, an Irishman born in Kerry and a doctor with a medical degree from Trinity College, Dublin, who set up a general practice in Chalk Farm in 1949. Reggie and Olivia were on his books as patients. Strikingly similar in appearance, Reggie and Jerry were staunch drinking companions and rugby fans. According to Johnny Slattery, who at our meeting in April 2009 generously shared her memories of Reggie and Olivia, it was a love of rugby matches (not Olivia) that brought the two men together—Jerry and Reggie would go off to games and then to the pub while Olivia stayed home to work, always, Johnny added, fiercely protective of her time and disciplined about her writing. When the four of them got together, it was usually to go out for drinks in the St John's Wood and Hampstead pubs, and then to supper at a local restaurant. Early in our conversation, Johnny Slattery dismissed talk of Olivia and Jerry having been lovers as malicious gossip and declared Reggie was not the energetic philanderer many believed him to be: from her perspective, he would have run a mile if someone got serious and said let's go to bed. His openness, generosity, and tremendous verve made him very different from Olivia, who tended to be much more guarded. The endurance of their marriage Johnny Slattery attributed to his steadfast appreciation of Olivia's talent and to her reliance upon his criticism of her writing; in return, she admired tremendously his love of language and his serious moral commitment to advancing the work of new dramatists and talented but unrecognized actors such as Dylan Thomas, Peter O'Toole, and Harold Pinter.[59]

Francis King, Olivia's intimate friend from the time they met in 1957 until her death in 1980, declares unequivocally in his autobiography, 'Jerry would visit Olivia every afternoon, however busy she might be on a book and however busy he might be in his practice. He was clearly devoted to her; but he was no less devoted to his quiet, patient, highly intelligent wife. Of the four people involved in this odd situation, none showed any jealousy or hurt. They would entertain each other, take holidays together, behave to each other with unalloyed affection.'[60] Persuasive support for Francis King's assertion is to be found in a letter from Olivia rehearsing familiar complaints about Kay Dick: 'Early on in my affair with Jerry, I took him to the house in Heath Street. Kay, of course, realized we were intimate and as we left I saw her watching us balefully from the window. She then spent the afternoon ringing up Johnny Slattery, pretending she wanted to contact Jerry, saying she had seen us go off together and where could Jerry be?'[61] To be sure, Olivia was a great show-off to Francis of her sexual conquests (actual or not), but in this case Jerry Slattery does not belong on the list of literary luminaries with whom she claimed to have had affairs, and taken for granted in this censure of Kay Dick is King's long-term knowledge of Olivia's intimate relationship with Jerry Slattery.

---

[59] Author's conversation with Johnny Slattery, 10 April 2009.
[60] *Yesterday Came Suddenly*, 241.
[61] Olivia Manning to Francis King, 31 August 1978, FKC/OM, HRC. The house in Heath Street to which Olivia refers was inhabited at the time by Kay Dick and Kathleen Farrell.

Finally, the playwright and screenwriter Julian Mitchell recalls vividly an incident that took place in 1962 when he was living in the basement flat at 26 Queen's Grove ('rather squalid' was how he described it) and at a time when, as he put it, Jerry was almost publicly acknowledged as Olivia's lover. The door between his basement flat and the shared hallway was generally unlocked and on 28 October 1962, the day the Russians backed down, Mitchell was glued to his radio listening to the final tense moments of the unfolding of the Cuban Missile Crisis. Eager to share this reassuring news, Mitchell rushed up from the basement, banged on the door to the upstairs flat, and shouted for Olivia: in a few minutes, Jerry appeared, hastily adjusting his clothing, with Olivia behind him, in her turn wrapping herself in her dressing gown.[62] It does seem, then, that Olivia's love affair with someone who looked remarkably like Reggie (big, burly, with glasses) is a matter of plausible likelihood rather than gossipy speculation. And Jerry not only became her lover, he also became an astute financial advisor: with his help, she built up an impressive stock portfolio, a reassuring hedge against fears of a return to the scrimping of her early years in Portsmouth and in London before the war.

In 1956, Olivia published in *Punch* a series of amusing vignettes about a barely disguised Reggie that were later published in book form as *My Husband Cartwright*. In a tone of wry tolerance and occasional annoyance, the 'wife' portrays Cartwright as a lovable and foolishly trusting man who has never grown up. Cartwright's love for his fellow men is 'very widespread,' covering people of all races, creeds, and right-minded convictions, a love so 'thickly spread it quite obliterates for him those interstices of character that influence the judgments of others. He sees people through a blur of love.'[63] Cartwright/Reggie is a lovable buffoon, always ready to buy someone a drink, lend them money, or share a hotel room with a fellow who snores. He has acquaintances all over the globe but he has almost no close friends: 'If he likes someone, he ceases to be aware of them. He likes almost everyone.' On the fringes of his vast circle of acquaintances there seem to be many who believe that the 'functions of an old and prized friend are the performing of favors, the lending of money, and the listening to long, tedious confidences. Many of these old friends are

---

[62] Author's conversation with Julian Mitchell, 6 May 2010.
[63] *My Husband Cartwright*, 15.

a great nuisance' (p. 101). Reggie laughed uproariously at Cartwright's deficiencies, ever generously tolerant of whatever Olivia did, said, and wrote.

And who else is Cartwright but Guy Pringle? In the mid-1950s, Olivia began work on the first novel in her Balkan trilogy, *The Great Fortune*, and in the *Punch* sketches about Cartwright we find the lineaments of Guy's character, based, of course, on Reggie Smith. Exhilarated, as she wrote to Kay Dick, that her 'new novel has started to come to life,' she sat down to work, ever frugal and writing always on the paper that Reggie brought home from the BBC and consulting notes about characters that she made on the backs of used envelopes. At that moment, she forgot about the 'booksey boys' and the Angry Young Men writing about working-class life, and went back twenty years to Bucharest and World War II.

9

Watching History

'You are watching a history, Doamna Preen-gal. Stay, and you will see a country die.'

Olivia Manning, *The Spoilt City* (p. 348).

'It was a bad time ... because we lived under the black shadow of the mushroom clouds ... we were all living in a kind of nervous hysteria.'

Eric Hobsbawm.[1]

The bomb

When Olivia Manning began writing *The Great Fortune* in 1956 she conceived it first, of course, as a novel, but it was also to be an autobiographical narrative anchored in recollection of the time from her marriage in August 1939 to her departure from Romania for Greece in April 1941. Always more comfortable with a fictional character as stand-in than with an unmediated depiction of her life, she settled on the name and character of Harriet Pringle, the 'Doamna Preen-gal' who is told by a weary German refugee economist named Klein that she will see a country die. In *The Doves of Venus* Ellie Parsons had been Olivia's fictional understudy and Quintin Bellot her disenchanted version of Hamish Miles. Now, in 1956, after reviewing regularly for *The Spectator* from 1947 to 1949 and then concentrating almost entirely on her own fiction rather than writing about the work of other writers, she had five post-war novels behind her.

---

[1] Eric Hobsbawm in conversation about the 1950s with Peter Hennessy, 16 October 2002. Quoted in Peter Hennessy, *Having it So Good: Britain in the Fifties*, 133.

Although more often drawn to long fictional narratives than to short stories, she had toyed for a while with the idea of persuading Heinemann to republish her 1948 collection, *Growing Up*, perhaps with a few additional short stories, a possibility encouraged by Henry Green, who wrote to say that although he did not like stories about children he could say 'with absolute conviction, what I really do feel—that you do it better than anybody else.'[2] Reggie, however, believed she should devote herself to another novel, and, unworried about a revelation of his imperfections if Olivia embarked on a frank account of their marriage (he had, after all, laughed uproariously at *My Husband Cartwright*), he suggested she write about her life from the beginning of the war.

Pointing out that in *The Doves of Venus* she had drawn vividly upon her own mid-1930s London years and that in *Artist Among the Missing* and *School for Love* she had created with great skill male protagonists facing war in the Middle East, Reggie urged that she begin the new novel with her (and his) arrival in Romania. Why not make a young woman rather like herself the narrative center of a book about World War II? Since she could reasonably expect to publish such a work in 1960, which would be twenty years from the beginning of the war and thus good timing for some lively publicity, she should contact the head of Heinemann, Dwye Evans, to see what he thought. Evans gave Olivia an enthusiastic go-ahead and she set to work, bothered only by the difficulty of finding a satisfactory cleaner for Queen's Grove. Writing to Kay Dick in early August 1956 that her new novel 'had started to come to life' and that at heart she was a 'slut,' she announced she was not inclined 'to waste time on chores.'[3] Promising to be quite long, she added, the novel only required the 'labour' of writing it. Much to her relief, she soon found Alex to take care of the cleaning (she remained with Olivia for many years) and *The Great Fortune* began to take shape. Vowing to undertake no more book reviewing for *The Spectator* (she did not review again for them until July 1961), doing just a few pieces for *The Observer* that appeared in 1957 and 1958, and appearing as Guest of the Week on the BBC program *Woman's Hour* in February 1957 when she talked about her work in progress, for the duration of writing *The Great Fortune*, Olivia pretty much disappeared from print and from the public.[4]

---

[2] Henry Green to Olivia Manning, 12 December 1955, OMC/C, HRC.

[3] Olivia Manning to Kay Dick, 9 August 1956, OMP, UT, Series 1, Box 1, Folder 6.

[4] For Olivia's negotiations with the BBC to appear on *Woman's Hour*, see Olivia Manning Contributor Talks 1951–1982, BBC Written Archives Centre, Caversham.

As Olivia had planned, the story of her surrogate Harriet Pringle became a story of World War II as witnessed by one particular individual. But despite the familiar and justified ascription of autobiographical material to the trilogies, they are also very much narratives about the time in which they were written. In other words, just as *The Doves of Venus* registered Olivia's combative reaction to the prominence of the Angry Young Men in the early to mid-1950s, the six novels in the trilogies, at different moments and in different registers, suggest her troubled preoccupation with contemporary politics and history as they unfolded from 1956 to 1980. She may have been holed up in St John's Wood but she was sharply attuned to current events, an interest fed, of course, by Reggie's BBC work and connections. In addition to being a record of her marriage, in their graphic depiction of the dislocation and devastation of war, the novels also disclose Olivia's political fears and preoccupations while she was writing them. The Suez crisis, an uprising in Hungary, anxiety about the Cold War, and an ambivalent response to the decline of British imperial power, replaced the anxious aftermath of wartime fears of German invasion and permanent exile from England that had dogged her from 1939 to 1946.

To be sure, Olivia was just one of many post-war British writers whose fiction reflected, directly or not, contemporary political preoccupations: George Orwell's *1984* (1949) famously depicts suppression of the individual by Cold War totalitarianism; C. P. Snow's *The New Men* (1954), as Alan Sinfield points out, is a novel permeated and confused by Cold War paranoia as it describes the work of British scientists in developing an atomic bomb.[5] In this connection, Andrew Hammond argues forcefully that *The Balkan Trilogy* helped 'to reinstall the traditionalist modes of balkanism during the Cold War period' and that in its references to Russian encroachment on Romania, it participates directly in Cold War politics: that is to say, Olivia relies upon stereotypical images of 'Eastern' lassitude and dirt for her evocation of Bucharest and exaggerates Romanian fears of Russian invasion. It seems to me, however, that the engagement with Cold War politics to be discovered in *The Balkan Trilogy* is located less in Olivia's conscious need to 'reinstall' 'balkanism' than in two other matters:

Olivia talked again on *Woman's Hour* in June 1957 on the subject of 'Discipline' and described her working habits.

[5] Alan Sinfield, *Literature, Politics, and Culture in Postwar Britain*, 96.

one, her verifiable recollection that Romanians in the early 1940s
actually did fear a Red Army advance, and, two, that writing in the
late 1950s, she was understandably worried about nuclear warfare.[6]
Olivia was not alone. In a different sphere, threaded throughout the
passionate dissection of women's lives in the middle of the twentieth
century to be found in Doris Lessing's *The Golden Notebook* (1962) are
newspaper accounts of the H-bomb, McCarthyism, and the Suez
crisis. To remain faithful to a recollection of her wartime experiences
Olivia obviously could not incorporate commentary on the political
crises of the mid-1950s into her writing: however, the trilogies'
graphic delineation of Balkan demagoguery, German invasion, and
desert warfare in the Middle East disclose her uneasy state of mind at
the time of writing in a way similar to how Lessing's *The Golden
Notebook* reveals her anger and despair at what was happening when
she was writing her novel.

In late July 1956, Gamal Abdel Nasser thumbed his nose at the
British and nationalized the Suez Canal. Almost immediately Royal
Navy ships were dispatched to the Middle East, accompanied by
blustering threats from the Tory government headed by Anthony
Eden. From early August onwards, the Egyptian position became
increasingly recalcitrant, and after Israeli tanks and armored cars
entered Egypt on 29 October, Eden announced in the House of
Commons that Nasser had been given twelve hours to withdraw his
troops from Suez or face military reprisals. The Tory press congratulated Eden on his tough stance but the *Manchester Guardian*, the
newspaper of choice for Reggie, Olivia, and most of their friends,
declared, 'The Anglo-French ultimatum to Egypt is an act of folly
without justification in any terms but brief expediency. It pours petrol
on a growing fire. There is no knowing what kind of explosion will
follow.'[7] With every loud noise evoking the sound of German bombers over Athens and never forgetting the sight of wounded Greek
troops packed on lorries streaming into the city after defeat in the
north, Olivia was understandably unsettled at the prospect of renewed
warfare.

---

[6] Andrew Hammond, '"The Red threat": Cold War rhetoric and the British novel,' 46.
[7] Quoted in David Kynaston, *Family Britain*, 681.

From a political perspective opposed to the *Guardian*'s, the tabloid *Daily Sketch* declared: 'Suez for us means survival or ruin . . . if Britain were now forced into an ignominious retreat by a frenzied reaction at home, then indeed would our nation be eclipsed and our standing in the world lost for many years to come.'[8] Dominating the news, then, as Olivia began the Balkan trilogy was the threat of renewed conflict in a part of the Middle East well known to her and Reggie. By the time British and French governments had sent paratroopers into Egypt and the British had commandeered Port Said, Olivia's dread of another war became so acute that she took herself off to Brighton to visit Kay Dick and Kathleen Farrell in the hope of distraction from the crisis, a breath of sea air, and some good fish. Her arrival precipitated the household into fear and worry and prompted Kay to write to Stevie Smith, 'We need cheering up: yesterday, like a minor tooth-grinding goddess, Olivia descended on us and depressed us UTTERLY.' She added a PS with a warning that Olivia was on her way also to 'depress you.'[9] But Olivia's anxiety, unquestionably insignificant in terms of that felt by those with global responsibilities in the Suez drama, was soon lessened by the threat of the United States to withhold financial credit from Britain unless there were to be a ceasefire. The United Nations delivered an ultimatum to Anglo-French forces to withdraw by 22 December and the Suez crisis ended in a political fiasco for Britain, the resignation of Anthony Eden as Prime Minister, and the selection of Harold Macmillan as his replacement. Leaving Brighton and a much relieved Kay and Kathleen, Olivia returned to Queen's Grove to resume work on *The Great Fortune* and to do some imaginative tooth grinding as she traced Romanian acquiescence in fascist expansion.

Having lived in the Middle East for four years, Olivia and Reggie had followed the unfolding Suez crisis with a particular awareness of time and place: they had lived in the British colony in Egypt and they had witnessed the tinderbox struggles in Palestine. But the uprising in Hungary in 1956 took on a different kind of personal meaning, particularly for Reggie: Russian suppression of the revolt led him to resign from the Communist Party after some thirty years of loyal membership. On 5 November 1956, the *Manchester Guardian*

---

[8] Quoted in Kynaston, *Family Britain*, 682.
[9] Postcard from Kay Dick to Stevie Smith, 15 November 1956, SSP, UT, Series 1 Book 3, Folder 1.

headlined its Hungary story as follows, 'SOVIET TANKS CRUSH RESISTANCE,' and on that same Sunday morning Reggie realized that his belief in Communism as a decent political system (a belief formed at the University of Birmingham in the mid-1930s) had been definitively demolished by the news from Budapest. That the British Communist Party immediately issued a statement declaring that the Soviet Union 'in responding to the appeal made to them to help defend Socialism in Hungary, is also helping to defend peace and the interests of the world working class,'[10] did not dispel his disillusion with the Soviet Union and his sentiments were identical with those expressed by the journalist Peter Fryer in the *New Statesman* a few days later. Having been in Budapest at the time of the uprising, Fryer was disgusted by the *Daily Worker*'s toadying to its Communist Party ownership: 'From start to finish the *Daily Worker*—or rather the Stalinists who control it—has lied, lied, lied about Hungary . . . Shame on the newspaper which can spit on a nation's anguish and grief. Shame on party leaders who can justify with smooth clichés and lies the massacre and martyrdom of a proud and indomitable people.'[11]

A seasoned book reviewer for the *New Statesman* and sympathetic to its middle-of-the-road liberal politics, Olivia was delighted by Fryer's condemnation and relieved when Reggie decided to resign from the Party, a decision in which he was hardly alone. Not only did he join Doris Lessing as an ex-CP member, but, as David Kynaston notes, in the aftermath of the Soviet suppression of Hungarian dissidents some seven thousand individual members resigned from the British Communist Party, representing approximately one-fifth of the membership.[12] In 1962 Olivia obliquely expressed her continued relief at Reggie's resignation when in a review of a novel by a Russian satirist (*The Bluebottle* by Ivan Valeriy, unpublished in Russia and brought to the England by a journalist) she quoted him as asking, 'If Communism is happiness for all why are people so beastly to each other?' and responded pithily, 'Why indeed?'[13] Never having taken Reggie's Communist Party membership very seriously, feeling, as did one of his colleagues at the BBC, John Tydeman, that he was a kind of

---

[10] Quoted in Kynaston, *Family Britain*, 688.

[11] Kynaston, *Family Britain*, 692.

[12] Kynaston, *Family Britain*, 692.

[13] 'A brilliant Russian satirist,' *Sunday Times*, 4 November 1962.

'romantic socialist' who loved most of all the rowdy demonstration, the conviviality of it all, nevertheless, in the heat of the Hungarian revolt, she was eager for him to dissociate himself from Russian suppression of dissent. Although there is no evidence that she discussed Reggie's Communist Party membership with Adam Watson, their friend from Athens and Cairo days (whom they continued to see in London), lacking Reggie's almost naïve idealism, she would have been in complete accord with Watson's much later assessment of Stalin: 'During the war, we had built up this man, though we knew he was terrible, because he was an ally ... Now the question was, "How do we get rid of the Good Old Uncle Joe myth built up during the war?"'[14]

Suez and Hungary were not the only contemporary political events in the 1950s that unsettled Olivia's often shaky psychological and physical equilibrium. Like Eric Hobsbawm, she lived 'under the black shadow of the mushroom clouds,' almost perpetually nervous about the possibility of nuclear warfare. After returning to England emotionally wounded by the trauma of being a refugee, albeit a lucky one in that she and Reggie were never arrested or interned, and then being hospitalized for a nervous breakdown, Olivia had resumed her book reviewing for *The Palestine Post.* As I noted earlier, one of her immediate post-war reviews was of Storm Jameson's *The Journal of Mary Hervey Russell,* an unusual autobiographical novel that rejects conventional narrative in favor of a surrogate protagonist, a strategy that Olivia, of course, eventually adopted for the trilogies. Preoccupied by the devastating aftermath of the atomic bomb attacks on Hiroshima on 6 August and on Nagasaki on 9 August 1945, Olivia declared in her review that Jameson's work is not only a record of a life but of 'the emotions of a generation that has known more anxiety and suffering than any past generation': she adds, 'if the atomic bomb permits us a future, the world will be so unbearably horrible that people will look back on the time between the two world wars as a calm stretch between two storms.' Whether, in fact, there would be a 'future' for Britain, the United States, or, indeed, the world, became a matter of increasing worry during the period now known popularly as the Cold War, a time of political conflict, military tension, and

---

[14] Adam Watson, telephone interview with Frances Stonor Saunders, August 1998. See Saunders, *The Cultural Cold War,* 58–9.

economic competition which did not truly end until the collapse of
the Soviet Union in 1991. It was at various moments until 1980 that
Olivia worked on her best-known fiction.

As Peter Hennessy observes, fear of the capabilities of a hydrogen
bomb between one thousand and fifteen hundred times more devastating than the atomic bombs that had been dropped on Japan in 1945
spread and intensified in the 1950s. The prospect of a Third World
War that loomed large in Whitehall, in the British press, and in the
minds of the British population, led to the formation of numerous
anti-nuclear-warfare organizations, and the terrifying prospect of a
nuclear attack on Britain became so acute that small ad hoc groups of
writers began meeting in each others' houses to organize themselves
into public demonstrations; 26 Queen's Grove became one gathering
place and Olivia and Reggie regularly attended meetings in other
locations. It was at such small meetings in the mid-1950s that the
Campaign for Nuclear Disarmament (popularly known as CND)
began to take shape and it was in December 1957 that CND emerged
from a cluster of peace and anti-nuclear groups, brought into robust
being by an article that appeared in the *New Statesman*, J. B. Priestley's
'Britain and the Nuclear Bomb.' Olivia's admiration of Priestley's
article buttressed the anti-war sentiments of *The Great Fortune*, indeed,
of the entire Balkan trilogy.

Priestley ended his article by saying that in a desperately insecure
world, Britain continues to muddle along, 'never speaking out, avoid-
ing any decisive creative act . . . as the game gets faster, the competition
keener, the unthinkable will turn into the inevitable, the weapons will
take command, and the deterrents will not deter.' Appealing to British
pride in having 'alone' defied Hitler, he urges all people to defy a
nuclear madness 'into which the spirit of Hitler seems to have passed,
to poison the world.' No longer must the British people hide their
decent, kind faces behind masks of sullen apathy or sour, cheap
cynicism: 'something great and noble in its intention' must make
them feel good again—and that something is a complete renunciation
of nuclear weaponry that will offer an example of moral integrity to
the world.[15] In January 1958 CND came into official being with the
appointment of an executive committee and plans for an inaugural

---

[15] Priestley's article appeared in the *New Statesman* on 1 November 1957.

meeting at the Methodist Central Hall, Westminster, which took place on 17 February. On 4 April 1958, on the coldest Good Friday for forty-one years, Reggie joined four thousand people as they set off from Trafalgar Square to march to the Atomic Weapons Research Establishment at Aldermaston in Berkshire (Olivia stayed home, fearful of large crowds). During these months of fervent press coverage of the ban-the-bomb movement and daily bulletins brought home by Reggie from BBC colleagues, she was hard at work on *The Great Fortune*, a novel that from its opening descriptions of European preparations for war to its closing image of Harriet and Guy Pringle turning their backs on a map of France with the swastika at its center, everywhere recounts the misfortunes of war. As one journalist, Alan Brien, reported in the politically conservative *Daily Mail*, the Aldermaston marchers were mainly middle-class and professional people—'the sort who would normally spend Easter listening to a Beethoven concert on the Home Service, pouring dry sherry from a decanter for the neighbours, painting Picasso designs on hardboiled eggs, attempting the literary competitions in the weekly papers, or going to church with their children.'[16] In sum, these marchers were Olivia's readers, and *The Balkan Trilogy* became her response to Priestley's call to speak out as prevention against the 'unthinkable' turning into the 'inevitable.' She dedicated the first novel in the trilogy to Johnny and Jerry Slattery.

A historical eye

'Somewhere near Venice,' Olivia writes in the first sentence of *The Great Fortune*, 'Guy began talking with a heavy, elderly man, a refugee from Germany on his way to Trieste.' This nameless refugee, eager to share his story of exile with a sympathetic listener, has escaped Germany and hopes to find asylum in Italy. But when the ticket collector enters their carriage, he is unable to produce his passport: panting and sweating, he pleads with the official, who remains unmoved by yet another tiresome story of a lost identity card, a missing pocket-book, and an absent passport. We never learn whether, in fact, the German

---

[16] Quoted in Peter Hennessy, *Having it So Good*, 528.

refugee ever possessed these crucial tools of survival: all we know is that he is taken from the train, never to reappear in the novel and, in the historical actuality that Olivia represents, probably never again to appear in the world he has left behind. This opening scene sounds the first chord in the trilogy's controlling motif of dislocation and exile. Although Guy and Harriet Pringle possess all the essential cards of identity and are on their way to a country not yet invaded by German forces, they have already become exiles from England, destined as British citizens to find themselves on arrival in Bucharest officially at war with Germany. The scene also compels the reader to witness the tragic, brutal effects of war upon one single individual—a German (in all likelihood Jewish) without country, resources, or cards of identification.

Immediately following this opening scene of refugee despair, we are introduced to Yakimov, an émigré from Yugoslavia who arrives in Bucharest with two suitcases, a crocodile dressing-case, and a sable-lined greatcoat, which may or may not have been given to his father by the Tsar. Always brilliantly attentive to the vivifying effect of small details in constructing a narrative or characterizing an individual, Olivia describes him as wearing a clean shirt, a dirty suit, and an ancient blue tie, 'now so blotched and be-yellowed by spilt food, it was no colour at all. His head, with its thin, pale hair, its nose that, long and delicate, widened suddenly at the nostrils, its thin clown's mouth, was remote and mild as the head of a giraffe' (p. 10). His whole sad aspect is 'made sadder' by the fact that he has not eaten for forty-eight hours, an especially taxing trial since he hungers throughout the novel for the rich delicacies he once enjoyed before being hounded, as he puts it, out of one European capital after another. When he manages to scrounge an invitation to a fancy party being given at the Hotel Athénée he almost faints with desire at the sight of a buffet set up with roasted turkeys, gammons baked with brown sugar, crayfish, salmon coated with mayonnaise, and piles of autumn raspberries.

Having traversed western Europe attaching himself along the way to multiple minor officials in various British legations, he is now in search of Dobbie Dobson (Adam Watson), and, creating a Dickensian panorama of urban life, Olivia describes Yaki trudging through the Bucharest streets, mesmerized by a window display of peaches and apricots in syrup, discomforted by the sight of Orthodox Jews 'with ringlets hanging on either side of greenish, indoor faces,' frightened by tailors in gas-lit rooms no bigger than cupboards thumping their irons and 'moving behind bleared windows like sea creatures in tanks' (pp. 12–13). Yakimov sidles throughout *The Great Fortune* as a clown-ish, pathetic image of dislocated and disenfranchised privilege, no longer the pampered social darling with his Hispano-Suiza, Savile Row suits, and wealthy patrons. In him Olivia creates a pitiful and unsavory symbol of a once-gilded Europe now invaded by German forces in search of fresh territory to conquer and abundant resources to plunder. In a treacherous act, he betrays Sasha Drucker to the author-ities when he learns that Harriet and Guy have been hiding him on the roof of their apartment building and that he, Yaki, might be dislodged from his smelly occupancy of their spare room. Coherently with her creation of Yakimov as a rich symbol of Europe pandering to power, Olivia allots him the role of Pandarus in Guy Pringle's production of *Troilus and Cressida*, a play frantically rehearsed and performed as news arrives in Bucharest of the fall of Paris to the German army.[17]

It seems as if the dregs of seedy Europe have coalesced in Bucharest. For example, Galpin, a freelance journalist, embodies a Fleet Street type Olivia despised: she paints him as a repulsive man with a whiny nasal voice who, when he talks, rubs at 'his peevish yellow, whisky-drinker's face. Over his caved-in belly, his waistcoat was wrinkled, dirty and ash-spattered. There was a black edging of grease round his cuffs: his collar was corrugated round his neck. He sucked the wet stub of a cigarette. When he talked the stub stuck to his full, loose lower lip and quivered there' (p. 73). And Dubedat, one of Guy's followers and as far as Harriet is concerned a despicable toady, is described by Olivia as giving off a 'sour smell' and displaying 'yellow and decaying teeth.' The creases in his nostrils are greasy and pitted with blackheads, crusts of scurf are caught in the roots of his hair, his fingers are stained yellow with nicotine. The physical revulsion inspired by these characters, painted with cutting skill by Olivia, evokes the small ways in which war erodes civilized habits. Of course, Olivia witnessed scenes of appalling brutality (real-life counterparts of the Jewish banker Drucker

---

[17] Olivia refused to tell Francis King on whom she had based Yakimov: 'the original is still alive and is as big a scrounger as ever, so I can take no risks with him.' FKC/OM, HRC, 30 March 1966. On the back of a photograph of 'Bunty' Scott Moncrieff, vintage car enthusiast and restorer in the 1930s, taken in 1939 and found in Olivia's papers after her death, someone (not Olivia or Reggie) has written 'Bunty used by Olivia as part of YAKIMOV.'

being dragged out of their apartment houses), but it was in these small things that she showed how characters beset by war, hounded by authorities, stranded in alien European capitals, harshly embody the physical neglect of self caused by wartime conditions. This peeling away, as it were, of the social codes that hold communities together in a reasonably civilized manner was attested to by an old friend from Athens days, Eric Gifford, who wrote to say that he 'burnt midnight electricity' to finish *The Great Fortune*: Olivia's novel 'shattered the romantic illusions' he used to have about pre-war Bucharest.[18]

Always impeccably well-groomed and taking great pleasure in furnishing her houses with beautiful objects, Olivia was repelled by a disfiguring ugliness in individuals and living spaces that reminded her of the frugality at Laburnum Grove and the seediness of London bed-sitting rooms. Without question, Commander Manning was a trim and sprightly figure and her mother so fastidious a housekeeper that she dusted the ornaments in the front room every single morning, but there was a metaphorical grayness about it all that Olivia throughout her life kept at bay with attractive clothes and elegant antiques. The stress of wartime conditions brings about a bizarre squalor particularly redolent in the stale magnificence of Bucharest in *The Balkan Trilogy*. War not only kills and tortures, it also reduces human beings to an elemental physical state, and this condition is something Olivia forces upon her reader in her descriptions of unappetizing physical bodies. And bodies were much on her mind during the writing of *The Great Fortune*. She not only coped with disturbing memories of wartime Romania but also was painfully reminded of her missed abortion in Palestine in 1944. Having suffered intermittently from hemorrhaging after she returned to England, she went to the Dollis Hill Hospital in December 1959 for yet another of the multiple curettages she had undergone to stem the irregular bleeding. Jerry Slattery assured her, she told Kay Dick, it would be 'nothing,' just a quick procedure, so, armed with Vladimir Nabokov's recently published *Lolita*, she took a mandated break from her work.[19]

In writing about *The Balkan Trilogy* in *The Novel Now* (in 1967, two years after publication of the last of the three novels), Anthony Burgess declared that overall it was 'the most important long work of fiction to

---

[18] Eric Gifford to Olivia Manning, 21 April 1960, OMC/C, HRC.

[19] Olivia Manning to Kay Dick, 2 December 1959, OMP, UT, Series 1, Box 1, Folder 7.

have been written by an English woman novelist since the war . . . one
of the finest records we have of the impact of that war on Europe.'[20]
Much later and retrospectively, Jeremy Treglown concurred, saying
that 'no other novelist has described these crucial arenas of the war
with such scope and immediacy.'[21] Burgess was astonished by the
variety of gifts to be discovered in the trilogy since it is 'rare' that a
contemporary woman writer possesses 'humour, poetry, the power of
the exact image, the ability to be both hard and compassionate, a sense
of place, all the tricks of impersonation and finally, a historical eye'
(p. 5). Putting aside the slightly patronizing view of women novelists
that lurks in his praise and bearing in mind Olivia's own contempt for
what she termed a 'flaccid feminine style,'[22] in his understanding of
how she can be both 'hard and compassionate' Burgess identifies
exactly that cold eye with which she views many of her characters—
hard in her delineation of their physical awfulness and compassionate
in her understanding of the wartime conditions that have brought
them to that pass. The *New York Times* reviewer of *The Great Fortune*,
Virgilla Peterson, while cogently identifying a 'miasma compounded
of bravado and fear, extravagance and hunger, pretense and anguish,
chicanery and stoicism, which hung over all the little, rumor-hung
capitals before their doom,' nevertheless deemed the success of the
novel more in the realm of reportage than of fiction.[23] Failing to
understand that Olivia had carved out new territory where the literary
imagination transforms recollected experience into fiction and positions it in the context of recent European history, Peterson concluded
that the novel 'floats in a limbo.' *The Great Fortune*, however, is neither
entirely personal history nor completely invented fact. Rather, it is a
hybrid form. For Olivia, the charge that she worked more in the realm
of journalism than art was offset by Charles Poore's comment in the
New York Times Sunday Book Review that appeared two weeks later:
the intensity of her 'brilliantly perceptive writing is controlled by a
serene style.'[24]

---

[20] *The Novel Now*, 94.

[21] Jeremy Treglown, 'Olivia Manning and her masculine outfit,' 151.

[22] Olivia Manning, Review of *An End to Running* by Lynne Reid Banks. *Sunday
Times*, 7 October 1962.

[23] *New York Times*, 16 July 1961.

[24] *New York Times*, 1 August 1961.

John Davenport, reviewing the novel in *The Observer*, detected a significant difference in Olivia's writing from her earlier work: whereas her earlier novels were '*grisailles*,' the Balkan setting seems to have brought out a Russian quality, a kind of 'colour of comedy' that makes the novel a 'balanced, subtle, witty, and humane work of art.' Plus, it was wonderfully entertaining. The anonymous reviewer in the *TLS* (Marigold Hunt Johnson) praised Manning for her brilliant control of a large and varied collection of characters and, sounding somewhat like Anthony Burgess, lauded her skill in not being 'by any means a feminine novelist.'[25] Added to her gift for penetrating the masculine mind, she possesses 'an objective, analytical approach which displays the futility of so much conversation . . . Her direct and ironic sense of style, never "literary" but professional as a Mozart quartet is what one expects from so unsentimental a writer.' If she continues in this same unsentimental and masculine vein, although 'a less intricately leisured writer' than either Lawrence Durrell or Anthony Powell, she will become a novelist on a similarly grand and humorous scale.

Good reviews for *The Great Fortune* led John Lambert, the literary editor of the *Sunday Times*, to invite Olivia to become a regular contributor, and she was happy to agree, hoping to knock 'the glamour girl' Iris Murdoch from her prominent pedestal (she greeted every review of a new Murdoch novel with the wry comment that yet again everyone was in for a 'Murdoch Benefit Week'). From June through December 1962, her witty, erudite pieces appeared almost every week—as they also did in *The Spectator*. Three of Olivia's amusing reviews written during this period show her having a grand old time with the male writers Irving Stone, John Updike, and Lawrence Durrell. After plowing through Stone's *The Agony and the Ecstasy* (for her, combined 'Renaissance guidebook, art-appreciation lecture and do-it-yourself manual of sculpture and fresco'), Olivia confesses herself astonished to learn that Michelangelo was a man like other men. Stone's most embarrassing lapse, she concludes, is his failure to distinguish between the chisel and the male member: at work, Michelangelo needed 'the thrust, the penetration, the beating and pulsating upwards to a mighty climax'; in bed with a woman (an unlikely possibility given Michelangelo's homosexuality, although Olivia fails to note Irving

---

[25] *TLS*, 29 January 1960.

Stone's misplaced fantasy in this regard), 'it was like penetrating deep into white marble with the pounding live thrust of his chisel beating upward through the warm living marble.' The implications of all this are flattering and reassuring, she concludes: 'sex is art and art is sex—we can all do it!'[26] In *Rabbit, Run*, Updike's notorious sex passages are as stimulating to the reader as posting a letter and his pastiche of Molly Bloom's night-thoughts is 'as vapid under the teeth as uncooked suet in a pudding.'[27] Olivia's nemesis from the Cairo poets-in-exile days, Lawrence Durrell, having been foolish enough to allow *The Dark Labyrinth* to be re-issued (it was first published in 1947), has only himself to blame for the reader's sense that he has taken an old hat from a dusty box: the hat emits a stale scent from the 1920s as if someone had 'spilt Willa Cather and Aldous Huxley all over it.'[28] Only Olivia's newly acquired basement tenant, Julian Mitchell, escapes her sarcasm: in reviewing his second novel, *A Disturbing Influence*, she praises his ability to 'organise his thoughts and present them with style.' At a time when so many young writers, she says, try to evade the sheer hard work of novel writing by tangling themselves up in 'pseudo-poetry, metaplasm, beatnik guff, half-baked metaphysics,' Mitchell's work is a breath of sensible fresh air.[29] And Ivy Compton-Burnett concurred: Olivia told Mitchell he had made 'quite a hit' with the formidable Ivy and that she 'breathlessly' wanted to see him again.[30]

One of Olivia's close friends, Peter Luke, among other things a scriptwriter and producer for ABC Television in London, wrote to her immediately after publication of *The Great Fortune* that it was in his 'private category of "Can't-put-it-downers!"'[31] and that he looked forward to the remainder of the trilogy, or even a quartet. J. G. Farrell (a writer Olivia much admired) had a similar experience: in August 1968 he wrote to a friend that he had been reading the 'splendid' Balkan trilogy and 'enjoying it guiltily when I should be writing me own novels.'[32] Predictably never entirely gratified by the praise that

[26] 'Pounding marble,' *The Spectator*, 21 July 1961.

[27] 'Faces of violence,' *The Spectator*, 15 September 1961.

[28] 'Daring too much,' *The Spectator*, 13 October 1961.

[29] 'Under the influence,' *The Spectator*, 30 March 1962.

[30] Olivia Manning to Julian Mitchell, 13 July 1962, Julian Mitchell private correspondence.

[31] Peter Luke to Olivia Manning, 22 February 1960, OMC/C, HRC.

[32] J. M. Farrell to Carol Drisko, *J. G. Farrell in his Own Words*, 140.

came her way, Olivia wrote back to Peter Luke expressing all sorts of doubts about her achievement, wondering anxiously whether she would ever be able to write another novel, let alone complete a trilogy. Luke assured her that he did not think her treatment of characters was 'dreary' (something she had feared) and that she had 'performed a small miracle' in making them more lively than they ought to be, a judgment based on his belief that British Council and Foreign Office types tend to erect a 'thick sheet of plate glass between *their* small world and the large, untidy, active one outside.' Emphasizing his admiration of *The Great Fortune* to assuage Olivia's neurotic self-doubt about her work, he added that it was packed with creative skill and sensitivity and sheer good writing: 'It wasn't anything *you* did wrong: on the contrary, you depicted them all with singular faithfulness.' Don't worry, he adds, about his general dislike of British Council types and don't let his remarks 'throw any grit into a really fine piece of work-in-progress.'[33]

Soldiering on, then, with that work-in-progress and despite all her worries about picky reviews, in early 1960 Olivia began *The Spoilt City*. 'The great fortune is life. We must preserve it,' says Harriet to Guy at the end of the first novel in the trilogy, and Olivia, recalling her great fortune in escaping Romania ahead of the Germans, conserved it through narrative in her next novel. She also began driving lessons, and on gaining her license in the name of Mrs Olivia Mary Smith proudly sent a postcard to William Gerhardie asking if she could take him out for a drive. He was delighted to accept, as was Reggie when she offered to drive him almost every morning to the BBC, whizzing down St John's Wood High Street and along Regent's Park to Portland Place. According to Johnny Slattery, Olivia actually learned to drive because she feared Reggie's easy distractibility would lead to accidents or worse should he ever get behind the wheel of a car. Her first long driving excursion out of London, however, ended with a summons for careless driving issued on 2 October 1960 by the Police Court in Stratford-upon-Avon, where she and Reggie had gone to see Peggy Ashcroft in *The Winter's Tale* and from where she wrote to Kay Dick on the following day 'This has been *quite* a holiday. I developed malaria as soon as we arrived.'[34] The malaria attack, a souvenir of her

---

[33] Peter Luke to Olivia Manning, 10 April 1960, OMC/C, HRC.
[34] Olivia Manning to Kay Dick, 3 October 1960, OMP, UT, Series 1, Box 1, Folder 7.

days in Egypt, passed quickly, and one month later she was fined £10 and had her license endorsed.

On her return to London, her days now fell into a regular pattern: drive Reggie to the BBC, do some shopping on the way home, settle down to her writing, and sometimes enjoy a late afternoon rendezvous with Jerry Slattery, either at Queen's Grove or in the flat of an understanding friend. At the weekends, she and Reggie usually had lunch with the Slatterys—these 'legendary parties' were especially jolly when Ireland played at Twickenham according to Louis MacNeice, who was also a regular along with sundry St John's Wood actors, writers, and politicians.[35] But the comforting affair with Jerry and the success of *The Great Fortune* did not dispel Olivia's obsessive fears about a coming apocalypse, fears that she displaced into almost gleeful predictions that the world as she and her friends knew it was falling apart: arriving at the opening of Ian Norrie's High Hill Bookshop in Hampstead in September 1961, she greeted Angus Wilson with the news (erroneous) that the publishers Secker and Warburg had gone completely bankrupt, a sign of the incipient collapse of the English publishing industry along with the coming economic meltdown. As Wilson's biographer Margaret Drabble observes, 'Manning was not one of his favorite people, though he relished her particular brand of exaggerated pessimism.'[36]

Wrecked on the edge of Europe

Dedicated to Ivy Compton-Burnett, *The Spoilt City* begins with a description of Bucharest summer heat so fierce that the grass withers in the public parks, leaves fall from the chestnut trees burned by a furnace breath, and the roads ooze tarmac. An ochre-colored dust floats in the hot air like the creeping fog that blinds the eyes and throats of Londoners in the first few paragraphs of Dickens's *Bleak House*. It is June 1940, and just as nine months previously Polish refugees had poured into the city, now hordes of German landowners from Bessarabia, warned by the German Legation, arrive in dust-covered cars strapped over with luggage. They have fled not in fear

---

[35] *Letters of Louis MacNeice*, 684.   [36] *Angus Wilson: A Biography*, 281.

of the Russians but of the Romanian peasants who they know will turn upon them when German forces begin their invasion from the north. Memories of that fear of invasion felt so powerfully by Olivia when she was in Bucharest in 1940, were, in the late 1950s as she worked on *The Spoilt City*, heightened by lingering worries about the British political situation. As David Kynaston observes, the last days of the Suez crisis revealed a number of disturbing political realities: Britain seemed unable to act independently of her American ally; colonial resistance was eroding illusions of imperial hegemony; and the British electorate's often deferential faith in its leaders was crumbling under the pressure of waning international prestige.[37] In the late 1950s, Britain, of course, was under no threat of invasion, but the unsettled political atmosphere troubled Olivia and Reggie and led each of them to different forms of distraction: in her case, to a renewed dedication to working on what was now definitely going to be an anti-war trilogy, and in his, to even longer sessions in the pubs around Portland Place drinking beer with his innumerable friends.

As we know, it is not only the city of Bucharest that is spoiled in the second novel of *The Balkan Trilogy*: the marriage of Harriet and Guy, if not rotting away, undergoes a disruptive transformation brought about by an erosion of Harriet's need for Guy's protection and her unhappy education in his blind indifference to her needs. On the one hand, he is a model of admirable gregariousness, happy to chat with anyone regardless of differences in nationality, wealth, or social class, but on the other, his indiscriminate geniality seems to leave nothing for his wife. This, of course, was Olivia's recurrent complaint about Reggie: loving everyone indiscriminately, he had nothing left for her. *The Spoilt City* traces Harriet's unhappy recognition that Guy is happiest when at the center of a group (preferably male) and that if her marriage is to continue, she must accept her role as bemused and sometimes cynical outsider. Unlike Olivia, who garnered recognition and cultural prestige for her work, Harriet is a kind of negative image of what Olivia might have been had she not succeeded as a working writer. Harriet has no career and seemingly no occupation other than mingling on the edges of the admiring circle that surrounds Guy. Not only, then, does Olivia express through Harriet's feelings for Guy the

[37] *Family Britain*, 693–4.

disappointments of her marriage, she also creates an image of a younger self lacking the talent, drive, and instinct for survival that made her the admired novelist she had become by the time she was writing *The Spoilt City*. In a sense, she imagines the self she was determined never to be, and she makes Harriet virtually identical with herself, it seems to me, in order for us to recognize that the writer is *not* unambiguosly the character. Harriet, of course, learns 'the resort of her own reflections,' and comes to the unhappy conclusion that what Guy lacks is 'a fundamental interest in the individual' (p. 515). It is the audience that interests him, that feeds his ego, and that reassures him as he and Harriet are 'wrecked together on the edge of Europe.' She learns to keep her thoughts to herself.

Olivia's description of Harriet's childhood spent with a nagging aunt strongly resembles her distressing recollections of her mother. 'Skinny and charmless' as an adolescent (as was Olivia), Harriet becomes 'aggressive and withdrawn' (as did Olivia): when her parents divorce, neither of them finding it 'convenient to give her a home,' she is given over to the care of the resentful aunt, who constantly urges her to make herself more pleasant to people. Instead, Harriet retreats into moody silence just as Olivia retreated to her drafty bedroom in Laburnum Grove when told by her mother that she was sullen, no longer pretty, and a miserable wet blanket in the household. Guy, with his 'large, comfortable, generous, embraceable' physical being, enfolds Harriet into his life, warms her, makes her feel safe and secure, but eventually, of course, relegates her absentmindedly to a kind of honorary membership in his circle of admiring friends. Remaining withdrawn, even sullen, recognizing ruefully that she will never become the sole recipient of Guy's attention and affection, Harriet becomes the sharp-eyed observer, her thoughts a projection of Olivia's narrative voice: dry, detached, ironic. The anonymous *TLS* reviewer of *The Spoilt City* (again Marigold Hunt Johnson) perfectly summarizes Guy's character: 'a childish idealist of the most dangerous sort—a man who is ready to befriend the world without realizing that charity also involves facing unpleasant facts, a self-sufficient escapist who is too easily impressed by the second-rate and content in his cocoon of vague optimism to let events pass him by.'[38] Evidence of Reggie's innate good

[38] *TLS*, 11 May 1962.

nature and unfaltering belief in Olivia's 'genius' became clear in his refusal to take offence at this description of a character so clearly modeled upon himself. Johnson concluded her review with the sensible note that the significance of the trilogy cannot be assessed without the final volume, but that *The Spoilt* City secured Olivia 'a place among the dozen most distinguished English novelists who can claim to be much read as well as much written about.'[39]

Predictably, glowing praise from the *TLS*, together with Anthony Burgess's admiration of the 'immense literary skill' apparent in *The Spoilt City* and Francis King's assessment that 'there are now few novelists at work in England who can be regarded as superior to her,'[40] got sidelined in Olivia's obsessive ledger of good and bad reviews. She was particularly annoyed by the failure of *The Listener* (the now defunct BBC cultural magazine) to review *The Spoilt City*. Writing to Jocelyn Brooke, an English writer whom Olivia much admired, she related a complicated narrative of how Vernon Scannell, the book reviewer for *The Listener*, had defended himself for failing to take notice of Olivia's latest work by saying someone in his office had made off with the review copy with the excuse that his wife wanted to read it: 'I felt pretty annoyed, chiefly because so many BBC people noticed that I had been left out... What the truth of the story is, I do not know and no longer care. Fuck the lot of them.'[41] Not only disregarding the *TLS* praise in this letter to Jocelyn Brooke, she declared further that she believed *The Spoilt City* was 'laboured, dull and too long' and that she should have combined it with *The Great Fortune*, and made considerable cuts in the process.

On 12 December 1962, Olivia and Reggie moved from Queen's Grove to a house not far away, 36 Abbey Gardens, St John's Wood—a change forced upon them by the Eyre Estate, leaseholders of Queen's Grove. Moving day was disastrous. Everything went wrong, Olivia wrote to William Gerhardie, on a miserably foggy morning when the builder they had hired to make crucial renovations to the new house refused to budge because of poor driving conditions, when the plumber also refused to appear to deal with a flooded kitchen, and

---

[39] 'Before the Deluge,' 11 May 1962, *TLS*.

[40] Anthony Burgess, 'Stone turned to flesh and blood,' *Yorkshire Post*, 17 May 1962; Francis King, 'Better and better,' *Time and Tide*, 10 May 1962.

[41] Olivia Manning to Jocelyn Brooke, 6 June 1963, OMC/C, HRC.

when they were handed a claim from the Eyre Estate for 'dilapidations' at Queen's Grove. So excessive were the claims, Olivia added, they were 'worried to death, Reggie has no money at all and I am steeped in debt. I wonder if I will ever have sufficient peace of mind again to start the 3rd. part of the trilogy.' Approached in early 1963 by the Harry Ransom Center at the University of Texas, Austin (the humanities center, library, and archive), she decided to send off two of the three complete manuscripts she had not yet foolishly given away—'As you know, we badly need some money,' she wrote again to Jocelyn Brooke.[42] Presented with ten pages of claims amounting to £3,000, she and Reggie had been turned out of their home 'for nothing,' and were now being 'dunned for vast sums which we have not got—And on top of it all—the weather!'[43] In February 1963, threatened with a writ from the Eyre Estate, compelled to find money to pay for the dilapidations at Queen's Grove, and driven, as always, by her ambition, as soon as the new house was reasonably in order, Olivia got down to work on the third novel in the trilogy, which she dedicated to Dwye Evans (the managing director of Heinemann who had encouraged her to begin the first novel) and his wife Daphne. Working was made easier by the fact that she had found a decent tenant for the garden flat in the new house, which was actually a much more attractive property than 26 Queen's Grove (and remains so). After the fractious dealings with Tony Richardson, she was delighted when Julian Mitchell, a young novelist and screenwriter, not only proved to be a responsible housekeeper and charming tenant; he was also known to her through their book reviewing for *The Spectator* and the *Sunday Times*. The hallway at Abbey Gardens was filled regularly with piles of books ready for reviewing by one or other of them.

Writing to Julian Mitchell in July 1962, while the house in Abbey Gardens was being decorated and before he could move in, Olivia assured him there would be blankets, but no china or linen; she did promise, though, to try to rustle up something in the way of sheets. When I spoke with him about Olivia in April 2010 in his elegant Chelsea flat with expansive views over the chimney pots of Draycott Avenue, Mitchell admitted that the Abbey Gardens basement was a bit

---

[42] Olivia Manning to Jocelyn Brooke, 12 June 1963, OMC/C, HRC.
[43] Olivia Manning to William Gerhardie, 6 December 12, 1962. Correspondence of William Gerhardie, Cambridge University Library.

squalid: small, ill-heated, and a little damp. But he was fond of Reggie and touched by his pride in Olivia's talent. Olivia he found a little frosty, at that time in her mid-fifties, gray-haired, poised, and elegant, and it was clear to Mitchell that she must have been pretty when young. For him, what spoiled her appearance was a kind of turned-down mouth that expressed her resentments of the world, her sense of not getting what she deserved. But she could be touchingly frank about her unhappiness and also surprisingly kind: writing to console him for a rather bad review in October 1966, she began by saying, 'I am about twice your age—and have never had a prize, and probably now I never shall have one. I sometimes feel so low that it seems to me I have wasted my whole life. I have just had some long overdue money for a MS from Texas and I was wondering if I could help with a loan?'[44] Vulnerable about her looks, her age, and her talent, Olivia in middle age was a far more complex figure than the easy dismissal of her as interested only in besting her female contemporaries would allow. She was often a loyal and generous friend, as a letter to Kay Dick written in August 1963 discloses: desperately unhappy about her failing relationship with Kathleen Farrell, deeply in debt, and without any prospects for employment, Kay Dick confided to Olivia her suicidal thoughts. Get your own life, writes Olivia: get back to writing, stop moaning about yourself, try to get an administrative job with the BBC—and in all this, Olivia vowed to support her old friend.

Set entirely in Athens, *Friends and Heroes* chronicles the period in which Olivia and Reggie lived an increasingly precarious existence as the Germans prepared to invade Greece from the north and the novel concludes with the escape of Harriet and Guy on a creaky cargo ship that takes them to relative safety in Egypt. During the six months in Athens, Guy and Harriet have 'learnt each others' faults and weaknesses: they had passed both illusion and disillusion.'[45] As the precarious boat nears the African coast, Harriet thinks of those they have left behind: no friends remain except one of 'the vainest and the emptiest' (Ben Phipps), a hanger-on always ready to entice Guy into 'the realms of folly' (p. 1021). For Marigold Hunt Johnson, again reviewing for the *TLS*, the main theme of *The Balkan Trilogy* becomes clear: 'the irony of survival

---

[44] Olivia Manning to Julian Mitchell, 3 October 1966. Letter in the possession of Julian Mitchell. Author's conversation with Julian Mitchell, 6 May 2010.

[45] *Friends and Heroes*, 1003.

in the midst of destruction,' something very much in Olivia's mind at the time of writing as she wondered whether civilization as she knew it could survive nuclear warfare. With astonishing mastery, says Johnson, the trilogy provides 'microcosmic examples of how the whole history of political thought and events interact upon each other.' Even more enthusiastic about the third novel in the trilogy than about the previous two, Johnson is amazed that Manning, with a skill 'rare among women writers', has covered an amazingly full and colorful canvas with people and scenes 'so real and so authoritatively recalled that it hardly seems like fiction.'[46] This, of course, is really the principal point about Olivia Manning's work. Shaping with great authority recollection of her own experience into fiction, she creates novels so much like life that they seem not to be works of fiction, which, of course, they are and are not. Olivia had been initially uncertain whether she wished to write a third volume, and while she was writing it she had a generally exhausting time: now, when it was written, she felt lost, unanchored without anything to do— 'I think it is probably the best of the three,' she wrote to Jocelyn Brooke, but what to do next immediately became an obsessive preoccupation.[47]

And thoughtful and admiring reviews of *Friends and Heroes* did little to assuage Olivia's neurotic belief that the literary establishment still shunned her work in favor of younger, more intellectual, and more decorative women writers. Even her closest friends were not exempt from charges that they neglected her, conspired against her, and curried favor with more glamorous creatures such as Edna O'Brien. In the early 1960s, Muriel Spark's success became particularly irksome. Writing to Francis King in November 1961, she complained that his review of 'Muriel's book' had made her (Olivia) sound 'very difficult,' but she did agree with his criticism that Spark was 'pouring out too much and is too eager for publicity.' As far as she was concerned, *The Prime of Miss Jean Brodie* was 'an amusing short story, but no more.' (Olivia sent a copy of Francis King's review to Kay Dick, noting she (Olivia) got only 'bleak mention'.) As Spark's biographer Martin Stannard observes, Francis King 'carped about Muriel's word selection, and prompted a sharp exchange of letters in *Time and Tide* by shrewdly suggesting she was promoting her public image.'[48] Olivia's

---

[46] *TLS*, 4 November 1965.
[47] Olivia Manning to Jocelyn Brooke, 6 May 1965, OMC/C, HRC.
[48] *Muriel Spark: The Biography*, 253.

envy of Muriel Spark remained unalloyed for many years: in March 1972, writing to Anthony Burgess, who was living in Rome at the time, she cattily noted that she had heard Spark aimed 'to be taken up by the Onassis circle. She is our female Icarus.'[49] Edna O'Brien, not yet famous enough to incur Olivia's sour envy nor ambitious enough to fly too close to the Onassis circle, she deemed to be 'pure butter with a filling of steel,' unlike Muriel Spark, who failed miserably in depicting the emotions.[50] Despite a restful holiday in Ireland in 1965 and despite the admiring reviews, Olivia remained disappointed and discontented.

A writing sex

Reviewing novels by Mary Hocking and A. S. Byatt in *The Spectator* in December 1963, Olivia began, 'Time was when women writers hoped to be mistaken for men or, like Ouida, they wrote, "All rowed fast but none as fast as stroke," and were treated as a joke. Now the Feminine has become an autonomous literary province and women, discovering the poetry of woman's life, are opening up the dark continent of domesticity.' In earlier years, Olivia had certainly spoken and written to friends in no uncertain terms about her desire not to be pigeonholed as a 'female' or 'feminine' writer, and she had been gratified when critics had praised a certain supple masculinity in her prose. But it was not until the early 1960s, when women's liberation movements were gathering steam on both sides of the Atlantic, that she ventured to have her say about the woman writer, even if it was somewhat inaccurate to argue that the 'dark continent of domesticity' was only just being explored. That mysterious realm had been invaded by Jane Austen with *Pride and Prejudice* in 1813 and the autonomous literary province of the 'Feminine' had been sensitively explored by George Eliot in her two great novels, *Middlemarch* and *Daniel Deronda*. But to be fair to Olivia, this was a brief review, not an academic essay about the depiction of domesticity in fiction written for women and by women.

---

[49] Olivia Manning to Anthony Burgess, 8 March 1972, International Anthony Burgess Foundation.

[50] Olivia Manning to Francis King, 28 November 1961, FKC/OM, HRC.

One month after publication of this review, *The Times* featured a revealing interview in the tenth of a series, 'Speaking of Writing,' in which Olivia elaborated at length her thoughts about women novelists. First, they are at a disadvantage when it comes to writing about the great world of affairs, of politics and science, she says, which came as a surprise to the Special Correspondent since 'Miss Manning is hardly a "woman novelist" given her achievement in the first two volumes of the Balkan trilogy in finding a perfect balance between imaginative scope and intellectual balance. This is an achievement which most male novelists might well envy.'[51] When asked whether she felt herself limited in any way by virtue of being a woman, Olivia responded thoughtfully that all writers are inevitably limited by what they are, and their sex has something to do with this, 'though not I believe by any means as much as is often supposed.' Insisting that she was not in any way a 'feminist' writer—nothing more dreary than the woman in life or in her writing who 'takes up a suffragette stance about her rights and abilities'—Olivia advanced an original category she felt might be adopted as an alternative to the deadening division of writers into male and female: 'a sort of third sex, intellectually speaking, all living in the same sort of circumstances, moving in the same sort of society, doing the same sort of job, irrespective of sex, and there is no inherent reason why men should be mysteries to women and beyond their power to treat convincingly in a novel, or vice versa.' Admitting that she probably has a 'more masculine than feminine mind as a writer,' she confessed that she much preferred to write from the man's point of view than from that of a woman, and added that when beginning a novel she wrote 'out of complete confusion.' The novels grow as she writes them and take shape as she rewrites—the key to all writing is 'rewriting' (a truth known to all authors). Finally, unable to resist a dig at the woman writer she disliked more than any other, she added, 'How I sometimes envy writers like Muriel Spark who can see a whole book clearly from the start and just write it straight off in six weeks!'

A quartet of Olivia's female contemporaries figures prominently in a series of letters she wrote to Jocelyn Brooke between June 1963 and September 1964. Only Pamela Hansford Johnson escapes her barbed

[51] 'Olivia Manning, "From our Special Correspondent,"' *The Times*, 30 January 1964.

critique: 'a powerful, inventive and very varied writer,' she has not been appreciated as she should be, having suffered more than most from the 'prejudice against women.' On an ironic note, Olivia describes someone 'who had, for some reason, been induced to try and read one of my books' writing to her to say that he or she had thought she was just 'another one of those lady writers like Pamela Hansford Johnson.'[52] Despite Iris Murdoch's fierce intellectualism and privileged education (always resented), she might actually be more of a 'lady writer' than Hansford Johnson, Olivia wrote to Brooke a few weeks later: the problem with Murdoch, she announced, is that she has it both ways, touted as a 'tremendous intellectual by her male intellectual admirers' and at the same time promoted as a best-seller. Here I have, she goes on to say, been slogging away for years, and now on the verge of old age can scarcely afford to have a roof over my head (Olivia was hardly on the verge of old age but at the age of fifty-five she exaggerated her infirmities and wrinkles). If Murdoch actually were another George Eliot, as her male admirers declare her to be, then she would gracefully take a back seat; but Murdoch is 'quite bogus.' Cut off from reality as well as from criticism since she never reads her own reviews and is able to retire to her 'ivory tower' to write while her husband runs the household, Iris Murdoch, says Olivia, leads a life utterly unlike her own. Olivia obsessively read all her reviews more than once and, with Reggie off at the BBC all day and disinclined to shoulder any household duties, was forced to do the shopping and supervise the cleaning lady.

Murdoch's success continued to rankle, and the sight of her face 'again spread large over the Sunday papers' led Olivia to berate Jack Lambert (literary editor of the *Sunday Times*, with whom she had established a good relationship, at least to this point) about the disjunction between the quality of her writing and the VIP treatment she received from the press, to which Lambert snapped back (according to Olivia) that whatever she thought, Murdoch wrote 'enjoyable and readable books. And I was left with the painful thought that—I did not.' The final blow came from *The Spectator*, from whose literary editor Olivia had expected a degree of loyalty since she had been reviewing for them for close to twenty years, when it declared Murdoch to be a second Ivy Compton-Burnett: 'Rather hard on Ivy' was

[52] Olivia Manning to Jocelyn Brooke, 6 June 1963, OMC/C, HRC.

Olivia's acid comment.[53] It is not the 'provincial boys,' she wrote to Julian Mitchell, who are 'the real enemies of the novel'—Iris Murdoch with her pretentious intellectualism was the one who was doing it in.[54] Of all her contemporaries, it was only Ivy Compton-Burnett who was exempt from Olivia's querulous envy. Reviewing *The Mighty and Their Fall* in September 1961, she deemed her to have achieved 'greatness' through a combination of unique talent and intellectual cogency. 'An acknowledged authority on family tyranny,' Compton-Burnett's wit is unimpaired, the concise pertinence of her dialogue as telling as ever, and her ability to make 'incident flow from precursor like figures in a dance' superlatively brilliant.[55]

When the glamorous Edna O'Brien began receiving critical attention, Olivia revised the views expressed earlier to Francis King that her work had a steel-like core in contrast to Muriel Spark's sentimental flabbiness. What a disgrace, she wrote to King, that 'your friend Karl [Karl Miller, then literary editor of the *New Statesman and Nation* and in 1979 founding editor of the *London Review of Books*] has really given himself to the Edna O'Brien Benefit Society. First a full-length review, then 1½ pages of Edna talking about herself on TV with front page picture, and now a whole page of some Irish critic talking about Edna's New Novel—as though it were some great work that must be introduced to the waiting world.'[56] One might think that what Olivia resented most about Edna O'Brien was her Irish good looks (apparently Lord Snowden was smitten when she posed for him) and this is in part true, but what compounded her resentment was, quite simply, the fact that O'Brien was twenty-two years younger than herself and possessed a polished Irish identity and beauty, whereas Olivia was in her mid-fifties and disinclined to claim her mother, the daughter of a Northern Irish publican from Bangor, as an Irish connection. Her envy of Edna O'Brien reveals the fundamental insecurities with which Olivia struggled all her life: she had no exotic family background about which she could boast (barely getting by in suburban Portsmouth lacked a certain cachet), she lacked any kind of formal

---

[53] Olivia Manning to Jocelyn Brooke, 13 September 1964, OMC/C, HRC.

[54] Olivia Manning to Julian Mitchell, 3 June 1961. Julian Mitchell Private Correspondence.

[55] 'A world and its weakness,' *The Spectator*, 11 September 1961.

[56] Olivia Manning to Francis King, undated letter from Abbey Gardens, OMC/C, HRC.

education, and her sexual attractiveness was of the irregular sort (when she first met Olivia in the mid-1960s, Margaret Drabble was struck by her beautiful complexion, slim figure, and silvery hair but thought the angularity of her bird-like face tended to make her appear witchy-looking). What Olivia had in her favor was a very sharp mind, a quick wit, and a fierce ambition. Déclassée by virtue of her introduction to a London world of writing, editing, and publishing through Hamish Miles and then through her immersion in a circle of British Council types through her marriage to Reggie, she forged her own social and cultural identity. Close friends such as Francis King, who appreciated her wicked wit and tenacious loyalty, admired and loved her. Others, particularly women, alienated by the sour resentment of her contemporaries' success, dismissed her as spiteful and malicious.

Probably because of her jealousy of other women writers, Olivia tended to be admired more by men than by women. For example, John Tydeman, who first met her in 1961 when he became Reggie's colleague at the BBC, believes that she actually preferred being with men and that she thought most women were silly, inconsequential, and uninteresting. For Tydeman, she was a well-dressed and acutely intelligent woman who had a great deal to put up with: Reggie was notoriously unreliable with her and with everyone—for instance, he would leave the control room at the BBC to go and place a bet on a horse—and he generally disregarded or failed to understand Olivia's feelings. Tydeman recalls going with them to a performance at the Old Vic and afterwards being shepherded to a local pub frequented by actors: Olivia loathed the smoke and noise of crowded pubs and refused to go inside. Reggie blithely proceeded and Olivia went home. An actress who worked on BBC documentaries with Reggie in the 1950s, Helen Miller-Smith, has never forgotten her first meeting with Olivia at 'The George,' Reggie's BBC local. At one end of the long bar was Reggie surrounded by laughing colleagues and at the other end was Olivia, a discontented expression on her face and making no attempt to join the group. Yet Helen always remembers Reggie saying to her, 'I may go off with another woman but there's no one like your wife.' From all accounts, Olivia and Reggie appeared to their friends as inseparably bound by his pride in her work and by her need for his support.[57]

---

[57] Author's conversation with John Tydeman, 7 May 2010; Author's conversation with Helen Miller-Smith, 15 July 2011.

For Margaret Drabble, Olivia in the 1960s was an entertaining and charming companion whom she recalls meeting at a Weidenfeld and Nicolson book party. By then Olivia had switched from Heinemann. Touchingly eager for affection and very much part of the literary social scene, she was always keen to come round to supper, often uninvited and perhaps a little more frequently than Drabble would have preferred. Drawn primarily, of course, by Drabble's considerable achievements (her third novel, *The Millstone*, won the John Llewellyn Rhys Memorial Prize in 1966 and *Jerusalem the Golden* won the James Tait Black Memorial Prize in 1967),[58] she also seemed in need of a kind of maternal warmth, behaving almost like a surrogate daughter despite the fact that she was older than Drabble by some thirty years. It was difficult, though, for Olivia to curb her jealousy of other writers, even when having a jolly supper in Drabble's kitchen with her three children: the moaning about not being nominated for the Booker prize became intolerable, as did her griping about mutual friends. When the British editor Anthony Godwin died in 1976 after a distinguished career at Penguin Books and Weidenfeld and Nicolson, Olivia started gossiping about his private life: seriously troubled by this insensitivity, Margaret Drabble told Olivia with a characteristic bluntness to shut up, a directness that she believes Olivia reluctantly appreciated. As did Reggie, who Drabble recalls as extremely generous in promoting people for jobs at the BBC; he would thank Drabble for being so nice to Olivia, an indication to her that there were many people who were not. For Drabble, little literary imagination went into the creation of Guy Pringle: Guy is Reggie and Reggie is Guy, and Jerry Slattery, in turn, was very much like Reggie—both of them big jolly blokes who liked a drink and made no attempt to hide their shared enjoyment of Olivia. When she was not with one, she was with the other.[59]

In a remarkably candid interview with Kay Dick, Olivia, at the age of fifty-five, admitted that she did not like getting old, a hardly surprising admission for her or anyone else of a certain age, but what

---

[58] Writing to Olivia from Rome in 1972, Anthony Burgess admitted that he had tried to read Margaret Drabble but 'always' failed: he 'stabbed at' *Jerusalem the Golden* at least nine times but eventually gave up, finding 'the style and the technique so old-fashioned.' Anthony Burgess to Olivia Manning, 9 April 1972, International Anthony Burgess Foundation.

[59] Author's conversation with Margaret Drabble, 29 April 2010.

is interesting about the conversation is an elaboration of how she feels. 'I hate seeing my face go to pieces. A lot of the excitement goes out of life as you get older. One sees all these attractive young men, and you think, well not for me. I must take a motherly attitude towards them . . . I photograph in two ways, either I come out looking like a gargoyle, or my face is so blotted out that I look like a film star.'[60] Middle age, she continues, is a very painful time: one is no longer at center stage; where once one might have been the most attractive girl in the room, the man to whom you are talking admires a lovely young thing ten years younger than you, and you realize you have been displaced. Olivia's preoccupation with aging had received a particular charge with a visit to Highgate Cemetery in 1961 after Ian Norrie, who for many years ran the High Hill Bookshop in Hampstead, asked Olivia to contribute an essay to a forthcoming book, *Heathside Book of Hampstead and Highgate*. On a midwinter morning when all was frozen into 'stillness,' Olivia discovered the inscription 'The Once Beautiful Eliza' on the gravestone of a 'lady of St. James's, wife of one George Fish,' who died at thirty-six. Here, Olivia discovers, time has devoured not only the flesh, but also the stones raised in its 'perpetual memory': broken columns have toppled and broken again, urns lie up-ended, cherubs are lost in grass. Chilled not only by the winter but also by the sight of a 'gigantic cedar stretched black as a crow against the livid sky,' she walked the circular passageway between vault and vault, and then, feeling 'the pressure of the grave', fled the scene, scurried home to Abbey Gardens, 'lone and chill as the dead.'

Shortly after her visit to Highgate Cemetery and publication of her essay in Ian Norrie's book, Olivia appeared on the BBC radio program *Woman's Hour* to give a talk on the 'Miseries of Human Life.' Aging is not listed as one of the 'miseries' and neither is a winter walk through a deserted cemetery. For Olivia, there are three categories of wretchedness with which one must contend: 'Domestic,' 'Social,' and 'Travel.' Under the rubric of domestic, she speaks comically about the sardine tin key that breaks half way, the nylon garments that have to be hand washed, the cat that is always on the wrong side of the door; the social miseries include the frenzied dog that rushes at you when you enter a strange house, the foreign maid who speaks no English but loves

---

[60] Kay Dick, *Friends and Friendship*, 36.

answering the telephone, and the hostess who announces she must separate you from someone with whom you are getting on; and the miseries of travel predictably include the delayed plane that takes longer than the train, the car in front of you looking for a parking meter, and the only available parking meter that proves to be out of order.[61] These are the small things that annoy and are nothing along the lines of a crisis in Suez, a revolution in Hungary, a fear of atomic warfare. By the early to mid-1960s, despite the fact that the Cold War continued and that the Soviet Union and the United States came frighteningly close to military combat in the Cuban crisis of 1962, Olivia began to feel less fearful that the secure world she had built around herself after 1945 would be annihilated in another war. Her life became safely grounded in her writing and in her settled domestic existence. Working regularly in her pleasant study in Abbey Gardens, surrounded by beautiful objects and pictures secured on trips to the King's Road with Francis King, making love regularly with Jerry Slattery and perhaps occasionally with Reggie, she no longer lived under the black shadow of the mushroom clouds. Taking great satisfaction from Anthony Burgess's designation of *The Balkan Trilogy* as 'one of the finest fictional productions that Britain has seen since the war,'[62] she worked on some new short stories and began a book about cats—*Extraordinary Cats*, published in 1967.

Olivia's modest and quite beautifully illustrated little book chronicles her devotion to cats from the time she listened to her father's stories of Siamese kittens scampering the decks of HMS *Venus* (a ship on which he sailed before she was born) to her 1960s adoration of the third of the four cats in her life, Choula, a gorgeous Siamese. The first had been the gift of a Siamese kitten from a friend when she and Reggie were living in Baker Street right after the war; the second was Faro, an offspring of the Baker Street cat and named for Felix Latimer's treasured kitten in *A School for Love*; the third was Choula; and the last Miou, a Burmese, who outlived Olivia by six weeks. 'For the cat lover the Siamese cat is the concentrate of addiction,' she wrote in her longhand notes for the book: cats are man's last link with nature, creatures who when domesticated 'become something more than an

---

[61] Olivia Manning Contributor Talks, 1951–1982, 10 January 1962, BBC Sound Archives, British Library.

[62] 'The Pringles all entire,' *The Spectator*, 11 May 1965.

animal. The change is brought about not merely by human fantasy and human need: the animal itself is drawn out of its animal world and advances to meet our wider understanding.'[63] Stevie Smith, though, was of a different mind when reviewing Olivia's book in the *Sunday Times*; no harm in liking cats, she says, but one can take this liking too far—as did the Egyptians and as does her old friend when she uses her love of Siamese and Burmese 'as a stick to beat about with' when attacking vivisection. As always, Stevie sighs, when writing about controversial subjects, 'Miss Manning is apt to be more agitated than original.'[64] Surprisingly, in light of Olivia's complaints about Stevie's 'bitchiness,' she did not let this bother her and remained a vocal opponent of vivisection throughout her life.

When it came to 'agitated' public protest against pollution of the environment and the ancillary damage to animal life, Olivia also did not keep quiet. In a letter to *The Times* in 1967 about the extermination of otters by pesticides dumped into England's rivers, she ridiculed claims that polluted waters controlled otter reproduction. On a visit to Oxhead in Norfolk in May 1967 to observe otters at work, as it were, she learned that by taking slow or diseased fish they actually improved stocks, that they eat large quantities of eels who are 'the chief predators of fish spawn,' and that 'if they are wiped out a more destructive force will take their place.' Now is the time, she concluded, for 'enlightened landowners to defend whenever possible these harmless, beautiful and sadly rare mammals.'[65] Also, in a notably prescient protest against damage to the environment by oil spillage (one thinks, if nothing else, of the BP Gulf of Mexico oil spill that occurred on 20 April 2010), Olivia announced in early February 1970 that she was selling her oil shares in protest against the widespread fouling of seabirds and that she planned to give the profit of £450 she received to any charity dealing with preservation of wildlife: 'I couldn't take this profit while these creatures are suffering . . . I am thinking particularly

---

[63] *Extraordinary Cats*, 77.

[64] *Sunday Times*, 26 November 1967.

[65] Kay Dick was a strong ally in the otter campaign: on a postcard to Olivia dated 14 August 1978, she asks, 'Did we ever achieve anything for those lovely otters?' OMC/C, HRC. Olivia would have been heartened by an article in the *Guardian* that appeared on 18 August 2011, 'Otters are back': 'It has been a long and perilous journey, but otters have finally managed to swim back from the brink of extinction and into every county in England.'

of the wiping out of an entire colony of eider ducks in Northern
Scotland by oil from a wreck.'[66] Until the end of her life, Olivia
continued to protest cruelty to animals and desecration of the environment. Immediately after publication of *Extraordinary Cats*, however, she set to work on her most extraordinary and least appreciated
novel: *The Play Room*.

---

[66] 'The Times Diary,' *The Times*, 5 February 1970. Whether Olivia ever actually
received a profit of £400 from selling her oil shares is uncertain: she received many letters
appealing for funds (among them, a request from the 'Advisory Committee on Oil
Pollution of the Sea'), but the only record of anyone receiving funds is an organization
named 'Oil Pollution South East Kent.' A Mr Trevor Dixon thanks her for a donation in
the sum of £10 and expresses regret 'for the misfortune of your oil shares.'

10

A Strange Decade

'*Mrs. A., timidly*: But isn't Olivia Manning dangerously highbrow?

We explain: Olivia Manning, Mrs. A., is an o.k. name, and that, in this context, is what matters. To read one of her books right through might indeed be dangerous and could even unfit you for your chosen life.'

Marghanita Laski.[1]

Cast away by the BBC

Back in 1942, when Olivia was working in Cairo as a Public Information Officer at the American Embassy, reviewing regularly for *The Palestine Post*, and polishing her book about Stanley and Emin Pasha, BBC Radio broadcast for the first time what is now its longest-running program: *Desert Island Discs*. Guests are invited to imagine themselves cast away, Robinson Crusoe style, on a desert island, but whereas Crusoe had only what he could salvage from the wrecked vessel breaking up on the rocks, visitors to the BBC's desert island are imaginatively provided with a gramophone (well, it was a gramophone in the early days) and eight records of their own choosing (now, of course, they are offered compact discs). When they get tired of listening to their eight pieces of music, they can read through the

---

[1] 'Is this your problem?' *The Observer*, 23 October 1960. In this parody of book reviewing, Marghanita Laski argues that the books one displays will create a more powerful impression for one's guests than the books that one actually reads. The inside of books is unimportant: 'It is what is *outside* them that matters.'

Complete Works of Shakespeare and the Bible, plus one other book of
their own choosing, and, finally, enjoy a 'luxury,' again of their own
choosing.

On 25 August 1969 Olivia was picked to have her turn to be cast
away, to choose her music, and to select her books. Initially, she was
not exactly a cooperative guest, as one can hear from her languid
response to the question as to whether music played a big part in her
life: 'I can't say it does,' she replied, 'I'm not very musical.' Confessing
rather grudgingly that she had no musical gifts, that she had been
'forcibly taught the piano' but 'it didn't take,' and that she hardly
ever played records, she then declared that she actually preferred
silence to listening to music.

Finally, after being prodded by a very patient host, Roy Plomley,
she managed to kick things off by choosing some Romanian gypsy
music and moved on to John McCormack singing 'She moved
through the Fair' (for her, 'The greatest of Irish songs'), a spot of
Sibelius, and Mozart's Quintet for Clarinet and Strings (Olivia explained the choice of Mozart by evoking her first stifling months in
Cairo when Adam Watson played the Quintet 'again and again and
again and all through that extraordinary heat of summer').[2] At this point
in the program, Plomley, eager to keep her talking, asked, 'Olivia, what
are your writing habits? Are you a disciplined writer?' The response was
ironically self-deprecatory: ' . . . being a married woman and a housewife
and not being very rich I have to do quite a lot of other things . . . but
I usually manage to write in the afternoons.' By 1969, Olivia Manning
was hardly identified by her friends and the English literary establishment as a married woman and a housewife, usually in need of money,
who managed to toss off a few paragraphs in the afternoon: if nothing
else, her reputation as an intelligent and authoritative novelist had
been secured by reception of *The Balkan Trilogy*. When it became
time to pick record number five, however, Olivia's irony gave way to
unguarded enthusiasm: she loved 'Penny Lane' by the Beatles.

For her, the lyrics to 'Penny Lane' captured the poetry of the 1960s:
'I mean the sort of mystery and beauty of our urban world. That
phrase, "Very strange . . . " I mean that's what life is. It's really

---

[2] In *The Danger Tree*, Harriet Pringle listens as, 'All through the late afternoons and
evenings of mid-summer the questing notes of the clarinet filled the flat as Dobson
[modeled, as we know, on Adam Watson] played and replayed his new record' (p. 144).

strange.'[3] That Olivia was struck by the very strangeness of life at the close of the 1960s is affirmed by much of her writing during that decade, not all of it situated in an 'urban world.' In her collection of short stories, *A Romantic Hero*, published in 1967, the reader encounters a woman morbidly terrified of 'the darkness at the end of the street,' a bisexual young man fatally mesmerized by a gorgeous fellow he meets on a train, and a young woman recalling an eerie childhood memory of her drug-addicted dentist seated in an old dental chair, hypodermic needle stuck in his arm. And in the very strangest of Olivia's novels (*The Play Room*, published in 1969 and to be discussed in the latter part of this chapter), we read of two children enticed by a male transvestite dressed like a tarted-up Queen Mary who shows them his collection of naked and anatomically correct life-size dolls posed in various sexual positions. The dolls occupy a padlocked shed on the Isle of Wight.

During these years, the center of Olivia's very strange 'urban world' became known as 'Swinging London' as hordes of young men and women (aiming to be 'Dolly Birds') flocked to Carnaby Street to deck themselves out in 'mod' fashion and more privileged young things floated up and down the King's Road in Chelsea, popping into the Biba boutique to try on the latest Mary Quant and Ossie Davis number. At a historical moment that both fascinated and unsettled Olivia, the 'Sexual Revolution' took off, fueled by relaxed standards of sexual morality and an eased availability of birth control. If a gutted England in 1945 had proved a difficult adjustment when she and Reggie had struggled to recover from the war, and if the 1950s had challenged everyone with Austerity and Cold War worries and Olivia in particular with the emergence of the Angry Young Men bent on appropriation of the modern novel, then in the 1960s she was confronted with a youth culture in which she seemed to have neither visibility nor voice. In *The Doves of Venus* she had faced down her fears about growing old through a compelling projection of such anxiety on to Petta Bellot, a narcissistic fading beauty, but ten years later an alarming contrast between what she felt was her waning attractiveness and the fresh bloom of young people she saw every day when she was out fulfilling her duties as the 'housewife' she claimed she was on

---

[3] I am grateful to Gerry Harrison for sharing with me a transcript of *Desert Island Discs*, recorded 15 August 1969, 14:00–16:45, and aired on 27 August 1969.

Desert Island Discs, rattled her confidence as a middle-aged woman. In 1965, she was nearing sixty: not, for her, a happy prospect. How to carry on and what next to write became compelling questions.

First, she decided to go on Arts Council tours around the country, along with other writers. During the day, the group would visit schools and colleges to see short dramatic performances that were then discussed by the group and the performers. In the evenings, the writers gave public readings from their own works and from their own particular favorite novelists and poets. Although for Olivia the money was welcome (£120, first-class travel, and £7 subsistence per day), she found it exhausting, rather like being on tour in an acting company. But she remained game, even if to her friend and companion on most of the tours, Margaret Drabble, she often seemed worn out by the dreadful wait at railway stations, the lugging around of suitcases, and the tiresome moves from one grim provincial hotel to another. On one particular trip with Drabble, the playwright Arnold Wesker, and the poet Adrian Mitchell, Olivia declared that the four of them were being shunted around like refugees (something she could speak about with authority). She also objected, jokingly, to her photograph on the pamphlet announcing one of the tours: signing it for Arnold Wesker, she wrote 'Love from Olivia (but I don't look like this. I'm much more beautiful!).' 'And so am I,' wrote Adrian Mitchell.[4] But she relished chumming around with fellow-writers and having her make-up done before they went on, gleefully telling Margaret Drabble that they looked fantastic with their 'pancake' faces.[5] The second strategy she decided upon for finding a place in a culture besotted with youth and sexual license was to make that culture the subject of her next novel. Unhappy as she may have been as she neared her sixtieth birthday, she knew she was by no means finished as a sharp observer of social mores.

Tony Judt argues that the Sexual Revolution was, for most people, a 'mirage,' a construction of the media eager to manufacture superficial comparisons between a loosened sexual style in the sixties and the 'moral rectitude and constipated emotional restraint' that popularly characterized the fifties.[6] Popular journalism in the decade in question was notably preoccupied with circulating salacious sexual gossip and

---

[4] 'Writers on tour,' Tees Area, 1970, OMC, HRC.
[5] Author's conversation with Margaret Drabble, 29 April 2010.
[6] *Postwar: A History of Europe Since 1945*, 396.

documenting the excesses of a promiscuous youth culture. For example, in the early 1960s a juicy scandal almost brought down the government when the Secretary of State for War in Harold Macmillan's cabinet, John Profumo, was revealed as a patron of Christine Keeler, an up-market call girl with other clients besides Profumo, which should have come as no surprise to anybody. Had a Russian diplomat named Captain Ivanov not also been one of her customers, the Profumo affair would probably have disappeared after the tabloids had their profitable fun with his private life. But rumors reached the Lord Chancellor's office. In the House of Commons Profumo vehemently denied any involvement with Keeler, then admitted he lied, and was eventually cleared of any breach of security. *The Times* wrapped up the affair with a sanctimonious lament about a decline in national moral standards.[7] Open discussion of the private lives of adulterous politicians and of the promiscuity of randy teenagers became significant for Olivia as she made notes about the sexual behavior of her friends' teenage children and mulled over ideas for her next novel.

After the third novel in *The Balkan Trilogy*, *Friends and Heroes*, was published in late 1965—rather too close for comfort to Iris Murdoch's *The Red and the Green*—Olivia imaginatively departed from Romania and Greece as Guy and Harriet Pringle set sail for Africa and returned to a thinly disguised Portsmouth and a recognizable Isle of Wight as the settings for her new novel. Delighted by praise from her old friend Walter Allen, who had judged the trilogy 'a major achievement in the English novel,' and also laid low by some disparagement of her work as boringly 'traditionalist,'[8] she vowed to remember the praise and ignore the criticism (a definite achievement on her part, given her tendency to dwell morosely over every review of her work). She also overcame the unpleasantness of having been sued in early 1965, along with Heinemann and Panther Books, by Barbu Calinescu, the only son of Armand Calinescu, a former Prime Minister of Romania. In *The Spoilt City*, on the basis of her research in newspaper archives, Olivia had implied that the entire Calinescu family had been wiped out by the Iron Guard: Barbu Calinescu, however, escaped to England, which allowed him to sue for damages on the grounds he had been made to

[7] Alan Sked and Chris Cook, *Post-War Britain: A Political History*, 186.
[8] *New York Times*, 28 November 1965.

appear an imposter. The matter was settled with a public apology and Heinemann's agreement to have a correction slip inserted in future editions.[9]

The Calinescu business out of the way, Reggie and Olivia traveled to Venice in the summer of 1966 with June and Neville Braybrooke for a two-week holiday. Jerry and Johnny Slattery joined them for the second week. Immediately on arrival at a well-known *pensione*, Casa Frollo, in the Giudecca district, Olivia wrote to Kay Dick that 'This "glamour puss" of a city looks as lovely as ever,' but in the second week of the holiday she came down with a malaria attack and her bad behavior put a damper on everyone's spirits. Throwing slippers at the maids, refusing to eat, and complaining about Reggie's non-stop drinking and inconsiderate habit of disappearing down Venetian alleyways when the fancy took him, she threw the normally serene Casa Frollo into confusion. Recovering sufficiently, however, to visit Peggy Guggenheim holding court at her palazzo, later that evening Olivia was able to join everyone for dinner at a local trattoria, where the phenomenally rich patron of the arts insisted that everyone pay for their own meal.[10] Olivia derided this absurd frugality but she remained fond of Venice until the end of her life, despite the city's tendency to trigger malaria attacks, a troublesome souvenir of her years in Egypt.

On the return to London, Olivia decided to cut back on the book reviewing she had conducted with little interruption for the previous twenty years (apart from the hiatus when she worked on *The Balkan Trilogy*), and to approach the BBC Radio Drama Department with a proposal for adaptation of Fanny Burney's *Evelina*, a somewhat courageous move on her part given the unhappy experience with BBC readers who had savaged most of her earlier projects. But she needed the money (she claimed she *always* needed the money) and was prepared to delay the writing of the next novel in order to pump up the Manning/Smith bank account. Reggie, like most BBC producers, did not earn a high salary and Olivia's income from reviewing, royalties, and savvy investments suggested by Jerry Slattery, essentially financed everything except food expenses. Having reread Burney's novel, she offered to write eight installments, each thirty minutes in length, for which she would be paid forty guineas per episode—not

---

[9] *The Times*, 2 April 1965.
[10] Neville and June Braybrooke, *Olivia Manning: A Life*, 197–8.

bad remuneration for the time. But the richness of the novel proved uncontainable within eight episodes, and she produced twelve. The BBC was not pleased: a reader's report written for Hallam Tennyson, assistant head of drama to Martin Esslin and a great-grandson of Alfred Tennyson, assessed the episodes as far too drawn out, as mere conversation pieces, and as displaying no sign that Olivia knew how to place and plant characters: overall, 'a most disappointing piece of work.' Tennyson then wrote to Olivia claiming that the BBC had been wrong to agree to twelve episodes, that the whole thing needed pruning, and that it had been very difficult to read her typed scripts as they were in 'an uncorrected state and with, in places, whole lines missing.' The project went nowhere, and yet once more Olivia terminated negotiations with BBC Radio Drama (or they with her) by delivering a barbed accusation that they paid writers very poorly.[11]

So, she returned to reviewing, accumulating notes about 'Swinging London' and the 'Sexual Revolution,' and working on her short stories. The reviews published in the 1960s sustain Olivia's reputation as a witty and often merciless judge of contemporary fiction, usually American. For example, Morley Callaghan's short stories fall into the trap of 'a vacuous repetition of the sort of "sensitive" story for which *The New Yorker* is famous' (Olivia's cracks at the *New Yorker* were fed in part by jealousy of Muriel Spark's highly remunerative relationship with its literary editor). Taking a sarcastic swipe at Philip Roth, Olivia declared that the cavalier attitude demonstrated by Goethe when he offered to extend a serial by including some pages of an old diary seemed to be 'playing havoc with the American novel today': in *Letting Go*, Roth's inflation of a moderately engaging story into two hundred and fifty thousand words leads to repetitive narrative and 'a literary dinosaur.'[12] To be fair, Olivia's scorn was not reserved for American writers: Colin Wilson, for example, who made a tremendous cultural splash in 1956 with *The Outsider*, a mélange of literary and philosophical criticism offered from a position of eccentric dislocation from the cultural mainstream, got roasted for a lame detective novel, *Necessary Doubt*—Olivia was unsure whether Wilson is still '*the* outsider' but as

---

[11] Olivia Manning Scriptwriter 1943–1982, BBC Written Archives Centre, Caversham, 28 July 1965; 2 June 1966; 13 October 1966; 17 October 1966.

[12] 'The Memoirs of Alan Sebrill,' *Sunday Times*, 12 August 1962; 'Leaving out,' *Sunday Times*, 18 November 1962.

far as mystery fiction is concerned he is 'right on the inside with a collection of characters that were Old Favourites long before he put pen to paper.'[13]

In Olivia's collection of short stories, *A Romantic Hero*, published in 1967, eight of the fourteen stories were reprinted from the 1948 collection *Growing Up* and of the remaining six, three were written between 1948 and 1953 and the final three rewritten or written in the 1960s. Strange and unnerving experiences unsettle the lives of the characters in the last three stories in the collection. The first of the final three, 'The End of the Street,' tells the story of Marion Partridge, a vicar's daughter who moves to London in the mid-1930s, where she is enthralled by the theaters and the blazing shop windows. What she fears is the 'emptiness' of isolated villages, 'the darkness at the end of the street... the loneliness of death.' Nothing much happens in the story. Marion and her husband Peter drive into the country to visit her parents at Christmas time, she heaped with shawls and he driving his vintage car through the icy darkness with the solid confidence that attracted her to him when they first met. As they stand on the glimmering grass outside her parents' Georgian house, looking in at people living their lives, she says, 'It's like being dead and watching the living doing things that you used to do yourself.'[14] Troubled by her mood, Peter asks whether, if she dies first, she will wait for him: her response to this peculiar question is to wonder if he thinks he could find her after her death, how he would recognize her without her body. This morbid remark fills him with regret for the way he neglected his now dead mother, and compels him to search every woman's face 'for that sad, forsaken face somewhere again' (p. 214). Marion's awareness of the desolation of death, symbolized in the darkness at the end of the street, infects their perfect world and ruins their marriage.

'A Romantic Hero' tells the dismal story of Harold, 'A tall man with a thin constricted look' impelled 'to prefer first the company of one sex, then of the other' and doomed to romantic failure with both. As always, Olivia writes perceptively about sexual attraction between men without making their sexual preference the sole defining mark of her characters. On a train to the seaside to stay with his long-suffering

---

[13] *The Spectator*, 21 February 1964.
[14] 'The end of the street,' *A Romantic Hero*, 213.

girlfriend, Harold becomes infatuated with a beautiful young man whose golden curls, mesmerizing blue eyes, and lean physique excite him almost to the point of choking with pleasure. Together with his physical attractions this young man speaks with 'an educated voice,' which to Harold is very much superior to the regional accents becoming acceptable in the mid-1960s. When Olivia rewrote this story, first drafted in 1939, in 1965, she made it current with reference to such things as a waning belief that the accent of an upper-middle-class person living in the Home Counties signaled inherent superiority. Having grown up over a grocery shop in Bradford and having been denied by his parents a university education (even at the neighboring red-brick, a note indicating Olivia's 1960s revision), Harold had been apprenticed to a gentleman's outfitters. Now, having trained as an elocutionist, he is proud of his polished accent and appalled by the sight of his girlfriend, Angela, waiting for him on the station platform: 'dumpy, badly dressed and lower middle class.'[15]

Poor Harold, mistakenly encouraged by the young man's laconic friendliness, visits him at a cottage where he is studying for the Oxford entrance exam (a detail that glamorizes him further in Harold's eyes) and slides an arm around his neck. Instantly rebuffed with the calm admonition to pull himself together and suffering from a miserable cold, he trudges back to Angela, to her 'feminine warmth and sympathy' that were now to him 'the most desirable things in the world.' She consoles him with the cheerful observation that everyone is full of anxiety, worried about 'what hangs over them': and it's 'not just the bomb' she adds. The success of the story rests in its unsentimental view of homosexual desire: Harold fancies himself some sort of 'romantic hero' but, as Angela wearily observes, he exaggerates his sufferings, his sensitivity, and his attraction to men in order to place himself above 'the common run.' In actuality, he is a boring, self-absorbed, whining snob and his homosexual longing is merely part of him, not the governing determinant of his behavior.

The last story in the collection was written in 1966 and recounts the memories of a young woman named Emily of childhood visits to the family dentist, Mr Limestone, a man with 'sandy hair and a nose that looked overlarge because it was almost the whole of his face. His

---

[15] 'A romantic hero,' *A Romantic Hero*, 221.

cheeks, brow and chin seemed to have receded, leaving the nose in possession.'[16] Adding to the strangeness of Mr Limestone, his patients' waiting-room is lined with cupboards containing electro-plated toast racks, jam dishes, cheap china statuettes of tall girls leading Alsatian dogs, and miniature models of small girls cuddling bunnies. Investing these commonplace objects with a menacing resonance, Olivia deftly conveys the sinister ordinariness of the room. On the occasion of Emily's final frightening visit to Mr Limestone, he begins to fill a cavity and then disappears downstairs leaving her with her mouth stuffed with cotton wadding: desperate to leave, she ventures to the basement and discovers him with a hypodermic needle stuck in his arm and a blissful smile upon his face. Twenty years later, reminded of this bizarre incident, she thinks that his may not have been an innocent pleasure, 'yet it seemed to her the pleasure of the innocent' (p. 252).

But despite good reviews of the short stories, whose eeriness floats menacingly throughout Olivia's next novel, *The Play Room*, she remained dissatisfied with her long-term publishers William Heinemann: in 1965, she complained that her royalty arrangements were unfair and discriminatory since she received only 12½ per cent on the first 3,000 copies of her novels, whereas other novelists started at 15 per cent. Heinemann met her demands in the mid-1970s but she moved to Weidenfeld and Nicolson, who published the first novel in *The Levant Trilogy*, *The Danger Tree*, in 1977. To John St John, a friend at Heinemann and later its historian, she confessed she wished she had stayed with 'the old firm.' As far as St John was concerned, Olivia was 'a most distinguished writer,' but, as he told her once at lunch, she was 'not one of the easiest in the world to publish for!'[17] For her readers, her next novel was certainly not one of the easiest in the world to digest.

The horrors of the doll shed

That Olivia Manning was an accomplished novelist not terribly well known beyond a band of devoted admirers was the principal point made by Ruth Inglis in an interview that appeared in the *Observer*

[16] 'Innocent pleasures,' *A Romantic Hero*, 242–3.
[17] *William Heinemann: A Century of Publishing*, 446; 345.

Colour Supplement in April 1969, a few days before publication of *The Play Room*. This was a big publicity event for Olivia and she dressed for it well, donning a bright fuchsia tweed suit picked up from the Oxfam Shop in Marylebone High Street (always a canny shopper, she acquired a substantial part of her wardrobe from Oxfam). Knowing Olivia to be 'a writer of prodigious gifts' who regularly received 'fulsome praise' from discerning critics, Inglis prepared herself for the interview by asking people whether they had, in fact, ever heard of Olivia Manning: the muddled answer was usually something along the lines of the name rings a bell but can't quite place her.[18] Inglis kicked things off by asking that since the forthcoming novel contained transvestism, lesbianism, and rape, was it not likely that loyal readers will yearn for 'the calm, the cool stylistic fineries' of *The Balkan Trilogy* and assume that sensationalism was the novel's primary attraction? Absolutely not, responded Olivia, after which Inglis conceded that if readers were to make such an assumption, they would be missing Manning's pitch-perfect capture of contemporary teenage anxiety in a time of sexual revolution. Altogether, Olivia presented an enigmatic figure: although impeccably well-mannered and a little aloof, her penetrating black eyes belonged 'to no comfortable English drawing-room matron.'

Aiming to fathom Olivia's uniqueness in the ranks of modern women novelists, Inglis ventured that her pursuit of a somewhat lonely course—'reflections on historical events, contemporary violence, loneliness'—precluded affiliation with feminist writers of the 1960s who were devoted almost exclusively to representation of women's inequality and articulation of its remedies. Rather, by virtue of her cool and elegant mastery of language, her irony, her lack of hysteria, she may be said to have a 'man's mind,' that 'ultimate fatherly compliment.' Halfway through the interview, her 'black eyes now flashing fire' and abandoning her reserve, Olivia launched into a lively celebration of female superiority: what man could deal with menstruating every month, could cope with the possibility of feeling ill for nine months just because he went to bed with someone? Biologically and in their behavior, women are altogether superior. They don't need to prove themselves, they don't need to overtake everyone on the road,

[18] Ruth Inglis, 'Who is Olivia Manning?,' *Observer Colour Supplement*, 6 April 1969.

and they are not hobbled by inferiority complexes like men. Here, Olivia's delivers her fulsome tribute to female superiority in the drily ironic tone of Harriet Pringle.

The interview with Ruth Inglis that appeared in *The Observer* was one of several Heinemann arranged for publication of *The Play Room*, most of them occurring in March and April 1969. Auriol Stevens, a reporter for the *Guardian*, like Ruth Inglis, noted the fuchsia tweed suit and Olivia's 'tall, slightly mouldering, comfy, cluttered house in St John's Wood.' Warned she should tread carefully as Olivia could be 'well, a bit difficult,' Stevens was surprised to find her 'shy,' prone to self-effacing confessions that she is not much of a talker. But, cradling her cat, Olivia seems to have chattered away quite happily, sometimes saying things grounded in fact and at other times not. For example, she ruefully drew attention to the somewhat dilapidated state of 36 Abbey Gardens and confessed that she longed 'to have a really lovely house in Hampstead,' which was certainly the case since she and Reggie were fed up with seemingly endless plumbers' and builders' bills. But she also insisted her new novel was not autobiographical. Given that *The Play Room*'s principal character is a teenage girl with literary ambitions desperate to escape a depressing seaside town, this insistence seems a little suspect. What's more the girl endures the plaintive nastiness of a nagging mother, suffers the painful sight of an improvident father, and struggles to master murderous fits of jealousy occasioned by her mother's favoritism of her only son. It may have been difficult for people to reconcile the well-mannered lady-like figure from St John's Wood with the author of a novel about sex, teenage girls, and violence, but its powerful evocation of adolescent experience owes a good deal to Olivia's Portsmouth girlhood.[19] She dedicated it 'with love' to Jane and Jonathan, the children of Jerry and Johnny Slattery.

Like Olivia, the principal female character, Laura Fletcher, has an oval face and clear skin, 'and viewed from the front, she was *almost* pretty. But her nose was too long, her chin too short, her arms and legs thick, her head small and she had dark unbiddable hair.'[20] As a teenager, although she did not have thick arms and legs, Olivia worried about her beaky nose and receding chin—in fact, she worried about these facial irregularities all her life. Like Olivia, who subscribed

---

[19] Auriol Stevens, 'Olivia Manning and her new novel,' *Guardian*, 13 March 1969.
[20] *The Play Room*, 54.

to the *TLS*, Laura ostentatiously carries the latest issues to school, only to be told that men don't like girls who read 'papers like that,' a reproof virtually identical with that uttered by Olivia's mother. Like Olivia, who boasted to her schoolmates of Anglo-Irish connections, Laura constantly invents romantic stories about herself. Claiming to have been brought up by a nurse, she counts among her interesting ancestors John Fletcher—this after reading about Beaumont and Fletcher in *The History of English Literature*. Like Olivia, whose torments of jealousy when her brother was born led her mother to bemoan the loss of her pretty appearance and charming personality, Laura, after the birth of *her* brother, ceased being 'pretty and charming and clever, and became instead a skinny little rat of a thing, unco-operative and given to boasting' (p. 39). Finally, the Fletcher family lives in Camperlea, again clearly Portsmouth.

Olivia clearly modeled Laura's father upon memories of Oliver Manning. Taunted by a schoolmate (the daughter of a radio repair shop owner) that she is actually 'nothing,' even if she thinks she is 'someone' because her father was an officer, Laura endures insults about Commander Fletcher having begun his career by swabbing decks. Handsome, well built, and light on his feet, Commander Fletcher when on active service had crowds of friends. When he marries late in life 'as a safeguard against shore life with its household worries,' he loses his small pension in piddling investments and becomes to Laura a figure 'helplessly trapped within her mother's agitated vortex' (p. 22). Mrs Fletcher, having adored her domineering father, scorns her husband's sentimental nature: he is 'a fool and an old fool' as far as she is concerned. She rejects her daughter and lavishes all her love on her son Tom. What's remarkable about *The Play Room* is Olivia's imaginative manipulation of this very familiar autobiographical material in order to shape a narrative that is anything but familiar in its depiction of sexual perversity.

A short novel, *The Play Room* is divided into two uneven parts: 'The Island' takes up the first third and 'The Play Room' the other two thirds. 'The Island' traces a visit by Laura and Tom Fletcher to the Isle of Wight, a place much loved by Olivia from the time of day trips as a child (the Mannings could barely afford the cost of a ferry ride let alone a summer holiday on the Island's beaches) to the last years of her life when she and Reggie would visit their friends Neville and June Braybrooke and stay either with them in Cowes or in a rented summer cottage, often next door to Helen Miller-Smith, who acted in BBC documentaries directed by Reggie in the 1950s. Taking the ferry from Southampton to Cowes, they would climb Castle Road to the large 1835 Braybrooke house thought to have been designed by John Nash, who retired to East Cowes in the early 1830s and died there in 1835. In June 1970, Olivia wrote to June Braybrooke about a recent visit to Alum Bay, a famous area near the westernmost point of the Isle of Wight noted for its multicolored sand cliffs: 'I often think of that wonderful afternoon we had there with the very delicate mist hanging over everything and the foghorn going and our trip round the Needles. All the summers of one's life add up in the end to a few exquisite days like that.'[21] The week that Laura and Tom Fletcher spend on the Isle of Wight in the first third of *The Play Room* begins with 'exquisite' days exploring the sands of Alum Bay.

The Fletcher children have traveled alone to the Island to stay with a Mrs Button who once worked for their mother in some kind of cleaning capacity. Forgetful and fond of the local pub, Mrs Button neglects to meet them on their disembarkation from the ferry but they manage to find their way to her shabby little house whose sitting room is very small and very hot and into which Mrs Button has crammed a table and chairs, a three-piece suite, a cocktail cabinet, a television set, and a new gas fire. Like the peculiar and menacing atmosphere in the dentist Mr Limestone's waiting room, the cluttered heat of Mrs Button's sitting room radiates something sinister and perplexing to the children. Mrs Button herself is very new: her hair is dyed red and she wears some remarkable glasses set with *diamanté*: 'Her red jumpersuit matched the red three-piece suite and her teeth, once brown and broken, were as white and even as a three-strand pearl necklace (p. 29). The next morning she appears in a tomato-colored housecoat of quilted nylon, trimmed with gold.

Mrs Button is one of several peculiar women (or people who appear to be women) connected by the red imagery that Olivia threads throughout the novel. Two of the Fletchers' neighbors in Camperlea, Mrs Everest and her daughter, aged eighty and sixty respectively, are greeted flirtatiously by Commander Fletcher as he walks his children to the ferry to take them to the Island: 'They looked like film stars of

[21] 'Isobel English,' Introduction to *The Play Room*, p. x.

the old days, dead but embalmed; their red hair, skin of unearthly whiteness and lips like plum jam, all preserved intact. Long nylon lashes swept about their faded eyes' (p. 23). The strangest of all of the very strange figures in this novel is Mrs Toplady, a transvestite who dresses in red satin and is like no other character in Olivia's fiction. When working on the novel, Olivia almost certainly culled Mrs Toplady from memories of her precocious teenage reading in Havelock Ellis when holed up in her bedroom in Laburnum Grove. She read all of Ellis's *Studies in the Psychology of Sex* and became very interested in Ellis's descriptions of what he termed 'sexo-aesthetic inversion.' Tom and Laura meet Mrs Toplady when exploring the Island, having been instructed by Mrs Button to amuse themselves during the day and not to return for tea until five o'clock.

They discover palm trees, landfalls, and the fascinating colored sands of Alum Bay and late one afternoon find themselves trapped in a desolate rock-strewn cove from which there is no outlet. The tide is coming in, the water is too deep for them to wade back to safety, and they have no alternative but to climb up the soft cliff face. When they make it to the top they discover a leveled lawn with garden chairs gazing seawards towards the mainland and a house with large French windows; they also discover a very large lady seated just inside one of these open French windows who beckons them forward. 'She's weird,' whispers Tom—and indeed she is. Wearing a crimson satin dress that reveals her vast shoulders and arms and a sort of Queen Mary pearl choker clasping her thick neck, and sporting silver polish on her stubby fingers, she is drinking whiskey from a tumbler and smoking a cigar. Doubting that she belongs to the human race, Laura and Tom liken this grotesquely top-heavy creature to a fairy-tale giant or a dame from the Christmas pantomimes. To Laura, who fancies herself a sophisticated young person of the world, she also seems 'a woman of liberal concepts,' but to Tom she resembles a sloppy predatory aunt drooling over his boyish beauty.

Soon, though, Laura sees that this vast improbable creature who has introduced herself as Mrs Toplady wears a dress that is stained and burst open at the seams, that even though her curls are golden, coarse ginger hair grows in her armpits, and that her make-up is smudged and sticky and powder has settled into the pores of her nose. On her big, loose mouth she has drawn a tiny red mouth with peaked upper lip and under lip like a cherry. The sex of Mrs Toplady is settled for Laura when the effort of pressing a squirming Tom to her vast bosom dislodges one of her pink plastic breasts, sending it up and out of her stained satin bodice. Offering an invitation to come and see the Play Room and grunting with the effort of hoisting her enormous body out of her chair, with her yellow hair, highly colored face, and long red dress, she seems to Laura 'like one of the ships' figureheads that Camperlea naval men put into their gardens' (p. 46). The Play Room turns out to be a padlocked shed into which are crowded many wind-up 'life-sized doll children, naked, lying and standing in odd positions.' Laura sees immediately that 'the figures are too complete for dolls' and realizes she has never seen children in such strange attitudes. Tom shrieks in fear and they both escape Mrs Toplady's sticky clutches, scrambling through the bushes and managing to catch a bus back to Mrs Button's.

The rest of this strangely sinister novel takes up Laura's return to school and her infatuation with one of her classmates, Vicky Logan, the pampered daughter of a lascivious local architect and his fatuous wife. Vicky's experiments in bisexuality shape the second phase of Laura's introduction to sex: the 'disturbing and equivocal' vision of Mrs Toplady brings a realization that 'Experience was what she needed' (p. 53) and she determines to get that experience after hearing moaning cries, 'rising and eddying up in ecstatic agony,' from the play room that is Vicky's bedroom, where she has retreated with another friend, Gilda. Laura hears a living, breathing actualization of what she has seen at Mrs Toplady's (two girl dolls wrapped in a sexual embrace) and when she enters Vicky's bedroom after hearing her 'ecstatic' cries, she sees her 'perfect body, her long arms and legs sprawled on the cornflower-patterned counterpane.' Immediately, she thinks of 'Those abominable dolls' (p. 111). The next level, as it were, of her education in sex takes the form of witnessing Vicky's obsession with a working-class boy from a seedy, derelict part of Camperlea named Saltmouth. A furtive observer, she watches avidly as they coil themselves around each other at a local dance and follows them to a rendezvous in an isolated, abandoned seaplane hangar.

According to June Braybrooke, Olivia conducted research for this novel by quizzing the teenage children of her friends about their sex lives, recording their idiomatic chatter in her notebook, and even venturing alone into a disco. For the most part, the dialogue is creaky—the teenage girls constantly scream 'Beyond Dreams!' and

'Grief!' and the loutish Clarrie Piper mumbles aggressively, sounding as if Olivia modeled his speech patterns on those of Marlon Brando in *On the Waterfront*. Alternately enticed and rebuffed by Vicky, Clarrie eventually rapes and murders her. Laura leads the police to the body and 'in a feverish transport' insists hysterically that the dead body is not that of Vicky: 'It was too grotesque. Its pose was unnatural. It had been artificial, a manufactured object, like those dolls in the Play Room.' And when she had watched Vicky dancing with Clarrie, she saw him put his hands on her shoulders, shaking her 'as though trying to shake her into some kind of rhythm.' Like a doll, she hangs 'limp under his hands' (p. 157).

How then to connect the extraordinary Mrs Toplady, her kinky wind-up sex dolls, and the body of Vicky Logan? If we remember that Laura's adolescent unhappiness, sexual curiosity, and infatuation with Vicky form the narrative frame of the novel, then we see a violent trajectory from exposure to sexual perversity, through homoerotic fantasies, to a brutal literalization of what Laura has witnessed in the Play Room. Much more willing than her brother to investigate strange sex toys, and desiring Vicky as the perfect, breathing sexual object, Laura is educated in an over-determined narrative of desire and revenge: Clarrie Piper, driven by sexual frustration and also by class rage, murders the unobtainable, beautiful, and privileged object. A sexual and class-based reading of the novel, however, does not necessarily accord with Olivia's own interpretation of what she was trying to do.

In an introduction to the American edition (titled *The Camperlea Girls*), she says that the novel 'is a study of what we may call the New Young, but it is also a study of middle age.' This latter group has power and money but cannot deal with their own children. Self-defeated because they are afraid of being old, 'they cannot belong to the new autonomous world of the young and they suffer from a sense of exclusion. They have no confidence in the status of middle age and the wisdom that should go with it.'[22] Bearing in mind Olivia's worries about her diminished sexual appeal, she could well be writing about her own sense of exclusion from what was going on in 'Swinging London' during the 1960s. Lacking 'a fixed morality,' the young are

[22] Quoted in Braybrooke, *Olivia Manning: A Life*, 210.

bewildered and revolting in a vacuum, and the middle-aged whose responsibility it is to provide this 'fixed morality' are merely 'trotting downhill to the grave.' Yet all this talk about 'morality' and adult responsibility hardly accords with the droll skepticism we associate with Olivia Manning's fiction. These emphases, however, inform an introduction Olivia wrote in 1968 for a Pan Books edition of Jane Austen's *Northanger Abbey*. Taking a break from writing *The Play Room*, she praises Austen's strict moral sense, declaring that 'her concern with kindness, honesty, reason, and right conduct, inform her novels with a goodness that we recognize as moral inspiration.'[23] If we read *The Play Room* as in some sense a moral fiction, then it would appear that Olivia intended this novel about sexual perversity and violence to expose a world quite distinctly *not* ruled by 'kindness, honesty, reason, and right conduct.' In *Northanger Abbey*, the heroine Catherine Morland discovers that girlish fantasies formed by reading too many sensationalistic gothic novels of imprisoned women and dastardly villains are, in fact, nothing but fantasies, and that the true villainy in the world lies in schemes of arranged marriage, financial settlements, and advantageous alliances. In *The Play Room* Laura discovers that her sexual fantasies about Vicky Logan are nothing compared to the graphic violence that she sees has been executed upon her languorous body.

An equally terrifying aspect of *The Play Room* may be found in Olivia's brilliant evocation of place. Depressing Rowantree Avenue, where Laura lives, is painfully reminiscent of Laburnum Grove: although by no means a run-down street, it is dispiritingly different from avenues in the more up-market area of Portsmouth, in *The Play Room* named Flamingo Park, where Vicky Logan lives with her architect father and her silly mother. In a truly menacing experience for Laura, more terrifying in its way than the sight of the wind-up dolls or the glimpse of Vicky's raped and brutalized body, she is abandoned by Vicky and Clarrie and forced to walk home through the underbelly of Camperlea, past brickfields and chalk-pits with rats rustling in the grass in the light of a gibbous moon that rises quickly and lights up the brickfield and its chimney—'a threatening phallus'—and the distant grayish clay hills: 'Here, in the purlieus of the gas-works, were the

[23] Olivia Manning, Introduction to *Northanger Abbey*, Pan Books, 1968.

dismal offices that Camperlea kept out of sight: the lunatic asylum, the old workhouse and the Fever Hospital that was empty because no one had fever nowadays... then there came the railings of Camperlea cemetery, slabs and crosses glimmering inside. Opposite was the gas-ometer and all the paraphernalia of the gas-works' (p. 174). This is the dreariness of Portsmouth that Olivia, as a teenage girl so much like Laura Fletcher, longed to escape.

Laura dreams of Carnaby Street, of the metropolis where everyone is 'swinging... not just young people, but old people like our mothers,' she says to Vicky (p. 70); she imagines herself walking in night-time Soho through a street dazzling with lights, lined with dance clubs, cafés, and coffee bars, being eyed by young men 'with lean pliable bodies and hair curling on their shoulders, as beautiful as arch-angels, in clothes all colours' (p. 71). Olivia invests Laura's fantasies with a rueful recognition that she is not part of 'Swinging London,' that the 1960s is distinctly not her decade. As far as Ivy Compton-Burnett was concerned, Olivia's palpable unfamiliarity with her sub-ject was the real trouble with The Play Room: while full of 'very good descriptions,' it showed Olivia writing about things from a position of vicarious obsession rather than intimate knowledge. What Compton-Burnett misses, of course, is the autobiographical nature of this novel and what she fails to acknowledge is that even if Olivia tried too hard to deliver teenage jargon, she describes with great psychological clarity a girl's education in ugly sexuality. Not caring much for 'description,' Ivy Compton-Burnett told Robert Liddell that The Play Room was really not her cup of tea.[24]

Claire Tomalin, despite being 'still enthralled by Miss Manning's intelligence,' indicated she, too, was less than captivated by Olivia's foray into depictions of teenage lust, by her invention of a clichéd seaside town Grand Guignol story. But, Tomalin observes percep-tively, a perennial theme running throughout Olivia's work is that 'of the child or young woman who seeks for and needs love and is never given quite enough. Most of these insufficiently loved creatures possess small, white faces, and many of them have sharp wits and tongues.'[25] Olivia herself, of course, had the smallest if not the whitest face, given her olive complexion—and the sharpest wit and tongue. In pointing to a few brilliant compensatory touches in *The Play Room*, Tomalin admires 'the feline comedy of Laura's growing up,' the enlightenment that comes from seeing through her father's seedy charm, from overhearing lesbian rustling through a bedroom door, and from an experiment with foam rubber breasts (Laura fashions them from Woolworth's place mats): as Tomalin notes, 'like Mrs. Toplady, Laura feels under-endowed.' The shocking climax she reads as a deliberate intention on Olivia's part to tell her reader 'no amount of ironic detachment can preserve us from the corruption of innocence, from blood and death.' If Tomalin is correct, then consciously or not Olivia undercuts her own particular brand of ironic detachment, although the narrative voice in this novel is notably non-ironic. When she was working on the proofs, she wrote to Kay Dick that she was going to have to 'appear with those brilliant girls Muriel and Edna, both of whom are probably putting out short novels packed with wit,' an implicit admission that she had fashioned this novel in a darker, heavier register than her early fiction.[26]

'Marking time' was how Janice Elliott, the reviewer of *The Play Room* in *The Times*, put it, speculating that Olivia, finding herself at loose ends after completing *The Balkan Trilogy*, decided to rework a not terribly original theme (adolescent education in a rapacious adult world). Yet Olivia's skill as an honest, unshowy writer 'enables her to write coolly and compassionately about some very strange and nasty things and, preferring 'a thundering failure to a modest success,' Elliott welcomed Olivia's unsentimental evocation of family squabbles, factories, middle-class poverty, teenage frenzy, even while she regarded the theme as 'small.'[27] Labeling Olivia a 'woman novelist,' the *TLS* declared that 'Schoolgirl passions and schoolgirl language are notorious literary traps' for such writers and that Olivia had fallen headlong into a world of clichéd teenage slang: for this reviewer, the best parts of the novel describe the seedy gentility of Rowantree Avenue and the Isle of Wight beaches. Finally, happy as she was to be placed at the top of Francis King's column in the *Sunday Telegraph* during the same week that Norman Mailer's *Why Are We in Vietnam?* appeared, Olivia was bitterly disappointed that she had not received a 'solo' review. Although she knew that when Anthony Curtis, the literary editor,

[26] Olivia Manning to Kay Dick, 15 July 1965, OMP, UT, Series 1, Box 1, Folder 8.
[27] Janice Elliott, 'Coming of age,' *The Times*, 12 April 1969.

assumed King would lead off his column with the Mailer book, King
had insisted Olivia's was the better choice, she did not know what
King later admitted to friends: that this was not really his opinion and
he had acted out of loyalty to Olivia.[28] The only unqualified praise for
The Play Room came from John St John at Heinemann's: for him it was
an experience which 'engaged my enthusiasm, interest and the thrill of
reading a work of art in which there is not a word too much . . . every
character rings true, including the truly terrifying Mrs. Toplady. I shall
never be able to look at any South Coast town in quite the same way
again.'[29]

Olivia's strangest novel had an interesting afterlife as a possible film
when the director Ken Annakin bought a six-month option for £500.
A firm believer that the best film scripts adapted from novels came
from the authors themselves, Annakin, whose recent box-office suc-
cesses had included *The Battle of the Bulge* and *Those Magnificent Men in
their Flying Machines* (both 1965), instructed Olivia to get to work. She
produced three scripts, neither of which led to a finished film, and
received £2,000 for eight months' continuous writing and rewriting.
And not only was Olivia disappointed and annoyed that her work
came to naught, she was appalled by the distortions in a letter Kay Dick
wrote to *The Times* in late May 1970. Protesting that the Arts Council
grants given to Olivia and Paul Scott should have been given to writers
more in need (that is to say, people like herself), Kay Dick announced
that Olivia had just been paid £7,000 for film rights, and, moreover,
that Reggie earned a high salary at the BBC. Both of these claims were
completely bogus. Paul Scott was as stunned as Olivia by Kay Dick's
letter, especially (Olivia wrote to June Braybrooke), since he had been
very generous to her and had borne 'endless hysterical calls.'[30]

Still hopeful in March 1971 that the project would go forward,
Olivia told Anthony Powell that after a long delay the script had
become 'a very sexy story about girls in Malta' in which Laura and
Tom arrive at Mrs Toplady's in a kayak and that several young
American actresses were being considered for the part of Vicky
Logan, but as Neville and June Braybrooke recount the story, Olivia
eventually acknowledged that 'Everything fizzled out . . . I wasted a lot

[28] Braybrooke, *Olivia Manning: A Life*, 209.
[29] John St John, *William Heinemann: A Century of Publishing*, 445.
[30] Olivia Manning to June Braybrooke, 2 June 1970, OMC/C, HRC.

of time and that is something which you cannot afford to do when you are sixty [actually she was sixty-two] ... My true calling is that of a novelist and I must return to it.'[31] As Olivia related the sorry finish of this saga to Anthony Burgess, Ken Annakin had a stupendous row with the principal financial backer of the project and left Malta for Capri, where the police seized all his equipment for non-payment of bills and wages. As she congratulated Burgess on the success of Stanley Kubrick's film of *The Clockwork Orange* and expressed a wish to see him soon, 'back in the grimy old Soho pubs,' she plaintively wondered whether he had heard the story of her own 'poor little film.'[32] But she had long known it was all over, and told June Braybrooke she felt 'useless, bored and depressed,' that she seemed condemned to the position of 'never quite making it ... I will have to get over this sense of failure before I can do anything else, but perhaps, being so old, I will never get over it—perhaps I will never write again.' The last statement was as veracious as Kay Dick's claim that Olivia was earning pots of money writing film scripts.

The horrors of the *Struma*

So Olivia, of course, eventually returned to fiction-writing; however, the return was hobbled by a serious bout of depression, not unusual when she finished a novel, but in this case particularly acute because *The Play Room* had, in general, been dismissed by critics as an embarrassing experiment. At the end of 1969, Olivia wrote to Francis King that she was feeling particularly low since she was the only writer whose work had been omitted from the *Sunday Times*'s list of the year's fiction: 'I wonder why I am treated this way? I know Margaret Drabble is now the coming successful writer and that she is very good, but ... I have become so depressed by this sort of thing that I very much doubt whether I shall be able to write another novel. I simply cannot face the misery that results.'[33] Like George Eliot and Iris Murdoch, she could, of course, have declined to read her

---

[31] *Olivia Manning: A Life*, 214.

[32] Olivia Manning to Anthony Burgess, 5 January 1972. Quoted by permission of the Trustees of the Estate of Anthony Burgess.

[33] Olivia Manning to Francis King, 29 November 1969, FKC/OM, HRC.

reviews—but the eagerness for approval overrode such a sensible course: each review was gleaned for its pluses and minuses which were then entered in her ledger of allies and enemies. As always, she also tallied the attention accorded to her contemporaries. The amount of attention given to Doris Lessing's *The Four-Gated City* in 1969, for example, precipitated dark thoughts: 'Another thing that has depressed me,' she wrote to June Braybrooke, 'is the amount of space given to Doris Lessing's latest. I know it is mean to be cross about it but she is a really dreary writer and I can see no reason at all why she should be more adulated than Yours Truly.'[34] Correctly or not, Olivia believed that over the years 'a succession of left-wing Unknowns have gone to great lengths to prove that Doris was vastly superior to me as a writer.' Singling out David Craig, 'a left-wing poetaster', for his biased selection of quotations from her own and Lessing's work to show Lessing could do supremely well 'what I could not do at all, i.e. write,' she sweetly and sarcastically wondered how Lessing felt about another woman writer being 'repeatedly maligned' for her own elevation.[35]

As a way, perhaps, of staving off the misery that would result if she published another novel, Olivia in the late 1960s turned to a subject that she had long wished to write about: the fate of seven hundred and sixty Romanian Jews who in the autumn of 1941 had been packed into an aging, broken-down hulk called the *Struma* and promised that they would be taken to Palestine. From the time of her return to England in 1945, Olivia had regularly approached newspapers and magazines with an offer to write about the *Struma*, but for reasons mostly to do with journalistic fears of unearthing unfortunate history (the British Mandate does not emerge well from this narrative) she had been turned down. Getting nowhere with print journalism, in 1950 she had written to Laurence Gilliam, Reggie's boss and Head of Features at the BBC, recounting her research at the Jewish Agency, her accumulation of official documents and letters, and adding that Arthur Koestler had suggested she write the story. Gilliam turned the project down as too graphically awful for a BBC audience. But in early 1970, the *Observer Colour Magazine* decided the story could now be told and Olivia received the go-ahead to write a long piece (when it appeared in

---

[34] Olivia Manning to June Braybrooke, 7 July 1969, OMC/C, HRC.
[35] Olivia Manning to Raleigh Trevelyan, at Michael Joseph, 8 January 1968, OMC/C, HRC.

March 1970 it ran to some ten pages with copious illustrations). She received £250 for her work.

Determined, as she put it to Francis King, to keep her 'pro-Arab feelings out of it' and not to air her views about the 'pretty bloody history' of Israel and its 'legend of God promising' all the land of Palestine to the Jews, she spent several weeks in the British Library reading various histories of the Jews and re-acquainting herself with fascist Romania.[36] Olivia begins her suspenseful and harrowing narrative by recounting how on Christmas night 1941 a Royal Navy cruiser on a goodwill visit to the Bosporus discovered in its searchlights a derelict ship crowded with white unsmiling faces. This was the *Struma*, once a barge that had transported cattle on the Danube, its passengers now refugee Jews. At best, the ship might have carried two hundred in 'reasonable discomfort,' as Olivia puts it, but there were seven hundred and sixty-nine people on board, six with visas for Turkey, five with immigration certificates for Palestine, and the rest traveling on Romanian passports. They were all refugees not so much, as one might expect, from the Nazis but from the Romanian Iron Guard: as Olivia explains authoritatively from personal recollection, the Germans were more interested in Romania as a source of raw materials and less committed to eradicating its Jewish population. They left that dirty work to the Iron Guard, which persecuted Jews with a ferocious intensity that almost outdid the Germans' own efforts.

Nowhere sparing *The Observer*'s readers the horrors perpetrated by the Iron Guard, Olivia describes how wealthy Jews (figures like the banker Drucker in *The Great Fortune*) were arrested and their property confiscated, and how others were rounded up and driven to the city slaughterhouse, where they were first mutilated, then killed, and then hung on hooks beneath a sign that read 'Kosher meat.' Synagogues were burned, women raped, and men cut to pieces in front of their women. It was no surprise, then, that when an advertisement appeared in Romanian newspapers announcing that a transport ship would leave Constanza in December 1941 and sail to Haifa under the flag of Panama, hundreds of terrified Jews bought tickets, among them, Olivia records, fifteen or twenty doctors, twenty-five lawyers, thirty

---

[36] Olivia Manning to Francis King, n.d., FKC/OM, HRC.

businessmen, ten engineers, and a group of young men eager to work on the land in Palestine.

Each passenger was asked to sign an undertaking never to return to Romania, and as they passed through customs, officers confiscated jewelry, clothing, canned goods, and medicines. Most went on board with little but the clothes they were wearing. Much worse awaited them when they explored the one-hundred-and-twenty-year-old *Struma*: there was no food, no storage of water, and only one lavatory; the ship's timbers were rotten, the wireless apparatus unusable, the searchlight broken, and there were no lifeboats or life-belts. Almost immediately the engine broke down (it had been salvaged from a sunken vessel and submerged in water for years), and the ship drifted in darkness in the Black Sea, its Bulgarian crew of seven helpless and besieged by frantic passengers. But finally on 24 December, after much stopping and starting, the ship reached Istanbul, which is where it was sighted by the Royal Navy cruiser, and everyone on board surged to disembark and make their way overland to Palestine. Port authorities came on board and declared that the ship was in transit and that no one would be allowed to enter Turkey. It must leave Turkish waters without delay. When editing Olivia's manuscript, the features editor of the *Colour Magazine* notified her that he was 'asking the Turkish Embassy for comments but I personally don't expect they will be anything other than non-committal,' which turned out to be the case.[37]

For eight days the passengers sent out appeals to anyone who might be able to help, most importantly to the Palestinian authorities under the control of the British Mandate; offering the excuse that there might be Nazi agents masquerading as Jewish refugees on board the ship, the Mandate refused permission for the refugees to immigrate. As Olivia notes, news of what was happening to the *Struma* reached the Jewish Agency in Jerusalem in the middle of January 1942 and immediately the Agency approached the Chief Secretary to the Government of Palestine with an appeal to admit the refugees as legal immigrants. The appeal was refused. At this point in her narrative, Olivia recalls hearing about the *Struma* when she arrived in Jerusalem in 1942 with Reggie when he took charge of the Palestine Broadcasting Service.

[37] Nigel Lloyd to Olivia Manning, 22 December 1969, OMC/C, HRC.

'Furious discussions' about what should be done were heard in almost every café, but, Olivia notes, 'even those who knew most about it seemed unable to sort out from among the misunderstandings, resentments and bitterness that existed everywhere, the prime cause of the rejection of this one boatload of wretched people.'[38]

Clearly unwilling to charge any one particular group with sole responsibility for the *Struma* tragedy and wishing, rather, to indict everyone involved, Olivia argues that the three communities in Palestine during World War II—Arab, Jew, and British—suffered the tensions of an 'exploded country kept entire by an outside pressure: the pressure of war.' The Palestine police were on the side of the Arabs and had no sympathy for the Jewish terrorists who were killing British police and officials: 'the Stern Gang and Irgun had roused the police to a state of baffled rage.' Declaring firmly that Arabs possess a 'natural tact and hospitality,' Olivia asserts that in return for their aid against the Turks on behalf of the British in World War I when they were promised domestic autonomy and control of Iraq, Syria, and Transjordan, they were now being asked to share their country with alien settlers who aimed to dispossess them. Then, aiming to be equally sympathetic to the Jewish position, Olivia writes that many of the newly arrived Jews in Palestine in the 1930s were 'exiled Europeans, insecure in a strange place,' who even if they 'displayed the aggressions of insecurity' were, quite simply, homeless, dislocated, hounded out of home and country.

By the middle of February 1942, conditions on board the *Struma* had become appalling. Some Istanbul Jews had sent food to the ship so each passenger received one hot meal a week but dysentery had spread and all the decks became slimy with feces. Since less than a third of the passengers could get on to the deck at one time, the rest were forced to stay below in foul and fetid darkness. By now the Turks were sick of the stench that was wafting from the *Struma* and began to fear the pestilence on board would spread to the mainland. A pitiful number were allowed to leave the ship: holders of immigration certificates for Palestine and a woman in labor. Seven hundred and sixty refugees remained on board. When the few who had been released reached Jerusalem in mid-February and told their story, the Chief Rabbis went

---

[38] '*Struma*: The ship that never had a chance,' *Observer Colour Magazine*, 1 March 1970.

to the British authorities to plead once more for the stranded passengers to be admitted: the government announced that children would be allowed in but adults not. Wartime scarcity of food in Palestine would make it impossible to take close to eight hundred people.

The end followed quickly on 23 February when after two months of unimaginable horror a Turkish tug came alongside the ship bringing a large group of police and harbor engineers. Without food, water, fuel or means of propulsion, the *Struma* was towed back through the Bosporus and left to drift into the Black Sea. The next morning, acting on orders to sink all neutral and enemy shipping entering the Black Sea to reduce the flow of strategic materials to Germany, a Russian submarine fired a torpedo into the *Struma*: from shore, smoke and flames were seen coming from the engine room, her wooden super-structure fell apart, and in a few minutes the *Struma* sank, taking with her everyone on board, except for one single survivor who was rescued by the crew of a Turkish lighthouse. His name was David Stoliar and, after making his way to Egypt, he joined the British army and served with the Eighth Army in Africa.[39]

At the end of a compelling and brilliantly managed narrative of wartime atrocity fueled by her eyewitness experiences of Iron Guard brutality in World War II, Olivia recounts asking a young friend if he had heard of the *Struma*: a river in Bulgaria? he ventured. She closes by saying, 'Everything has changed, of course. The Jews hold most of Palestine and they call it Israel. The Arabs are the refugees now. The Mandate is ended but officialdom goes on, impedient, intractable; cold as the sea.' A fortnight after the *Struma* piece appeared, Olivia wrote in a fury to Francis King about some remarks delivered by Sonia Orwell at a pro-Israeli luncheon: the speech contained 'sweeping inaccurate statements about the beauty of the Israelis and the wonders of their achievements etc. As these achievements have depended on American money while the poor wretched Arabs had nothing, I began to feel rather cross and said at last that I thought the Arabs had been disgrace-fully treated.'[40] It is to Olivia's credit that the *Struma* article records unflinchingly the unspeakable anti-Semitism that led to the *Struma*

---

[39] The *Observer* carried the Stoliar story separately but embedded within Olivia's piece. Stoliar, forty-six and living in Tokyo at the time Olivia's story appeared, alleged that the Turks torpedoed the ship.

[40] Olivia Manning to Francis King, 19 March 1971, FKC/OM, HRC.

tragedy and also documents, where she believed it appropriate, a prejudice towards Arabs, people whom she admired and with whom she lived in World War II. For all her efforts to be fair (if that is possible, in allotting blame for such horrors), Olivia was rewarded by an attack from the Romanian Legation in a letter to *The Observer* for representing 'the entire Romanian nation as anti-semitic because of a small minority, who came to power only because the Nazis rode high in Europe at that time.' A defense of her position came from a Mr R. Ainsztein who declared he found her description of Romanian anti-Semitism 'very subdued.'[41] Olivia, then, ended what was for her a decade of feeling old and sidelined by a youth culture and also of writing some very strange fiction about sexual perversity, by going back to the Balkans and to World War II. In the early 1970s she began work on what many believe to be her best novel, *The Rain Forest*: a strongly felt political work about political corruption and global desecration of the environment.

[41] Ion Ratiu, Chancellor at the Romanian Legation, *The Observer*, 15 March 1970; R. Ainsztein, *The Observer*, 29 March 1970.

11

A Deteriorating World

'I am working in a new way . . . More and more my subconscious is taking over.'[1]

'Darling, It's a novel of great imaginative power, always readable, lively, amusing, and vibrant with the tensions you feel resolved in a poem. I feel sure it is a *development*: it touches a deeper layer than any of the other books.

Love, Reggie.'[2]

Down in the dumps

The year 1970 did not begin well for Olivia. Suffering from a nasty bout of influenza, she had had a miserable Christmas and in the New Year caught one dreadful cold after another. The endless coughing and sneezing took her back to the drafty Portsmouth days when to escape her mother she would hole up in her unheated bedroom reading 'unsuitable' books and the *TLS*. These gloomy memories deepened her melancholic state of mind. What's more, her always frail constitution seemed to be on its last legs: her arthritic knees made trudging up the stairs at Abbey Gardens increasingly difficult and a drooping eyelid had become so debilitating she could hardly see out of her left eye. Still feeling rather under the weather but realizing she could delay no longer, in the early spring of 1970 Olivia underwent successful eye surgery. No sooner did she recover than she was laid low by severe

---

[1] Olivia Manning to Neville Braybrooke, *Olivia Manning: A Life*, 217.
[2] Reggie Smith to Olivia Manning, 1974, OMC/C, HRC.

pain in her right hand and thumb, which she attributed incorrectly to arthritis and which Jerry Slattery quickly judged to be simple 'neuritis.' Today, in all likelihood, Olivia's symptoms would be diagnosed as carpal tunnel syndrome. However, it needs to be said that almost fifty years of typing—initially as a secretary in Portsmouth, then as a clerk in London, and from about 1940 turning out all her own manuscripts and reviews— would not necessarily have caused the problem. Rather, long bouts at the typewriter might have worsened the pain of what is now recognized as a genetic disposition to develop carpal tunnel inflammation. Misdiagnosed or not, the pain in Olivia's hand and thumb became so severe that she wrote to June Braybrooke that at times she felt there was so much wrong with her that she'd rather be dead.[3] Always solicitous of Olivia's health, Jerry advised surgery, but a terror of hospitalization led her to wait until August 1974 to go into the Royal National Orthopaedic Hospital. The corrective procedure enabled her to write and type without pain, even if her hand remained swollen, but by the mid-1970s she began to feel like one of the walking wounded. She turned sixty-five in 1973.

Never physically tough, Olivia had been a delicate teenager, and when living in London in the mid-1930s had virtually starved herself while subsisting on a meager lunch and tea and toast in the evening. During World War II, while in the Middle East she had suffered from serious bouts of amoebic dysentery and malaria, and in 1944 had endured the delivery of her dead child, which left her subject to uterine bleeding and frequent hospitalizations for curettage. On her return to England in 1945, she suffered a nervous breakdown ('anxiety, terror, depression' was how she characterized her symptoms to Kay Dick) and from that time onward she experienced recurrent bouts of stomach trouble and mild malaria attacks. In sum, Olivia Manning was not a healthy woman and from 1974 until her death in 1980 she underwent three more surgeries after the carpal tunnel operation: one for gallstones, and two for a broken hip. The physical trials were compounded, and perhaps even caused at times, by her recurrent worries about money and her nagging resentment of other women writers, together with lapses into depressive episodes so serious she often felt unable to work. It was only with the writing and publication of the novel to which Reggie refers in the epigraph to this chapter, *The*

---

[3] Olivia Manning to June Braybrooke, 29 May, 1973, OMC/C, HRC.

Rain Forest (1974), that Olivia achieved the degree of psychological
serenity and professional security that enabled her to write *The Levant
Trilogy* in the last six years of her life. Although for the most part
negatively reviewed and imperfectly understood, for Olivia *The Rain
Forest* was a truly cathartic novel: its fusion of harrowing autobiography, piercing political criticism, and descriptions of rich local color
reveals her imaginative sublimation of private fears and global worries
into compelling fiction. In writing this novel, she confronted head-on
the loss of her child, engaged with political issues that were tremendously important to her, and freed herself for the future. Unlike *The
Balkan Trilogy* novels that directly represent the actual experience of
a woman at war, *The Rain Forest* is Olivia's combative testimony in
a battle against destruction of the environment and the demon of
low spirits.

Olivia's depression, always hovering, never entirely dispatched,
became particularly severe in the summer of 1970. On 17 September
she wrote to her old friend William Gerhardie to apologize for having
been such a neglectful correspondent: 'I have been going through a
long period of depression and uncreativeness and find it very difficult
to do anything.' But, she added, she was just beginning to 'come out'
of it and resume work, the revision of two short stories promised to
Penguin and the *Sunday Times*.[4] A few months previously, having
heard about the squalid conditions in Gerhardie's flat behind Portland
Place, she had gone there with other Gerhardie friends to see if they
could help. Appalled by what she discovered, Olivia wrote to June
Braybrooke that the place was absolutely filthy—dusty books stacked
everywhere on every available surface and in the hallways, and the
bathroom filled with empty boxes from Selfridges' food hall.[5] Recognizing Gerhardie's inability to take care of himself, let alone get himself
to a doctor, she persuaded Jerry to take him on and to send him by post
his various prescriptions when needed; Gerhardie, however, failed to
send the necessary stamped addressed envelopes and ended getting no
help from Jerry other than a promise, delivered through Olivia, that he
would 'faithfully' pierce his heart to ensure that he was well and truly
dead (Gerhardie suffered from a morbid fear that he would be buried

---

[4] Olivia Manning to William Gerhardie, 17 September 1970, Correspondence of
William Gerhardie, Cambridge University Library.
[5] Olivia Manning to June Braybrooke, 15 July 1970, OMC/C, HRC.

alive). Until his death in 1977, Olivia remained Gerhardie's devoted friend. She regularly offered to take him out for a drive in her blue Morris Minor, and a few years before her discovery of the wretched squalor of his flat, she had written a letter to *The Times* lamenting the absence of any official recognition of his achievements: 'When Mr. Gerhardie is no longer with us, there will be many to recognize his genius. Might we not, rather, reward him while he is still alive?'[6] (she probably had in mind a CBE, an award which she received in 1976). Always eager to promote Gerhardie's work, in 1973 she offered to BBC Radio an adaptation of his best-known novel, *The Polyglots*, but in the long tradition of BBC rejections of her proposals, the reader (Richard Wortley) deemed it unsatisfactory: far too many fidgety scenes, too many crude link-ups, and altogether rambling.[7] They did, however, think more highly of her adaptation of Gerhardie's *Futility*, and it was aired in December 1973.

By October 1970, beset by her various ailments, Olivia fell into the familiar pattern of agonizing at repetitive and tiresome length to her close friends about an inability to work, a paucity of ideas for a new novel, and the callous indifference of editors and critics to her talent. Uncertain about what to do after *The Play Room*, she toyed with the idea of starting a novel about Cairo but wrote to Francis King that her customary discipline had deserted her and that going 'back to the past again,' after the foray into contemporary Britain with *The Play Room*, filled her with disgust: 'I feel defeated by the modern world . . . In fact I feel a failure and very tired and wondering what it is all for, anyway.'[8] A week later she wrote to June Braybrooke with pretty much the same worry: should she pursue the idea of a fourth novel to follow *The Balkan Trilogy*, which would, in effect, turn it all into the Balkan quartet? Would it not be a 'mistake' for her to continue writing 'that sort of fictionalized history'?[9] As things turned out, she did not return to 'fictionalized history' until beginning *The Danger Tree* (the first volume of *The Levant Trilogy*) after finishing *The Rain Forest*.

[6] *The Times*, 17 April 1966.

[7] Olivia Manning Scriptwriter 1943–1982, BBC Written Archives Centre, Caversham.

[8] Olivia Manning to Francis King, 7 October 1970, FKC/OM, HRC, Box 1, Folder 6.

[9] Olivia Manning to June Braybrooke, 28 July 1970, OMC/C, HRC.

In 1970, all of Olivia's anxieties, fed by her continuing ill health, seemed to coalesce into a maelstrom of anxiety. In addition to the chronic worry about her aches and pains, an inability to start another novel, and her failure to become the literary darling of the popular press, Olivia added to the list concerns about the state of the British economy. What she exaggerated morbidly as Britain's perilous financial state fed a dread of poverty that stemmed from many years of scrimping, from her childhood to marriage to Reggie in 1939. In particular, she feared that as a consequence of the newly elected Prime Minister Edward Heath's decision to cut spending, 'galloping inflation [would] set in almost overnight as in the Weimar republic.' This could mean, she wrote in great alarm to Francis King, that 'the only thing that had value would be your piece of property and the mortgage would be chickenfeed, too. It is something one must consider.'[10] As a hedge against the coming inflation, she urged him to get in touch with the Harry Ransom Center at the University of Texas, Austin, since their financial arrangements were 'very elastic' and he would surely be able to arrange for acquisition of his papers.[11] Out of continued disgust with Edward Heath's failure to settle the miners' strike and put the country back to work, in the 1974 General Election she voted Liberal for the first time in her life.

Most probably because she was in the grip of anxiety and depression, when Stevie Smith died of brain cancer in March 1971 and the *Sunday Times* asked if she would write a narrative of their friendship, in the manuscript notes that survive for this assignment, Olivia obliterated her memories of Stevie's steadfast friendship before and during the war and painted a sour picture of a spiteful and manipulative woman who made good use of her friends. Whenever Stevie came to a party in central London she arranged to spend the night with someone, Olivia related, and this meant 'hot milk in bed for S., breakfast in bed next morning and the bath made ready by some member of the household.'[12] Soon after they returned to England, she and Reggie had Stevie to dinner and she was 'extremely annoyed to find the food was

---

[10] Olivia Manning to Francis King, 18 November 1970, FKC/OM, HRC, Box 1, Folder 6.

[11] Olivia Manning to Francs King, (n.d., probably early 1970s), FKC/OM, HRC, Box 1, Folder 6.

[12] Manuscript notes, untitled, OMC, HRC.

pilchards. We had had so little to eat in Palestine that tinned pilchards were a luxury to us but not to S. She looked at the pilchards with disgust and said, "Look at them! Look at them looking at me!"' Olivia resorted to giving her the household's egg ration for the week. At Stevie's memorial tea party held at the Ritz Hotel, Elisabeth Lutyens recalls catching Olivia's eye when someone declaimed 'in passionate sincerity, a Blake-like innocence for Stevie.'[13] They almost winked, says Lutyens, since they both knew their Stevie, and anyone less 'innocent' they had yet to meet. In her manuscript notes, Olivia recalls that when the group was told Stevie was 'a fey, child-like character,' Elisabeth Lutyens said to her, 'Like hell she was!'

Feeling always the wallflower, Olivia's perennial resentment of other women writers also reached an alarming pitch in the early 1970s. Iris Murdoch's amazing popular success completely mystified her: easy enough, she would announce darkly at drinks parties, to account for the intellectual appeal but the media popularity was inexplicable. She eventually ascribed it to the extraordinary 'physical strength' that enabled Murdoch to write continuously and lecture widely.[14] Muriel Spark seemed to have everything Olivia envied: critical admiration, good looks, nice clothes, and plenty of money. 'No wonder the film industry is flat on its back,' she wrote sarcastically to Francis King on hearing that Spark's most recent novel, *The Driver's Seat*, was to be made into a film (with the title *Identikit* and starring Elizabeth Taylor, it came out in 1974).[15] Muriel, Olivia reported with gleeful envy to her friends, had arranged her financial affairs so brilliantly that she pays no income tax at all—'What a fortune she must have put away, apart from the diamonds! I have seen some extraordinary pictures of her advertising her new Penguins. She looks like an intellectual film star . . . What a fantastic creature she is!'[16] So fantastic, in fact, that Olivia remained mesmerized by the designer wardrobe, the jewelry, and the glamorous Italian friends. But as compulsively preoccupied as she was with Spark's celebrity, she also declared she was 'totally wrapped up in herself—and abysmally silly with it.' Despite

---

[13] Frances Spalding, *Stevie Smith: A Critical Biography*, 313.

[14] Olivia Manning to June Braybrooke, 17 September 1971, OMC/C, HRC.

[15] In March 2010, *The Driver's Seat* was one of six novels nominated for the 'Lost Booker Prize' of 1970: the contest had been delayed by forty years because changes in the competition's rules disqualified many high-quality novels from consideration.

[16] Olivia Manning to Francis King, 23 June 1970, FKC/OM, HRC, Box 1, Folder 6.

Spark's similarity to the notoriously extravagant Ouida who ran up enormous bills at the Langham Hotel in the 1860s, Ouida, Olivia announced, 'cared for animals and worked devotedly on their behalf and wrote passionately against vivisection.'[17] In Olivia's moral scheme of things, a devotion to animal rights militated against many failings and for her Spark's narcissism and ambition to fly, Icarus-like, with the Onassis jet set lacked any such leavening.

Shortly after warning Francis King about the looming dangers of galloping inflation, Olivia joined him at the Silver Pen Awards Dinner on 26 November 1970 at the Café Royal. Having been one of the judges in the 'Novel' category (the others were Elizabeth Taylor and John Raymond), she was thoroughly miffed not to be seated at the top table and provided an entertainingly malicious account of the evening for June Braybrooke. Why Elizabeth Taylor should have been seated with the 'Nobs' (and she not) she cannot fathom, unless the organizers believed that Taylor 'was also the much moneyed film star,' a misperception shared by Reggie, she added; other 'lady writers' at the top table were Rebecca West, Rosamond Lehmann, and Lettice Cooper—'In fact, your poor friend was the only lady writer not there.' Olivia spares Lettice Cooper, her old friend from Ivy Compton-Burnett tea-party days, but has a grand old time describing Rosamond Lehmann. Looking like Lady Hamilton in decline, 'she is simply gigantic, with an enormous bosom, a mass of elaborately done white hair, a great big glazed-looking pink and white face and an expression of utter idiocy.' Done up in pink chiffon and sporting the largest pair of diamond earrings Olivia had ever seen, she is a waxwork figure, a creature who bears an uncanny resemblance to Mrs Toplady from *The Play Room*. Had Olivia not already written and published this novel, one could easily imagine that Rosamond Lehmann provided the model for that bulky transvestite creature decked out in red satin and pearls. Rounding out her report of Lehmann's appearance, Olivia writes that as soon as Rebecca West set eyes on her she whispered to her neighbor, 'My God, she thinks she's Danny La Rue.' Olivia ends by saying that she thought this comment 'unkind to Danny.'[18]

---

[17] Olivia Manning to Francis King, 7 October 1970, FKC/OM, HRC, Box 1, Folder 6.

[18] Olivia Manning to June Braybrooke, 27 November 1970, OMC/C, HRC. Danny La Rue, who died in 2009, was, in the 1970s, an immensely popular and very tall female impersonator. His wardrobe and jewelry were especially flamboyant and memorable.

Apart from Ivy Compton-Burnett, only three of Olivia's contemporaries were ever exempt from her jealousy: Alison Lurie, Margaret Drabble, and Beryl Bainbridge. Lurie she greatly liked and admired, having taken to her immediately when she met her at a garden party; she was impressed by her intellectual vitality and 'wonderful energy, physical and creative. Like Margaret Drabble, she not only writes but runs a home and three children. I could never do it.'[19] (Reggie was less enthusiastic and found Lurie a little too tart for his taste, which is surprising given Olivia's droll wit.) Equally in awe of Beryl Bainbridge's support of three children and a husband with her writing, Olivia liked her enormously on first meeting: 'she is a plain young woman and friendly and unpretentious. I can see that much of her success has come from the fact that she is pleasant and unassuming.' In 1977, Bainbridge sent a sharply worded letter to the editor of *Private Eye* correcting their assertion that she had formed a 'new' friendship with Olivia: 'I have been fortunate to know her for three years. She was kind enough to encourage me when I was virtually unknown and to be generous about my writing.'[20] It is clear, then, that Olivia did praise other women writers—although it needs to be said this was generally when they posed no threat. She also maintained cordial relationships with a number of women authors who, not being novelists themselves, presented less of a challenge to her frail self-esteem. Claire Tomalin, for example, she much admired and they worked well together when Tomalin assigned book reviews for the *New Statesman*. Tomalin reciprocated, writing to her in December 1973 to thank her for a 'kind' letter written about the death in the Yom Kippur War of her husband, the journalist Nicholas Tomalin: 'Nick admired you and Reggie so much (as I do too!).'[21]

Margaret Drabble's cheerful hospitality and Alison Lurie's unassuming friendliness tempered Olivia's chronic competitiveness. Right from the start of her friendship with Drabble, Olivia had been drawn to the welcoming warmth of her London house: to her, Drabble was 'angelic' and in 1972 she was delighted to accept her invitation to participate in a project dreamed up by the Literary Panel of the Greater

[19] Olivia Manning to Francis King, 14 April 1970, FKC/OM, HRC.
[20] Typewritten letter to Olivia Manning from 42 Albert Street, n.d., enclosing copy of her letter to *Private Eye*, OMC/C, HRC.
[21] Claire Tomalin to Olivia Manning, 8 December 1973, OMC/C, HRC.

London Arts Association: twenty writers were asked to contribute a chapter, to be written in five days, to a communal novel to be published under the title 'London Consequences.' Olivia joined Melvyn Bragg, Julian Mitchell, Piers Paul Read, among others, and, of course, the editors: Drabble and B. S. Johnson, who wrote the first and last chapters respectively. Olivia's chapter (number ten) is a beautifully managed satire of London literary life, a composite send-up of all those arts editors who had not given her a solo review, had not put her on the front page of the Sunday color supplement, and who had promoted Muriel Spark, Iris Murdoch, and the rest of the favored female gang.

Set in a Soho restaurant clearly based on the 'Ivy,' the reader joins Anthony Sheridan, a political journalist, at a lunch of colleagues and arts editors, the vainest and most self-satisfied being 'Daniel Tuffkin,' the literary editor of the 'Daily Gripe.' Olivia describes him as 'small, spidery, dark man, distinguished by a drooping eyelid that made him appear one-eyed' (she would have known exactly what this looked like, having had such a drooping eyelid the year before): Tuffkin says little during the lunch and only comes to life when debating with the waiter whether to have the *Faisan à la Cauchoise* or the *langoustines à la crème au gratin.* Since the bill is to be settled by a rich and washed-up Foreign Office type, Tuffkin quickly orders all the wines: a Johannisberger Holle '65, a Volnay-Santenots '47, and with the pudding perhaps a glass of Château Yquem. Nothing much happens: everyone tucks in, Tuffkin remains sullen, and, lunch over, sidles into a taxi after morosely wondering why a Charing Cross Road bookshop has failed to display his latest book in its window.[22] Julian Mitchell remembers that the first meeting of the contributors to *London Consequences* was a hilarious occasion as people exchanged ideas (not all of them publishable for fear of libel): Olivia, he recalls, was principally interested in how much money the project might accrue and how it would be distributed.[23]

With Alison Lurie, Olivia shared many of the habitual self-doubts about her work. Having had no success in beginning another novel about 'present-day problems,' she felt she had no choice but to go back to the war years and write about the Middle East, a prospect she had, of

[22] Olivia Manning (anonymous), Chapter Ten, *London Consequences*, 77–84.
[23] Diary Notes of Julian Mitchell, shared with the author in May 2010.

course, run by June Braybrooke and Francis King earlier in the year. But a return to what she termed 'fictionalized history' induced a 'terrible sense of failure and of being too old to understand the world as it has become. I do not want to retreat. I feel forced to do it by my total inability to make sense of things as they are. It is a terrible admission and I am very depressed.'[24] Reading Saul Bellow's most recent novel (*Mr Sammler's Planet*, 1970) plunged her deeper into self-doubt and she wonders why she goes on writing at all, 'because he has done what I want to do.' Although Olivia fails to specify precisely what it is about *Mr Sammler's Planet* that she finds both inspiring and intimidating, given her well-developed admiration of superb style, it's virtually certain she was bowled over by Bellow's powerful, eccentric, and utterly unique narrative voice. For her, he was one of her two contemporaries who offered a 'fabric' in which she could lose herself. The other was Patrick White. Olivia may have been a spiteful critic of certain women novelists but she knew a brilliant writer when she read him, or her. And she was equally enthusiastic about novelists perhaps less brilliant than Bellow (at least to her mind), such as J. G. Farrell: she liked him and his work 'enormously' and found him 'very gentle, agreeable, and of course highly intelligent.'[25]

Despite her gloomy forecasts of impending poverty for the Manning/Smith household that would be caused, she feared, by a slide into a national economic decline similar to that of Germany in the 1920s, Olivia always managed to take Italian holidays, spend money on landscaping her St John's Wood garden, and have people over for drinks parties on a regular basis. In July 1971 she spent a week on Capri, ten days in Venice, and then, when the Italian weather turned nasty, a few days in Paris. She also began to lobby actively on behalf of causes about which she felt strongly: in October 1970, her name appeared in an advertisement demanding 'No Arms for South Africa' that was sponsored by the Movement for Colonial Freedom and in the same month she spoke before a group called 'The Hampstead Council Against Factory Farming.' Vehemently vocal about the cruelty of apartheid and the abuse of animals, she highlighted these concerns in *The Rain Forest* (the novel she was working on at the time, to be discussed later in this chapter). On the island that is the setting for this novel, we find a

[24] Olivia Manning to Alison Lurie, 12 October 1970, OMC/C, HRC.
[25] Olivia Manning to June Braybrooke, 2 February 1974, OMC/C, HRC.

racial hierarchy headed by British colonialists, followed by Arabs and Indians, and ending up in a swamp-infested slum with the descendants of former African slaves. The principal female character in the novel refuses to visit a turtle factory, declaring she cannot bear to see the things human beings do to animals: 'I can't bear cruelty to anyone, but especially to animals and children. I loathe vivisection and experiments on living creatures. I can't bear animals being hunted by human im-beciles and show-offs.'[26] Shortly after *The Rain Forest* was published, Olivia found it chillingly ironic to see a woman clad in a leopardskin coat step out of Hatchard's in Piccadilly clutching a copy of *The Balkan Trilogy*. She was torn between accusing the woman of complicity in cruelty to animals and congratulating her on her choice of reading matter.

When Choula, the beloved Siamese, died in September 1971, Olivia decided to devote herself to animal rights causes rather than to one particular domestic pet. What's more, she felt, it would be pleasant to have a little freedom in her old age from lugging around a cat carrier and special food whenever she visited friends in the country (as things turned out, she acquired one more cat before she died, Miou, a Burmese). Sympathetic as she might have been to animal rights, however, she was a little less tolerant when dealing with actual human workmen and with disputed invoices. Ever contentious when it came to paying her bills, she wrote angrily to a local St John's Wood landscaper in July 1970 to complain about a charge of fifteen guineas for 'only' six hours work while the garden remained unweeded and the cuttings uncollected. And she wrote to Messrs Pugh and Carr Ltd., another St John's Wood landscape gardener, to announce icily that she was 'bewildered' by a recent bill for work at Abbey Gardens and could only assume it had been sent to her in error (the disputed amount was 27s. 6d., by today's accounting approximately £16 or $25—not exactly a hefty sum). In the face of Olivia's frigid prose, Messrs Pugh and Carr retreated quickly and admitted there had been some 'misunderstand-ing' about their charges.[27] Judging from one of Reggie's BBC

---

[26] *The Rain Forest*, 95.

[27] Olivia developed a mastery of complaint letters to various authorities. In December 1972 she protested to the North Thames Gas Company about an outrageous amount of £5 being charged for installation of a new thermostat on her gas stove. In July 1973 she wrote to the London Electricity Broad to chide them about 'the confusion that appears to

colleagues, Rayner Heppenstall, this uncooperative frostiness extended to dealings beyond local tradespeople: in recollecting his experience as one of the judges for the Katherine Mansfield short story prize in 1971, he describes how a lack of enthusiasm for any of the stories led the judges half frivolously to agree they would select a winner on the basis of whether they would be 'agreeable company.' Olivia was thought 'to be particularly unlikely' to fit the bill.[28]

During these months of inability to decide upon the subject for a new novel, or whether, in fact, she should bother to write at all, Olivia tried yet once more to get work from the BBC, despite the difficulty she had experienced in getting the Gerhardie radio adaptations off the ground. That she continued to pester the drama department suggests at least two things: that she felt no embarrassment in being constantly rejected by Reggie's colleagues and that, despite the worries about her health, the Manning/Smith household's perennial search for more income, and her failure to dislodge Muriel Spark from her glamorous, diamond-laden perch, she was determined to soldier on. At sixty-two, beset as she was by depression and all her other worries, she still possessed the guts that took her from Portsmouth to London and sustained her throughout the war, and so she sent to the BBC an adaption of one of her short stories, 'Ladies Without Escort,' which had appeared in *Penguin Modern Short Stories* in 1972. The reader's report on her proposal was withering: the story creaks along like an old hulk, is loaded down with irrelevant details, it lacks any dramatic tension, and is written in wordy, clichéd language: 'I suspect that if Olivia Manning were allowed to turn this into a play it would be a very antiquated one indeed.'[29] Undaunted, she also volunteered yet once more to write scripts for the long-running radio drama *Mrs Dale's Diary*, an assignment for which she had applied back in the early 1950s (and had been turned down). When she learned that one of the script editors in the drama department had laughed uproariously at the prospect of the author of *The Balkan Trilogy* writing about Middlesex suburban life, she wrote indignantly to say that 'intellectuals' are too

reign in your office,' and informing them that if they wished to continue corresponding with her they should send stamped addressed envelopes.

[28] Rayner Heppenstall, *The Master Eccentric*, 75.

[29] Olivia Manning/Drama Writer's File, BBC Written Archives Centre, Caversham.

easily cut off from popular writing. She closed by saying that with two overdrafts, she needed the work.[30]

The following year, however, saw a momentous turnaround on the part of the BBC in regard to Olivia's work. Radio Drama decided to commission an adaptation of *The Balkan Trilogy* entailing eight fifty-two-minute episodes. The reader assigned to assess the viability of the adaptation declared that he could 'think of no other woman novelist who has celebrated in book after book with such irony and perception her own *happy* marriage,' and felt sure that despite the formidable problem involved in covering such a wide canvas and also presenting many small scenes, the series was sure to succeed.[31] And succeed it did, so spectacularly that in the Christmas 1974 edition of *The Listener*, Antonia Fraser selected it as the best radio feature of the year: 'When I heard that Olivia Manning's Balkan Trilogy was to be done over, I hesitated as to whether to listen at all. I had just finished rereading all the three books in the new paperback edition and I wondered if radio could really add anything to Olivia Manning's subtle and exciting masterpiece. How wrong I was!'[32] Two years earlier Olivia had written testily to Anthony Burgess that Antonia Fraser was now 'queen of the literary world' and was running everything from the Booker award to the Arts Council, but her resentment of a woman described by the head of the Arts Council as 'young and beautiful' diminished considerably with praise of *The Balkan Trilogy*.[33]

Reggie 'tholing'

In the early 1970s, after nearly thirty years with the BBC as a producer, Reggie became restless and distracted by wishful fantasies of becoming a full-time writer, but, as Olivia wrote to June Braybrooke, 'the actual

---

[30] Olivia Manning to Charles Lefeaux, 3 December 1962, OMC/C, HRC.

[31] Olivia Manning Copyright 1945–1972, BBC Written Archives Centre, Caversham, 3 July 1971. Report written by Arnold Hinchliffe. Confirming the difficulties involved in dealing with a broad historical canvas and many characters, the script editor reported to Olivia in October 1972 that the actual script-writing was taking longer than anticipated but that Radio 4 had now firmly decided on a three-part adaptation, each part to last ninety minutes.

[32] Braybrooke, *Olivia Manning: A Life*, 244.

[33] Olivia Manning to Anthony Burgess, 19 February 1972, International Anthony Burgess Foundation.

writing' would be too much of a bore for him. Long an astute analyst
of Reggie's personality, she added that what he really liked best is to
'talk and be with people, and he is also very keen to see things.' Were
he to stay at home and try to write, he would not only do no work but
would 'stop me from working. When he comes home he drives me
mad with his noise and restlessness.'[34] He also drove her mad by
keeping both the television and the radio tuned at full volume to
sports programs, even when she was working. It was around this
time that Richard Griffiths, the well-known British actor, met Reggie,
and Griffiths' memories of their friendship, shared with me in a long
conversation backstage at the National Theatre, helped shape his
performance as Hector in Alan Bennett's *The History Boys*, which
premiered in May 2004 and for which Griffiths received the Olivier
Award for best actor.[35] In an Associated Press interview just before
opening in the American production of Bennett's play in the spring of
2006, Griffiths described Reggie as 'very roly-poly'—a big fat guy,
very amiable, and 'an absolute god of memory of English verse and
poetry.'[36] Olivia he never met but he remembered vividly that Reggie
was extremely proud of her and spoke often of her extraordinary
talent.

Griffiths first met Reggie right after he graduated from drama school
in the late autumn of 1970 and, as the result of a competition for an
internship, got a six months' job at the BBC. When Griffiths arrived in
London after spending the summer working at the Harrogate Reper-
tory Company and earning the pitiful sum of about £12 a week,
Reggie was the chief producer of radio drama. For Griffiths, he was
a remarkably generous and likeable person, beloved by all who met
him, astonishingly gifted with a mastery of verse that enabled him to
finish any poem if someone uttered just one line, and a wonderful
singer to boot. Big and burly and sporting little glasses like 'Piggy' in
William Golding's *The Lord of the Flies*, Reggie always wore a suit
(a little shiny here and there, Griffiths recalled), poorly laundered shirts
whose collars curled up, and rumpled ties always askew. Reggie's
unkempt appearance suggested to Griffiths and to many others that

---

[34] Olivia Manning to June Braybrooke, 17 September 1971, V.O.-E.

[35] The author's conversation with Richard Griffiths occurred on 1 May 2010.

[36] Connor Ennis, 'Griffiths enjoying life as a teacher in *The History Boys*,' Associated
Press, 1 June 2006.

no one took care of him, that is to say, did his laundry, took his suits to the cleaners, and checked his appearance before he left the house.

Two instances of Reggie's generosity and talent remain particularly vivid for Griffiths. The first is of New Year's Eve 1971 when, as he put it, he was a poor fat bloke with no money and no girlfriend, and all alone decided to take a walk down Regent Street: Reggie suddenly appeared, took pity on his lonely state, and escorted him to a nearby pub where he introduced him to other waifs and strays. What was remarkable was that Reggie would disappear for ten minutes or so and then return with an additional person until, through his remarkable gift for conviviality, he had assembled a large group of lonely people now ready to drink together and be happy together on New Year's Eve. The second vivid memory is of being with Reggie in Belfast after he became Professor of Liberal and Contemporary Studies at the New University of Ulster in 1973, where he stayed until he retired in 1979 (Olivia told friends that this appointment meant a great deal to him). At a reading and lecture on the poetry of Louis MacNeice, Reggie took the podium with a sheaf of crumpled notes to which he made no reference whatsoever over a two-hour period; instead, he recited from memory many of MacNeice's poems, interjecting along the way fascinating commentary on the literary scene in Birmingham in the 1930s.

In his recollections of Reggie, Richard Griffiths recurred frequently to imagery of 'flowing': verse seemed to flow spontaneously out of Reggie as he swam through life like a great mammal in love with literature, poetry, and theatrical gossip (never malicious, always gentle). Rather like a fishbowl that is lovely to look at and fascinating to watch, but in which one cannot really see the fish, Reggie seemed to have something hidden about him, something rather sad, which was not to suggest, Griffiths assured me, that he was devious and that his gregariousness was a façade, but that not everything about him was made apparent to the world. He 'tholed' through life, perhaps endured an unhappiness never to be spoken that he covered with his genuinely decent bonhomie. Griffiths last saw Reggie sometime around 1976, running into him on the street and receiving his characteristically affectionate greeting of 'Hello, darling, how are you?' and then seeing him run off to watch a cricket match.

If there was one person among Olivia's friends who was utterly different from Reggie, it was Kay Dick: suspicious where he was trusting and spiteful where he was generous, she had begun a turbulent friendship with Olivia after the war. In the early 1970s, after twenty-five years of editing various literary magazines, working for numerous publications, and acquiring an impressive roster of literary friends, she decided to interview half a dozen or so novelists and publish the interviews as a book about writers and their writing habits. Olivia agreed to be one of those interviewed, an act of 'charity' as she described it to her New York correspondent Robert K. Morris: Kay, she wrote, is 'a rather sad, brave character who struggles along on almost no money at all, has made one suicide attempt and we feared, if she did not get something published might make another.'[37] Starting in the 1950s, Olivia complained regularly to her friends about Kay Dick's behavior—her drunkenness, her physical violence, her abusive treatment of her long-time partner Kathleen Farrell, and her scrounging and extravagance (something particularly galling for Olivia, whose worries about being poor never left her). But despite all this, she remained deeply fond of her and she was touchingly frank in her interview. Her comments offer considerable insight into a troubled childhood and her fears of aging. And Olivia talks not only about Portsmouth, her wartime years, her work, and her dislike of growing old, she also articulates a number of political views about which, by the early 1970s, she felt strongly, and which at the moment she was talking to Kay Dick were being folded into *The Rain Forest*.

In response to a question about a rapidly changing world and the emergence of globalism, Olivia declared, 'the most terrifying thing that has happened is the sudden revelation of the effects of over-population.' Not only is man destroying the planet through an inability to balance population and available resources, 'animal life is being sacrificed in order to feed such an enormous number of people.' The world is 'deteriorating,' she warned, a prediction of catastrophe very much on her mind as she worked on her new novel in the early 1970s. At times, too, it seemed that her own private world was falling apart. Not only had she received little relief from her various physical ailments since 1970, the domestic cocoon so happily established after returning to England in 1945 began to unravel. The ramshackle Abbey Gardens house had become difficult to manage, the stairs were proving

---

[37] Olivia Manning to Robert K. Morris, 9 May 1974, OMC/C, HRC.

a trial, and in 1973 Reggie left the BBC to take up his appointment in Northern Ireland. As Olivia confided to Alison Lurie, he did not wish her to join him there because of the political unrest, and she was happy to acquiesce in that desire: 'As I spent some years of my childhood in that cold, wet, windy north among a narrow, very bourgeois society, I feel no urge to move there.'[38] But she and Reggie had barely been separated since 1939, and now that he was away from London for six months at a time she found herself lonely in the big house in Abbey Gardens. It was time to leave, and in 1973 they moved to a sunny first-floor flat at 71 Marlborough Place, not very far away.

Apart from the unwelcome fact that in March of that year she turned sixty-five and thus became an old age pensioner, Olivia settled cozily into three rooms that she decorated with her Syrian paintings and rugs, and she sketched plans for a sun-room and terrace where she hoped to plant old-fashioned roses. The sole unpleasantness came from people living on the ground floor, a Maltese family named Vella—husband, wife, and four children. The children, Olivia claimed, constantly bounced their ball against the door of her flat when they played on the stairs; Mrs Vella would jostle her with bulging shopping bags if they tried to enter the house together through the downstairs front door; and the Vellas complained to the landlord that Olivia had no right to have a terrace, something she vehemently denied since she had cleared its construction with the owners of the house and had obtained permission from the local authorities. Permission for Development was granted on 21 March 1974. In Olivia's version of a particularly ugly contretemps as she related it to June Braybrooke, Mrs Vella banged on her door, screamed that she had no right to tell her children where they could play, and called her a 'cunt—a word I have never expected to hear one woman call another.'[39] After writing to Mr Vella that she would tolerate no more 'insults' and issuing a warning that if Mrs Vella 'makes one more remark of the sort she made this morning' (one assumes the 'cunt' appellation), she would take the entire family to court, Olivia sued them for abusive language and harassment (and won the case). The Vellas continued to yell ugly demands for quiet when Olivia had drinks parties on the terrace, but eventually everyone at Marlborough Place settled into sullen tolerance.

[38] Olivia Manning to Alison Lurie, 10 January 1973, V.O.-E.
[39] Braybrooke, *Olivia Manning: A Life*, 238–9.

While working on *The Rain Forest* (which she did from 1970 to 1973, producing two longhand and one typescript versions), Olivia agreed to give a talk in November 1970 to the Shaw Society on Dickens and his Characters. Her preparatory notes for this talk (in typescript) reveal how deeply she immersed herself in his fiction and biography during the summer of 1972.[40] They also disclose her admiration of his narrative genius and her identification with his stories of neglected children such as David Copperfield, Florence Dombey, and Pip. Dickens's scarred childhood resonated with her own, and she acknowledged the influence of his fiction upon her post-war writing when asked by her close friend Jeremy Trafford in which literary tradition she would wish to place herself: 'Why in that of Dickens, of course,' she replied. Through her skill in creating large social canvases and memorably strange characters such as Yakimov, Miss Bohun, and Mrs Toplady, she enrolled herself in a Dickensian tradition of social realism heightened by historical particularity and vivid characterization.[41] Just as she worshipped Saul Bellow for his brilliant style, she adored Dickens for his mastery of compelling narrative. Olivia knew she could never be as good as either of them but she revered them nonetheless.

'What a magnificent novel,' she noted after reading *Nicholas Nickleby*, 'packed with all the excitement of youth' and featuring a character who, whether Olivia admitted it or not, resembled her own mother: 'the embodiment of muddled thinking and wounded class consciousness.' Admitting she has never been able to get through *Barnaby Rudge* 'because of a dislike of historical novels' (an interesting confession since many critics today would characterize the Balkan and Levant trilogies as 'historical' fiction), she dismisses it very quickly and moves on to the 'great glory' of *Dombey and Son*, although she found the death of Paul Dombey completely unforgivable. *Great Expectations*, for Olivia and for many of Dickens's readers, is his greatest achievement: the most unified, it has no extraneous characters, no

---

[40] The following summary of Olivia's notes is taken from her typescript, OMC, HRC.

[41] Neville Braybrooke's working notes for *Olivia Manning: A Life*, OMC/C, HRC. Jeremy Trafford is the 'Jeremy' of the 2004 documentary film *Andrew and Jeremy Get Married* that tells the story of two men, very different in terms of social background and education, who marry after five years of living together. I'd like to think that Olivia would have enjoyed this film, given her unfailing affection for her gay male friends and her sympathetic yet never sentimental depiction of gay male characters in her fiction.

monstrosities, no grotesques. The superb integration of autobiography, social criticism, and memorable characterization that distinguishes so many of Dickens's novels clearly spurred Olivia to a form of mimicry and homage in *The Rain Forest*. In many ways, this is the most self-consciously literary of her novels, rich in Dickensian characters, Shakespearean allusions, and Conradian imagery. It is certainly the most politically arresting in its depiction of eroding imperialism, anti-colonial violence, and the prediction of a virus that will be transmitted from 'small creatures' to humans and that will compromise man's immunity to disease. Olivia aimed to warn her readers about the danger of ignoring protest on the part of the oppressed and dismissing the perils of environmental neglect. The political indignation of *The Rain Forest* affiliates it with the nineteenth-century novelistic tradition of social protest to be found in the work, say, of Elizabeth Gaskell, and, most prominently, in that of Dickens.

A little bit of England on the Equator

Set in 1953 on an island in the Indian Ocean off the east coast of Africa that strongly resembles one of the Seychelles (most likely Olivia had the island of Praslin in mind) and is named Al-Bustan (the garden), the plot of *The Rain Forest* traces the catastrophic experiences of an English couple named Hugh and Kristy Foster: he ventures into the back country of the island and barely survives to tell the tale, she loses a child at seven months in utero. He is an unsuccessful screenwriter and she is a published novelist whose working habits are notably similar to those of Olivia (rather than keeping notebooks she collects notes on slips of paper and on the backs of envelopes); together, they have fled London in hopes of rejuvenating their marriage and of making a fresh start for Hugh as newsletter writer for the local colonial government. They have a room at a genteel boarding-house incongruously named 'The Daisy' run by an alarming former music-hall entertainer named Mrs Gunner, who, like Olivia's frightening 'female' characters in *The Play Room*, Mrs Button and Mrs Toplady, has a fondness for the color red: 'Red, it seemed, was a colour favoured by Mrs. Gunner. She herself was in red. The chairs and sofas were covered in bright red haleskin, the curtains were red and at intervals, on an embossed cream paper smudged with gold, gilded cupids held out lights with red plastic shades.'[42] The eighty-one–year-old Mrs Gunner entertains her guests by turning cartwheels in the dining room and devotes herself to the growing of English lettuces: for her, they are 'A Little Bit of England on the Equator.' Inhabited by the leftovers of colonial governance, insufferably snobbish men and women who shun the Fosters, ignore them at the crucial cocktail hour, and refuse to acknowledge their presence in the dining room, the 'Daisy' is a rank emblem of a post-war imperial power fast losing its global significance.

Constructing a history of the island that is virtually identical with that of the Seychelles archipelago, Olivia's narrator tells the reader that Al-Bustan was initially controlled by Arabs who imported African slaves, then taken over by the British in 1810 in order to protect shipping in the Napoleonic wars; the British, in their turn, imported Indian labor in the common imperial practice of transporting workers from one part of the empire to another, in this case to work the profitable sugar plantations. The result is an island inhabited by a racial mixture of Arabs, Africans, and Indians, still ruled by the British colonial Governor, who is advised by a local cabinet composed of two Arabs and five Africans (the Arabs believe that when the British leave, which will be very soon, they wish the Africans to take over since they are more 'controllable' from Whitehall). 'Your people destroyed a way of life for us,' says Musa, a young privileged Arab, to Kristy as he escorts her through the dark passageways of the walled Medina in the center of the island (p. 188).

'The isle is full of wonders,' murmurs Kristy when they first arrive, Olivia's first allusion to *The Tempest*. The 'wonders' of the island are to be found in Olivia's talent for vivid visual description. Lush vegetation juts from every rock face, brightly colored fruits burst out of tree trunks, richly colored birds swoop through the canes of the sugar plantations, and the southern hemisphere night sky in the 'Daisy' garden is 'indigo, of a glassy clarity; and the stars so large they seemed to be rushing towards the earth, pulsing and scintillating as they came, and casting a bluish twilight over the garden' (p. 15). Transforming certain characters from *The Tempest* into parodic figures, Olivia describes Akbar, the Nubian head servant at the 'Daisy', serving its English inhabitants with Caliban's ferocious contempt for those who

---

[42] *The Rain Forest*, 11.

have displaced him from sovereignty over his island, yet he performs his fury with a comic intensity. Ambrose Gunner, the son of the owner of the 'Daisy,' is a public-school-educated, massively overweight, and perpetually sweating scrounger, unable to return to London because of debts and condemned to reside in a poky room off the kitchen in his mother's boarding-house. Always in search of money and frequently drunk, he lurches through the novel like a grotesque conflation of Trinculo and Stephano, those comically avaricious drunkards. The British Governor, Sir Beresford Urquhart, rules the island not with Prospero's rough magic but with a bureaucratic haughtiness under attack from colonial unrest and the incipient threat of terrorist violence. As Hugh's superior at Government House puts it, 'I'm old in the service. I've seen the empire go down. Once we were as gods (p. 217).'

Al-Bustan is not only an 'isle of wonders,' it is also an isle hospitable to staggering corruption, peopled by figures like the character Lomax, a Lebanese trader who entertains potential business partners at the luxurious Praslin Hotel located on the most beautiful beach on the island. With its basin for private yachts, luxurious lobby, and stupendous buffet lunches, the Praslin is patronized by wealthy tourists from South Africa: the men 'big, strong, brute creatures' who lounge by the pool smoking cigars, and the women oiled beauties stretched out on sun-loungers. When he first sees the tourists, Hugh thinks to himself that they are the 'devourers,' making such a 'ruthless demand on life' that the world 'was being squandered, its resources used up, its wildlife decimated, its seas polluted, the sea life destroyed, and the seabirds in their thousands killed by their accursed oil-tankers' (p. 124). Olivia also satirizes colonial bureaucrats hanging on at the fag-end of empire, their pathetic insignificance conveyed by her skill in characterization through closely observed physical detail. Hugh's boss, a pedantic sadist named Pedley, has eyes whose whites are 'dotted over with tiny yellow growths, like yolk crumbs from a hard-boiled egg. Repelled and fascinated by these growths, Hugh attributed them to a liver disorder that would account for Pedley's "unreliability"' (p. 67). At a ghastly Residency lunch Kristy is seated between a clergyman who pompously announces the Governor represents the British sovereign and must therefore be served before the guests, and the police chief, 'large, strong-bodied, red-faced, with police buttons on his khaki drill jacket,' who brusquely reproves her for disapproving of turtle soup (like

Olivia, Kristy loathes any form of cruelty to animals). Hugh is forced to cope with the widow of a former chief secretary. Her husband having died in office, she has remained on the island, like the characters in Paul Scott's *Staying On* (1977): notably similar to the skeletal relic Mrs Skewton in *Dombey and Son* (which Olivia was reading when working on *The Rain Forest*), she is 'a vivacious relic of an age when to be entertaining was a social duty' and, dressed in a large transparent hat and with a chiffon rose at her throat, she ardently throws up 'her old eyes' at Hugh, gazing 'at him whenever he spoke, and once or twice placed her skeleton hand on his arm' (pp. 76–7). The daughter of the Governor, a Miss Urquhart, watches them 'like a nice bull terrier observing human speech and trying to have a part in it' (p. 77).

The most disturbing and enigmatic figure in *The Rain Forest* is Simon Hobhouse, a non-practicing medical doctor and botanist who regularly ventures into a forbidden part of the island to investigate the ruins of an abandoned African slave village. Hobhouse is Conradian: a mysterious, reclusive, and sardonic Englishman with hard sapphire eyes who, like Kurtz in *Heart of Darkness*, has immersed himself in the menacing culture and geography of the wilderness. Surviving on cassava and plantain when he is in the rain forest, he traps ants, bees, mosquitoes, and tiny flies. Hugh finds him immensely attractive. As Kristy watches them together, like Harriet Pringle watching Guy and his British Council pals in *The Balkan Trilogy*, they appear 'jubilant. It was like a meeting of lovers.' She has 'no part' in their conversation: 'They were rejoicing in each other, a male co-operative designed to exclude her and all other females.... Hugh had what she called "a trick" of picking up men who, for a while became heroes to him, and using them as a shield against her' (p. 164).

On this occasion, what they are talking about, or, rather, what Simon reveals to a startled Hugh, is that the world 'could be due for another killer as all-pervasive as the plague' (p. 166). This killer, he continues, 'could be hibernating in some unexplored corner of the earth, some fragment of primitive forest, and carried by a creature so small no one has noticed it': could this be 'a new virus'? asks Hugh. Simon responds that it will be a virus that will cause 'a disease as contagious as smallpox, as virulent as plague, coming newly into a world without inherited immunity and no present knowledge' (p. 166). But rather than expressing alarm at the thought of the coming scourge, Simon declares he will welcome it since 'it could bring human numbers down at a very satisfactory speed' (p. 167). 'When one species has over-bred itself, as we have, nature strikes back with a decimating force,' he announces as he explains his interest in the rain forest. Although the term 'AIDS' was not coined until the early 1980s (in the UK and in the USA) and the term 'HIV' did not appear until 1987, clearly Olivia was thinking about some kind of imminent epidemic of a human immunodeficiency virus as she was writing *The Rain Forest*. And although there is no evidence that Olivia discussed this possibility with Jerry Slattery or other medical friends, one cannot rule out her awareness of such a virus: as early as 1972, for example, a Danish surgeon who had been working in Zaire developed symptoms of what would later be identified as AIDS.[43] What's more, Hobhouse's disgust with a global indifference to the consequences of over-population resonates with Olivia's remarks to Kay Dick in the interview for *Friends and Friendship*: just too many people on the planet.

While she watches the two men and listens to Simon's troubling predictions, Kristy unhappily contemplates her coming contribution to 'human numbers': contrary to her desire and intention, she has become pregnant and feels herself hobbled like a nursing cow whose function is to give suck: 'Good God,' she thought. 'No wonder the female sex was left standing at the post. We didn't stand a chance' (p. 144). Like Olivia in Jerusalem in the spring of 1944 who walked two or three miles a day through the Old City, Kristy plods up to the sugar plantations or trudges along the shore road to watch the flying-fish. But despite her daily exercise, several months of ravenous eating, and strict adherence to doctor's orders, the fetus dies at seven months. In a painfully exact reconstruction of her own tragic experience, Olivia describes 'the limp despair' of Kristy's body when, lying in the bath, she notices that the flesh across her distended belly has shrunk, and feels no kicking life inside her. Unlike Olivia, however, Kristy is not forced to carry the fetus to term; rather, the birth is induced by drugs, which signals Olivia's attention to changes in obstetric care from 1944 to 1953. Feeling 'like a walking cemetery,' Kristy goes to the hospital, where a pitocin drip induces labor, and, after a night of terrible spasms, she writhes in pain as the doctor at last

---

[43] Alex Shoumatoff, 'In search of the source of AIDS,' *African Madness*. I am grateful to Joseph Cady for sharing with me his extensive bibliographical knowledge of the history of AIDS and HIV.

manages 'to drag the unaiding foetus out of the birth canal . . . feeling a raw and crunching sensation as the flesh was pulled from her flesh, she ceased to control herself and screamed aloud' (p. 239). The fetus has died through the cord being entangled around its neck, or rather *her* neck since Kristy is told that the child was a girl, 'well-formed' adds the officious matron.

The next day, resting on the hospital balcony, Kristy hears tremendous explosions coming from the area of Government House, and as the noises swell into reverberations that strike the cliff behind the hospital she feels the whole building rattle and the sound of windows breaking. Anti-colonial forces have exploded several bombs. From her time in Jerusalem at the end of the war, Olivia was uneasily familiar with the sound of exploding bombs, and when Kristy leaves the hospital in frantic search of news she vivifies the scene of frantic British wives searching for their husbands among the wreckage with her memories of such scenes in Palestine, and also with more immediate recollection of such events as Bloody Friday in Belfast city center in July 1972 when twenty-two IRA bombs exploded, killing nine people and injuring some one hundred and thirty others. Many civil servants (British, Arab, and Indian) are killed and Hugh is thrown from the building. Retrieving his bruised body from the roadside, Simon Hobhouse takes him in his Land Rover into the rain forest, where, he promises, he will see extraordinary things. Olivia's spectacular descriptions of the forest take the reader into *Heart of Darkness* territory, as did her lush evocations of the African wilderness in *The Remarkable Expedition*. As Simon and Hugh hike along the banks of a steamy river, they are buzzed by wasps, bees, mosquitoes, and as they clamber over trees brought down by lightning they stumble on thick ligatures of creeper that stretch like nets around the tree trunks. A gray-green twilight hangs over them as they enter a 'region of romantic beauty where dragonflies skim the river and the trees are grown over with ferns, red, blue, and gold orchids, moss, and lichens.' Peering into the interwoven branches and creepers, Hugh can see 'only the inner darkness . . . For all he knew, the forest darkness was an eternity, like space, without habitat or goal' (p. 272). Wading through stagnant pools covered with emerald weeds, Hugh sinks into slime that throws up a sickening stench. The forest is literally and symbolically diseased, the trees deformed, lifeless and brittle, covered with fungoid growths that extend 'pink, like deformed hands' (p. 273).

Like Marlow who comes out of the darkness to tell his story, Hugh escapes from the forest, leaving behind Simon's corpse, already being invaded by ants who move through his black beard and into his delicate nostrils and over his fine pale lips (felled by a malignant spider bite, Simon murmurs as he dies, 'Could be significant. Not sure. Interesting. Wish I knew,' p. 279). Hugh takes the key to the Land Rover and in the last line of the novel sets out 'to find his own way back,' his story presumably to be told to a recovering Kristy and imaginatively, of course, by Olivia Manning. With its imbricated narratives of imperial decline, native violence, the possibility of the emergence of a devastating new virus, and the death of a child in utero, *The Rain Forest* powerfully fuses Olivia's political distaste for the colonial hubris she had witnessed first in Cairo during the war, her prescient sense that man's devastation of the environment will result in his own destruction, and her own private story of ruinous loss.

The Rain Forest was published on 1 April 1974 (just my luck, Olivia ruefully remarked, to have it come out on April Fool's Day): on the following day the *Guardian* ran a story about her that begins somewhat negatively by declaring that she 'tends to write out of her experience rather than spin some fine web out of her imagination.'[44] Yet that experience, the interviewer Hugh Herbert concedes, has enabled her to create some of the most memorably eccentric characters in twentieth-century fiction: the monstrous Miss Bohun, the voracious Yakimov in *The Balkan Trilogy*, and, now, Ambrose Gunner, based, Olivia confides in this interview, upon a literary journalist who was the most brilliant man of his year at university. Desperate for money and attention, Ambrose boasts that he plans to return to London where he has been asked to edit a magazine of the arts: it will be lavish, he trumpets, covering not only poetry, prose, painting, sculpture, and music, but architecture, interior decoration, and film. At the end of the *Guardian* interview, to 'cheer her avid followers,' Herbert is delighted to report that on Olivia's desk in her quiet flat in St John's Wood, one can see a large volume titled simply 'Cairo' and a Chatham House book on the chronology of World War II. The first volume of *The Levant Trilogy* was already in the works.

For the *TLS* reviewer it came as an 'agreeable surprise' to discover that after slogging its dreary way through a critique of imperialism and

---

[44] Hugh Herbert, 'Forest worlds,' *Guardian*, 2 April 1974.

representations of Arab resistance to British rule, Olivia's novel actually becomes exciting in the way that the fiction of Robert Louis Stevenson or John Buchan grips the reader: the best parts for this reviewer (D. A. N. Jones) are to be found in the last third recounting Hugh's journey into the rain forest with Simon. But the rest is forgettable.[45]

If the *TLS* review tends to condescend to Olivia's novel by dismissing her interest in political critique as less engaging than her talent for adventure narrative, then Peter Ackroyd in *The Spectator* deemed *The Rain Forest* dismally improbable: the characters are lifeless mannequins colliding with one another 'within what is suspiciously like a well-made play.'[46] Ackroyd's judgment that 'the ramshackle hut of empire is knocked down with a breath' reduces Olivia's serious and sustained representation of imperial decline to maladroit narrative manipulation, and it would seem Ackroyd is unwilling to take Olivia Manning seriously. For these (I fear, male) reviewers, she's best when imitating male adventure stories and inept when attempting to write a political novel. Having anticipated that reviews would not be positive, she was pleased to see that the *Sunday Telegraph Colour Magazine* had chosen it as the Book of the Week and termed it 'masterly,' the 'best' of her fiction: as she wrote to June Braybrooke, 'I suppose I must not grumble but I would like before I die to have reviews of my own in the Sundays. Perhaps that is asking too much.'[47]

Although it did not appear on a Sunday, the *Irish Times* did give her a splendid review, hailing *The Rain Forest* as 'beautifully written, buttressed by wisdom, judgement, keen observation, and knowledge of life.' Olivia's skill in characterization is likened to that of E. M. Forster: 'unfaltering in her observation,' she creates characters who write themselves, as it were, in their manners and behavior. Clearly having understood the political critique brusquely dismissed by other reviewers, the *Irish Times* asserts that there are very few modern novels that are 'so rich and significant, so much in accord with the Zeitgeist': were she 'more pretentious or bawdier she would probably be more richly rewarded.' The reviewer concluded that Olivia deserved

---

[45] 'Creeping pollution,' *TLS*, 5 April 1974.

[46] Peter Ackroyd, 'The enchanted forest and other fictions,' *The Spectator*, 13 April 1974.

[47] Olivia Manning to June Braybrooke, 2 April 1974, OMC/C, HRC.

'many respectful bows for her first class accomplishment.'[48] Further unconditional praise came from Ian Norrie, owner of the High Hill Book Shop: he wrote to her on 7 April to say that he was delighted to see her 'back in true form . . . Your prose is an absolute joy to read, as always, and your characters are real, real people.'[49]

When *The Rain Forest* made the long list for the Booker Prize, Olivia was not optimistic about making it to the next level since A. S. Byatt was one of the judges and on a recent radio program had termed Olivia's novel 'slow': as Olivia reported this to June Braybrooke, 'I would not have thought she went in for James Bond speed herself but "slow" was what she said.' Byatt was not exactly 'a sprinter', she added. Olivia was correct about not getting on the short list: for 1974, the novels were Kingsley Amis's *Ending Up*, Beryl Bainbridge's *The Bottle Factory Outing*, Nadine Gordimer's *The Conservationist*, Stanley Middleton's *Holiday*, and C. P. Snow's *In Their Wisdom* (Gordimer and Middleton shared the prize). The judges were Ion Trewin, Elizabeth Jane Howard, and A. S. Byatt. Olivia's tiresome obsession with making the Booker short list taxed Francis King's usually patient responses to her need for recognition. Already hurt and annoyed by her indifference to his hospitalization for severe psoriasis, he wrote to Neville Braybrooke that she had sent him proofs of *The Rain Forest*, together with 'pages about the Booker,' and that he was sweating over how to respond: 'It's one of those books in which between conception (magnificent) and actual execution (often unconvincing), some kind of death seems to have intervened.' *The Rain Forest*, then, was symbolically akin to the dead child Olivia had carried to term. Knowing he could not say this, King wrote a long critique, hinting delicately about the stillborn nature of her novel.[50]

Whether Olivia put him up to it or not (she claimed not), after the short list was published, Jerry Slattery sent a letter to *The Times*: signed Dr J. M. Slattery, it began 'Sir—I have been shocked and astounded to learn from articles in several papers that one of the judges of the Booker Award is the wife of a writer whose name appears on the shortlist for this very substantial prize.'[51] The wife in question, of

---

[48]   Terence de Vere White, 'Rain tropics,' *Irish Times*, 12 April 1974.

[49]   Ian Norrie to Olivia Manning, 7 April 1974, OMC/C, HRC.

[50]   Francis King to Neville Braybrooke, 4 October 1973, from St Joseph's Nursing Home, Beaconsfield, OMC, HRC.

[51]   *The Times*, 4 November 1974.

course, was Elizabeth Jane Howard, at the time married to Kingsley Amis. A few days later, a columnist in *The Spectator* observed sarcastically that the writer of this letter to *The Times* had not though it 'worth mentioning that he is a close friend of a lady novelist who is not on the shortlist.'[52] What had begun as a welcome if not totally positive recognition of *The Rain Forest*, even if the novel didn't get beyond the long list for the Booker in 1974, ended in the most petty kind of backbiting, something that Olivia, it must be admitted, rather relished. She loved literary gossip and was not averse to doing down her competitors, or having a surrogate do it for her, as was almost certainly the case with Jerry and his letter to *The Times*.

One month after publication of *The Rain Forest*, Olivia was again down in the familiar dumps, mired in depressive questioning of her worth as an author, of the usefulness of ever beginning another novel, and, if she managed to do so, of what kind of novel that should be. She was tired, she felt she had written too much about the past, and she disregarded suggestions from friends that she write about Cairo. Her life seemed to be falling to pieces, and, as she admitted to June Braybrooke, she was lonely when Reggie set off on jaunts such a trip to Dublin with Jerry Slattery and Peter O'Toole to watch an Irish–Welsh rugger match ('What a drunken spree that will be!').[53] And she was more affected by Reggie's departure for the job in Northern Ireland than she would have thought possible: 'He is maddeningly irritating when he is around but I do not like living alone. I become very depressed and often wonder why I have to wake up in the mornings.'[54] But wake up in the mornings she did, and one summer afternoon in 1974 she began the customary doodling on whatever scrap of paper was at hand when she knew that she was about to begin a novel but did not really know what she wanted to say. Eventually, this novel began with the sentence, 'Simon Boulderstone, aged twenty, came to Egypt with the draft,' and Olivia Manning, despite her initial unwillingness to do so, had returned to Cairo and to historical fiction. The novel became *The Danger Tree* and it was dedicated 'with love' to Reggie, whom she missed deeply even when most fully engaged by her work.

[52] *The Spectator*, 9 November 1974.
[53] Olivia Manning to June Braybrooke, 1 February 1974, OMC/C, HRC.
[54] Olivia Manning to June Braybrooke, 30 June 1974, OMC/C, HRC.

12

The Battle Won

'We had reached the dark side of the world.'

Olivia Manning, BBC Broadcast, 6 October 1963.

'It is a humbling thing to have to admit that the best, or at any rate the most convincing, descriptions of the War in the Desert have been written by a woman who cannot possibly have been closer than 100 miles to it.'

Auberon Waugh, 'Men at war—by a woman,' *Evening Standard*, 5 December 1978.

Writing out of darkness

Exasperated by condescending attitudes towards women writers, disgruntled by an influx of non-white immigrants into Britain, and (as always) preoccupied by what to write next, Olivia Manning in the mid-1970s became particularly difficult. Testily beginning a 1974 review for *The Spectator* of recently published books about women's writing, she reported that at a recent party an 'undistinguished male writer' had told her he never read novels written by women. In response to her baffled question as to why this was so, he responded, 'I can never get over the idea that women are here to serve men.' At that moment, the daughter of her American hostess (possibly Alison Lurie) entered the room wearing a sweatshirt emblazoned with that triumphant slogan, 'You've Come a Long Way, Baby!' Suspecting that in 1974 this was not, in fact, the case and that women still had a long way to go in achieving social, cultural, and political equality and that the world of 'telegrams and anger' was not yet their province (as

E. M. Forster put it in *Howard's End*), Olivia then enumerated the obstacles to progress. In particular, she berated women who hate their own sex: for example, the journalist who jeered at female Fellows of the Royal Society by saying they would have been better employed cooking their husbands' dinners and the critic who declared she loathed women who 'try to be men.'[1] But in Olivia's review, women are not, of course, the sole sexist culprits. Recalling a story told to her by Jonathan Miller, who asked E. M. Forster whether a few intelligent young women might be admitted into the Cambridge Apostles, and who was then told absolutely not since the presence of women would distract the men 'from the elevated mental state that was their aim,' Olivia wonders disingenuously whether England is now free of this 'inequity.' She concludes her review by remarking that although 'Baby' might have come a long way, she has not yet reached her destination. For Olivia's career, that terminus was critical recognition as an accomplished if not best-selling novelist with no further need to yearn for the solo review in the *Sunday Times* nor to pick her way through the sexist minefield of being a woman writer.

In contrast to the liberal sentiments expressed in this review, earlier in the year she had written an unsavory letter to Robert K. Morris, a professor of English literature at City College in New York and best known for a book on Anthony Powell that appeared in 1968. In it, she complained about literary factions 'hysterically loyal' to their own kind: in the United States, she writes, 'you are well advised to be a Jew or a black if you want to succeed as a novelist' and in England it is 'rather better to be a Roman Catholic or a Communist or both, like Graham Greene.'[2] Morris had become a regular correspondent after writing to tell Olivia of his admiration of her work and she confided in him her frantic worries about the world in general, and, in unappetizing racist outbursts, her fear that Britain was being overrun by non-white peoples. She complained to Morris about the loneliness caused by Reggie's decision to continue teaching in Northern Ireland for at least two more years (although she realized that if he gave up the job

---

[1] 'Olivia Manning on the perils of the female writer,' *The Spectator*, 7 December 1974. The books under review: Patricia Beer, *Reader, I Married Him* (1974), Elizabeth Hardwick, *Seduction and Betrayal* (1974), Mirabel Cecil, *Heroines in Love* (1974), Joan Goulianos, *By a Woman Writ* (1973).

[2] Olivia Manning to Robert K. Morris, 16 March 1974, OMC/C, HRC.

they would be unable to manage on his small BBC pension);[3] she shared her disquiet about the perilous state of Britain's economy (the stock market sinking and her savings fading away); and she expressed her disgust with the arrival in England of 'more bloody Kenya Asians...(we are swamped with every sort of coloured person already).'[4] Without question, the irascible intolerance articulated here seems inconsistent with the critique of imperialism threaded throughout *The Rain Forest*, but I tend to attribute the inconsistency to Olivia's general malaise in the mid-1970s rather than to sustained racism. She was dyspeptic, out of sorts, given to peevish and sometimes ugly outbursts.

But the presence of 'coloured' persons in England remained both-ersome. Writing to June Braybrooke in September 1976 about one of her Arts Council visits, this time to Yorkshire, Olivia says it was all reassuringly old-fashioned: 'There are no coloured people. It was like going back to the early '50s before everyone started to "swing." Life gets worse and worse here with violence and mugging and general chaos.' She had written to Anthony Burgess in 1972 that in London the 'muggings happen nightly' and that Anthony West (the son of Rebecca West and H. G. Wells) had popped out for cigarettes, been attacked, and had come home covered in blood.[5] Johnny Slattery, she reported to June Braybrooke, was mugged on Hampstead Heath; a 'coloured man' demanded her money and when she refused to hand it over gave her a violent blow to the face—'Since the riots at Nottinghill [*sic*] one has the sense that the coloured people are becoming an absolute nuisance.' What she does not need to spell out is that in the early 1950s immigrants from the West Indies, Pakistan, and former African colonies were barely visible in British life; by the mid-1970s many more of the formerly colonized had arrived in Britain and had gathered in communities such as Bayswater and Brixton, heavily

---

[3] Reggie regularly urged Olivia to visit since he thought she might find the university setting 'very attractive.' R. D. Smith to Mrs R. D. Smith, 24 February 1975, OMC/C, HRC.

[4] Olivia Manning to Robert K. Morris, 18 August 1975, OMC/C, HRC. Morris continued to admire Olivia's work, terming *The Sum of Things* (the third novel in the Levant trilogy) 'one of the most remarkable books published in the past twenty-five years.' 'Olivia Manning's *Fortunes of War.* Breakdown in the Balkans, love and death in the Levant,' 233.

[5] Olivia Manning to Anthony Burgess, 27 October 1972, International Anthony Burgess Foundation.

populated by West Indians, and Bradford in Yorkshire, an enclave for Pakistanis.[6] For many British people, not all of them, of course, as virulently racist as the politician Enoch Powell, who had warned in April 1968 that there would be bloodshed as a consequence of rampant immigration of 'coloured people,' the Notting Hill events of 1976 signaled a frightening breakdown of social order.[7]

As far as Olivia was concerned, Britain was going down the drain. 'Coloured people' were terrorizing white middle-class women taking a walk on Hampstead Heath; Iris Murdoch and Angus Wilson ('those perennial great writers,' she noted sardonically to Francis King) were basking in critical adulation; Doris Lessing, always 'boring' from Olivia's perspective, was receiving adoration from left-wing critics as 'the champion of women'; and Arthur Koestler, she reported, had declared the novel 'dead'—done in by women, it has become 'a feminine pastime, a craft, like knitting or basketwork. So much for Ivy and the rest of us.'[8] Predictably, she also remained preoccupied with the question that had plagued her (and almost all her friends) since finishing *The Rain Forest*: should she write a sequel to the Balkan novels? She wrote to Robert Morris that she had been 'trying to start another Trilogy—three novels about Cairo, but the sense of hopelessness in the air is very discouraging. It is difficult to believe there is a future to work for.' And to top everything off, London was full of rich Americans while the impoverished English were slinking about, terrified to take the tube for fear of 'American-style muggings, mostly by young blacks who make so much money by beating up people on the Underground that they do not even bother to draw national assistance.' The only consolation in August 1975 was a brilliantly fine summer, she writes to Morris, the best since 1955, 'which was the finest summer we ever had and I fell in love and was happier than I can

---

[6] The Notting Hill riots that occurred on 30 August 1976, the tenth year of the annual Carnival in West London celebrating Caribbean culture, resulted in injuries to some one hundred police officers and sixty carnival-goers. According to many eyewitnesses, the riots began when local West London youths (all of West Indian origin) came to the aid of a teenage boy being accused of pickpocketing by the police.

[7] Quoted in Zig Layton-Henry, *The Politics of Immigration*, 81. Speaking in the House of Commons on 29 April 1968, on the eve of the introduction of a second Race Relations Bill, Powell had announced that as he looked ahead, he was 'filled with foreboding. Like the Roman I seem to see the River Tiber foaming with much blood.'

[8] Olivia Manning to June Braybrooke, 2 September 1976, OMC/C, HRC; Olivia Manning to Julian Mitchell, 1 February 1968, Julian Mitchell Private Correspondence.

ever hope to be again.' It was in 1955, of course, that Olivia met Jerry Slattery.[9]

The predictions of economic doom and perpetuation of ethnic stereotyping that we hear in these letters signal a turn for the worse in Olivia's history of chronic discontent, allowing for the slim possibility (slim, since Olivia was no fool) that as a white middle-class woman of sixty-eight she might have been vulnerable to a good deal of alarmist journalism about the breakdown of British order and stalwart decency by the rapidly increasing population of people darker than herself. Yet as she aged, troubled also by her graying appearance and a painful hip, she became increasingly querulous. Meeting her for the first time in late 1974, Roy Foster thought her 'rather imperious and snappy' and, seated next to her at a dinner party in early 1978, a few months after the death of Jerry Slattery, was troubled by her obsessive preoccupation with his death. Even shopping failed to please. A trip to Liberty's in January 1977 turned up nothing decent on sale, the tights in Selfridges were not worth buying, and altogether the foray an absolute waste of time and money, she wrote to June Braybrooke. Struggling through crowds of foreigners in Marks and Spencer near Marble Arch, it seemed to her that English was becoming 'a forgotten language.' And in St John's Wood, all the shop signs were in Arabic.[10]

What's more, the familiar complaints about over-charging by almost every business that had billed her for various services became particularly acute.[11] Rather than buckling down to her writing, or if not that, then sketching out some ideas, she spent a lot of time heckling organizations such as 'The Reader's Digest Association'—in this case to say that she had received an album of gramophone records she neither ordered nor wanted, and that she did not even own a gramophone. 'This method of doing business is illegal,' she announced, adding that if the album was not picked up in ten days 'it will be sold to cover the cost of storage space.' To a doctor (M. R. Lawson) she wrote that for two visits to his surgery she had paid the 'large sum' of £12 and refused to pay any more for laboratory fees. To Clifford J. Tracy, Specialist Cabinetmakers and Restorers of Antique Furniture, she wrote to protest an 'exorbitant and unjustified' charge of £30 for a small repair

---

[9] Olivia Manning to Robert K. Morris, 8 August 1975, OMC/C, HRC.
[10] Olivia Manning to June Braybrooke, 5 January 1977, OMC/C, HRC.
[11] The following letters are all in OMC/C, HRC.

to a bookcase door, a job which, she declared, she could have completed herself. If Messrs Clifford J. Tracy decide to pursue this matter, she threatens, she will take them to court 'in order that this sort of over-charging should be brought to public notice.' The local gas company received a crisply worded letter in December 1975 informing them that she had no intention of paying a bill for £2 since the servicing promised for her boiler had never been performed; she and Reggie had suffered through several very cold days with no heat in the flat and 'the whole idea of a servicing agreement seems to me to have been a total failure.' At a dinner party at Margaret Drabble's, according to Julian Mitchell, Olivia was at her absolute worst: drunk, with bile 'erupting' from a mouth twisted with 'envy and disappointment,' she turned on him and asked why she had received no congratulations on *The Rain Forest* since she had watched and praised his TV shows.[12]

More successful, at least from Olivia's point of view, than her tiffs with local tradesmen were her negotiations with the film director Stanley Kubrick, with whom she had fallen into a dispute about who should pay the dealer's commission on a painting by his wife, Christiane Kubrick, which she had added to her art collection. Quite generously, he agreed in July 1976 to share the cost of the commission and sent Olivia a check for £62.50. Olivia, however, would not let it rest there and promptly responded with a long and pedantically worded letter itemizing various legal costs she had incurred in pursuing the matter: a writ to be served on Christiane Kubrick (subsequently withdrawn), transportation costs to the court to take out the writ and to withdraw it—'Both time consuming procedures' she added, in another nit-picking letter of 12 August 1976. She demanded that Kubrick send her a check for £25 to settle the matter, which he did promptly, happy to be rid of the matter and released from her peevish correspondence.[13]

During these difficult months, Olivia assuaged her anxiety by weekly outings with Francis King. They would drive in her blue Morris Minor to stalk antique bargains in out-of-the-way shops, stroll through the flower gardens in Regent's Park, take the tube out to Kew Gardens, or join friends such as J. G. Farrell for meals at Italian

[12] Julian Mitchell, Private Diaries.
[13] Correspondence between Olivia Manning and Stanley Kubrick, OMC/C, HRC.

restaurants in Victoria. As we know, Olivia was very fond of Farrell, admired his work, and dedicated the third novel in *The Levant Trilogy*, *The Sum of Things*, to his memory. They were affectionate friends and allies, as Farrell's account of a lunch party given for Olivia by Weidenfeld and Nicolson in December 1975 after she left Heinemann suggests: 'Olivia and I were agog because Antonia Fraser and Harold Pinter, who had just "run off" together (figuratively) were also there. They behaved with perfect decorum, however, under our four beady eyes.'[14] Earlier in the year, in a letter to Robert Morris, Olivia had said, 'Reggie likes Pinter and says he is merely shy, but I find him dull and pompous, so cannot understand what Antonia sees in him.'[15] Still, she and Reggie joined Harold and Antonia at a dinner party at the home of her editor at Weidenfeld, Christopher Falkus, in early January 1976, and she managed to enjoy herself, ignoring Pinter and focusing on conversation with Antonia Fraser, for whom she had developed great admiration after Fraser voted a BBC Radio adaptation of *The Balkan Trilogy* best feature of the year in 1974. But despite Olivia's interesting social life, worries persisted about the next book. It was only when by chance she came upon the transcript of a BBC Radio talk about Egypt she had given in October 1963 that she knew her next novel would return to Cairo. The title of the talk was 'The Dark Side of the World.' Olivia began to emerge from her slough of depression and prejudiced complaints.

In the talk, she recalls that when she and Reggie arrived in Cairo in April 1941, Egypt had become 'the final bolt-hole of Europe.' Its principal city was peopled by English soldiers and European refugees 'on edge with heat, dirt, din, stink and flies,' tormented by 'perpetual petty cheating, the persistent pestering of beggars, the pointless yells and hootings of the streets.'[16] Pervading every alley, infiltrating every café, lingering on every breeze was the sight and smell of death: in this city, the indolent indifference of the rich to take action against smallpox, malaria, plague, typhus, or typhoid was such that even a European 'stuffed with drugs, could die in the twinkling of an eye from a disease that was scarcely a name to him.' It was in Cairo that she and Reggie

[14] *J. G. Farrell in his Own Words*, 321.

[15] Olivia Manning to Robert K. Morris, 8 August 1975, OMC/C, HRC.

[16] 'The dark side of the world,' by Olivia Manning. Transmission: 6 October 1963. Producer: Joseph Hone. BBC Talks Department.

suffered the contamination of flies and the slow erosions of dysentery and lived with a visible presence of death, even if they escaped the more dramatic diseases. When they visited the City of the Dead, a showplace by moonlight to which one made 'an eerie jaunt' in a taxi, Olivia recalls that she shuddered at the sight of the little burial-houses clustered around the Mameluke tombs where families settled in with food and bedding until a newly departed spirit could accustom itself to the strangeness of death.

In *The Battle Lost and Won*, the second novel in *The Levant Trilogy*, Harriet and Guy Pringle visit the City of the Dead to make what Guy terms a 'courtesy visit' for the funeral of an ex-pupil. On an 'oppressive, fly-ridden' afternoon, they enter the tomb and Guy begins to weep. As she did in a Bucharest café watching Guy hold court at the center of a group of British Council pals, and as she did on the train carrying them across Europe when a crowd of Romanian women clustered excitedly around him, Harriet remains apart as a herd of Egyptians, 'emotional people who warmed to any display of emotion,' press Guy's arms, pat his back, murmur appreciation. Once more, Harriet feels, he was being 'disseminated among so many, there was little left for her' (p. 247). In 'The Dark Side of the World,' Olivia remembers that another arena of death pressed upon everyone in Cairo: 'the war at our elbow.' Back from the desert, men arrived with their clothes and faces ingrained with desert dust, begging for a bath: dried by the sun, thin, avid for a normal life, looking 'for a world that had been stolen from them.'

Reading the transcript of her 1963 BBC talk in the summer of 1974 seeded for Olivia the beginning chapters of *The Danger Tree*, and during the remaining six years of her life she confronted a 'dark side,' not just to be found in her memories of the Middle East but also in her fear of growing old and in her belief that she had suffered sustained discrimination in the literary world. In a sense, in *The Levant Trilogy* that was to come, she wrote through and against all the darkness that had shadowed her life. Before settling down to serious writing, however, she needed to have the hip-pinning surgery that Jerry had been urging for at least a year, and on 23 July 1975 she entered the London Clinic to be operated on by Mr R. L. Beare. Mr Beare sent her a bill for £400 and the anesthesiologist received £40. These were bills undisputed and quickly settled.

Recuperating at home after the operation, Olivia amused herself by doing a few reviews for *The Spectator*. What she has to say about Anthony West's *The Lives of Three Tormented Women* differs significantly from her earlier assessment of books about women's writing. In contrast to the writers discussed in 'Olivia Manning on the Perils of the Female Writer,' the women in West's book are not major players: a letter-writer (Madame de Staël), a little-known Dutch woman (Madame de Charrière), and 'an exhibitionist noted chiefly for amours' do not represent what poor Mr West terms 'writers as a class.' What about Jane Austen, Emily Brontë, and George Eliot, she asks: 'These were women writers who did not give vent to domineering histrionics or play furious games with unhappy lovers.' Announcing that there is 'a strong smell of male chauvinist piggery' in West's effort, Olivia notes slyly that not only women have suffered from hidden wounds: think of the humiliation endured by Napoleon because of his small and under-developed sexual organs. (In a later review, Olivia developed her theory about Napoleon's penis, at his inquest, found to be 'small and under-developed': 'There is no doubt that Napoleon's deep-seated resentment of women,' she deduces with great confidence, 'had its origin in his sexual inadequacy.'[17]) Lastly, Anthony West makes no attempt to explain 'success.' Why does one neurotic games-player become Proust and all the others take to the bottle? What is the driving imperative that raises one writer to greatness and that is lacking in others? Significant about this review of a not terribly interesting book are the questions that Olivia could well have been asking herself as she began *The Danger Tree*: was she merely a 'neurotic games-player' with no more fiction up her sleeve? Was she capable of 'greatness' in another novel?[18]

In the mid-1970s, besides devoting a good deal of reviewing prose to women's writing and women's lives, Olivia wrote a provocative article for *The Times* that was published on Christmas Eve 1975 supporting the election of women to the Christian ministry: 'The Thirteenth Apostle Has a Great Deal to Answer For.' In International Women's Year (1975), Olivia announced her horror at hearing Paul hailed as an 'authority' on the position of women since he was 'an hysteric, a fanatic, probably an epileptic and almost certainly

[17] Olivia Manning, 'Heavyweights,' *The Spectator*, 27 November 1976.
[18] Olivia Manning, 'The novelist as computer,' *The Spectator*, 8 March 1975.

a suppressed homosexual with a hatred, fear and envy of women.' Her intention in this article, she announced forthrightly, would be to address Paul's 'pronouncements on women that have echoed and re-echoed down the centuries as God-given authority for the suppression of the female sex.' More of a vengeful Old Testament prophet than a gentle Christian of the Acts of the Apostles, she says, his writings remind her of male Jews she saw in the old city of Jerusalem who 'spend their days in prayer, usually bumping their heads against the Wailing Wall while the women work to support these boobies.' Attacking the misogyny of reactionary 'Hebrew religion' that is deployed by the Catholic Church to deny women admission to the ministry, she describes sitting next to a Jesuit priest at a dinner party, whom she rather gratuitously describes as squat, elderly, and looking like a rhinoceros. She asked him why there was no Jesuit order of nuns: none would act as their priest, he answered, to which Olivia responded tartly that such a refusal was strangely inconsistent with the reverence of the Virgin Mary 'as the centre of the universe.' She concludes by saying that even if she has no desire to enter a profession that is 'the bolt-hole of the fool of the family,' she feels bound to support those women who are drawn to the ministry.

Putting aside for a moment Olivia's support of feminist politics (something about which she had long remained ambivalent), what is most interesting in terms of her life in the mid-1970s is the unmuted anger suffusing this article. It was an anger that brought down upon her ears 'a hornet's nest,' as she put it to Kay Dick: 'Threats of hell fire, exhortations to pray for forgiveness before God's terrible vengence [*sic*] descended on me, assurances that women *are* inferior and must accept the fact with humility.'[19] The sarcastic attack on Paul, however, did not rule out the award of a CBE on 24 November 1976 at Buckingham Palace, an occasion to which she had not looked forward, having heard that it was an exhausting and tedious business—hanging about in an anteroom, nowhere to sit, and the band playing 'Tea for

[19] Olivia Manning to Kay Dick, 11 January 1976, OMP, UT, Series 1, Box 12. Olivia Manning, 'The thirteenth apostle has a great deal to answer for,' *The Times*, 24 December 1975. Terming Olivia's article 'an astonishing attack on St. Paul, compounded of prejudice and misconceptions,' Morna Hooker, who had recently been appointed Lady Margaret's Professor of Divinity at Cambridge, responded in May 1976. She argued that almost all of Olivia's assertions were distortions and unsupported allegations. Morna Hooker, 'Laying the misogynist myth about Paul of Tarsus,' *The Times*, 21 April 1976.

Two.' But her greatest pleasure in receiving this honor, which came as a 'complete surprise' to her, vanquished the anxiety. She thought of how proud Commander Manning would have been to see the grand-daughter of an East End tradesman and a Northern Ireland publican make her curtsey before the Queen and sail out into Pall Mall with a medal pinned to her suit jacket.

In the long run, the scorn directed at the Thirteenth Apostle represented Olivia's most direct expression of feminist feeling: for the rest of her life, she wrote little about women's lives and women writers. In fact, in September 1976, reviewing Patricia Meyer Spacks's *The Female Imagination* and finding it limited in scope and critical analysis, Olivia concluded by saying, 'Perhaps we have had too much of this woman business. There is something claustrophobic about it, and the particular voice with which the feminist writer writes of her lot is beginning to sound like a whine. The battle may not be won but it would be pleasant now to have a rest from it.' Two years later, as a contributor to a forum on 'The State of Fiction' published in the *New Review*, Olivia pointed to the pleasing number of women to be seen among the outstanding writers of the mid-1970s: 'prejudice has been outfaced' by these women, she believes, but an unfortunate reverse side to this happy state of affairs remains: 'the female voice has its own music but when it takes on the moan of self-pity, it becomes a bore.'[20] Done with moaning, at least about gender inequal-ity, as she neared completion of the first volume in *The Levant Trilogy*, Olivia turned to other battles, those fought in the Middle East in World War II.[21] Initially the going was rough: the novel seemed to drag slowly on and she felt as if she was 'digging it out of complete darkness,' but, she insisted, it was better 'to write out of darkness than ignorance.'[22]

The 1976 New Year had not begun well for Olivia in terms of her health. Always vulnerable to infections, she was struck down with a nasty case of gastric flu, which left her in a 'coma' for three days as she related the incident to June Braybrooke: Jerry came in twice a day and brought food but for a week she ate almost nothing. When she recovered and was eager for company, she invited Alison Lurie and

---

[20] Olivia Manning, 'The state of fiction,' *New Review*, Summer 1978.
[21] Olivia Manning, 'Sisters?' *The Spectator*, 25 September 1976.
[22] Olivia Manning to June Braybrooke, OMC/C, HRC.

Francis King for supper, for which she made a 'lovely kiche' [*sic*].
No sooner had they arrived, however, than she felt a heavy, horrible
pain in the solar plexus ('her ghastly liver' starting up), and, after taking
a painkiller, promptly fell asleep on the sofa: Alison and Francis ate the
'Kiche.' But there *was* some good news to report to June: 'my novel
has begun to come together after a long struggle,' she added. And at
the end of 1976 she could write that *The Danger Tree* was finished:
'I put the last alterations in yesterday. Reggie read it when he was here
on Friday and was enthusiastic—thank goodness. He did not recom-
mend any cuts or drastic changes—he is extremely acute about any bits
being too long or not in keeping, but he seems satisfied by all of it.'[23]

Olivia as Orlando

As preparation for beginning *The Danger Tree* Olivia immersed herself
in several books about the war in North Africa that proved indispens-
able as she reconstructed the terrifying onslaught of strafing, sandstorms, and landmines that awaited Montgomery's 'desert rats,' the
British soldiers who fought the German Afrika Korps. First was Alan
Moorhead's *African Trilogy* (1945), which comprised three journals
documenting his experiences as a war correspondent—*Mediterranean
Front, A Year of Battle*, and *The End in Africa*; next was Keith Douglas's
Alamein to Zem Zem (1946), a personal narrative of his wartime service
in North Africa (since praising Douglas in her essay 'Poets in Exile' in
1944, the year of Douglas's death on the Normandy beaches, as a poet
on a par with the best of those writing in World War I, Olivia had
returned regularly to his World War II poetry and prose); Cyril Joly's
Take These Men (Echoes of War) (1955), a vivid first-person account of
desert warfare; and finally and most important overall, *The Memoirs of
Field-Marshal Montgomery* (1958). Almost all of the manuscripts and
typescripts for *The Levant Trilogy* are housed at the McFarlin Library at
the University of Tulsa, together with copious notes on scraps of paper
or on the backs of envelopes, many of them to do with questions she
needed to ask experts on World War II in the Middle East or with
problems in constructing her double narrative. One notebook contains

---

[23] Olivia Manning to June Braybrooke, 29 January 1976; 4 December 1976, OMC/C,
HRC.

extensive notes made from Montgomery's memoirs and indicates she had read them carefully more than once.

That Olivia immersed herself in first-person narrative accounts of the war in North Africa indicates a significant difference from her earlier work as a historical novelist. In *The Balkan Trilogy* she embedded the story of the Pringle marriage in a historical narrative grounded in her own memories of Romanian fascism and Athens under siege: for *The Levant Trilogy*, she was able, of course, to call up once more the personal recollections of wartime, but in order to take her reader to the sandstorms, the strafing, and the rotting bodies of desert warfare, she needed necessarily to rely on outside sources. She succeeded so splendidly in integrating this reading with her memories of the North African war that paradoxically *The Levant Trilogy* seems even more personally vivid than the novels about Bucharest and Athens. She actually seems to become Simon Boulderstone, the inexperienced young officer who shares the narrative with Harriet Pringle, and it is through this character that she confronts the worries that threatened to hobble the last years of her writing life: her fear of aging and death and her resistance to being categorized solely as a woman writer. By writing so magnificently about war, she confronted her terror of mortality and showed she could write as well as any man about male experience, perhaps even better.

As we know, the narrative structure of *The Danger Tree* alternates between chapters recounting the experiences of Simon Boulderstone and Harriet Pringle in Egypt, beginning with Simon's arrival right after the fall of Tobruk to the Germans on 21 June 1942, where the Axis forces captured some two and half million gallons of desperately needed fuel oil, as well as two thousand wheeled vehicles abandoned by the British. At the time of Simon's arrival, Harriet has been in Cairo for a year, working as an assistant press officer at the American embassy in a stopgap position until her official American replacement arrives. Her principal duty is to keep the color-coded push-pins up to date on a wall-size map of the entire World War II theater of war: blue for the allied forces, red for the Russians and Chinese, black for the Axis, and, after 6 December 1942, yellow pins for the Japanese.

Just as *The Balkan Trilogy* traced an incremental experience of displacement for Harriet and Guy Pringle, the first Levant novel picks up the theme of dislocation and elaborates it to the final point of Simon Boulderstone leaving Egypt to sail to Greece. Yoking several forms of dislocation as a means of linking her characters, Olivia opens *The Danger Tree* with the young and unseasoned army officer Simon arriving in Egypt on the *Queen Mary*; on board he has made two friends, 'the people nearest to him in the world' (p. 9), but he loses sight of them in disembarkation. He is alone, soon to become one the British soldiers trudging sweatily through the Cairo streets, 'browned off, not only because they were there, but because they felt no one cared whether they were there or not' (p. 90). His sergeant, Ridley, has lost *his* outfit after being wounded: discharged from hospital, he discovers that his company has been broken up and that 'he belonged nowhere' (p. 91). Later in the novel, Aidan Pratt, a former actor and one of Guy's many acquaintances, confides to Harriet his fear that when the war is over he will be 'verging on middle-age. Just another not-so-young actor looking for work. In fact, a displaced person.' Harriet quickly responds, 'We're all displaced persons these days,' adding that she and Guy 'have accumulated more memories of loss and flight in two years than we could in a whole lifetime of peace' (p. 167). Olivia's interest in her fiction in evoking the dismal atmosphere of boarding-houses, bed-sitting rooms, and European pensions speaks to this sense of displacement, of homelessness: one thinks of 'The Daisy' in *The Rain Forest* where Kristy and Hugh Foster are shunned by the snobbish English residents and then deprived of every piece of furniture in their room when the pension is taken over by an avaricious local businessman; in *The Danger Tree*, Harriet and Guy are housed in an establishment run by Madame Wilk, 'a shrunken little monkey of a woman with large brown eyes, faded and swimming with tears.' A long hall serves as a claustrophobic dining room and sitting room, which means nobody can sit there for very long. Windows are shuttered during the day to keep out the Egyptian sun and a door that is opened at dawn to let in some air is closed, locked, and bolted before guests arrive for breakfast.

Olivia based the character of Aidan Pratt on an actor and poet named Stephen Haggard who came to the Middle East in 1942 and joined the Department of Political Warfare. Reggie and Haggard immediately became fast friends and Reggie recruited him to play starring roles in his productions of *Henry V* and *Hamlet* on local radio in Jerusalem. In *The Danger Tree*, Harriet, chatting with Aidan alone while they await the perpetually late Guy, realizes that he was 'another victim of Guy's reassuring warmth. Each one imagined himself the sole recipient. Guy would remake the world for him, and for him alone. They clung to him and, in the end, he evaded them or asked her to protect him from them' (p. 103). Once more, Harriet is the ironic outsider. In actuality, Stephen Haggard shot himself in the corridor of a train traveling between Jerusalem and Cairo in February 1943, just as Aidan Pratt in *The Levant Trilogy* shoots *himself* in a train corridor, unable to bear the guilt and sorrow of having witnessed the tragic death of many young children. A conscientious objector at the beginning of the war, he becomes a steward on a ship taking women and children to Canada. The ship is torpedoed and Aidan hustles a group of nineteen children and two women, all in their nightclothes, into a lifeboat. Alone on the Atlantic, without blankets and in the midst of a storm, their only hope the presence of a retired naval officer who acts as pilot, they exist for four days on meager tinned rations and water. But then the rations and the water run out, and one by one the children die after falling into a coma from thirst and exposure. Each morning, one or two are found dead and their bodies tipped overboard. Eventually an American destroyer rescues Aidan Pratt, and for every moment in his life thereafter he is unable to forget the sight of the children's bodies floating in the water. In this episode we see how Olivia transforms the facts of Stephen Haggard's actual suicide into a fictive account of being a witness to the tragedies of war.

In *The Danger Tree*, Olivia writes that Cairo becomes 'the clearing house of Eastern Europe. Kings and princes, heads of state, their followers and hangers-on, governments with all their officials, everyone who saw himself committed to the allied cause, had come to live here off the charity of the British government' (p. 93). But with the rumored impending arrival of Axis forces, everyone is on the move again. English women and children are being shipped out of Suez, volatile Greeks, Free French, Poles, and German Jews fight to board trains out of Alexandria; all this is accompanied by the gleeful yells of porters flinging luggage on board the train: 'You go. Germans come. You go. Germans come' (p. 94). Simon Boulderstone receives instructions to join a desert convoy, and Olivia's descriptions of men at war disclose the breadth and depth of the reading undertaken as preparation for beginning *The Levant Trilogy*.

As in much of her fiction, Olivia excels in evoking a sense of place through precise attention to detail. For example, the reader seems to travel with Simon's truck as it moves into the desert: we see Simon helping his men load rations from platoon headquarters as they collect water-cans and sacks of supplies; we see and almost smell Simon in his sweat-soaked shirt, filthy shorts, and desert boots covered in sand. And we can almost feel the sand in our mouths and eyes as Simon and his men brew up and hunker down with their backs to the wind, waiting for a sandstorm to die down. 'Breathing sand, eating sand, blinded and deafened by sand,' the men pick sand from their noses and the interstices of their ears. As Francis King wrote to Olivia in August 1977 after finishing *The Danger Tree*, 'You manage atmosphere so marvelously—I really felt that heat and smelled all those smells and heard all those sounds . . . one feels that, Orlando-like, you must really have been there!'[24] That Francis King, her dear friend and sympathetic critic, suggested her re-creation of the North African desert resembled Virginia Woolf's brilliant feats of historical imagination in *Orlando* pleased Olivia tremendously. And she was grateful for his criticism as she planned the second volume in what was clearly going to be the second trilogy. 'Rather too great a proliferation of minor characters,' he suggested, and Olivia's treatment of the British Council 'was not entirely right. Everyone except Guy was either corrupt, inefficient or malevolent—the scales are too much loaded in one direction.' But together 'an auspicious start to the new series,' he concluded in this letter of congratulation.

In *The Danger Tree*, the need to survive is every British soldier's 'chief preoccupation': suffering the stupendous heat of the day, the biting cold of the night, the plagues of flies, mosquitoes, and sand-flies, they live with 'the stench of death that came on the wind.' Yet they not only survive, they flourish. Simon, strangely enough, begins to feel 'well and vigorous' mostly because he feels that he belongs 'to a world of men; a contained, self-sufficient world where life was organized from dawn to sunset' (p. 197). He not only learns to endure as a 'desert rat,' he learns to kill without qualms. Coming face to face with 'a blond, pink-skinned German youth,' he fires in his face, which opens and spills out 'redness, like a pomegranate' (p. 157). Then, he spots in the distance a man standing in the turret of a tank, as 'the pellucid silver of first light' rolls out like a wave across the sand; but this is not a man, it is 'a man-shaped cinder that faced him with white and perfect teeth

[24] Francis King to Olivia Manning, 2 August 1977, OMC/C, HRC.

set in a charred black skull. He could make out the eye-sockets and the triangle that had once supported a nose . . . ' (p. 202). On his return, he is told that his brother Hugo has bled to death in the sand after a direct hit from German guns: the 'man-shaped cinder' foreshadows this and many other deaths, and as Simon attempts to write a letter to his parents, he weeps, knowing they 'must live with their sorrow, perhaps for years' (p. 205). This scene concludes *The Danger Tree*, and expresses, I think, Olivia's long-lingering sadness for her parents' inconsolable grief over the death of her brother. When Reggie read a rough draft of the last volume in the trilogy, *The Sum of Things*, he insisted there must be more Simon Boulderstone, since in what was to become her last novel she had displayed once more her brilliant talent in creating believable male characters.

Overall, *The Danger Tree* did well, both critically and financially. Weidenfeld and Nicolson sold the rights to Atheneum in New York, who paid an advance of $3,500 dollars (now approximately $12,000) against royalties of 10 per cent to five thousand copies, 12½ per cent to seventy-five hundred copies, and 15 per cent thereafter; and Foyles Book Club produced their own edition with an initial print run of three thousand copies. They paid 10p a copy, not an amount that would 'make either of us very rich,' noted John Curtis at Weidenfeld, but good for promotion of the novel.[25]

The *Sunday Times*' reviewer, Anne Redmon, deemed *The Danger Tree* 'a flawless sequel' to *The Balkan Trilogy*: Redmon knew 'of no other woman writer who has achieved such a complete sense of a battlefield.' Every sentence is composed with a 'chiselled authority,' every image is introduced at precise intervals as if Olivia 'were writing a classical symphony in which she must now and then make discordant references to evil.' This was not the 'solo' review which Olivia longed to see in the *Sunday Times*, but it was a fine boost for her writing morale as she worked on the next novel, titled *The Battle Lost and Won*, even if in the *New Statesman* Jeremy Treglown was a little less enthusiastic, troubled by what he saw as the 'reluctance' of the narrative to take off and a certain laxness in Olivia's style—likening the character Angela Hooper's elegance to the polished sheen of her crocodile luggage struck him as especially lazy.[26] But Pamela Hansford Johnson

[25] John Curtis to Olivia Manning, 10 September 1979, OMC/C, HRC.
[26] Jeremy Treglown, 'Such style,' *New Statesman*, 12 August 1977.

much admired the book: Olivia's prose was as 'neat and sharp as a new-trimmed hedge,' her feeling for atmosphere 'intense.' She is 'one of the very best of our novelists' with a stoical voice of her own. Hansford Johnson particularly admired Olivia's ability to write 'excellently' about men, but then she interrupts herself to ask why a woman writer should be praised for doing this since no one wonders why Balzac wrote so magnificently about women. But if we put aside the implication that men write best about men and women write best about women that underpins Hansford Johnson's comments, we cannot deny Olivia's skill in creating male characters. If a reader new to her work and with no information about her sex were to venture a guess as to whether 'O. Manning' (or even better, 'Jacob Morrow,' her pseudonym from early Portsmouth days) were a man or a woman, he or she would find it difficult to arrive at an unequivocal answer.[27]

Throughout 1977, in addition to polishing *The Danger Tree* and seeing it through publication, Olivia kept her seasoned hand in as a reviewer. In the occasional review, she returned, mostly in a comic mode, to her views about women's lives and women writers. In eviscerating the memoirs of Dennis Wheatley (the best-selling author of thrillers and books about the occult was eighty years old when they were published), she ridicules his diatribe against the inability of women to hold a few drinks—for him, after a few vodkas they throw up in a taxi—and derides his jolly delight in describing chaps who engage in drinking bouts. A pretty good drinker herself when it came to keeping up with her male friends, Olivia pities Wheatley's inability to realize that few women possess the freedom or the money to engage in 'drunken sprees': in other words, they are not yet fully fledged citizens of the world of 'telegrams and anger.' He sounds off 'with the prejudices of a vanished age.'[28] Arthur Marwick's book about women's lives in World War I Olivia liked for its documentation of how women drove trams, swept roads, and operated heavy machinery, although she regretted to report that sixty years after women got the vote in 1919 the fight still goes on for equality between the sexes.[29]

---

[27] Pamela Hansford Johnson, 'Two novels,' *New York Times*, 9 October 1977.
[28] Olivia Manning, 'Way back,' *The Spectator*, 15 January 1977.
[29] Olivia Manning, 'Heroine trade,' *The Spectator*, 9 September 1977.

On publication day of *The Danger Tree*, Olivia was in University College Hospital having her troublesome hip re-set, and fretting about her beloved Burmese, Miou, all alone at home. She knew Reggie was there on leave from teaching, that friends were checking on Miou and that they were feeding him his beloved turkey breast (Olivia would buy it raw from Sainsbury's and scald it before letting him have it), but she also knew he looked for her every time one of those friends came into her flat. The pain of worrying about Miou compounded the pain of her surgery. She had re-fractured the hip when falling on wet grass in Regent's Park after William Gerhardie's funeral (he died on 15 July 1977), having gone there with a group of friends to scatter Gerhardie's ashes in the Rose Garden. To her friends, she used to joke that Gerhardie said he would continue to pull her leg after his death: the fall seemed to be a 'sign' from him, she insisted, and when, a few months later, she was given a dozen coffee cups and saucers in dark blue and gold with the Gerhardie crest on each, she believed that this splendid, unexpected present was also a 'sign.' The cups and saucers looked very impressive in her china cupboard.

On a chilly late November afternoon in 1977, Jerry Slattery returned to his house in Eton Villas NW3 after attending a rugger match with Reggie. Seeing that he was in need of a good meal after many hours out in the cold, Johnny prepared an early supper, the principal feature of which was a juicy piece of rump steak. As he tucked in, Jerry began to gasp for breath and Johnny understandably believed he was choking, but within minutes she realized he was having a heart attack. He died almost immediately and the next night Michael Laurence broke the news to Olivia. She remained almost preternaturally composed and merely uttered the commonplace phrase, 'It will be a great loss to us all.' But to June Braybrooke she wrote that she did not know how she would go on living without him and that she could 'scarcely bear to speak or even write' of his death; to Julian Mitchell a few months later, she confessed her continuing desolation: 'I do not feel anyone could replace him.'[30] Olivia ended the obituary she wrote for the *Hampstead and Highgate Express* by saying that the Slattery house had never been more crowded than on the Sunday when 'the news went round that our beloved physician was

---

[30] Olivia Manning to Julian Mitchell, 1 February 1978, Julian Mitchell Private Correspondence.

lost to us. Where shall we find another like him?'[31] To Kay Dick on 3 December 1977, she wrote, 'I do not need to tell you how much we love Jerry and I am still confused and devastated by his sudden death.'[32]

That Olivia should be severely low-spirited at the beginning of 1978 is understandable given Jerry's death in the previous November, and also, of course, she tended to become depressed every January. Something about the New Year, and the seasonal expectation that new projects would be set in motion and that new and better ways of conducting one's life would be initiated, put her down in the dumps. She felt in a dreadful state of low-spirited inactivity and found it almost impossible to think about writing. And even after the surgery to re-set her hip, she could hardly put her leg to the ground when she got up in the morning; but what's the point in 'sending one's depression around?' she wrote to June Braybrooke. Thanking June for having arranged a mass to be said for Jerry Slattery, she added that two or three of his Catholic friends did the same thing: 'Although he had turned against religion, I think he would have been pleased. I always said to him, "On your deathbed, you will call for a priest"—but, alas, there was no time. The Chinese say that only very good men are allowed so sudden a death—perhaps because they do not need repentence [sic].'[33] She was grateful that Jerry was spared the horrors of cancer: 'he would have hated it. He had one of those sinister black warts . . . and always feared it would turn cancerous. Thank goodness he did not suffer at all. I went round to the house the other morning and it seemed terribly empty without him. Johnny is so very brave, living alone there. I could not bear it.' But there was one spot of good news in this letter to June. She was managing to write again and getting on, as she put it, with the second volume of what was now officially *The Levant Trilogy*: this was to become *The Battle Lost and Won*.

Cheered by an improvement in the grim winter weather, by early April she was feeling very much better, only to be felled by news that she needed to re-enter hospital to have the hip re-pinned, yet again: X-rays showed that the bone was being eroded and that if she did not have the operation, she would require a complete hip replacement. So she went into the private Wellington Hospital (the best hospital food

[31] Braybrooke, *Olivia Manning: A Life*, 140–1.

[32] Olivia Manning to Kay Dick, 3 December 1977, OMP, UT, Series 1, Box 11.

[33] Olivia Manning to June Braybrooke, 7 January 1978, OMC/C, HRC.

in London, she crowed, and also full of possibilities to pick up a rich oil sheikh). One good thing, she noted to June Braybrooke, has come out of being disabled for seven months: 'I have written the new novel in (for me) record time and have now nearly finished the fair type-script.'[34] As she worked on polishing the final version, she relied on a valuable set of comments about the desert war that were sent to her by an old friend, Geoffrey Wheatley, who had fought in North Africa: he indicated, for example, that rather than saying Simon Boulderstone's column was accompanied by a mobile canteen, more accurately she should describe a NAAFI truck that traveled from column to column in the desert dispensing tea and bully beef. With a historian's mind, for almost all her novels Olivia would entwine ferretted facts, autobiographical recollection, and imaginative historical reconstruction.

Predictably, of course, Olivia agonized over forthcoming reviews, so much so that Francis King told her firmly that it was no use 'hungering and thirsting after fame—nice though it would be to have it. The thing to hunger and thirst after constantly is excellence and perhaps the fame will follow.' Apologizing for sounding senten-tious, he told her that, like Virginia Woolf, she worried too much about 'what totally worthless judges think . . . People who know about the novel, and have discrimination and taste admire you.'[35] Summing up, he warns her that yearning for the Booker is an unworthy pre-occupation for someone of her talent. And Kay Dick weighed in a few weeks later, telling Olivia to stop wasting her energy bothering about 'minority' publications that have failed to mention her name: what matters is that she was still writing books which a great number of people admire and read and buy. She should stop moaning and be pleased with the impact of her work upon the history of the post-war English novel.

Olivia, as one might expect, disdained Francis's sensible advice and dismissed Kay Dick's warm admiration as empty talk. She wrote to Francis that his letter had upset her tremendously and had seemed to her 'bitchy.' Displaying remarkable patience and also revealing the depth of his affection for her, Francis King responded that of course they would both like more recognition than they received, but on the

[34] Olivia Manning to June Braybrooke, 5 April 1978, OMC/C, HRC.
[35] Francis King to Olivia Manning, 10 August 1978, OMC/C, HRC.

other hand neither of them had done too badly, given the nature of their 'gifts': 'You are highly regarded, you have your C.B.E. and you occupy a definite place of your own in the literature of our times.' But for her own sanity and that of her close friends, she needed to cease the volley of complaints about insufficient mention in the newspapers: for example, he assured her that in a forthcoming piece in the *Sunday Telegraph* he would be giving her a mention, not, he emphasized, to placate her but because her work merited such recognition. She needed to be glad for what she had achieved and for what discriminating people thought of her—these were the sentiments in his original letter and written with nothing more than a wish to assure her that she *was* recognized and that she should be grateful for her long and successful career.

Happily for both of them, Olivia and Francis's friendship survived this most recent of her discontented outbursts and they continued to go to the theater together, to visit Kew Gardens, and to share gleeful delight in privately savaging the work of their least favorite authors: Kingsley Amis's *Jake's Thing* (1978), which traces the struggle of a fifty-nine-year-old Oxford don to overcome the loss of his sexual drive while keeping up a barrage of vitriolic sarcasm aimed at women, Francis deemed egregiously vulgar and likely to outsell his and Olivia's 'products.' He maintained that it was 'a nasty book,' full of prejudices of every kind and unremittingly sour. There was little love lost between the Amis family and Olivia. She insisted that 'bitchy' anonymous reviews of Margaret Drabble's work (and her own) were being spewed out by 'little Martin Amis himself, probably to please Daddy' and that all of the Amises (Kingsley, Elizabeth Jane Howard, and Martin) had had it in for her 'ever since Jerry wrote that unfortunate letter to the Times.'[36] And both Francis and Olivia valued the work of Nadine Gordimer considerably less than the committee in charge of assembling a short list for the Nobel Prize for Literature in 1978: Olivia wrote to June Braybrooke that Gordimer was 'Such a dull writer. She has managed to pick up every prize merely by being politically on the right side. At the Booker dinner, her speech, Francis said, was simply a list of the other prizes she had won.'[37] Olivia

[36] Olivia Manning to Kay Dick, 18 August 1977, OMP, UT, Series 1, Box 1, Folder 11.

[37] Olivia Manning to June Braybrooke, 4 September 1978, OMC/C, HRC.

objected particularly to the graphic donkey-beating scene in *Burger's Daughter.* 'I find that sort of writing sick.'[38]

On the brighter critical side, she much admired Beryl Bainbridge's most recent novel, *Young Adolph* (1978), an 'amazing book' that showed Bainbridge's remarkable gifts in evoking a dismal, lower-middle-class milieu and that so filled her with depression she felt as though she were back at her childhood home in Laburnum Grove.[39] The depression was lifted somewhat by a holiday with Reggie in Spain: they went to an expensive and traffic-ridden Madrid, loved the gardens in Toledo, and on the way home spent two nights in Paris. Olivia wasn't sure how she managed to see and do so much since she had to sit down very often and have a 'restoring gin.' She reported that the Spanish gin was not bad and very cheap and that Reggie got on very well with Spanish beer and brandy. All in all, she confessed, they probably drank rather a lot, but they did keep going.

A bureau of sexual exchange

In November 1978, the second novel in *The Levant Trilogy, The Battle Lost and Won*, was published and Olivia gave a large party for over forty people, delighted that she had been able to feed them all with stuff from the delicatessen in St John's Wood High Street and had spent only £60. Roy Foster so thoroughly enjoyed the evening that he and his bicycle had to be driven home, 'inert,' and in his bread-and-butter letter he congratulated her on publication of *The Battle Lost and Won*, which gave him 'an enormous amount of pleasure.'[40] Francis King became so enraptured with the novel that he neglected to feed his cat and when he finished it 'it was not with a desire for bed but with a desire for the succeeding volume.' The lucid prose and economical narrative alone would, he was sure, receive many hurrahs and 'super reviews' and he was convinced the book, like its predecessor, *The Danger Tree*, would reach the best-seller lists.[41] Frank Tuohy, the British writer, former British Council teacher, and mutual friend of

[38] Olivia Manning to June Braybrooke, 13 October 1979, OMC/C, HRC.
[39] Olivia Manning to Francis King, 2 September 1978. FKC/OM, HRC.
[40] Roy Foster to Olivia Manning, 11 December 1978, OMC/C, HRC.
[41] Francis King to Olivia Manning, 4 November 1978, OMC/C, HRC.

Francis and Olivia, wrote to say that she had worked out with 'the utmost effect' the contrast between Simon's world and Harriet's world and that the battle scenes were better than ever. He especially admired a scene with Angela Hooper and Harriet 'with their blokes' in the club, which he felt read like a modern string quartet, all 'jangling discords.' And, as always, she was tremendously good at presenting men: 'neither joked away . . . or painstaking furry constructs.'[42]

Almost all the reviews were equally enthusiastic. Rachel Trickett in the *TLS* declared Olivia had once more displayed 'her impressive talent,' produced prose that was 'spare, witty, and dry,' and created characters so convincing one was hardly aware of the skill and discretion that had gone into their making. She succeeds brilliantly 'in the unusual feat for a woman of describing war,' and sustains her unforgettable narrative by taking the reader to scenes of rusting tanks and machinery, sand-choked depots, and sunrise over the desert. Trickett's only reservation, and it's a slight one, is to do with a certain contradiction between the lassitude of Harriet, Guy, and most of the characters not at war in the desert, and the vitality of Simon, his fellow-officers, and their men, although it is entirely clear to her that Olivia displays no lassitude or uncertainty in her assumption of narrative authority.[43] Edith Milton in the *Christian Science Monitor* was much taken with the 'Spartan sophistication' of the writing,' which moves the reader more powerfully than if Manning had resorted to sensationalistic blood-and-guts exposition. Milton noted that Olivia, much read in England, deserves to be better known in the United States since she ranks among the finest women writers of the day.[44] Noting the somber preoccupation with death that invades almost every page of *The Battle Lost and Won*, Hermione Lee in *The Observer* declared that no other English woman novelist can write like this about war and that Olivia 'surpasses herself in her account of Alamein. It is a superbly precise and convincing reconstruction, and as moving about a young soldier's first experience of battle as *The Red Badge of Courage*.'[45] What Lee terms Olivia's 'exemplary lucidity and assurance,' though, is not just brought

[42] Frank Tuohy to Olivia Manning, 2 November 1978, OMC/C, HRC.

[43] Rachel Trickett, 'Obsessed with death,' *TLS*, 24 November 1978.

[44] Edith Milton, 'War's absurdity fought on a human desert,' *Christian Science Monitor*, 12 December 1978.

[45] Hermione Lee, 'The ultimate alien,' *The Observer*, 12 November 1978.

into the service of evoking the stench, fear, and sheer horror of desert warfare as experienced by young men. With equal lucidity and assurance, I think, she so brilliantly describes the lives of women in wartime in the Middle East (Angela Hooper and her desperate affair with Bill Castlebar, Edwina Little's obsession with a sadistic Irish peer) that it is safe to say she enters magnificently into the minds of *all* her characters, here in *The Battle Lost and Won* and in virtually all her fiction. But equally remarkable about this novel praised by critics and readers alike for its brilliant evocation of battle in the North African desert and for its description of men at war, is Olivia's quite graphic depictions of sexuality, both male and female. For Rachel Trickett, in the *TLS*, an 'odd aspect' of *The Battle Lost and Won* is 'its uniform association of sexual love with the comic, the mercenary or the sordid.'

In contrast to *The Balkan Trilogy*, where Harriet Pringle is the dominant female character alongside whom her friend Bela, married to a Romanian politician, and the predatory Sophie, on the lookout for a husband to take her out of the country, function as mere subordinates, in *The Battle Lost and War* Harriet's radical transformation from sardonic watcher at the male table to independent traveler in Syria is accompanied by the sexual adventures of four other women characters. At the beginning of the novel we meet Angela Hooper, the rich and brittle wife of Sir Desmond whose life is tragically altered by the brutal death of her nine-year-old son; Angela leaves her husband and takes up with Bill Castlebar, a chain-smoking, hard-drinking poet and journalist. Shortly thereafter, we encounter Edwina Little (the dishiest 'popsie' in Cairo, according to Simon's brother Hugo)—as a very attractive young woman, Edwina is in high social demand, but her sights are set on Peter Lisdoonvarna, who turns out to be married and interested only in Edwina's appealing 'popsiness.' And in the closing chapters of the novel Harriet joins Mort and Phil, 'capable and strong' female truck drivers on their journeys backwards and forwards between Cairo and Damascus. One of their jobs is to scrub out the ambulances that bring in the dead and wounded.

As increasingly dire predictions of Rommel's advance upon Cairo spread through the British colony, the Embassy orders all women and children to return to England and Harriet wonders if she should leave Guy alone: 'How did she know that Guy, under the easy-going, well-disposed exterior, was not secretive and sly, suggesting she return to England for his own ends, whatever they might be?' (p. 337). Having suffered through several bouts of amoebic dysentery Harriet thinks longingly of England, 'where there was no plague, no cholera, no smallpox, and the food was not contaminated,'[46] and she knows that if she returned she would regain her health. Everything has gone wrong since we got here, she thinks: the climate that preserves ancient remains disrupts the living; commonplace English couples, 'who at home would have tolerated each other for a lifetime,' turn into 'bored, lax, unmoral' complainers who abandon one partner for another. Cairo has become 'like a bureau of sexual exchange' (p. 337).

For whatever reason, Olivia chose not to include any scenes of sexual attraction, let alone anything more advanced, between Harriet and Guy in this or in any of the other novels in the trilogies. The extent of physical contact between them is the occasional consoling bear-like hug offered by Guy, usually accompanied by him taking Harriet's small hands in his and muttering 'poor little monkey paws.' Guy, Olivia writes, 'feeling a need to justify his civilian status,' works long hours, organizes lectures, and tries any activity that 'could give him a sense of purpose' (p. 241): sex with Harriet does not seem to meet that demand. Sex in Cairo happens elsewhere, and between other characters. It is in the infamous 'Berka,' the red-light district of Cairo, that an innocent Simon sees women, richly dressed and bejeweled from the waist up, leaning from windows to importune customers: he has arrived there with Harriet, Castlebar, and Angela Cooper— Angela determined to show him a side of Cairo nightlife so he'll have something to tell the boys back in the desert. The party witnesses a truly dismal and unexciting sex show in which a 'half-negro woman,' in a dirty pink wrapper, reclines on a bunk, legs apart, 'fat, elderly, bored and indifferent to the audience.' Within minutes a sexually aroused but painfully embarrassed young Egyptian fellow falls on top of her: 'The union was brief' (p. 231). The young man, it turns out, is a student of Castlebar's, and, once he is back in his trousers, approaches him to say, 'Professor, sir, you do not know me, but I know you. At times I am attending your lectures.' Castlebar asks if he often does these 'performances,' Angela, ever socially accomplished, gives him 'undue praise' for his efforts, and the young man replies that he does not often do this, that, unlike Europeans, Egyptians like to do such things in

---

[46] *The Battle Lost and Won*, 336.

private. Invested with comic horror, this scene discloses the initiation of the inexperienced Simon and Harriet into a world of unromantic sex, an education furthered for Harriet not just by watching, but also by listening, or trying not to listen.

When Angela Hooper leaves her husband and moves into the Dobson flat in Garden City, she quickly takes up with Castlebar: their noisy lovemaking can be heard through the wall separating the Pringle bedroom, where nothing seems to be going on, from that of Angela. Harriet is also treated to Angela's confidence that Castlebar keeps by the bedside a dish of water, 'because he's inclined to come too soon . . . when he's over-excited, he dips his wrist in the water and it cools him down' (p. 265). When Harriet accompanies Edwina Little and Peter Lisdoonvarna to the ruins near Memphis, she wanders alone among the fragments of fallen temples, eventually entering the Serapeum (a temple dedicated to the Hellenistic-Egyptian god Serapis and the burial place of bulls), and finds Edwina and Peter obscure in the shadows, their bodies pressed together as though each sought to merge into the other. In the most disturbing of her vicarious experiences of sexual desire, she overhears Edwina sobbing in the room next to hers and then the gruff voice of Peter telling her to shut up, followed by the noise of a slap and scuffle and his voice, 'contused with sexual intent,' saying hoarsely, 'Come on, you little bitch. Turn over.' Harriet crashes her chair against the wall in the hope of stilling their noise but she is doomed to hear the squeaks, grunts, and a rhythmic clicking of the bed 'until Peter gave out a final groan' (p. 322).

After several hospitalizations for amoebic dysentery, Harriet eventually caves in and agrees with Guy that she should return to England; it is Dobbie Dobson, with her when she left Athens, who convinces her finally that she must leave—'You look as though a puff of wind would carry you away. You might catch anything in this condition' (p. 371). Scheduled to sail from Suez in late December 1943, she boards the boat-train in Cairo, relieved to be leaving Guy, who she feels is draining her life as well as his own. But whereas he has the physical strength to survive she knows she cannot: she recalls him saying that the climate was killing her, but now, 'seeing the relationship from a distance, she felt the killing element was not the heat of Cairo but Guy himself' (p. 374). As the train pulls into Suez and she sees the name of her ship, the *Queen of Sparta*, it reminds her chillingly of her departure from Greece: she knows with a terrible foreboding

that she must and never will board the ship. Then, suddenly, as she
breaks from the queue to embark she sees Mort and Phil climbing into
their freshly loaded lorry; crying out 'Take me with you,' she runs into
their arms, jumps on board, and prepares herself for a bumpy ride
across Sinai. Told that she'll need to kip down among the ammunition,
Harriet laughs and says that she does not mind how she crosses Sinai
'for all the wonders of the Levant were on the other side' (p. 377). The
coda to *The Battle Lost and Won* tells the reader that a week after the
ship sailed, rumors reached Cairo that the *Queen of Sparta* had been
torpedoed off Tanganyika with the loss of all on board: 'This was the
last that Cairo heard of the *Queen of Sparta* and, the times being what
they were, only the bereaved gave further thought to the ship.' Freed
from the 'killing' closeness of Guy, happily throttling across the Sinai
desert to Damascus, Harriet Pringle finds independence in the company of a lesbian couple. Similarly, Olivia Manning freed herself from
her crippling fears of mortality by imagining the terror of death in
scenes such as the bloody end of Simon's brother and the tragic
drowning of some thirty or so shipwrecked children. She also challenged the conventional wisdom that women writers could not really
write about men and war. And in completing *The Battle Lost and Won*
with Harriet freely roaming around Syria, she freed herself to begin the
last novel in *The Levant Trilogy*. No more agonizing about what to
write next and no more striving to show that women writers do not
necessarily write best when writing about women, although in her case
she also did that very well.

13

The Stray Survivor

'Then, at last, peace, precarious peace, came down upon the
world and the survivors could go home. Like the stray figures left
on the stage at the end of a great tragedy, they had now to tidy up
the ruins of the war and in their hearts bury the noble dead.'

Olivia Manning, Coda, *The Sum of Things* (1980).

Tidying up

Kay Dick asked Olivia Manning in 1972 how she felt about death.
Feeling arthritic and under the weather, Olivia answered that she
would like to survive death in some magical way and find herself still
alive yet released from the miseries of her present physical condition:
'I hate the limitations of the physical world. I have an absolute loathing
of death. . . . I really love life as a force, and I do want to continue it.
I've no desire at all to be dead.'[1] Given the history of depression and
despair chronicled in Olivia's letters to close friends, it might seem
surprising to hear her affirm so fervently that she loves life, and that her
unhappiness stems from such things as the perennially bothersome hip,
rather than from emotional ups and downs. But for all the times she
questioned in her letters the point of going on with her life and her work,
she was never seriously suicidal, never really thought of packing it in.
Despite the delicate stomach that was a legacy of her days in Greece and
Egypt and despite the daily discomfort of the aching bones, she relished
her existence and all the talk about taking an overdose (mainly voiced to

---

[1] Kay Dick, *Friends and Friendship*, 44.

June Braybrooke) was part of the self-dramatization as unappreciated and unloved author. Above all else, it was writing that gave her the deepest reason to live, and it was writing that had sustained her through years of scrambling out of the literal and emotional ruins of war. In the late 1970s, she began the business of tidying up.

Undoubtedly, Olivia is one of the survivors evoked in the coda to *The Sum of Things*. By the time she completed her last novel in 1979, she was confident of her cultural recognition as one of Britain's most accomplished women novelists. Throughout her writing life, she had recurred regularly to stories of survival, whether, say, in the autobiographical documentation in *The Doves of Venus* of inventive ways to get by in London on limited resources, or in the narrative of Felix Latimer's struggle as a friendless orphan in Palestine at the end of World War II that is the subject of *School for Love*, or of trying to stay one step ahead of the Germans like Harriet and Guy Pringle in the trilogies. On the most painful level of surviving personal tragedy, Olivia had also endured the death of a child in utero and sublimated her grief into its fictional depiction in two of her novels.

If we remember Olivia's actual experience of endurance and an unfaltering dedication to a life of writing maintained under almost all circumstances, we can see, it seems to me, that her caustic wit, frosty demeanor, and querulous attitude often cloaked the cost of that endurance. Her closest friends knew what lay behind the brittle façade; in particular, Francis King, June Braybrooke, and Johnny and Jerry Slattery understood her vulnerability and tolerated her prickliness. In the last five years of Olivia's life, this small group was enlarged to include Michael Laurence, an orthopedic surgeon, and his Persian-born wife Parvin when they joined the regular Saturday and Sunday noontime gatherings at a pub in St John's Wood. This was a collection of haute bohemian types—actors, doctors, and journalists, mainly, who, after an hour or so of convivial drinking, would proceed to the Slatterys for a late lunch. It was there that the Laurences met Reggie and Olivia. In late 1978, Michael Laurence replaced the hip that had never been right since Olivia had fallen in Regent's Park after William Gerhardie's funeral, and as well as getting her back on her feet, he also became an valuable resource for details of recovery from paraplegic injuries similar to those suffered by Simon Boulderstone.

At these weekend gatherings, Olivia appeared to everyone as a slim and attractive woman with grayish hair and beautiful skin, who, even if she relished gossip, according to Parvin Laurence, remained almost fanatically loyal to her closest friends. She particularly appreciated the Laurences' generous offers of help when Reggie was away in Northern Ireland; for example, when she was recovering from the hip replacement surgery and feeling particularly miserable and lonely after Jerry's death, they took her by car wherever she needed to go, did her shopping, and in a raging snowstorm delivered a large packet of frozen hamburgers. Parvin Laurence was very fond of Olivia and understood intuitively that underneath the droll banter, she was actually very shy and nervous about almost everything—most of all, frightened she would betray her lack of classy social credentials and a university education. Yet she never denied the history of survival and making do that led to chronic worries about money, worries mostly unfounded, one might add, since she invested wisely and was highly frugal. But she complained tirelessly that Reggie never earned enough, that her royalties were inadequate, and that their flat was a constant financial drain. What was little known to anyone outside this St John's Wood circle of friends was that Reggie and Olivia basically lived off her royalties and investments: she made all the money, bought the flat in Marlborough Place, purchased the Morris Minor, and shopped for all of Reggie's clothes in Marks and Spencer. She paid for everything while he frittered away his BBC salary, handing it over if someone happened to be on their uppers or standing rounds for everyone in the local. Roy Foster recalls a telling incident when a rather lavish basket of fruit arrived at Marlborough Place, sent to Olivia by her publishers; Reggie happened to be entertaining a group of Iranian students at the time and much to Olivia's chagrin promptly gave away almost everything in the basket to his guests.[2] Long accustomed to Reggie's impetuous generosity, she merely smiled and helped herself to what was left.

If Olivia's cutting commentary on friends and acquaintances occasionally got out of hand, this stemmed, Parvin Laurence believes, from her chronic discomfort when around people whose social privilege and education she both envied and resented: she would often speak impulsively and without forethought, which led to a habit of clapping her hand over her mouth and lamenting immediately a tactless remark.

---

[2] Author's conversation with Roy Foster, 27 November 2008.

An awareness that she often spoke without thinking led to a paralyzing fear of performing in public, even when she had no choice and putting on a good show might have served her best interests. For example, for a BBC program featuring two writers talking about the book of the week Olivia joined the veterinarian/writer James Herriot. So painfully nervous that she could barely speak about the book under review, let alone make some graceful passing reference to her own work, her discomfort was so visible Parvin could barely watch. Occasionally, though, the impulsiveness also led to a refreshing if alarming frankness: at a book party, Olivia told Samuel Beckett that *Waiting for Godot* was a load of pretentious old rubbish (or words to that effect) and on another literary occasion announced loudly within hearing of Sonia Orwell that whenever George Orwell walked into a room a kind of fog descended.

As one might expect, Reggie was beloved by everyone in the St John's Wood crowd for his hearty gregariousness and his readiness to recite poetry or sing North Country folk songs for as long as anyone might wish to listen. An enthusiastic organizer of outings, he especially enjoyed rounding up volunteers for cricket parties and telling people how to bat, which struck everyone as comically inappropriate since Reggie was so shortsighted he could barely see the length of the cricket pitch. He also loved to cook but predictably was completely disorganized. None of Olivia's friends ever recall her having much interest in the kitchen (although she loved to go to good restaurants), but Parvin Laurence remembers vividly a weekend at her house on the Isle of Wight when Reggie had promised to arrive early on the Friday afternoon, do the shopping at the local supermarket, and cook dinner for everyone. Turning up at 6 o'clock with two bulging shopping bags, he cheerily reassured Parvin that all would be well, and it was, after he threw a joint and some not too well-scrubbed potatoes into the oven. Dinner was late but delicious, and Olivia, back in St John's Wood working on the third volume in *The Levant Trilogy*, was not there to sigh resignedly, 'Oh, Reggie!'

Olivia dedicated *The Sum of Things* to 'the memory of Jim Farrell taken by the sea August 1979' (Farrell had died in a drowning accident off the coast of Ireland). Olivia regarded his novel *The Singapore Grip* very highly, and in a radio program about his work recorded in March 1980 she spoke warmly of his writing. For her, he was one of the best British novelists and had he lived, she added in her throaty voice, it was impossible to say what further greatness he might have achieved.[3] In this novel dedicated to Farrell, she continued to interweave the individual narratives of Simon Boulderstone and Harriet Pringle. In the opening chapters, we learn that Simon is in an army hospital, 'a collection of huts in the sand,' and that he is paralyzed from the waist down after being hit by German mortar fire; Harriet, unaware that 'she was mourned for dead,' is being bumped in the back of a lorry as Mort and Phil drive across the Sinai bound for Damascus. News having reached Cairo of the sinking of the *Queen of Sparta* after being torpedoed, all assume that Harriet has drowned. The novel begins, then, with a motif of wounding and promised recovery: Simon has been the literal target of a lobbed German mortar and Harriet has been the emotional victim of Guy's benign indifference to her needs. The rest of the novel traces their respective journeys through rehabilitation and adventurous travel, through recovery and survival, to the point of Simon's departure for Greece and Harriet's return to Cairo and to Guy. Simon's journey to recovery takes him through the painful return of the use of his legs and Harriet's journey home assumes an Odyssean resonance as she traverses a roving route through Syria, Lebanon, and Palestine and suffers through various obstacles to a reunion with Guy. Penniless and without work, a European woman vulnerable to harassment in a male-dominated society, and, until she is rescued by Angela Hooper and Bill Castlebar, entirely without friends, she endures and survives physically unscathed and emotionally seasoned.

That Olivia benefited from Michael Laurence's advice about describing the physical after-effects of a serious injury to the legs is apparent from her description of Simon's first weeks with 'The Plegics,' which is how the paraplegic patients are described by one and all. After the early days of feeling no sensation whatsoever, Simon becomes subject to delusions: his knees seem to have a life of their own and someone seems to be pulling at his feet. Prevention of bedsores is attended to by the regular lifting of his buttocks and being rubbed with mentholated spirits; prevention of his bowels getting 'all bogged up,' which is how a young nurse describes it, is attempted by shifting him every two hours from one side to another.

---

[3] 'J. G. Farrell,' 24 March 1980. British Library Sound Archives, T2942R C1.

When he begins to show signs of recovery, he is handed over to a physical therapist whose approach is that of a sergeant drill-instructor in the regular army: placed on the parallel bars, Simon can hardly hold his body upright since his arm muscles are so wasted, and when he is forced to swing himself along he sees his legs hanging, but feels no sensation. In contrast to her reliance upon Michael Laurence's authoritative advice for describing Simon's injury and rehabilitation, for Harriet's journey across the Sinai, into Lebanon, and then to Jerusalem, Olivia, needless to say, needed no assistance other than her own recollection and the occasional contribution from Reggie.

In Egypt the sun shone every day in a cloudless sky, Harriet recalls, yet in Syria, close to the Mediterranean, the sky is 'blotted over with batches of cloud and the wind had an unfamiliar smell, the smell of rain.'[4] Jumping down from the back of Mort and Phil's lorry, she feels fit for the first time in months, recovered from her amoebic dysentery, and 'free in a new world.' The lorry has stopped on a rocky shoulder overlooking the sea and she notices Mort and Phil barefoot below her; about to call out to them, she is checked by the 'sense of intimacy between them' and she watches as they stand close together, looking into each other's faces. Their figures merge and they remain locked together for several minutes. Once more, Harriet is the outsider, left alone in the lorry just outside Damascus, as Mort and Phil, without a word, jump down and disappear into the shadowed hills for twenty minutes. Nothing more explicit than these brief details is needed to convey to the reader the sexual intimacy between the two women. Yet this scene is actually not a replay of Harriet's seemingly inescapable role as watcher while others have a good time: now, their intimacy reminds her of what was wrong with her marriage. Rather than walking off with her to have sex in the shadowed hills, Guy would have pressed on, eager to find a Damascus bar where he could have a beer and chat up whoever he might find there. In other words, witnessing the sexual connection between Mort and Phil brings home to Harriet the importance of Guy's reliance upon a crowd to sustain their relationship and a rueful acknowledgment that whatever sexual attraction fueled their hasty marriage has diminished considerably, if not disappeared entirely. Harriet realizes yet once more that to

[4] *The Sum of Things*, 402.

Guy she is merely one of that crowd, loved by him the best way he knows how. But to survive as a secure and independent individual, she needs more than the distracted hug, more than being accepted by a group of beer-drinking comrades, as did Olivia.

After being dropped off by Mort and Phil in Damascus, Harriet finds a cheap hotel, but realizes quickly that the £50 she was taking with her to England will not keep her going for very long; she thinks wistfully of how in London she had earned her own living, how she had told herself that 'any girl who could survive there, could survive anywhere in the world' (p. 469), which is, of course, how Olivia always remembered her days at Peter Jones and the Medici Society. But here in Damascus, Harriet must admit, 'her attempt at an independent life had reduced her to penury' (p. 469). Despite the efforts of a Syrian lawyer named Halal to entertain her with a tour of famous Damascus landmarks and despite some three weeks doing secretarial work for an overbearing Egyptologist named Dr Beltado (who leaves Damascus without paying her), she remains lonely and without money—that is, until she runs into Angela Hooper and Bill Castlebar in the lobby of the very posh Cedars Hotel. 'Don't worry about money,' says Castlebar. 'You'll be all right with us. Angie's a great giver. She loves to feel she's got us captive' (p. 486).

In captivity to Angela's money, Castlebar is perfectly happy. As we know from Olivia's Cairo days when she wrote the 'Poets in Exile' article for *Horizon*, she modeled Castlebar on Bernard Spencer, for her, she wrote in 1944, a poet who had long deserved a wider public. In *The Sum of Things*, as long as he is kept in a constant supply of cigarettes and whiskey and allowed to write the odd poem before lunch, Castlebar is in heaven. He settles in with Angela and Harriet at the King David Hotel (well known to Olivia from her Jerusalem days) and goes with them both to attend the ceremony of Holy Fire at the Church of the Holy Sepulchre. Harriet, battling her way through the crowds, suddenly sees a woman who was standing in the queue to board the *Queen of Sparta*: puzzled as to why this woman would be in Jerusalem and not in England, she is told tersely about the torpedoing and the survival of only three passengers. Realizing with horror that Guy must assume she is dead, Harriet returns immediately to Cairo and arrives at the Dobson flat just as the wedding reception for Edwina Little and a Major Brody is getting under way. Brody is a dull man without the desirable title Edwina longed for when she was sleeping with Peter

Lisdoonvarna, but at least she has a husband. In contrast, for Angela the novel ends in tragedy when Castlebar dies after contracting a form of virulent and fatal typhoid, just as the first novel in *The Levant Trilogy* begins with the tragic loss of her son.

Reunited with Guy, Harriet realizes that she sees the world 'as a reality and he did not,' and she wonders if she could have borne life with 'some possessive, interfering jealous fellow who would have wanted her to account for every breath she breathed': concluding that she could not, she admits that in 'an imperfect world, marriage was a matter of making do with what one had chosen' (p. 566). Placing this somber realization in the autobiographical frame of both trilogies, it seems fair to say that, judging from Olivia's letters and from the reminiscences of her friends, her marriage was much more than 'making do.' When she and Reggie returned to England after the war, their relationship might have lost the sexual excitement that brought them together in 1939, and as the years went on his unreliability and social promiscuity certainly became infuriating, but she never ceased to look to him for intellectual and emotional support. So at the end of *The Levant Trilogy*, Harriet survives and reconciles herself to her marriage, imperfect as it may be, just as Olivia, when she finished this novel, knew that she too had survived and come through. From the early days in her drafty Portsmouth bedroom when she wrote sensation stories for the local newspaper, and through all the years of her career, to the moment in 1979 when she finished *The Sum of Things*, feeling creaky and a bit cranky, it was writing that had framed her life. And it was to say how much he admired that writing life that John Gielgud came and sat at her feet at an 'Authors of the Year' party in March 1980, a thrilling moment that Olivia relayed to all her friends. In the same month, Penguin published a paperback edition of *The Balkan Trilogy*, 'well displayed at Charing X Station,' Olivia reported to June Braybrooke, although, she added, all she ever saw in bookshop windows was Kingsley Amis's *Jake's Thing*—'a sad, unfunny book, obviously about Kingsley's "thing."'[5] To celebrate completion of *The Sum of Things*, in the spring of 1980 Olivia and Reggie had a holiday in Spain and France: in Barcelona they saw the Sagrada Familia and the Gaudi Park Guell and in Paris drank a lot of wine and brandy.

---

[5] Olivia Manning to June Braybrooke, 23 March 1980, OMC/C, HRC.

Despite being in almost constant pain from the bothersome hip (and two surgeries), Olivia was game and in good spirits.

Coming through

When Reggie arrived at the Athens airport in October 1940, one week after Olivia had fled Bucharest, he carried a rucksack and a small suitcase: the rucksack was stuffed with shirts, underwear, and socks and the suitcase was full of books. When Olivia remonstrated about the minimal amount of clothing and the considerable number of books, Reggie replied that he needed to bring his precious signed copies and first editions, particularly those of D. H. Lawrence.[6] From his days at Birmingham studying classics with Louis MacNeice, Reggie had much admired Lawrence, and when he returned from Bucharest to London on a brief leave in the summer of 1939, when he wasn't having beers with MacNeice and other pals at the Museum Tavern or going to bed with Olivia in her Woburn Place bed-sitting-room, he was in the British Museum making notes for a possible book about Lawrence's verse. A particular favorite was 'Look! We Have Come Through!' and the title of this poem (also the title of the book of verse in which it appeared) seems particularly appropriate for describing the last year of Olivia Manning's life, the year in which she completed the aptly titled *The Sum of Things*. The speaker of Lawrence's poem takes quiet pleasure in the fact that 'All the troubles and anxieties and pain' are 'gone under the twilight,' and closes with the line, 'It is perfect enough, It is perfectly complete, You and I, what more—?' | Strange how we suffer in spite of this.' For Olivia, her marriage to Reggie was 'perfect enough.' What more could she want, in the 'twilight' of her life, even if she still suffered from the pains of her childhood, the terrors of the war, and the loss of her child, so long ago?

For many years until her death in 1980, Olivia and Reggie slept in separate bedrooms, an arrangement explained on the grounds that Reggie was a spectacular snorer, although a number of their friends (particularly Francis King) believed they no longer had a sexual relationship. Whatever the case, Reggie's bedroom at Marlborough Place

---

[6] Braybrooke, *Olivia Manning: A Life*, 88.

was bigger than Olivia's and for many years contained a large and heavy metal bed (Reggie was a big fellow), which, having become very dingy, was replaced in early July 1980 by a more practical item from Heal's in Tottenham Court Road. Removal of the old bed and installation of the new one, however, revealed a grubby floor, and on the morning of 4 July Olivia set to work to scrub it clean. The room was also crammed with old newspapers, scripts of plays, and mountains of books piled on rickety chairs and stacked against the walls. The floor scrubbed and the room tidied, Olivia, feeling tired from the work and lonely from Reggie being away in Ireland, called Parvin and Michael Laurence, who suggested immediately that she come to their house on the Isle of Wight, Billingham Manor, for the weekend. At four o'clock, with Miou in his cat box, she was ready to be picked up by the Laurences, and after driving to Southampton they caught the 5:30 ferry to East Cowes; on board they enjoyed a few gin and tonics as they crossed the Solent and proceeded happily to the house. Miou's needs always taking precedence, Olivia went directly to the scullery to fix his supper while Parvin remained in the kitchen preparing the dinner. Suddenly, Olivia cried out 'Oh, my head!,' vomited into the scullery sink, and collapsed on the floor covered in sweat, complaining of tremendous head pain.[7] It was obvious to Michael Laurence that she had suffered a stroke.

Parvin and Michael drove her double quick to the hospital in Ryde twelve miles away (where at the time there was no CT Scan equipment) and Michael called a neurologist colleague in Southampton for advice, who suggested that it was probably best to leave her be rather than risk a move, and for a few days thereafter she seemed to improve. Reggie came immediately from Ireland and stayed with an old friend from Birmingham days, Bobby Case. Every afternoon he came to her room and read the many get-well letters and postcards arriving at the hospital: the poet David Gascoyne commiserated with Olivia on her 'rotten luck,' the poet, political activist, and for many years poetry editor of the *New Statesman* (and also fellow-presenter on the Arts Council tours), Adrian Mitchell, wrote to say that he and his wife Celia were relieved to learn that she was 'much better,' and Margaret

---

[7] Details of Olivia's collapse and death gathered from author's conversation with Parvin and Michael Laurence, 4 May 2010.

Drabble scribbled a note before leaving for a trip to the United States
to say she was 'shocked' to hear of the illness.

For about a week Olivia seemed to be recovering her spirits. She
told June and Neville Braybrooke not to hang around her bed as if they
were waiting for a train and she spoke hopefully about a resumption of
writing when she left the hospital. But she was highly disappointed that
she would probably be unable to attend a Foyles Literary Luncheon
scheduled for 17 July where she was to be a guest of honour along with
eight other writers, one of whom she loathed (Kingsley Amis) and
another she much admired (V. S. Pritchett). But, after a few days, she
began dozing almost all the time, her voice sank to a whisper, and on
the morning of 23 July just before Parvin Laurence arrived at the
hospital, she became unconscious. She died at noon with Parvin
holding her hand. Reggie arrived at two in the afternoon, having
gone to London the day before since he felt he could no longer sit
by Olivia's bedside and watch her fade away.

According to the Laurences, Olivia's funeral on 28 July, which took
place at Whippingham Crematorium on the Isle of Wight, was a
miserable occasion, allowing, of course, for the unhappiness that
shadows such events. Reggie invited a couple of old Birmingham
pals and a few of Olivia's London friends came to the Island. Bobby
Case and his wife (with whom Reggie had been staying) and Reggie's
brother Roy and his wife barely said a word about the shocking
suddenness of Olivia's death. Only June and Neville Braybrooke,
Parvin and Michael Laurence, and Johnny Slattery seemed able to
express their deep sadness: Reggie remained mutely stricken and
refused to take the ashes after the cremation. The Church of England
service lasted a very brief fifteen minutes. Afterwards, the twenty or so
mourners proceeded to the Case house in Ryde for a pork pie lunch,
and around two in the afternoon Reggie took himself off to the local
pub. For the following six weeks or so he parked himself with various
friends around the country, refusing to enter the Marlborough Place
flat, and sporadically traveling to the University of Surrey, where he
had become a Visiting Professor of Literary Arts in the year before
Olivia's death (he remained there until 1983). It was not until early
September 1980 that he arrived in St John's Wood, accompanied by
Michael Laurence, who had insisted that he return if only to pick
up the mail accumulating in the hallway. As soon as they entered
the flat, Reggie collapsed on the sofa and burst into tears, forced to

acknowledge Olivia's death as he looked around at the furniture, books, and pictures they had collected over the years. In an ironic instance of Olivia's familiar fusion of autobiography and fiction, in real life Reggie wept for her loss just as in fiction Guy Pringle weeps for the presumed drowning of Harriet.

In her will, made two years before her death and prepared by the solicitors Farrer & Co. (the Queen's solicitors, she eagerly told her friends), Olivia left the flat and all her possessions to Reggie, whom she appointed one of her three literary executors, along with Neville Braybrooke and Francis King. The estate was valued at £167,000 (almost twice that of Ivy Compton-Burnett), an almost laughably large sum in light of Olivia's self-pitying complaints to her friends that she and Reggie were always on the verge of bankruptcy. As soon as she began accruing a good income from her writing, she had started making wise investments on the basis of Jerry Slattery's shrewd advice; driven by her childhood experience of scrimping and the years of barely supporting herself before the war, she had vowed never to want for money if she could help it. She bequeathed individual legacies of £500 to her literary executors, to Alex, who had been her loyal cleaning lady for many years, and to five animal welfare societies. This witnessed will was assumed to be her last, but when Reggie returned to the flat after many more weeks of mournful wandering, he discovered a later will dated 28 April 1978 in which Olivia had increased the legacies, including those to the animal charities, to £2,000 each. She also left instructions that after Reggie's death, she wished her shares and future royalties to be divided equally between the five animal trusts, June Braybrooke, and Johnny Slattery. When Reggie got in immediate touch with Olivia's solicitors, they agreed that her wishes should be honored and on 27 September 1982 a deed of variation was executed.[8] The details of the will seemed to Francis King a validation of something he had always suspected about Olivia—that she put human beings second to animals. Rather than leaving money to the Wood Green Animal Sanctuary, he thought she might more positively have made provision for indigent friends or given money to the Royal Literary Fund. He would often mutter to

[8] I am grateful to Victoria Orr-Ewing for allowing me to examine the notes made by Neville Braybrooke about the two wills.

friends that to gain Olivia's unconditional love you needed to be a seal or a cat.

On the weekend following Olivia's death, *The Observer* and the *Sunday Telegraph* ran signed obituaries by Anthony Burgess and Neville Braybrooke (Burgess's, interestingly enough, omitted the final sentence of his typescript—'She was a fine writer and a good friend').[9] The following Sunday Julian Mitchell's obituary appeared in the *Sunday Times* and those by Paul Binding and Francis King quickly followed in the *New Statesman* and *The Spectator*. All the obituaries seemed to get her age wrong, probably because she had always looked a few years younger than she actually was, and also because she had resolutely refused throughout her life to reveal her true birth date: 1908. Even Francis King was off by a few years in his *Spectator* obituary: discussing her pluckiness in coming to London in the mid-1930s with no job prospects and very little money, he says she was a mere twenty-three-year-old—in 1934 she was, of course, twenty-six. All the obituaries also referred to her acerbic wit and tactless outbursts: as Derek Mahon observed in the BBC Radio 3 memorial program broadcast on 21 November 1981, 'Never a Day Without a Line,' she was 'formidable with her provocative remarks' and did not suffer fools gladly.[10] On this same program, Reggie recalled an incident at the Gargoyle Club where he and Olivia had gone to lunch with Dylan Thomas and another poet, Brian Howard. Unwisely charging Thomas with having sold himself to the BBC, Howard became the recipient of a ferocious attack from Olivia, who was very fond of Thomas. 'You Common Awful Vulgar Little Swine—You Pederaster,' she cried in what Reggie recalls as a 'hard clear voice,' as she chased him out on to Dean Street.

Most of all, it was her vulnerability that made Francis King so fond of her: the touching eagerness to be admired and to be loved that coexisted with a sharp intelligence and a laser-like humor 'that irradiates even her saddest pages.'[11] All the obituaries were laudatory, of course, but none quite matched the cogent assessment of Olivia's

[9] Anthony Burgess, Typescript, 'A talent to remember,' International Anthony Burgess Foundation.

[10] 'Never a day without a line' featured multiple contributors: Neville Braybrooke, Kay Dick, Isobel English (June Braybrooke), Roy Foster, Victoria Glendinning, Francis King, and Reggie. Anna Massey read selections from the novels.

[11] *The Spectator*, 2 August 1980.

literary talent offered by Roy Foster in the *TLS* on 8 August 1980. Pointing to her 'exacting moral sense, her cool appraisal of the second-rate, of cruel and shabby attitudes, of the way people behave under pressure,' and praising her original wit, sharp, deft style, and 'a use of language almost bleak at times,' Foster aptly located Olivia's originality as a novelist in her brilliant depiction of the 'intricate interplay between historical and personal fortunes.' For Foster, the trilogies have the strength to remain 'the best evocation of the Second World War in English,' and Olivia's other novels, despite the self-acknowledged reliance upon private experience, transcend the merely autobiographical. But despite the CBE and the critical praise that accrued to the first two novels in what became *The Levant Trilogy* with the publication of *The Sum of Things* in late September 1980, Olivia's work, Foster concluded rather sadly, remains 'critically undervalued.'

In what she terms an ultimately futile attempt to separate *The Sum of Things* from its 'bleak circumstances' (it was published shortly after Olivia's death), Victoria Glendinning identifies disappearances, death, and loss as its principal motifs. This is not 'woman's writing,' she declares; rather, Olivia writes sexlessly about sexual relationships, and the ability to evoke a 'rackety wartime atmosphere' of this last, almost documentary novel cannot be over-stressed. But Glendinning ends her *TLS* review a little less than enthusiastically: the trilogies were a *succès d'estime* but that kind of achievement does not always survive an author's lifetime.[12] More positively, Hermione Lee, who had admired *The Battle Lost and Won* for its 'exemplary lucidity and assurance,' found Olivia's talent for historical reconstruction undiminished and her elegiac, dry prose as effective as ever in evoking the strangeness of places such as a bar in Tiberias where Australian soldiers go on a drinking binge and the dingy isolation of a run-down Damascus hotel on a rainy evening. For Lee, Olivia's 'deft understatement' remains the hallmark of her direct, unsentimental prose.[13] Writing in the *Sunday Times*, Peter Ackroyd (who had rather hammered *The Rain Forest*) much admired Olivia's remarkable evocation of a sense of place. Noting correctly her dislike of being termed a 'woman writer,' he elaborated the qualities in *The Sum of Things* that make her anything but that: the exploration of 'male' themes such as fighting and

---

[12] Victoria Glendinning, 'Ordeals of solitude,' *TLS*, 18 September 1980.
[13] Hermione Lee, 'A farewell to arms,' *The Observer*, 21 September 1980.

vainglory and a resolutely unsentimental prose. Reading her novels, he concludes, is like watching small human figures in the distance walking to an unknown destination, by which he means, I think, that we feel the powerlessness of Olivia's characters when they are caught in the grip of inexorable historical forces. When he reviewed *The Rain Forest*, Ackroyd had found the plot dismally improbable and the characters lifeless, like mannequins colliding with one another in a not very good play, but here the mannequins have become vulnerable human figures caught in the maelstrom of war, not entangled in a poorly constructed melodrama.[14] The only negative review of *The Sum of Things* that appeared in the major newspapers was that written by Jonah Jones in *The Times*. Not only unkind to the novel, he also queried Olivia's reputation—to his mind 'inflated' by people like Anthony Burgess. Despite the virtues one might expect ('accurate, superbly economical writing' for one), Olivia 'falls down on the little matter of character-ization': 'A bloodless Anthony Powell,' she creates characters who are nothing more than cardboard cut-outs. Had Olivia lived to read this review, one can be sure she would have been on the telephone to the literary editor of *The Times*, questioning his judgment in allowing someone better known as a sculptor than as a literary critic to review her latest novel.

In late 1981, Reggie married Diana Robson and she moved into the Marlborough Place flat and into possession of Olivia's books, paintings, and souvenirs of her time abroad during the war: 'With her combination of discriminating taste and financial acumen,' Francis King noted in his autobiography, Olivia collected many beautiful and valuable things. At the time King was recording his memoirs of Olivia, Diana and the man she married after Reggie's death in 1985, the artist Paul Hogarth, were living in 'Olivia's beloved flat among her beloved possessions. I often wonder what Olivia would say about that.'[15] According to Parvin Laurence, Diana had been very jealous of Olivia when she was alive and had hoped Reggie would leave her, but after they eventually married she was an adoring wife and nursed him devotedly during the six months that he lived after a diagnosis of cirrhosis of the liver received in late 1984. On his death on 3 May 1985, all the obituaries evoked his ebullience, good nature, optimism, gusto,

[14] Peter Ackroyd, 'A look at the Pringles,' *Sunday Times*, 28 September 1980.
[15] *Yesterday Came Suddenly*, 244.

and vitality. To both Parvin and Michael Laurence, Diana was an undeniably attractive successor to Olivia, yet they missed the vibrant figure who on lovely summer afternoons would sit with friends on the terrace at Marlborough Place while Reggie read aloud from her novels.[16]

On the August Bank Holiday weekend of 1987, June and Neville Braybrooke, Parvin and Michael Laurence, Beryl Bainbridge, Johnny Slattery, and Helen Miller-Smith (Reggie's old friend from the BBC and Cowes neighbor when Reggie and Olivia would visit for a summer holiday), together with a few other of Olivia's close friends, gathered in the garden of the Laurence house on the Isle of Wight. For the five years after Olivia's death, Reggie had been unwilling or unable to claim her ashes and they had remained at the crematorium, but now, two years after *his* death in 1985, everyone agreed it was time for them to be scattered. But where and how remained unsettled. Initially, Parvin placed them for safe storage in the grandfather clock in the hall of Billingham Manor and then, after a suggestion from June Braybrooke, all agreed that a beautiful old stone drinking trough facing the sea in the Laurences' garden was the ideal place. In a commemorative act that honored Olivia's fondness for anything geranium-pink, June Braybrooke wrapped the ashes in a pink scarf, and after Judy Gascoyne, Beryl Bainbridge, and Helen Miller-Smith had recited some poems and read from *The Balkan Trilogy*, the ashes were buried in the trough.[17]

As June and Neville Braybrooke observe in their biography of Olivia, the funerals and the memorial services for Olivia and Reggie were very different: her funeral on the Isle of Wight was sparsely attended and his at the Golders Green Crematorium drew over one hundred people; her memorial service arranged by PEN on 19 September 1980 and presided over by Francis King drew a respectable number of friends, but Reggie's held at the BBC concert hall on 31 July 1985 was packed. At Olivia's service, Margaret Drabble, Michael Laurence, and Antonia Fraser, among others, spoke of her achievements and shared their memories, and last to speak was Reggie; he talked about Olivia's shyness, her childhood, and her refusal to remain

[16] At the time of writing, Diana Robson now lives in Scotland. Her second husband, Paul Hogarth, died in December 2001.

[17] Braybrooke, *Olivia Manning: A Life*, 280–2.

silent when she perceived an injustice. At Reggie's service, John Hurt read a poem by Louis MacNeice, Anna Massey read extracts from *The Balkan Trilogy*, and Adam Watson reminisced about Reggie in Romania and Cairo (Watson, of course, was Olivia's model for Dobbie Dobson). After one of Reggie's fellow BBC producers sang his favorite sea shanty, 'The Golden Vanity,' Michael Foot recalled Reggie's record as a steadfast socialist and marveled at how well he had withstood some forty years of being observed by 'the most perceptive eye since Jane Austen.'[18] The remark credits the sharp economy of Olivia's writing but also implicitly salutes Reggie for having put up with her difficult temperament, a sentiment echoed by Godfrey Smith, a well-known journalist on the *Sunday Times*, who wrote to Neville Braybrooke in 1994, 'Reggie was always a hero of mine; indeed some people thought he was my elder brother and I wish he had been. I cannot truthfully say I was so keen on Olivia although I admired her talent.'[19]

Neither Reggie nor Olivia lived to celebrate the popular fame that accrued to her name and reputation after the BBC presented a seven-part television dramatization titled *Fortunes of War*, an adaption of the Balkan and Levant trilogies, that began on 'Masterpiece Theater' in January 1988. And by the time 'Fortunes of War' appeared, the autobiographical frisson that some readers had received from the trilogies had begun to fade, which in a sense made way for a more disinterested appraisal of Olivia's gifts as a novelist who fused autobiographical memory with historical fiction. Just after Reggie's death in 1985, Howard Moss in the *New York Review of Books* wrote a long appreciative review/essay of both of the trilogies newly reissued in Penguin paperbacks. He was surprised that more fuss had not been made of Olivia's writings about war, of her standing as 'dispassionate moralist' and 'inimitable storyteller.' Judiciously identifying a major theme in the trilogies, Olivia's alignment of petty personal betrayals and larger historical deception, Moss points aptly to how Guy in Athens is betrayed by the craven duo Lush and Dubedat and how the heroic Greek resistance to Mussolini is sabotaged by the blowing up of the port of Piraeus. But Moss ends his almost entirely positive review on a slightly sour misogynistic note: Olivia is a 'good girl forced

---

[18] Braybrooke, *Olivia Manning: A Life*, 277–9.
[19] Godfrey Smith to Neville Braybrooke, 20 January 1994, OMC/C, HRC.

to relay the bad messages the world keeps broadcasting.' Ultimately, although the trilogies have the 'subject, shape, and size of something epic,' they lack the 'poetry that goes with it.'[20] After her death, Olivia's reputation came to reside primarily in her work as a woman novelist who wrote brilliantly about men and women at war, which is fair enough given the tremendous success of the trilogies, but she also merits accolades, I would argue, for writing brilliantly about childhood, male anxiety, post-war austerity, and desecration of the environment. Finally, her work is at its most distinctive and remarkable in its seamless integration of personal recollection and public history.

If not quite an affirmation of Olivia's belief, articulated some twenty years earlier when reviewing three novels for *The Spectator*—'On his death, the achievement of every writer is acknowledged with conventional regrets; the reappraisal that follows after a decent interval is often much less kind'[21]—Howard Moss's judgment expresses the long-standing critical difficulty that Olivia presented to the world. One of a group of British women novelists who acquired considerable critical acclaim in the 1960s, she remains difficult to place. If neither as intellectual nor as well educated as Iris Murdoch, in her novels *Artist Among the Missing*, *A Different Face*, and *School for Love* she certainly depicts male experience as successfully as Murdoch does in *Under the Net* (1954); and although by no means as fierce a feminist as Doris Lessing, whose *The Golden Notebook* (1962) became essential reading for any self-respecting member of a consciousness-raising group in the 1960s, Olivia's novel *The Doves of Venus* depicts unflinchingly the physical and emotional perils confronted by young women living alone in London; and even if her dry and droll prose never soared to the heights of poetic lyricism found in the novels of Elizabeth Bowen, her writings about the effects of war upon civilian populations are certainly as chilling as that to be found, say, in Bowen's *The Heat of the Day* (1948). Descending less from the tradition of domestic fiction perfected by Jane Austen (a writer she fervently admired) and more from the literary lineage of Charles Dickens and Joseph Conrad, Olivia Manning wrote about male matters in a manner that shocked readers and critics out of their comfortable assumptions regarding appropriate subject matter for writers of different sexes: she wrote about

[20] Howard Moss, 'Spoils of war,' *New York Review of Books*, 25 April 1985.
[21] Olivia Manning, 'Revaluation,' *The Spectator*, 24 January 1964.

homoerotic attachments between men, about the blood from a fatally wounded man's body seeping into the Egyptian sands, about the terrifying whizz of German plans strafing Athens, about the sight of the fanatical Romanian Iron Guards forcing gypsies and Jews to flee the streets of Bucharest, and about a sixteen-year-old boy's education in adult sexuality. And her most political novel, *The Rain Forest*, is as powerful as any by Graham Greene (never a favorite) in its depiction of the lingering political effects of imperialism and the spoliation of nature brought about by rampant commercial development.

How, then, to place her, this highly intelligent, not-too-well-educated girl from Portsmouth who got herself to the metropolis, began hobnobbing with famous poets such as Louis MacNeice, lived through World War II, pushed herself relentlessly to succeed in the post-war literary world, and along the way published thirteen novels, several works of non-fiction, some fourteen or so short stories, and at least a hundred book reviews? In many ways, the difficulty of finding her appropriate literary slot proved to be the impetus for writing this biography. A woman at war with her provincial past and her melancholy temperament, she soldiered on and wrote about war with more skill, sympathy, and knowledge than any man or woman in the canon of twentieth-century British novelists. Finally, in some sense she is a conventionally androgynous figure: feminine in her elegant appearance and in her healthy enjoyment of female sexual pleasure, and masculine in her acute sensitivity to male experience and in her unsentimental skill in describing the intimate, graphic, and grisly details of war. The stray survivor who witnesses not the tragic end of Hamlet or Lear evoked in her coda to *The Sum of Things*, but of the Jewish banker brutalized by Romanian fascists and the ordinary soldier whose body is shot to pieces in the desert, Olivia was a witness to the ruins of war, the one who lived to tidy up the pieces through narrative and to tell the tale.

Bibliography

PUBLISHED WORKS BY OLIVIA MANNING

'The rose of rubies' ('Jacob Morrow'), *Portsmouth Evening News*, October 1929.

'Here is murder' ('Jacob Morrow'), *Portsmouth Evening News*, November 1929.

'The dark scarab' ('Jacob Morrow'), *Portsmouth Evening News*, December 1929.

'The Sunwaite ghost,' *Hampshire Telegraph and Post*, 29 December 1929.

'A scantling of foxes' (O. M. Manning), *New Stories*, Vol. 1, no. 5 (October–November 1934), Oxford: Basil Blackwell.

The Wind Changes, with a new Introduction by Isobel English, London: Virago Press, 1988 (1937).

'The Irish coast and Portsmouth,' *The Palestine Post*, 2 June 1944.

'Poets in exile,' *Horizon*, 10/58, October 1944, 270–9.

'Against the past,' *The Palestine Post*, 14 December 1945.

The Remarkable Expedition: The Story of Stanley's Rescue of Emin Pasha from Equatorial Africa, New York: Atheneum, 1985 (1947); original US publication: *The Reluctant Rescue*, Garden City, NY: Doubleday (1947).

Growing Up: A Collection of Short Stories, London: William Heinemann, 1948.

Artist Among the Missing, London: William Heinemann, 1949.

The Dreaming Shore, London: Evans Brothers, 1950.

School for Love, London: William Heinemann, 1951.

A Different Face, London: William Heinemann, 1953.

The Doves of Venus, London: William Heinemann, 1955.

My Husband Cartwright: With Illustrations by Len Deighton, London: William Heinemann, 1956.

The Great Fortune, London: Arrow Books, 2004 (1960).

'Buried alive,' *The Times*, 6 November 1961.

The Spoilt City, London: Arrow Books, 2004 (1962).

'The once beautiful Eliza,' *Heathside Book of Hampstead and Highgate*, ed. Ian Norrie, London: High Hill Books, 1962, 3–8.

'Speaking of writing,' *The Times*, 30 January 1964 (interview with Olivia Manning).

'The dark side of the world,' *Transatlantic Review* (Spring 1964), 101–5.

Friends and Heroes, London: Arrow Books, 2004 (1965).

'Cairo: back from the blue,' *Sunday Times Magazine*, 17 September 1967, 46–55.

Extraordinary Cats, London: Michael Joseph, 1967.

A Romantic Hero, and Other Stories, London: William Heinemann, 1967.

Introduction and notes, *Jane Austen: Northanger Abbey*, London: Pan Books, 1968.

The Play Room, William Heinemann, 1969.

Introduction, *Romanian Short Stories*, The World's Classics Series, London: Oxford University Press, 1971, pp. vi–xiv.

The Rain Forest, William Heinemann, 1974.

'Books I have read,' *Bookmarks*, ed. Frederic Raphael, London: Jonathan Cape, 1975, 116–24.

'Voyages around my father,' *The Times*, 24 May 1975.

The Danger Tree, London: Weidenfeld and Nicolson, 1977.

The Battle Lost and Won, London: Weidenfeld and Nicolson, 1978.

The Sum of Things, London: Weidenfeld and Nicolson, 1980.

UNPUBLISHED MATERIAL BY OLIVIA MANNING

'Guests at a marriage,' 1941, Harry Ransom Center, The University of Texas, Austin.

'Let me tell you before I forget,' Harry Ransom Center, The University of Texas, Austin.

'Soon to be forgotten,' Harry Ransom Center, The University of Texas, Austin.

ARCHIVAL MATERIAL

'As I was walking down Bristol Street,' BBC Television documentary narrated by David Lodge, 1983, Media Archive for Central England.

BBC Written Archives Centre, Caversham.

BBC Sound Archives, British Library.

Correspondence of William Gerhardie, Cambridge University Library.

Francis King Correspondence/Olivia Manning, Harry Ransom Center, The University of Texas, Austin.

'Never a day without a line,' BBC Radio 3, 21 November 1981, British Library Sound Archives, T4584R (Derek Mahon, Neville Braybrooke, Kay Dick, Isobel English, Roy Foster, Victoria Glendinning, Francis King, R. D. Smith, Anna Massey (reader))).

Olivia Manning Collection/Correspondence, Harry Ransom Center, The University of Texas, Austin.

Olivia Manning Collection, Harry Ransom Center, The University of Texas, Austin.

The Olivia Manning Papers, McFarlin Library, The University of Tulsa.

Oral History of the British Council, British Library Sound Archives.
'Poetry Now,' selected and introduced by R. D. Smith, British Library Sound
Archives, PR66TR C1.
The Stevie Smith Papers, McFarlin Library, The University of Tulsa.

OTHER WORKS

Allen, Walter, *As I Walked Down New Grub Street*, London: William Heine-
mann Ltd., 1981.
Allen, Walter, *Tradition and Dream: A Critical Survey of British and American
Fiction from the 1920s to the Present Day*, Harmondsworth, Middlesex: Pen-
guin Books, 1965 (1964).
Andras, Carmen, 'In-betweenness and intermediality in British images of
inter-war Bucharest (1930–1939),' *New Directions in Travel Writing and
Travel Studies*, ed. Carmen Andras, Aachen: Shaker Publishing, 2010.
Banham, Mary, and Hillier, Bevis, eds., *A Tonic to the Nation: The Festival of
Britain 1951*, London: Thames and Hudson, 1976.
Barbera, Jack, and McBrien, William, *Stevie: A Biography of Stevie Smith*,
London: William Heinemann, 1985.
Beaton, Cecil, *Near East*, London: B. T. Batsford Ltd., 1943.
Beauman, Nicola, *The Other Elizabeth Taylor*, London: Persephone, 2009.
Birkett, Jennifer, *Margaret Storm Jameson: A Life*, Oxford: Oxford University
Press, 2009.
Bolton, Jonathan, *Personal Landscapes: British Poets in Egypt during the Second
World War*, New York: St Martin's Press, 1997.
Bowen, Elizabeth, *The Collected Stories of Elizabeth Bowen*, New York: Alfred
A. Knopf, 1981.
Bowen, Elizabeth, *People, Places, Things*, essays edited with an introduction by
Allan Hepburn, Edinburgh: Edinburgh University Press, 2008.
Bowen, Roger. '"The artist at his papers": Durrell, Egypt, and the poetry of
exile,' *Twentieth-Century Literature*, 33/4, Lawrence Durrell Issue, Part II
(Winter 1987), 465–84.
Bowen, Roger, '"Monologue for a Cairo evening": A cultural landscape in
wartime,' *London Magazine*, December 1982/January 1983, 50–60.
Braybrooke, Neville, and Braybrooke, June, *Olivia Manning: A Life*. London:
Chatto and Windus, 2004.
Brittain, Vera, *Lady into Woman: A History of Women from Victoria to Elizabeth
II*, New York: Macmillan, 1953.
Burgess, Anthony, *The Novel Now: A Guide to Contemporary Fiction*, New
York: W. W. Norton & Co., 1967.
Connell, John, *The House by Herod's Gate*, London: Sampson Low, Marston &
Co., 1947.
Conrad, Joseph, *The Nigger of the 'Narcissus' and Typhoon and Other Stories*,
London: J. M. Dent, 1964 (1897; 1903).

Conrad, Joseph, *Youth, Heart of Darkness, The End of the Tether*, London: J. M. Dent, 1967 (1902).

Cooper, Artemis, *Cairo in the War, 1939–1945*, London: Hamish Hamilton, 1989.

Croft-Cooke, Rupert, *The Verdict of You All*, London: Secker and Warburg, 1955.

Cusk, Rachel, Introduction to Olivia Manning, *Fortunes of War: The Balkan Trilogy*, New York: New York Review of Books, 2010.

Dick, Kay, *Friends and Friendship: Conversations and Reflections*, London: Sidgwick and Jackson, 1974.

Donaldson, Frances, *The British Council: The First Fifty Years*, London: Jonathan Cape, 1984.

Drabble, Margaret, *Angus Wilson: A Biography*, London: Secker and Warburg, 1995.

English, Isobel, Introduction to Olivia Manning, *The Doves of Venus* (with Rosamond Lehmann, *The Weather in the Streets*, introduction Janet Watts; Antonia White, *Frost in May*, introduction Elizabeth Bowen), London: Virago Press, 1986.

Farrell, J. G., *J. G. Farrell in his Own Words: Selected Letters and Diaries*, ed. Lavinia Graecen, Cork: Cork University Press, 2009.

Fuller, Roy, 'The end of the forties,' *The Sewanee Review*, 99/2 (Spring 1991), 274–81.

Garfield, Simon, ed., *Our Hidden Lives: The Remarkable Diaries of Post-War Britain*, London: Ebury Press, 2005.

Hamilton, Patrick, *Hangover Square*, New York: Europa Editions, 2006 (1941).

Hamilton, Patrick, *The Slaves of Solitude*, New York: New York Review of Books, 2007 (1947).

Hammond, Andrew, '"The Red threat": Cold War rhetoric and the British novel,' *The Balkans and the West: Constructing the European Other, 1945–2003*, ed. Andrew Hammond, London: Ashgate, 2004, 40–56.

Hartley, Jenny, *Millions Like Us: British Women's Fiction of the Second World War*, London: Virago Press, 1997.

Hassan, Fayza, 'A betrayal of history,' *Al-Ahram Weekly*, 30 December 1995–5 January 2000, no. 462.

Hassan, Fayza, 'In search of Amy,' *Al-Ahram Weekly*, 30 March–5 April 2006, no. 788.

Hennessy, Peter, *Having it So Good: Britain in the Fifties*, London: Allen Lane, 2006.

Hennessy, Peter, *Never Again 1945–1951*, New York: Pantheon Books, 1993.

Hensher, Philip, 'The lady's not for exhuming,' *The Spectator*, 30 October 2004.

Heppenstall, Rayner, *The Master Eccentric: The Journals of Rayner Heppenstall 1969–81*, ed. Jonathan Goodman, London: Allison and Busby, 1986.

Heron, Liz, *Truth, Dare or Promise: Girls Growing up in the Fifties*, London: Virago, 1985.

Hewison, Robert, *Under Siege: Literary Life in London, 1939–1945*, London: Weidenfeld and Nicolson, 1977.

Hodgson, Vere, *Few Eggs and No Oranges: The Diaries of Vere Hodgson 1940–45*, London: Persephone Books, 1999.

Holroyd, Michael, 'Tepid tea and raspberry jam,' *The Times*, 28 February 1981.

Hornsey, Richard, *The Spiv and the Architect: Unruly Life in Postwar London*, Minneapolis: University of Minnesota Press, 2010.

Howard, Elizabeth Jane, *Slipstream: A Memoir*, London: Pan Books, 2002.

Judt, Tony, *Postwar: A History of Europe since 1945*, New York: Penguin Books, 2006.

King, Francis, *Yesterday Came Suddenly: An Autobiography*, London: Constable, 1993.

Koven, Seth, 'Borderlands: Women, voluntary action, and child welfare in Britain, 1840–1914,' *Mothers of a New World: Maternalist Politics and the Origins of Welfare States*, ed. Seth Koven and Sonya Michel, New York: Routledge, 1993.

Kynaston, David, *Austerity Britain: 1945–1951*, London: Bloomsbury Publishing, 2007.

Kynaston, David, *Family Britain: 1951–1957*. New York: Walker and Co., 2009.

Lassner, Phyllis, *Colonial Strangers: Women Writing the End of the British Empire*. New Brunswick: Rutgers University Press, 2004.

Layton-Henry, Zig, *The Politics of Immigration: Immigration, 'Race', and 'Race Relations' in Post-War Britain*. Oxford: Blackwell Publishers, 1992.

Leader, Zachary, *The Life of Kingsley Amis*, New York: Pantheon, 2006.

Lessing, Doris. *Walking in the Shade: Volume Two of my Autobiography, 1949–1962*, London: Harper Collins, 1997.

Liddell, Robert, 'Notes on Ivy Compton-Burnett,' *Twentieth-Century Literature*, 25/2 (Summer 1979), 135–52.

Livezeanu, Irinia, Review of Luminita Machedon and Ernie Scoffham, *Romanian Modernism: The Architecture of Bucharest, 1920–1940*, *Slavic Review*, 61/22 (Summer 2002), 388–9.

Lutyens, Elisabeth, *A Goldfish Bowl*, London: Cassell, 1972.

Machedon, Luminita, and Scoffham, Ernie, *Romanian Modernism: The Architecture of Bucharest, 1920–1940*, Cambridge, Mass.: MIT Press, 1999.

MacKay, Marina, and Stonebridge, Lyndsey, eds., *British Fiction after Modernism: The Novel at Mid-Century*, Basingstoke: Palgrave Macmillan, 2007.

MacNeice, Louis, *Collected Poems*, ed. E. R. Dodds, London: Faber and Faber, 1979.

MacNeice, Louis, *Letters of Louis MacNeice*, ed. Jonathan Allison, London: Faber and Faber, 2010.

MacNeice, Louis, *The Strings are False: An Unfinished Autobiography*, London: Faber and Faber, 1982 (1965).

Marcus, Laura, and Nicholls, Peter, eds., *The Cambridge History of Twentieth-Century Literature*, Cambridge: Cambridge University Press, 2005.

Mengham, Rod, 'The thirties: Politics, authority, perspective,' *The Cambridge History of Twentieth-Century Literature*, ed. Laura Marcus and Peter Nicholls, Cambridge: Cambridge University Press, 2005, 359–78.

Montgomery, Bernard, *The Memoirs of Field-Marshal Montgomery of Alamein, K.G.*, Barnsley: Pen and Sword Military, 2007 (1958).

Mooney, Harry J., Jr., 'Olivia Manning: Witness to history,' *Twentieth-Century Women novelists*, ed. Thomas F. Staley, Totowa, NJ: Barnes and Noble Books, 1982, 39–60.

Morris, Robert K., 'Olivia Manning's *Fortunes of War*. Breakdown in the Balkans, love and death in the Levant,' *British Novelists since 1900*, ed. Jack I. Biles, New York: AMS Press, 1987.

Munton, Alan, *English Fiction of the Second World War*, London: Faber and Faber, 1989.

Murdoch, Iris, *Iris Murdoch: A Writer at War, Letters and Diaries 1939–45*, ed. Peter J. Conradi, London: Short Books, 2010.

Ovenden, Keith, *A Fighting Withdrawal: The Life of Dan Davin, Writer, Soldier, Publisher*, Oxford: Oxford University Press, 1996.

Patmore, Derek *Invitation to Roumania*, London: Macmillan & Co., 1939.

Patten, Eve, 'Olivia Manning, imperial refugee, *That Island Never Found: Essays and Poems for Terence Brown*, ed. Nicholas Allen and Eve Patten, Dublin: Four Courts Press, 2007.

Phillips, Mike, and Phillips, Trevor, *Windrush: The Irresistible Rise of Multi-Racial Britain*, London: HarperCollins, 1999.

Piette, Adam, 'World War II: contested Europe,' *The Cambridge History of Twentieth-Century Literature*, ed. Laura Marcus and Peter Nicholls, Cambridge: Cambridge University Press, 2005, 417–35.

Pixner, Stef, 'The oyster and the shadow,' *Truth, Dare or Promise: Girls Growing up in the Fifties*, ed. Liz Heron, London: Virago Press, 1985.

Popescu, Carmen, Review of Luminita Machedon and Ernie Scoffham, *Romanian Modernism: The Architecture of Bucharest, 1920–1940, Journal of the Society of Architectural Historians*, 59/3 (September 2000), 403–5.

Porter, Ivor, *Operation Autonomous: With SOE in Wartime Romania*, London: Chatto and Windus, 1989.

Pritchett, V. S., 'Letter from London,' *New York Times*, 8 May 1949.

Raphael, Frederic, ed., *Bookmarks*, London: Jonathan Cape, 1975.

Rebellato, Dan, *1956 and All That: The Making of Modern British Drama*, London: Routledge, 1999.

St John, John, *William Heinemann: A Century of Publishing 1890–1990*, London: William Heinemann, 1990.

Salwak, Dale, and Amis, Kingsley, 'An interview with Kingsley Amis,' *Contemporary Literature*, 16/1 (Winter 1975), 1–18.

Saunders, Frances Stonor, *The Cultural Cold War: The CIA and the World of Arts and Letters*, New York: The New Press, 1999.

Shoumatoff, Alex, *African Madness*, New York: A. A. Knopf, 1988.

Sinfield, Alan, *Literature, Politics, and Culture in Postwar Britain*, Berkeley: University of California Press, 1989.

Sissons, Michael, and French, Philip, eds., *Age of Austerity 1945–1951*, Harmondsworth, Middlesex: Penguin Books, 1964.

Sked, Aland, and Cook, Chris, *Post-War Britain: A Political History*, Harmondsworth, Middlesex: Penguin Books, 1979.

Smith, Stevie, *Novel on Yellow Paper*, New York: New Directions, 1994 (1936).

Social Insurance and Allied Services: The Beveridge Report in Brief, London: HM Stationery Office, 1942.

Spalding, Frances, *Stevie Smith: A Critical Biography*, London: Faber and Faber, 1988.

Stannard, Martin, *Muriel Spark: The Biography*, London: Weidenfeld and Nicolson, 2009.

Starr, Joshua, 'Jewish citizenship in Rumania (1878–1940),' *Jewish Social Studies*, 3/1 (January 1941), 57–80.

Thane, Pat, 'Women in the British Labour party and the construction of state welfare, 1906–1939,' *Mothers of a New World: Maternalist Politics and the Origins of Welfare States*, ed. Seth Koven and Sonya Michel, New York: Routledge, 1993.

Thirkell, Angela, *Love Among the Ruins*, London: Moyer Bell, 1947.

Thirkell, Angela, *Peace Breaks Out*, New York: A. A. Knopf, 1947.

Treglown, Jeremy, 'Olivia Manning and her masculine outfit.' *British Fiction after Modernism: The Novel at Mid-Century*, ed. Marina MacKay and Lyndsey Stonebridge, Houndmills, Basingstoke: Palgrave Macmillan, 2007, 145–56.

Wakeman, John, ed., *World Authors*, New York: H. W. Wilson, 1975.

Williams, Gwyn, 'Durrell in Egypt,' *Twentieth-Century Literature*, 33/3 (Autumn 1987), 298–302.

Woolf, Virginia, *The Essays of Virginia Woolf*, Vols. 1–4, ed. Andrew McNeillie, London: Hogarth Press, 1986–94.

Woolf, Virginia, *Moments of Being*, ed. Jeanne Schulkind, New York: Harcourt, Brace, Jovanovich, 1985.

INTERVIEWS

Francis King, 30 April 2008.

Roy Foster, 27 November 2008.

Doreen (Johnny) Slattery, 4 April 1009.

Victoria Orr-Ewing, 8 April 2009.

Elizabeth Jane Howard, 26 April 2010.
Roy Foster, 28 April 2010.
Margaret Drabble, 29 April 2010.
Victoria Orr-Ewing, 30 April 2010.
Richard Griffiths, 1 May 2010.
Parvin and Michael Laurence, 3 May 2010.
Francis King, 5 May 2010.
Julian Mitchell, 6 May 2010.
Anna Davin, 6 May 2010.
John Tydeman, 7 May 2010.
Helen Miller-Smith, 15 July 2011.

Index

The following abbreviations are used in the index : OM = Olivia Manning; RS = Reggie Smith. Page numbers in bold refer to figures.